ORGANIZATIONAL CHANGE THEORIES

To my students.

ORGANIZATIONAL CHANGE THEORIES

A SYNTHESIS

CHRISTIANE DEMERS

HEC Montréal

SAGE Publications
Los Angeles • London • New Delhi • Singapore

For information:

Sage Publications, Inc.
2455 Teller Road
Thousand Oaks,
 California 91320
E-mail: order@sagepub.com

Sage Publications Ltd.
1 Oliver's Yard
55 City Road
London EC1Y 1SP
United Kingdom

Sage Publications India Pvt. Ltd.
B 1/I 1 Mohan Cooperative
 Industrial Area
Mathura Road, New Delhi
India 110 044

Sage Publications Asia-Pacific Pte. Ltd.
33 Pekin Street #02-01
Far East Square
Singapore 048763

Printed in the United States of America.

Library of Congress Cataloging-in-Publication Data

Demers, Christiane, 1953–
Organizational change theories: A synthesis/Christiane Demers.
 p. cm.
Includes bibliographical references and index.
ISBN 978-0-7619-2932-1 (pbk.)
1. Organizational change. I. Title.
HD58.8.D45 2008
302.3′5—dc22   2007004816

This book is printed on acid-free paper.

07 08 09 10 11 10 9 8 7 6 5 4 3 2 1

Acquisitions Editor:	Al Bruckner
Editorial Assistant:	MaryAnn Vail
Production Editor:	Diane S. Foster
Copy Editor:	Halim Dunsky
Typesetter:	C&M Digitals (P) Ltd.
Proofreader:	Scott Oney
Cover Designer:	Bryan Fishman
Marketing Manager:	Nichole M. Angress

Contents

Preface   ix

Introduction   xi
   The Field of Organizational Change: An Historical Account   xi
   The Focus of This Book   xii
   Organization of the Book   xiv

PART I. ADAPTATION OR SELECTION?   1
   Do Organizations Really Change?   1

1. Adaptation and Growth Perspective   5
   Rational Adaptation Approaches   6
      Contingency Theory   6
      Discussion   8
      Purposeful Action Approaches: Strategic Choice
         and Resource Dependency   11
      Discussion   12
   Organic Adaptation Approach   13
      Discussion   16
   Life-Cycle Approach   17
      Stages of Development   18
      Patterns of Change   20
      Discussion   21
   Conclusion   23

2. Selection and Imitation Perspective   25
   Population Ecology   26
      Organizational-Level Change   28
      Discussion   30
   The "New" Institutionalism   32
      The Process of Institutionalization   34
      Discussion   35
   Conclusion   38

Conclusion to Part I: Looking at Change From the Outside   40

PART II. TRANSFORMATION OR EVOLUTION?   43
Is Transformation Always Revolutionary?   43

3. The Configurational Approach   47
Momentum and Revolution: The Punctuated Equilibrium Model   50
Design Archetypes: From Punctuated Equilibrium to Theories
     of Stability and Change   54
Discussion and Conclusion   55

4. The Cognitive Approach   61
Organizational Change as Reframing   62
     Reframing as a Change of Knowledge Structure   65
     Reframing as a Social Interaction Process   68
Discussion and Conclusion   71

5. The Cultural Approach   75
Culture and Change: Functionalist and Interpretive Perspectives   76
     A Functionalist Framework   79
     An Interpretive Definition of Culture   81
Cultural Change Processes   84
     Managing Cultural Change: Revolution or Evolution?   84
     Cultural Dynamics: From Integration to Fragmentation   87
Discussion and Conclusion   89

6. The Political Approach   93
Power and Change: From Resistance to Renewal   95
     Top-Down Incremental Change: Politics Viewed as a
       Force Against Change   96
     Bottom-Up Incremental Change: Politics Viewed as a
       Force for Change   98
     From Change to Changing: Politics as a Reproduction
       and Transformation Process   101
Discussion and Conclusion   106

Conclusion to Part II: Looking at Change From Above   110

PART III. NATURAL EVOLUTION OR SOCIAL DYNAMICS?   115
How Do Organizations Renew Themselves?   115

7. The Natural Evolution Perspective   121
The Behavioral Learning Approach   122
     Routine-Based Change   124
     Cross-Level Learning   126
     Linking the Behavioral and Cognitive Approaches
       to Learning   128
     Discussion   132

The Evolutionary Approach 135
    Organizational Genealogy: Producing the New From
      the Old 137
    Intraorganizational Ecology: A Bottom-Up Process of
      Change 143
    From Evolution to Coevolution 147
    Discussion 150
The Complexity Approach 154
    Chaos and Punctuated Change 155
    Complex Adaptive System Theory and Power Law Patterns
      of Change 158
    Change as an Emergent Phenomenon 162
Discussion 168
Conclusion 170

8. The Social Dynamics Perspective 177
    The Radical and Postmodern Approaches 179
      Change: From Emancipation to Language Games 180
      New Organizational Forms: Transformation or
        Reproduction? 185
      Discussion 187
    The Discursive and Practice-Centered Approaches 190
      Discourse and Change: From Interpreting to Narrating
        and Translating 193
    Situated Change: From Structuring to 207
      Improvising Discussion 215
    Conclusion 218

Conclusion to Part III: Looking at Change From the Inside 222

Conclusion 229
    Looking for an Elusive Object 229
    Culmination or Dissolution? 233

References 235

Index 267

About the Author 277

Preface

A book of this nature is, by definition, a long-term project. I guess it has been in the back of my mind since the mid-1990s, when I started teaching a course on organizational change at HEC Montréal. I had been lucky to witness, since my early days as a doctoral student, the rapid growth and transformation of the field of organizational change. In less than 15 years, it had moved from a peripheral topic of research to a major field of inquiry encompassing an increasing diversity of theoretical approaches. Fascinated by the breadth of the field, I decided to build a course that would help students take advantage of all this richness. I wanted them to develop the curiosity and open-mindedness that would allow them to explore change from multiple points of view, to develop their own point of view on the subject. I was fortunate enough to have wonderful students who, with their questions and comments, helped me to clarify my ideas and test the usefulness of the framework I had developed. A few years later, when I finally settled down to write this book, I had no idea that I was embarking on a journey that would take me more than 3 years to accomplish. It was an inspiring adventure, because it gave me the occasion to deepen my understanding of the work of scholars in my field coming from different horizons.

Naturally, although I am solely responsible for any misunderstanding or faulty interpretation of others' work, I benefited from the help of many people along the way.

First of all, I owe a lot to Henry Mintzberg, who supervised my doctoral research. His masterly syntheses have inspired this work, and his thinking has influenced me in many ways. I will forever be grateful for his enthusiastic support. I also want to thank Alain Chanlat for helping me get started on this path. Taïeb Hafsi and Nicole Giroux, colleagues and friends, with whom I collaborated on numerous research projects, have also taught me a lot. Many of the ideas developed here emerged in my work with them, and they have contributed greatly to their elaboration. The many discussions with Ann Langley, Linda Rouleau, Francine Séguin, and Martine Vézina on the study and teaching of strategic change have helped sharpen some of my ideas. I have also greatly benefited from ongoing conversations with other colleagues at HEC Montréal. I particularly want to thank Jean-Pierre Béchard, Richard Déry, Jean-Pierre Dupuis, and André Kuzminski for their encouragement and their friendship. They had the patience to listen to my arguments as they were evolving over the years and to give me feedback and support. Yvonne Giordano, of the University of Nice at Sophia-Antipolis, was a wonderful host and made my stay a pleasant and beneficial experience. During my visit, she gave me the opportunity to share my ideas with participants in a workshop on organizational change. Finally, Carole Groleau, research collaborator and dear friend, read the entire manuscript and helped me clarify my thinking and regain my confidence when I felt I was going nowhere. I want to thank her for her generosity and her great sense of humor.

I want to thank the people at Sage for their professionalism, particularly Al Bruckner, my editor, for his unfailing belief in this project and for his patience, and MaryAnn Vail, Diane Foster, and Halim Dunsky for their graciousness and their efficient work. HEC Montréal provided resources, a congenial work atmosphere, and a sabbatical that allowed me to get a good start on the project. I also benefited from the assistance of doctoral students Ryad Titah, who read some of the early chapters and made judicious comments, and Marcos Barros, who helped with the references.

However, my deepest gratitude goes to my family. To my parents, Madeleine and Pierre Demers, who are my greatest source of inspiration, and to Georges and Charlotte for being who they are. They make it all worthwhile.

—Christiane Demers
Montréal, Canada

Introduction

What people think about social change is crucially important in moving them to action, and hence it crucially influences the very course and prospects of social change. In this sense, enriching theoretical knowledge about change is by the same token practically relevant for producing change. Ideas about change become a resource for introducing change. The richer such resources are, the wider the variety of available concepts, models and theories, the deeper and more critical their mastery, the more informed and self-aware human actions become, both the everyday actions of common people, and the change-oriented programmes of task-groups, organizations, social movements, governments and other collective actors.

(Sztompka, 1993, p. xv)

The Field of Organizational Change: An Historical Account

Anyone interested in organizational change cannot help but have noticed the phenomenal number of books and articles dealing with this subject that have been written over the years. This topic continues to be one of the most important for scholars and practitioners alike. But reading the literature on organizational change can be a frustrating experience. As a doctoral student in the 1980s, when I became interested in this topic, I had the feeling that the field was highly fragmented, due to the diversity of the vocabulary and models employed. But, after a while, I started having an impression of déjà-vu and noticed that different terminology often masked very closely related notions. Later, as a university professor having to teach a course in organizational change to graduate students, I had to organize this vast body of literature. My aim in this book is to present the framework I have developed to synthesize the literature on this fascinating topic.

This book is a guided tour to the field and its evolution. This historical account is one way of organizing the literature that I think has the advantage of presenting each school of thought on its own merits, allowing readers to develop their own point of view on the subject. Because it includes both summaries of the major approaches and examples of studies and relevant research questions, I believe the book can be of interest to a wide range of people interested in organizational change—scholars and practitioners alike.

To be sure, I am not the first to attempt this difficult task. Over the years, excellent reviews proposing syntheses or typologies of the field have appeared in scholarly journals or handbooks (Child & Kieser, 1981; Meyer, Goes, & Brooks, 1993; Rajagopalan & Spreitzer, 1997; Starbuck, 1965; Van de Ven & Poole, 1995; Weick & Quinn, 1999). As well, several authors, such as Aldrich (1999), Pettigrew (1985a), and Huff, Huff, & Barr (2000), have discussed extant literature before presenting their own perspective on organizational change. These efforts, although very interesting, offer only brief accounts of the field. To my knowledge, no one has yet written a comprehensive treatment of the scholarly literature on organizational change with the purpose of exposing its variety and richness.

The Focus of This Book

Some probably think that it is foolish (or presumptuous) to embark on such a journey, considering the diversity and the sheer quantity of work to be covered. To make the project more manageable, I have decided to focus on theoretical works and empirical studies about organizational change. I have therefore excluded most of the enormous prescriptive and practitioner-oriented literature on organizational development and change, because there already are a number of extensive reviews of organizational development (OD) literature (Burke, 2002).

This decision might seem surprising, because, for a number of people, OD is synonymous with organizational change. This perception is perhaps even stronger now, as the boundaries between the OD and organizational change literatures have blurred considerably. Over the years, as OD has extended its scope to include all types of large-scale organizational change, it has become more difficult to define what OD is (Boucher, 1995). I share the view of authors such as Starbuck (1965), Child and Kieser (1981), and Pettigrew (1985a), who define OD as a movement "concerned with helping managers to adapt organizations" (Child & Kieser, 1981, p. 28) and therefore focusing on theories of intervention, that is, theories about how change should be managed. In contrast, the literature discussed in this book address the issue of why, how, and what kind of change, both planned and emergent, occurs in organizations. Having said this, the distinction between prescriptive and analytical writings is not always easy to make. Some works on organizational change, though normative in tone and written for managers, also present a theoretical framework that has had such an influence on the field that it must be included in this synthesis.

Furthermore, a lot of work in organizational behavior, concerned with changes at the employee or the workgroup level, will not be included in this review. This research—for example, studies of psychological reactions to organizational change—is based essentially on individual-level theories of change. Although such research is very relevant and interesting, this book is about theories of organizational change, not theories of change in organizations.

In short, this is a multidisciplinary project drawing predominantly on the fields of organization theory, strategy, sociology, and social psychology. This book aims to classify, present, and discuss the contributions and the limits of the major theories of organizational change using an historical perspective as its organizing scheme.

My objective is neither to describe in detail the sequence of appearance of all theories of change nor to trace exhaustively all the links among them. Rather, I believe that, by situating the main theories of organizational change in a general historical context, a better understanding of the evolution of this field of inquiry will be gained. In this sense, my synthesis of the literature can be viewed as a complement and extension of other recent reviews. For example, like Weick and Quinn (1999), I see the distinction between episodic change and continuous change as a major feature of the field (Demers, 1999). However, while Weick and Quinn present these as two opposing views of the management of change, my aim is to show how different conceptual threads have been woven together over time to produce this contrast in conceptions of planned and emergent change. Another example is the review article by Van de Ven and Poole (1995), who integrate all theories of organizational change and development into four generic types or "motors": life-cycle, teleological, dialectical, and evolutionary. While I agree with their classification and find its parsimony useful, it doesn't reflect the wealth of perspectives found in the literature. In this book, theories representing the four different types will be presented with the objective of exposing their variety and richness.

Particularly, the theories that describe how change is managed, which are all subsumed under the teleological motor, will be discussed in more depth, since they account for the vast majority of the studies in the field. Finally, in another literature review (Rajagopalan & Spreitzer, 1997), the authors uncover three conceptual lenses behind the numerous studies of strategic change: the rational, cognitive, and learning lenses. These perspectives, although defined somewhat differently, are among those that are discussed in this book.

The literature on organizational change has evolved tremendously over the years, yet also shows, as we shall see, remarkable continuity. For the sake of simplicity and clarity, I have segmented the literature into three major periods.

The first, beginning after World War II, emphasizes growth and adaptation. The second, which developed at the beginning of the 1980s, is more concerned with organizational transformation. Finally, in the current period, which began at the end of the 1980s, the themes of learning and innovation have taken center stage in the broadly defined literature on organizational change.

Although these different themes can be found, more or less explicitly, through all the periods, this historical reconstruction seeks to highlight the evolution in the importance and meaning given to them at different times. For example, the organizational learning approach is presented in the third period, even though discussions of learning appear much earlier in the field (Argyris & Schön, 1978; Hedberg, 1981; March & Olsen, 1976). My argument is that it became a dominant theme in the early 1990s with the popularity of topics such as knowledge management, the learning organization, and the knowledge economy. In a sense, in that period, learning and innovation became synonymous with organizational change.

Finally, I don't intend to suggest that earlier approaches are replaced by later ones or that the latest theories are better than earlier ones. Rather, I see the field as evolving through a process of sedimentation where earlier theories continue to coexist with more recent approaches. Basic epistemological, theoretical, and methodological differences remain that maintain the conceptual diversity of the field. Recent work from each theoretical perspective will be presented when its evolution is discussed. But, as we shall see, some of the most recent studies integrate elements from various previous perspectives, therefore leading to a certain convergence among different streams of research.

As already mentioned, a number of authors (Demers, 1999; Weick & Quinn, 1999) have characterized the field as divided between transformational, or "episodic," and incremental, or "continuous," views of change. As we shall see, the first of these, for the most part, focuses on planned changes driven by top managers using formal organizational processes, while the second emphasizes emergent changes, which are the (more or less unanticipated) result of multiple local actions. My basic argument is that the most recent theoretical perspectives on organizational change attempt to bridge these two competing conceptions of change. Furthermore, I suggest that it is the difference in the conception of agency that now separates the two major streams of research on change: the natural evolution and the social dynamics perspectives.

Organization of the Book

The book is divided into three parts, each section covering one period. Each part has roughly the same structure. First I introduce the period, articulating the general conception of change that is prevalent at the time and briefly discussing the economic and social context that frames the evolution of the themes and theoretical perspectives. I then present the theoretical perspectives that are dominant in that period, sometimes briefly describing more marginal perspectives that will become more prominent in later periods. My aim in placing the theories in the socioeconomic context in which they emerged is not to suggest a cause-and-effect relationship but to observe the parallels in the evolution of the environment in which organizations live and the preoccupations of scholars in our field.

Each era is characterized by a major debate that forms the basis of the narrative around which that part of the book is constructed. Within each part, the presentation of the various theories or approaches is articulated around the following questions: Do organizations really change and why (or why not)? What is meant by organizational change? How do organizations change? Who is involved? What are the consequences of organizational change? Naturally, the answers to these questions depend, in large part, upon the conceptions of the organization, the environment, and the actor that authors of the various perspectives adopt more or less explicitly. I thus include in the presentation each theory's definition of these concepts. However, the structure of each chapter is adjusted to reflect the main features of the approach in that period. I conclude the book with a synthesis of the field as a whole, a comparison showing the links between schools in the three periods, and a discussion of what I see as the main issues in the continuing evolution of this field of organizational inquiry.

PART I

Adaptation or Selection?

> Although development can be considered as the natural mode of
> organizational behavior, there is no theoretical consensus as to
> which forces generate development or hold it back. There is a debate
> as to how far one should seek to interpret the development of orga-
> nizations as the product of external forces rooted in the social and
> economic system, as opposed to interpreting it as the product of idio-
> syncratic purposive behavior on the part of those within organiza-
> tions who decide on strategies.
>
> (Child & Kieser, 1981, p. 2)

Do Organizations Really Change?

From the post–World War II years to the late 1970s, this question is central to
the reflection on organizational change and is framed in terms of adaptation.
For most of this period, the answer to this question is a resounding yes. There
is little doubt in most practitioners' and scholars' minds that organizations
really can change deliberately and that their main goal is adaptation through
growth. *Growth* and *development* are the preferred terms for talking about
change. For example, Child and Kieser, in their 1981 review of the field, define
development very broadly as "a change in an organization's condition" (p. 28)
over time.

This era, starting after the World War II,[1] is first characterized in the
literature by an optimistic view of change. For the most part, change is viewed
as benevolent, positive—it equates with progress. There is a definite sense that
change equals expansion and that expansion is a natural phenomenon, as
can be seen in the various papers edited by Starbuck in 1971 under the title
Organizational Growth and Development. During that period, change is more
or less explicitly conceived as a process of gradual adaptation. Except for a small
group of scholars who view change as emergent, the dominant view is that

1

adaptation is largely controlled by management reacting to either internal or external pressures.

This view of change is totally in accord with the glorious postwar years, epitomized by the phenomenal growth and great economic stability that prevail until the mid-1970s. Companies in the West, American firms in particular, are enjoying a long period of prosperity and expansion. Socially and politically, human rights and democracy are at the forefront, most likely in reaction to the tragic events of the Second World War. It is also a period of social ferment that gives rise to a questioning of the traditional social order. The growing popularity of the Organizational Development movement, promoting change based on humanist values, is part of that trend. Until the mid-1970s, this "social revolution" combines with the new abundance to create the impression that anything is possible.

But this period of optimism ends abruptly with a recession brought about, according to most accounts, by the 1973 oil embargo.[2] The first oil crisis, followed by a second one in the early 1980s, plunges the world into the worst economic downturn since the Great Depression of the 1930s. From 1973 to 1979, the annual growth in U.S. productivity, which had reached 4%, drops to about 1.5% (Wren, 1994); inflation rates rise from 5.8% in 1976 to 13.5% in 1980, and interest rates go from 5.25% to 12.87% in the same period.

At about the same time, authors challenging the dominant view on organizational change are starting to be heard. Hannan and Freeman (1977), for example, assert that most organizations are too rigid to be able to adapt to environmental change. They argue that environmental selection is a better explanation than purposive adaptation for the changes witnessed in populations of organizations. Furthermore, their view of organizational change is pessimistic. They affirm that large-scale change is dangerous, making organizations more vulnerable. Their answer to the question "Do organizations really change?" is that most organizations don't really change, because of high inertia, and that those who try risk dying in the process.

The first period of evolution of the field, thus, culminates in a debate over whether organizations can change deliberately to adapt to their evolving environment or are simply constrained by environmental forces that determine which forms of organization will survive. This opposition between the advocates of voluntarism and environmental determinism (Child & Kieser, 1981; Hrebeniak & Joyce, 1985) is still part of the debates that characterize the field to this day (Aldrich, 1999; Baum, 2002).

Actually, a variety of positions, on a continuum ranging from the strategic choice perspective defended by Child (1972) to the natural selection argument proposed by Hannan and Freeman (1977), make up this first period. For the sake of clarity, they are divided into two chapters. Chapter 1 presents various perspectives on growth and adaptation: the rational adaptation and organic adaptation approaches and life-cycle theory. In spite of their differences with regard to the freedom of action afforded managers, they all view change as organizational adaptation. Chapter 2 introduces the other side of the debate and features the population ecology and neo-institutionalist theories as the more environmentally deterministic view of organizational change (see Figure I.1).

Despite these divergences, as we shall see, most of the work of that period focuses on the study of organizational change as a *difference* between states and/or forms over time, rather than as a *process* (Van de Ven & Poole, 1995). The observation and explanation of the differences in structure, strategy, or management style are emphasized over the discussion of the dynamics of change. Even though some case studies that describe the process of change mark that era, most often, causal explanations of adaptation are derived from large-sample cross-sectional studies.

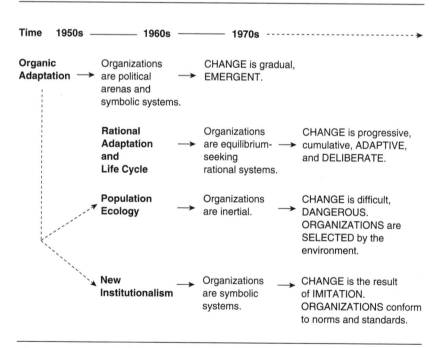

Figure I.1   First Period: Adaptation or Selection?

Notes

1. I have chosen this date as the starting point for my analysis because in the extensive literature review of the topic done by Starbuck in 1965 only 16 of the 246 references predate 1945.

2. In 1973, OPEC (Organization of Petroleum Exporting Countries) imposes an oil embargo on certain countries, including the United States, that sends oil prices skyrocketing and causes inflation to rise dramatically. As a consequence of this crisis, the international system of fixed exchange rates (the Bretton Woods Agreement) is terminated. Fluctuations in international exchange rates and a rapid increase in interest rates follow (Hafsi & Demers, 1989).

1

Adaptation and
Growth Perspective

U ntil the 1970s, most scholars interested in organizational change conceive it in terms of growth and development, linked to deliberate efforts at adaptation. This conception of change is exemplified in a collection of articles edited by Starbuck in 1971. In the book's introductory survey, first published in March's 1965 *Handbook of Organizations,* Starbuck argues:

> Growth is not spontaneous. It is a consequence of decisions. . . . The relationships between specific decisions and ultimate expansion of the organization may be tenuous, but expansion is necessarily dependent upon some decisions and the actions that follow them. (Starbuck, 1971a, pp. 13–14)

Noting the positive connotations associated with organizational change in that era, Child and Kieser (1981) mention that "development is usually interpreted by people in organizations as indicating innovation, growing capability and increased size" (p. 28). Growth is, therefore, seen as the normal evolutionary path for organizations, because larger size is associated with economies of scale, higher profits, and higher survival rates, as well as more prestige, power, and job security for executives (Starbuck, 1971a). But among researchers who explain organizational development and growth in terms of internal forces, there are three trends. First, there is a group of authors who favor more or less voluntaristic explanations of organizational growth and adaptation, such as Penrose (1952), Thompson (1967), Child (1972), and Pfeffer and Salancik (1978). A second group view adaptation as a more emergent phenomenon (Cyert & March, 1963; Selznick, 1957). These two bodies of work are respectively labeled, after Hirsch and Lounsbury (1997), the rational adaptation and the organic adaptation approaches. Finally, a third group of authors develop life-cycle models (Greiner, 1972; Stopford & Wells, 1972). In the following pages, these views are presented with a focus on how each one treats the following themes: the determinants of change, the nature of change, the process of change, and the actors involved.

Rational Adaptation Approaches

Child and Kieser (1981), in their literature review on organizational development, include references to numerous theories that, following Hannan and Freeman (1984), we will label rational adaptation theories (see Table 1.1). Among these, one finds contingency theory (Lawrence & Lorsch, 1969; Thompson, 1967), resource dependency theory (Pfeffer & Salancik, 1978), and the strategic choice perspective (Child, 1972). While these various perspectives adopt different positions with regard to the level of discretion granted to managers, they all agree that organizations can change to pursue goals that are adaptive. But the extent to which they explicitly focus on organizational change is very different from one perspective to another, as we will see in the following sections.

CONTINGENCY THEORY

The structural contingency approach develops in the 1960s and achieves dominance in the 1970s in the field of organization theory. The main assumption of contingency theory, which is part of the functionalist tradition,[1] is that the structural components of the organization must be integrated for the organization to survive. Therefore, a change in one structural element must be followed by adaptive changes in other elements for coherence to be maintained. Moreover, contingency theorists argue that performance is dependent on the achievement of a match between various situational features (such as technology, environment, size, and age) and structural features (Khandwalla, 1973; Lawrence & Lorsch, 1969; Pugh, Hickson, Hinings, & Turner, 1971). Even if contingency theorists don't discuss explicitly the passage from one set of organizational characteristics to the other, they imply that managers, as rational decision makers, are responsible for modifying the organization's characteristics to adapt it to its environment.

Starting in the 1960s, first in Britain with the studies of Burns and Stalker (1961) and Woodward (1965), and then in the United States with the work of Thompson (1967) and Lawrence and Lorsch (1969), scholars develop a situational approach to organizational adaptation. Viewing organizations as open

Table 1.1   Rational Adaptation Approaches

RATIONAL ADAPTATION		
General model of change:	MISALIGNMENT – Environmental change	ADAPTATION – Organizational adjustment	ALIGNMENT Return to stability

Focus: Level of discretion of managers in achieving adaptation

Antecedent: Sociology

	CONTINGENCY THEORY
Organization:	Rational, flexible tool; structured system
Process of change:	Reactive, deliberate, piecemeal, gradual change of strategy and/or structure to achieve functional equilibrium in reaction to change in contingencies (e.g., environment, technology, size)
Authors:	Burns & Stalker (1961); Lawrence & Lorsch (1969); Thompson (1967); Donaldson (1996b)
	PURPOSEFUL ACTION APPROACHES
	Resource dependency
Organization:	Rational, flexible tool; black box
Process of change:	Planned responses to preserve autonomy in the face of environmental constraints, ranging from avoidance to compliance and manipulation
Authors:	Pfeffer & Salancik (1978); Oliver (1991); Sherer & Lee (2002)
	Strategic choice
Organization:	Rational, flexible tool; structured system
Process of change:	Proactive, deliberate, gradual change aimed at achieving strategic fit by choosing or influencing the environment
Author:	Child (1972, 1997)

systems, they associate organizational survival and growth with the adoption of a design appropriate for a given environment. According to them, there is no internally prescribed sequence of change, but the options open to management are still severely constrained by environmental and situational exigencies.

In this approach, the organization is conceived as an integrated system inter-acting with its environment, as well as an instrument in the hands of rational managers. In most studies, the organization is described in terms of macro-structural variables (such as centralization, formalization, and standardization) and macro-organizational features (such as scale, functions or activities, and systems) (Lawrence & Lorsch, 1969; Pugh et al., 1971). The role of the environment is predominant; it is defined mainly as the task environment comprising the various organizations such as suppliers, customers, competitors, and regu-latory groups that matter to the organization (Thompson, 1967, pp. 27–28). In most studies, it is measured in terms of its levels of uncertainty (i.e., degree of predictability), stability (i.e., frequency and rhythm of change), complexity (i.e., degree of heterogeneity and interaction), and/or threat (e.g., degree of compe-tition) (Burns & Stalker, 1961; Khandwalla, 1973; Lawrence & Lorsch, 1969).

Contingency studies, apart from a few early in-depth case studies (Burns & Stalker, 1961; Lawrence & Lorsch, 1969), rely on cross-sectional analyses that try to establish the contextual determinants of different types of structures. For example, Burns and Stalker show that a stable environment requires a central-ized bureaucratic structure (the mechanistic system of management), whereas turbulent conditions call for a flexible decentralized structure (the organic system of management); pioneering case studies such as these spawn a large number of related quantitative studies (Donaldson, 1996b).

The types of change discussed in the contingency approach are therefore mainly structural responses to specific contingencies. As mentioned before, a systematic study of the process of change itself is not part of contingency theory, but the assumption behind those studies was that "organizational managers were strategic thinkers who could rationally plan and direct performance-enhancing changes" (Hirsch & Lounsbury, 1997, p. 81). It is also clear from the normative conclusions derived from this work that management's role is viewed as reacting to the environment by gradually and continuously adjusting the organization's design (Lawrence & Lorsch, 1969). The organizational change process is conceived to be a deliberate but reactive and constrained process of gradual adaptation.

DISCUSSION

In the 1970s, contingency theory starts to draw some criticism both in Europe (Child, 1972; Crozier & Friedberg, 1977) and in the United States (Meyer & Rowan, 1977). Although it is generally agreed that it is an improve-ment over classical management theory and its search for the "one best way"

(Child & Kieser, 1981; Wren, 1994), the assumption of severe environmental constraints on managerial choice inherent in this view is strongly challenged, particularly by European scholars. Child and Crozier and Friedberg, for example, criticize the fact that contingency theorists develop causal explanations of environmental determinacy on the basis of statistical correlations. They oppose the notion that the environment is a given, a constraint over which organizational members have no control. They argue that the contingency view underestimates the importance of human agency. According to Child (1972), " 'strategic choice' extends to the context within which the organization is operating, to the standards of performance . . . and to the design of the organization's structure itself" (p. 3). Crozier and Friedberg, also proponents of human agency, criticize the monolithic and apolitical view of organizations that characterizes contingency theory.

A second challenge comes from American authors such as Meyer and Rowan (1977), who oppose the functionalist reasoning underlying contingency research. Although they agree with contingency theorists about the environmentally driven nature of adaptation, they argue that adaptation is the result of social influence processes that emphasize legitimacy, rather than the outcome of a rational process leading to more efficient organizations as implied by contingency theory (Tolbert & Zucker, 1996).

Contingency theorists are also berated for producing inconclusive results (Meyer, 1979; Wren, 1994); for example, Child and Kieser (1981) note: "There is no evidence yet to suggest that matching organizational designs to prevailing contingencies contributes importantly to performance" (p. 56). A fourth related criticism concerns the fact that most contingency studies have examined individual contingencies—for example, one independent contextual variable correlated with one dependent structural variable. This type of research gives results that are difficult to synthesize; these results have led some to suggest that contextual and structural variables should be conceived as interdependent, forming a gestalt or configuration (Child & Kieser, 1981; Mintzberg, 1979). This configuration approach, conceiving change as radical transformation rather than incremental change, becomes an important perspective on organizational change in the 1980s and is presented in the second part of this book.

Donaldson (1996a), a passionate advocate of structural contingency theory, refutes these criticisms. For instance, he argues that his research studying the link between strategic change and structural change, taking into account intermediate stages between the changes, validates contingency theory's view of change (Donaldson, 1996b). In the conclusion to his book aptly titled *For Positivist Organization Theory* (Donaldson, 1996a), he insists that incremental rational adaptation in which an organization adjusts its structure little by little over time is a coherent explanation for most structural changes. He argues that "over time, this series of growth spurts allows an organization (if the environment permits) to change considerably growing from, say, a small firm to a large, diversified corporation" (p. 169). Donaldson also rejects the configuration view with its emphasis on radical change, criticizing its reference to vision and charismatic leaders as reliance on "quasi-religious processes" for explanation (p. 170).

Furthermore, despite the attacks, in the 1980s and 1990s, contingency-style functionalist research remains prominent in the field, as it moves from structural contingency to a contingency approach to strategy and strategic change (Donaldson, 1996b). Authors such as Smith and Grimm (1987), Grimm, Corsi, and Smith (1993), and Wiersema and Bantel (1992) study the determinants and consequences of strategic change based on what Rajagopalan and Spreitzer (1997) call a "rational lens perspective." Essentially, these large-sample statistical studies operationalize strategic change as discrete changes in content or direction of strategy (e.g., change in strategic type or in degree of diversification). Most of this research looks at the link between environmental variables (e.g., munificence or uncertainty or specific changes such as deregulation), organizational variables (e.g., size, age, prior performance), and strategic change, and the impact of strategic change on performance. Others examine the relationship between the likelihood of strategic change and the top management team's characteristics, such as age, tenure, and diversity (Grimm & Smith, 1991; Wiersema & Bantel, 1992).

According to Rajagopalan and Spreitzer (1997), the results of these studies are often inconclusive or contradictory. In their exhaustive review, they conclude that this is due, in large part, to the underspecified model these authors use. The rational adaptation model treats "managerial actions and cognitions as a 'black box' " (Rajagopalan & Spreitzer, 1997, p. 55) and presumes that strategic change is the result of the planned actions of rational managers reacting to objective environmental and internal pressures. These actions and the motivations behind them are not studied; only their outcomes (i.e., the change in strategy content) are measured. For example, even Wiersema and Bantel (1992), while they situate themselves in the strategic choice perspective by explaining strategic change as a result of the top management team's cognitive perspectives, finally adopt contingency reasoning. Their study using measures of certain demographic characteristics such as age, tenure, and heterogeneity as a proxy for managers' cognitive perspectives associates them more with the contingency school and its notion of fit than with the strategic choice perspective. Although their theoretical explanation emphasizes the role of managers' cognitions in initiating strategic change, their methodological choices favor contingency reasoning—that is to say, associating specific objective characteristics of the top management team with an increased likelihood of strategic change.

However, despite these shortcomings, the contingency view still continues to contribute to our understanding of organizational change by making us more aware of the influence of environmental and other contextual factors on organizational development, in particular on choice of organizational design and of strategy. And, as such, it offers normative solutions that go beyond classical management theory's one best way of organizing (Child & Kieser, 1981; Wren, 1994). But as an organizational change theory, it is a theory of fit that helps answer the question "What kind of change is appropriate?" rather than a theory of process. In addition, most of this research, both the early studies on structure and the more recent ones on strategic change, tends to assume the environmental context is "deterministic and immutable" (Rajagopalan & Spreitzer, 1997, p. 56), which is what distinguishes it most from the adaptation theories that are discussed next.

PURPOSEFUL ACTION APPROACHES: STRATEGIC CHOICE AND RESOURCE DEPENDENCY

Some authors elaborate alternative adaptation theories that assume more freedom of action for managers. Among the better known are Child (1972), who proposes the strategic choice model of decision making, and Pfeffer and Salancik (1978), who develop resource dependency theory. These authors' works, which, following Child and Kieser (1981), I label the purposeful-action approach, are not, strictly speaking, theories of organizational change; they are more general. Decision-making models are concerned with decisions about change but are much broader in scope. After all, not all or even most decisions result in change. In the same way, resource dependency can be used to explain stability as well as change. For example, Pfeffer and Salancik discuss organizational responses to environmental pressures, such as avoidance and manipulation, which, in fact, are ways not to change. As theories of adaptation, they see the relationship between organization and environment as bidirectional in contrast to the previous adaptation perspectives. According to these views, environments can be adapted to organizations, just as organizations adapt to the environment. I will present these views briefly in the following paragraphs because of the influence they have on the future evolution of the literature on organizational change.

As Child (1972) mentions in his famous paper, he is interested in developing a theory of strategic choice as a decision-making process where ideology, expectations, and power relations, among other dimensions, play an important role. He believes that influential decision makers—which he refers to as the "dominant coalition," following Cyert and March (1963)—have the power to make choices that are only partially constrained by environmental and organizational contingencies. He asserts that managers are not prisoners of their environment, but that they have the capacity to influence it. For example, large organizations have the power to create the demand for their products. By diversifying, they are even choosing the environment in which they want to evolve. Similarly for organizational design, Child refutes the notion that managers are forced to adopt a specific structure. According to him, ideology, goals, and power relations play as important a role as issues of organizational fit in determining the choices made. Child adopts a voluntarist position that places him at the opposite end of the continuum from the authors who adopt a deterministic point of view.

Pfeffer and Salancik (1978) occupy a middle ground between the environmentally deterministic and the free will perspectives. On the one hand, they begin their book by arguing for the adoption of an external focus on organizations and by strongly criticizing most organization theory as being too centered on the organization's internal functioning. For example, they assert that even contingency theory, which acknowledges the importance of the environment, remains essentially concerned with internal adjustments. Their position is that the main problem of organizations is survival, which they view as depending on the acquisition of resources from the environment. They go so far as saying that the role of management is mostly symbolic and that individual action explains very little variance in organizational behavior, which seems to imply a fairly deterministic view. On the other hand, however, the contextual perspective they propose on organizations aims to understand both the "effect of environments on organizations and the effect of organizations on environments" (p. 11). Furthermore, they specify that "constraints are not predestined and irreversible" (p. 18) and develop an "image of the manager" that emphasizes his role as "an advocater, an active manipulator of constraints and of the social settings in which the organization is embedded" (p. 19). Finally, like Child (1972), they argue that the environment is not a given, but has to be perceived and interpreted by managers, and that it is on the basis of this created or "enacted" environment (Weick, 1979b) that managers act. This view of the environment, as a phenomenon that is perceived subjectively and socially constructed, rather than an objective reality, also distinguishes these authors from contingency theorists.

This difference is significant because it implies that, for understanding organizational change, it is important not only to measure discrete changes, but also to understand why and how changes are made. In fact, the theoretical frameworks these authors develop suggest that it is critical to study the *process* of change. Moreover, this affects not only the questions asked but also the methods of research that are used. In a sense, these authors set the stage for the next period, which focuses on how organizational change is actually managed.

DISCUSSION

Not surprisingly, one of the staunchest critics of Child's strategic choice perspective is Donaldson (1996a), a contingency theorist. He labels strategic choice an "anti-management organization theory" and refutes its validity. He argues that "managers may go through the subjective process of choosing" (1996a, p. 51), but that the outcome is already determined by the need for objective fit to various contingencies. Therefore, there is no real strategic choice. On the other hand, as part of the rational adaptation approach (Hannan & Freeman, 1984), the purposeful-action perspective, like contingency theory, is criticized for assuming too much intentionality and predictability in organizational behavior (March, 1981). This reaction against the dominance of the "rational view" of organizations is not new. It starts in the 1950s with authors such as Selznick (1957), Cyert and March (1963), and Braybrooke and Lindblom (1963), who view as unrealistic the depiction of adaptation as deliberate programmed change. They argue that organizations are not technical instruments in the hands of omniscient managers, and they develop models of "organic adaptation" (Hirsch & Lounsbury, 1997).

Another related limit of the purposeful action approach is that it is essentially a top management perspective (Demers, 1993). Crozier and Friedberg (1977), for example, criticize Child's (1972) strategic choice model for its emphasis on top management (the dominant coalition) and on strategic decision making, at the expense of the organization as a pluralistic entity and as an organized action system.

Alternatives to the dominance of the rational perspective emerge both in the late 1950s and the late 1970s. The first wave, the organic adaptation approach, despite its relative marginality in the field of organizational change at the time, has seen its influence rise over the years. The "new" institutionalism and population ecology, the second wave, with their radically different vision of change, provoke immediate reactions and rapidly gain popularity in organization studies. And, as will be seen, their influence on the field of organizational change increases in the 1990s.

Organic Adaptation Approach

As Hirsch and Lounsbury (1997) note in their insightful essay, this early organic adaptation approach, with its focus on internal organizational dynamics, is completely overshadowed by the emergence of contingency theory. But it offers a vision of organizations and change whose impact can be felt to varying degrees in more recent perspectives, such as the cultural and the political approaches. I will briefly present its most influential representatives, who diverge in many respects but share a pluralistic view of organizations[2] (see Table 1.2).

Cyert and March (1963), characterizing the firm as an "adaptively rational system rather than an omnisciently rational system" (p. 99), propose a decision process theory that seeks to explain how organizations adapt. In their view, firms are not malleable instruments in the hands of omnipotent managers. Rather organizations are political arenas constituted by subgroups with diverse interests, in which adaptation is an emergent process that depends on "what

Table 1.2   Organic Adaptation Approach

ORGANIC ADAPTATION	
General model of change: ADAPTATION/DRIFT Functional or dysfunctional, gradual, emergent change	
Focus: Nonrational conception of organization and change	
Antecedents: Sociology, political science, social psychology, behaviorism	
	Behavioral theory of the firm, disjointed incrementalism
Organization:	Political arena
Process of change:	Step-by-step gradual process of bargaining leading to emergent results
Authors:	Cyert & March (1963); Braybrooke & Lindblom (1963)
	"Old" institutionalism
Organization:	Political and symbolic system
Process of change:	Process of institutionalization of values or drift (i.e., natural, emergent change stemming from compromise and conflict)
Author:	Selznick (1957)
	Theory of organizing
Organization:	Loosely coupled socially constructed system
Process of change:	Ongoing collective sense-making process leading to continuous emergent change
Author:	Weick (1969, 1979b)

goals are currently evoked and what part of the system is involved in making the decision" (p. 100). In their view, organizational response is governed by procedures and decision rules and is influenced by the dominant coalition.

While Cyert and March (1963) develop a general model of organizational decision making, Braybrooke and Lindblom's (1963) "disjointed incrementalism" and Selznick's institutional approach (1957) are explicitly concerned with organizational change. Building on two dimensions—the scope of change (incremental or large) and the type of situation (low or high understanding)—Braybrooke and Lindblom construct a typology of four types of change. Influenced by the experience of the government sector, they argue that a rational, programmed approach to change only works for incremental change in situations of high understanding (i.e., routine decisions). Viewing organizations as political arenas, they suggest that, in a situation of low understanding, a piecemeal, incremental approach to adaptation—"disjointed incrementalism," also known as "muddling through" (Lindblom, 1959)—is more realistic and is likely to give better results.[3] In this view, change is a step-by-step process, the result of bargaining "along regularized circuits among players positioned hierarchically" (Allison, 1971, p. 162).

Selznick (1957), the most prominent representative of the early institutional school, elaborates a theory of organizational change as a process of institutionalization. Criticizing most organization theorists for being overly concerned with routine decisions resulting in static adaptation, he focuses on what he calls "dynamic" adaptation, actions that result in basic institutional changes. Opposing the concept of organization (a technical instrument, "an expendable tool") to that of institution (a "product of social needs and pressures—a responsive, adaptive organism") (p. 5), he defines leadership as the art of institution-building. He conceives the process of institutionalization as infusing the organization with "value beyond the technical requirements of the task at hand" (p. 17), as "the area of 'character-defining' commitments, which affect the organization's capacity to control its own future behavior" (p. 35).

As noted by Hirsch and Lounsbury (1997), Selznick "thought of leaders as statesmen . . . required to manage a wide complex of interests" both inside and outside the organization (p. 81). However, Selznick's position is ambiguous. He acknowledges that the change process is usually emergent, "not . . . a result of conscious design but a natural and largely unplanned adaptation to new situations" (Selznick, 1957, p. 12), but he also sees the leader's role as avoiding the natural tendency toward institutional drift (Lodahl & Mitchell, 1980).

These models of organic adaptation all share a political view of organizations and conceive of change as largely emergent, different from what anyone intended, resulting instead from compromise, conflict, and confusion among actors with diverse interests and unequal influence. Still, they retain a resolutely managerial perspective through their emphasis, respectively, on the role of the dominant coalition (Cyert & March, 1963), the pragmatic analyst (Braybrooke & Lindblom, 1963), and the statesman (Selznick, 1957).

A last contribution that can be added to the emergent vision of change is Weick's (1969, 1979a) model of organizing that depicts organizations as loosely coupled systems continuously re-created in interaction. This process view of change places great emphasis on actors' potential for action by calling attention to the way they subjectively create the environment to which they respond. Weick, in contrast to the previous authors, stresses the cognitive process through which shared interpretations are created, rather than the political dimension of collective action.

DISCUSSION

One of the limits shared by these early perspectives is that they remain focused on internal dynamics, neglecting the environment (Hirsch & Lounsbury, 1997; Pfeffer & Salancik, 1978). Even institutional analysis, renowned for the rich contextual and historical description of its case studies, is centered on what occurs within the boundaries of the focal organization (DiMaggio & Powell, 1991). However, in the 1970s, influenced by contingency and life-cycle theory, Swedish authors Rhenman (1973) and Normann (1977) integrate Selznick's institutional approach in their theory of organizational growth and extend it to explicitly include the environment, which they also define in terms of its value system. These authors, who use the language of growth and development characteristic of the first period, show through in-depth case studies the influence of the value systems of the organization and of the environment in framing the development of the organization. They go beyond contingency theory, with its reasoning in terms of rational efficiency and its mechanical model, to explain organizational change as a rational learning process. Rhenman and Normann are part of a group of Scandinavian scholars who become influential in the 1980s, particularly as the strategy process literature gains importance in the field of organizational change.

While Braybrooke and Lindblom's influence is particularly important in the political perspective on change (Johnson, 1988; Quinn, 1980), Cyert and March's behavioral theory of the firm is one of the theoretical foundations of the behavioral (or adaptive) learning school, which gains momentum in the 1990s (Glynn, Lant, & Milliken, 1994). This last theoretical framework is criticized for succumbing to a form of action or behavioral determinism because its view of actors is not sufficiently elaborated to support true human agency. As argued by Whittington (1988), they present an undersocialized view of actors as atomized agents, whose action is governed by psychological traits and individual interests (pp. 524–525). According to Allison (1971), actors become prisoners of the system, and behavior is understood "less as deliberate choices and more as outputs of large organizations functioning according to standard patterns of behaviour" (p. 67). On the other hand, Weick (1969, 1979a), whose work becomes increasingly popular in the 1990s, is faulted for his neglect of structure in favor of a strong position for agency (Whittington, 1988). As will be discussed in the third part of this book, starting in the 1980s but culminating in the 1990s, although this debate between voluntarism and determinism continues, new responses are constantly elaborated that are attempts at bridging them (Garud & Karnoe, 2001; Reed, 2003; Whittington, 1988).

Early institutionalism, for its part, is criticized for its functionalist framework (Tolbert & Zucker, 1996). Neo-institutionalists, while influenced by Selznick, disagree with his view of institutionalization as a functional requirement (i.e., environmental support depending on an organization showing "consistency between core values of the organization and those in the larger society") (Tolbert & Zucker, 1996, p. 178). Rather, they argue that legitimated models (i.e., taken-for-granted scripts, rules, and typifications) are unconsciously adopted through imitation. Finally, Perrow (1986), adopting a critical stance, criticizes the moral ambiguity of this perspective, which favors the established order.

In summary, the influence of scholars within the organic adaptation approach, while fairly limited in the organizational change literature of the time, can be felt in various recent approaches to change. More important, their conception of change as an emergent process becomes characteristic of the third period of evolution of the field. However, until the late 1980s, the vision of change as a deliberate process remains dominant in the literature, largely because of the dominance of contingency theory (Thompson, 1967) and of the transformational perspective on change (Tushman & Romanelli, 1985) that replaces it in the early 1980s.

Life-Cycle Approach

The life-cycle model gains popularity in organization and management theory in the early 1970s. It has been applied, for example, to product development and marketing, operations planning, project management, and strategy. The idea that organizational development follows a predetermined sequence of stages from birth to maturity, sometimes followed by decline and death, is one of the most intuitively appealing metaphors for explaining organizational change. Haire (1959) was one of the first to explicitly use biological models to suggest that organizations are like living organisms and that growth is a natural process following its own internal laws. According to life-cycle theory, development is a cumulative process, with each preceding stage leading the way to the next one in a movement toward increasing organizational complexity and specialization. This generic model proposes a typical path of development; it identifies the common stages of growth, focusing on age and size as critical variables (see Table 1.3).

In the life-cycle approach, the organization is viewed as a unitary entity (Van de Ven & Poole, 1995). Like a living organism, all its parts have a specific function and evolve in an integrated fashion following the same direction. This model adopts the point of view of the anatomist, in the sense that it focuses on identifying each phase and its defining characteristics. Differences in the organization's typical activities, structure, and processes at each stage, as well as the sequence of such changes, are described, but not the process of transition itself.

Because organizational development is conceived as driven by an immanent logic, a preexisting internal program, the role of the environment is viewed as

Table 1.3   Life-Cycle Approach

LIFE CYCLE
General model of change: SEQUENCE OF STAGES Transition between predetermined stages Focus: Generic developmental pattern and common important phases Antecedents: Sociology

Organization:	Living organism
Process of change:	Progressive, natural evolution through a series of fundamental transitions, from birth (entrepreneurial phase) to adolescence (specialization phase) to maturity (decentralization phase).
Authors:	Cameron & Whetten (1993); Chandler (1962); Stopford & Wells (1972)

peripheral. It can act as a catalyst, speed up the rhythm of evolution, or accelerate a transition, but it won't change the basic pattern of organizational growth. This pattern is explained by logical or natural order (Van de Ven & Poole, 1995).

The type of change discussed in a life-cycle model is, therefore, the modification in the particular combination of organizational features, such as strategy, structure, and leadership style, that characterize each stage. Interestingly, most of the research and writing on life-cycle theory deals only with birth, youth, and maturity; stages of decline and death are underrepresented in the literature (Cameron & Whetten, 1993, p. 51). Most models, therefore, tend to present a view of change that is associated with progress. It is only in the 1980s, in a context of recession, that decline and death start to be explored. To better understand the nature of the changes involved, a presentation of the stages-of-development models is necessary.

STAGES OF DEVELOPMENT

Cameron and Whetten (1993), in their review of the literature on life-cycle models, comment that, despite the different dimensions included in the models, they all suggest a very similar sequence of stages. The earliest models tended to focus on the "patterns in size and structure" (Starbuck, 1965). Later models also considered goals pursued, product–market scope, leadership styles, control mechanisms, and group dynamics. A typical model is the well-known three-stage model, with its startup or entrepreneurial phase, its professionalization or specialization phase, and its decentralization or multidivisional phase (Scott, 1971; Stopford & Wells, 1972). Child and Kieser (1981), later, add a fourth phase, the matrix organization.

The generic model suggests that at birth an organization goes through an entrepreneurial phase during which it is entirely under the control of its owner, who directly supervises all operations with little formalization. A startup only needs a simple structure because flexibility is what it requires to establish its product in a niche market. If it is successful, the organization will grow rapidly, and soon the owner will be unable to cope with all the new demands brought on by expansion. This will lead to Stage 2, the specialization phase, with the establishment of functional departments, each one in charge of a specific set of activities, such as marketing, finance, or production. In this type of design, the top manager's role is the coordination of these interdependent activities, which are now formally organized. This hierarchical functional structure, staffed by professional managers, can accommodate considerable growth, as long as the organization remains in the same domain of activity (Chandler, 1962) and doesn't expand geographically beyond exportation (Stopford & Wells, 1972). All that is needed is further specialization through the creation of additional functional subunits.

In Stage 3, the decentralization phase, diversification and/or geographical expansion has increased organizational complexity to the point where top managers can no longer control the development of the organization as a global concern. They don't have sufficient information and knowledge about the new activities and are too involved in day-to-day operations to develop an overall strategy and reap the benefits from diversified operations or international activities. A new multidivisional structure, composed of several quasi-autonomous functional divisions organized on a product or geographic basis, becomes necessary. The divisions are managed by corporate headquarters, which are responsible for deciding the overall strategy and allocating resources among divisions. Finally, in the fourth stage, diversification is so extensive that a matrix structure is necessary to handle the multiple and often conflicting pressures for differentiation (autonomy of the specialized units) and integration (overall coordination).

Chandler (1962),[4] in his masterly historical account of the reorganization of Dupont, General Motors, Sears & Roebuck, and Exxon following their diversification, documents the creation of the large multidivisional firm that is typical of the third stage of organizational development. He argues that it is the change of strategy through the addition of new product lines and new markets that eventually forces the unwitting managers to create a new structure that can handle a degree of complexity incomparable to anything ever seen. While Chandler's analysis concluded that structure follows strategy, others have argued that structure also constrains strategy (Stopford & Wells, 1972). The existing structure being resistant to change influences the type of strategic decisions taken. In any event, this brief presentation clearly shows that life-cycle models are concerned with changes in the overall design of an organization, and as such are particularly concerned with macro-organizational dimensions of the organization.

As mentioned by Child and Kieser (1981), the notion of developmental stages also draws attention to the issues of transition patterns between phases as well as the processes by which such transitions occur. The next pages present the approach of life-cycle theory to these issues.

PATTERNS OF CHANGE

The question of "how organizations change" is mostly treated in terms of whether the transition between phases of the cycle is gradual and smooth or metamorphic (Aldrich, 1999; Starbuck, 1971b). Most authors (Child & Kieser, 1981; Greiner, 1972; Starbuck, 1971b) see the pattern of change as metamorphic and emphasize the discontinuity between stages. Child and Kieser, for example, argue that "the theory of stages in organizational development implies that it is not a smooth, continuous process, but involves abrupt and discrete changes in organizational policies, contexts, and structures" (p. 51). It should be noted that this interpretation of the discontinuous nature of change relates to the *content* of the change, the scope and magnitude of the differences between states, and is not derived from a systematic study of the process of change itself.

Actually, most pure life-cycle models don't take into account the process of transition. They are more concerned with the antecedents and outcomes (or results) of the change process than the dynamics of change over time. Although some authors acknowledge organizational resistance to moving from one phase to the next and the difficulties involved, they still present the process as a natural progression with the previous phase being the prerequisite, and setting the stage, for the next one (Stopford & Wells, 1972). The shift may be difficult, but it is the leader's role to facilitate this internal restructuring. Greiner (1972), who developed a four-stage metamorphic model of growth, distinguishes for each phase a specific management crisis. For example, the creativity phase engenders a crisis of leadership, the direction phase a crisis of autonomy, the delegation phase a crisis of control, and the coordination phase a crisis of red tape. The solution he offers to these crises is a change of structure and often a change of the management team itself. But again the process of change is left unspecified, and the actions taken to move the organization from one phase to the next are reduced to a few generic solutions, such as increasing specialization, formalization, or delegation (Aldrich, 1999).

In that view, change is rare, but predictable, and managerial action is restricted to a limited range of options: "In each revolutionary stage it becomes evident that this stage can be ended only by certain specific solutions; moreover these solutions were different from those that were applied to the problems of the preceding revolution" (Greiner, 1972, p. 45). The goal of these changes is to reestablish the internal equilibrium by adapting the organization's functioning to the requirements of its particular stage of development.

While stages-of-development models have been elaborated on the basis of longitudinal case studies such as the one by Chandler (1962) that describe the transition process in some detail, life-cycle theory itself has relatively little to say about these processes of change. It is in the next period, with the increased interest in understanding how organizational change is managed, that authors adopting configurational, cognitive, political, and cultural perspectives on change start theorizing in more depth about the change process.

DISCUSSION

Life-cycle theory, despite its wide popularity, has always been controversial. Its reliance on a biological analogy has given rise to many criticisms (Cameron & Whetten, 1993; Child & Kieser, 1981; Kimberly & Miles, 1980). Some, like Child and Kieser (1981), debate the usefulness of the life-cycle metaphor in the case of organizations because, unlike living organisms, "many organizations seem to survive at an arrested stage of organic development, while most of the organizations attaining a mature level of development then avoid the transition into decline and death" (p. 46). This skepticism over the validity of the metaphor is exacerbated by the lack of empirical evidence. Starbuck (1971a) asserts, "The greatest part of what we think we know about organizational development over time is based upon case studies of single organizations" (p. 203). More than 10 years later, Cameron and Whetten suggest that the continuing controversy is due to the fact that "organizational development models have not been based on systematic empirical investigation" (1993, p. 51). Finally, in 1999, Aldrich reports that, after studying 63 stage models of organizational growth, Levie and Hay (1998, cited in Aldrich, 1999) conclude that such models have persisted despite their failure to empirically predict patterns of organizational growth.

Another line of attack has come from those who question the predetermined nature of organizational development inherent in the life-cycle analogy. One of these critics is Penrose (1952), an economist, who explains growth by management's quest to maximize profits. In her view, growth is dependent upon the availability of managerial resources. Like life-cycle theorists, she emphasizes expansion and the ensuing modifications to organizational structure. However, she attributes the increasing operational complexity brought on by growth, not to an immanent drive, but to management's will. Kimberly (1980), in the introduction to *The Organizational Life Cycle*, cites Penrose's argument:

... we have no reason whatsoever for thinking that the growth pattern of a bio-logical organism is *willed* by the organism itself. On the other hand, we have every reason for thinking that the growth of the firm is willed by those who make the decisions of the firm. . . . We know of no general "laws" predetermining men's choices, nor have we as yet any established basis for suspecting the existence of such laws. By contrast, . . . we have every reason for thinking that these matters are predetermined by the nature of the living organisms. (Penrose, 1952, pp. 808–809, cited in Kimberly, 1980, p. 11)

To the preceding criticisms, Kimberly answers that using the life-cycle model in a strict sense is misguided. The usefulness of the life-cycle perspective is in raising interesting questions about organizations and their history and bringing researchers to develop theories for explaining developmental processes, for example those of birth and decline (Kimberly et al., 1980, pp. 11–12).

Other researchers agree with Kimberly; Cameron and Whetten (1993), com-paring organizational life-cycle models to group development models, suggest amendments to the generic model. They argue that, in older organizations fac-ing crises, a phenomenon of recycling to earlier phases can occur: "This recy-cling phenomenon explains why some writers find evidence that sequential transitions are characteristic of organizations whereas others argue that sequen-tial change does not occur" (p. 58). They also propose that the pure model is mostly useful to describe young organizations, but that in mature decentralized organizations, different subunits could be in different stages of development. More recently, Van de Ven and Poole (1995), discussing life-cycle models, com-ment that "there is no reason to suppose organizational systems could not have such processes as well" (p. 515). They argue that it is by using multiple models, including this one, that more complete explanations of organizational change can be developed.

To summarize, apart from distinguishing different stages in structural terms, life-cycle literature has also focused on identifying the strategy (Child & Kieser, 1981; Normann, 1977; Stopford & Wells, 1972), the leadership crises (Greiner, 1972), the type of managers (Cameron & Whetten, 1993), and the type of pol-itics (Mintzberg, 1983), as well as the criteria of organizational effectiveness (Cameron & Whetten, 1993) specific to each stage. More generally, this stream of research has been concerned with establishing what constitutes a coherent response to a particular stage of development.

Since its heyday in the mid-1980s, the life-cycle analogy has continued to stimulate scholars. One research trend is the study of specific settings rather than using the life-cycle model as a universal model. For example, the wine industry (Beverland & Lockshin, 2001) and the banking industry (Metzger, 1989), as well as small businesses (Dodge & Robbins, 1992) and family businesses (Gersick, Lansberg, Desjardins, & Dunn, 1999), have been studied from a life-cycle per-spective. Another trend has been to study the relationship between organizational life cycle and other organizational features, such as the composition of boards of directors (Johnson, 1997) and accounting systems (Moores & Yuen, 2001), and to extend its use to organizational processes like learning (Miller & Shamsie, 2001; Oliver, 2001) and change itself (Mintzberg & Westley, 1992). Over the years, the life-cycle metaphor has been used more and more loosely and can be viewed as including all stage and cyclical models (Van de Ven & Poole, 1995).

To conclude, the life-cycle model is an interesting framework for emphasizing certain regularities in the development of organizations and, as such, can be a useful tool for managers and students of change. It also has had the merit of drawing attention to certain critical events in an organization's life, thereby stimulating research on the dynamics of birth (Van de Ven, 1980), growth (Lodahl & Mitchell, 1980), decline (Weitzel & Jönsson, 1989), and death (Sutton, 1987). But as an organizational change theory, because it is acontextual and aprocessual, it needs to be completed by other approaches.

Conclusion

This overview of the literature from the 1950s to the early 1980s shows us that change is conceived essentially in terms of growth and rational adaptation. Authors of the rationalist approach, which dominates during that period, view the organization as an instrument in the hands of managers who deliberately adjust the organization's structure and systems in reaction to internal or external pressures to maintain its efficiency. In contrast, the more marginal organic adaptation approach sees change as the emergent result of regulated processes, bargaining, or interpretation processes. But whether adaptation is conceived as intended or emergent, it is for the most part conceived as an expansive, gradual change that is internally driven (even if in reaction to environmental pressures). One could argue that this view is consistent with the relative stability and favorable economic context that characterize most of that period. However, in the context of the environmental turbulence that marks the end of the first period, organizational change is reconceived as an issue of selection or imitation.

Notes

1. Sociologists of the functionalist school view the main goal of any social institution as survival. Theirs is a sociology of social order (Burrell & Morgan, 1979). For example, antecedents of the contingency school in organization studies can be found in the work of scholars such as Merton (1948), Gouldner (1950), and Blau (1955). They studied organizations as small societies with the goal of "assessing the dynamic balance between dysfunctional and beneficial outcomes of given structural arrangements" (Tolbert & Zucker, 1996, p. 176).

2. While the authors of the purposeful-action approach also have a political view of organizations, they focus more on the dominant coalition. Therefore their vision of organizations is more unitary than pluralistic.

3. They also comment that a situation of large-scale change and high understanding is utopian and that situations of large-scale change and low understanding, such as revolutions, crises, and grand opportunities, call for a method yet to be formalized. It is interesting to note that they concentrate on gradual, piecemeal change, which is more characteristic of that era.

4. Although Chandler's empirical work was used for developing the life-cycle model, he isn't a life-cycle theorist himself. His landmark studies were also interpreted by contingency theorists as confirming their point of view (Lawrence & Lorsch, 1969, pp. 195–197). But Chandler (1962), an historian, cannot be easily classified. His comparative analysis is sensitive to cultural, historical, and contextual influences. He also emphasizes the role of managers' creative action in organizational change.

2

Selection and Imitation Perspective

I n the late 1970s, some authors begin to question whether purposeful adaptation really is the main force behind the changes witnessed in organizations. These theorists see the scope for managerial action as severely limited and the environment, either through selection or imitation processes, as the major force behind organizational change (Hirsch & Lounsbury, 1997).

Two approaches stand out as being particularly important because they question some of the basic assumptions shared in the field: population ecology (Aldrich, 1979; Hannan & Freeman, 1977, 1984) and neo-institutional theory (DiMaggio & Powell, 1983; Meyer & Rowan, 1977). In contrast to adaptationist theories that explain the transformation of the organizational landscape over time by individual organizations' unique adaptation to their context, these theories develop explanations of change at the population or field level and offer different accounts of the mechanisms by which this occurs.

Both approaches are concerned with the issue of the diversity of organizational forms but approach it from opposing points of view. Population ecology's founding article by Hannan and Freeman (1977) starts with the question: "Why are there so many kinds of organization?" On the other hand, the "new" institutionalism's equally notorious article by DiMaggio and Powell (1983) begins by questioning this notion and stating that it is rather a tendency toward homogeneity among organizations that is observed over time. Population ecology sees competitive selection, the law of the jungle, as the main process behind both diversity and isomorphism. Individual organizations don't adapt; new organizations having the characteristics required by the environment are selected and the ones that are maladapted disappear, leading to a transformation at the population level. Influenced by authors of the organic adaptation perspective, these authors conceive organizations as "recalcitrant tools" (Hannan & Freeman, 1989, p. 6), which are too slow to adapt to environmental change. One example would be the disappearance of small local retail stores and their replacement by large discount chains, such as Wal-Mart. Neo-institutionalism, for its part, focuses on institutional isomorphism, viewing external pressures to conform to normative, cultural, or legal standards as the critical mechanism leading to homogeneity. In reaction to the dominant view of organizations as rational technical tools, held by contingency theorists, they highlight the symbolic and social nature of organizations. Here, organizations change not by devising unique responses but by copying legitimate managerial practices and adhering to institutional norms. For example, the presence of United Way, acting as a centralized financing institution, has led to the homogenization of structures and practices in the field of humanitarian organizations in conformity with prevailing business norms (Bégin, 2000).

This brief presentation could lead us to conclude that these theories are not particularly relevant for understanding organizational-level change, but it doesn't do justice to the richness of these approaches, in terms of their treatment of different dimensions of change. In particular, while their views of change are elaborated on conceptions of the organization and the environment that differ from the dominant perspective, their influence on later conceptions of organizational change is very significant.

Population Ecology

Population ecology, like the life-cycle model, is based on ideas borrowed from biology. But this time it is biological evolution, conceived as a cycle of variation, selection, and retention of species, that is used as a model for organizational change at the population level. As popularized by Hannan and Freeman (1977) and their followers, population ecology conceives individual organizations, foremost, as members of populations where different organizational forms are viewed as species. It is change at the population level of analysis (i.e., the replacement of organizational forms) that their theory seeks to explain (see Table 2.1).

While they recognize that each organization is distinctive, they believe that classes of organizations can be identified. A population represents a class of organizations having a typical form, that is to say, a particular configuration of goals, structures, and activities. Variation, the emergence of new organizational forms, is mostly assumed to be blind or random with regard to selection. Selection is conceived as a competitive process whereby organizations that are better adapted to fight for the scarce resources available in a given resource space survive or, in other words, are selected by the environment. Retention

Table 2.1   Population Ecology

POPULATION ECOLOGY		
General model of change: VARIATION – SELECTION – RETENTION Birth of new organizational forms — Competition between forms in a niche — Survival of selected forms, death of old ones		
Focus: Inertia, which makes it difficult for established organizations to change their core structural features. Change at the population level.		
Antecedents: Sociology		
Organization:	Inertial system, tightly coupled hierarchical form	
Process of change:	Change is rare, difficult due to inertia, and dangerous because it makes organizations vulnerable and accelerates their demise if they don't succeed	
Authors:	Hannan & Freeman (1984); Amburgey et al. (1993); Baum (1996)	

refers to the forces that maintain and perpetuate certain organizational forms over time. In consequence, change is explained as the result of "the creation of new organizations and the demise of old ones" (Hannan & Freeman, 1989, p. 12). Organizations don't adapt, they fail and are replaced by newcomers better suited to the new environmental conditions. According to Van de Ven and Poole (1995), they propose a Darwinian theory of evolution, where change is intergenerational (i.e., only new organizations acquire new traits), as opposed to a Lamarckian perspective, where new traits can be learned within a generation (i.e., existing organizations can change by learning and imitation). However, they dissociate themselves from earlier social evolution theory that viewed change as necessarily leading to progress, stating: "We are not convinced that change in populations of organizations reflects a unilinear evolutionary process of the sort described by sociocultural evolutionists" (Hannan & Freeman, 1989, p. 36).

Ecologists focus on organization–environment relations. They describe the environment in terms of the varied nature and relative quantity of resources that are available for organizations and view it as a competitive arena. They operationalize the concept of ecological niche, which they define as "all those combinations of resource levels at which the population can survive and reproduce itself" (Hannan & Freeman, 1977, p. 946), to develop mathematical models that allow for empirical testing. Populations are usually defined as "aggregates of fundamentally similar organizational entities" (Baum & Singh, 1994b, p. 17).

Using powerful mathematical models, the ecological approach has spawned a large number of empirical studies of organizational demographics—the "vital rates" (entries and exits) of populations. Based on data collected on a large sample (or whole populations) of organizations, these studies seek to understand, for example, the link between various environmental changes and rates of founding and mortality, the relationship between age, size, and death rates (through disbanding or mergers) for different kinds of population, and the effect of niche width on population dynamics (Carroll & Hannan, 1989; Delacroix & Carroll, 1983; Freeman, Carroll, & Hannan, 1983; Freeman & Hannan, 1983). Sectors such as the newspaper industry in different countries, the semiconductor industry, California wineries, labor unions, and daycare centers were studied using this perspective.

This voluminous research (see Baum, 1996, for a recent review) concentrates on testing this theory of change at the population level and is beyond the scope of this book. However, the ecologist perspective doesn't exclude the possibility of change at the organizational level. As will be seen in the next paragraphs, Hannan and Freeman also elaborate a vision of organizational-level change in terms of both the nature of change and the process involved.

ORGANIZATIONAL-LEVEL CHANGE

In a 1984 article titled "Structural Inertia and Organizational Change," Hannan and Freeman react to criticism about their claim that organizations rarely change by clarifying their view on the subject. Their argument is that organizations are basically inertial. Like organic adaptation theorists such as Cyert and March (1963) and Selznick (1957), they conceive organizations as complex and resistant instruments. Because of internal pressures arising from such elements as sunk costs, rules and procedures, politics, routines, and values, as well as external pressures such as barriers to entry and exit and legal and legitimacy constraints, organizations are severely limited in their capacity to change. Moreover, this structural inertia is a result of selection, which "favors form of organizations with high reliability of performance and high levels of accountability" (Hannan & Freeman, 1984, p. 154). In other words, structural inertia is assumed to be the consequence of acquiring essential competencies, which "require that organizational structures be highly reproducible" (p. 153). In this sense, inertia, "a by-product of selection," is positive; it is survival-enhancing. Adopting a life-cycle point of view, Hannan and Freeman also propose that structural inertia increases with age and size, while death rates decrease. As a matter of fact, they explain the "liability of newness" hypothesis by suggesting that new organizations are more vulnerable (i.e., have higher mortality rates) because they are too variable (not inertial enough).

However, as Hannan and Freeman (1984) point out, "To claim that organizational structures are subject to strong inertial forces is not the same as claiming that organizations never change" (p. 151). What they argue, instead, is that most mature organizations change too little and too slowly, in relation to the rate of change of the environment, to be able to adapt. Therefore, if change proves to be adaptive for an organization, it is more the result of chance than of managerial foresight, and, in any case, such occurrences are too rare to have an impact at the population level.

Following Parsons (1960), Hannan and Freeman (1984) argue that organizational entities or structures "are composed of hierarchical layers of structural and strategic features that vary systematically in flexibility and responsiveness" (p. 156). They describe this hierarchy, from core features to periphery, as being composed of stated goals, forms of authority, technology, and marketing strategy, pointing out that the likelihood of change declines as one moves up the hierarchy. This leads them to view organizational change, or what they call fundamental change (i.e., change in core features), as relatively rare and, more important, hazardous. They claim that "such changes are both rare and costly and seem to subject an organization to greatly increased risks of death" (p. 156).

Hannan and Freeman (1984) go on to discuss the process of fundamental change itself. They introduce in their model the notion of state of reorganization, pointing out that "the processes of dismantling one structure and building another make organizational action unstable" (p. 159); the longer it takes and the more resources it uses up, the more it increases the risk of failure. Moreover, they think that fundamental change and the process of reorganization it entails are, in fact, similar to the creation of a new organization, therefore subjecting it to the "liability of newness." In short, in contrast with previous perspectives that paint a positive picture of organizational change, they view organizational change as disruptive, at least in the short term, arguing that organizations may die more quickly as a direct consequence of their attempt to survive in the long run.

However, this part of their theory, which is most relevant for the field of organizational change, has not been subjected to much empirical validation, except for a few studies mostly done in the early 1990s (Baum, 1996). Furthermore, because of the type of methodological approach favored by population ecologists, studies of the process of transformation would be reduced to a measure of duration and effect.

But Hannan and Freeman's structural inertia theory has drawn attention to a particular type of change, fundamental or radical change, and the difficulties of reorganization it entails, which will be the focus of the next period in the evolution of the field of organizational change.

DISCUSSION

Despite its growing importance in the field of organization theory in the 1980s and 1990s, population ecology remains isolated from the mainstream in the field of organizational change. Notwithstanding its self-definition as a theory of organizational change (Hannan & Freeman, 1984, p. 149), it is viewed by others as a structural theory "largely irrelevant to the study of organizational change" (Hirsch & Lounsbury, 1997, p. 80) because of its lack of concern for action in organizations. When it first appears in the early 1980s, population ecology provokes a major controversy, its adversaries accusing this approach of being overly deterministic (Astley & Van de Ven, 1983; Child & Kieser, 1981; Hrebeniak & Joyce, 1985; Perrow, 1986). For example, Astley and Van de Ven summarize their view on the free will and determinism debate by stating, "To conclude that the environmental constraints determine organizational life incorrectly underplays the role of voluntarism since organizational members are independent actors as well as involved members of a larger collectivity" (p. 245).

For their part, Child and Kieser (1981), while acknowledging that this determinism applies only to populations of organizations, argue that

> it fails to account for imperfections in selection whereby certain organizations find protected niches. . . . Nor does it allow for the possibility that the leaders of some organizations may be able to negotiate with or dominate external parties. (p. 29)

To this criticism, Hannan and Freeman (1989) respond that their models are not deterministic but probabilistic, adding: "In no sense do we think that the history of organizational populations is preordained to unfold in fixed ways . . . the ecological approach treats processes of change as contingent but also as random" (p. 40).

Concurring with Hannan and Freeman, Baum (1996) adds that the criticism also originates from confusion in level of analysis. Ecological approaches do not imply that individuals are not important for organizations; rather, they suggest that their actions "matter more to their organization than they do to their organization's population as a whole" (p. 78). And it is because population ecology neglects organizational-level change that the wealth of empirical studies it inspires in the next decade has few repercussions in the field of organizational change itself.

As we have seen, the bulk of research is concerned with testing the validity of the selection argument with studies of global population dynamics, using increasingly sophisticated methodology. Although the concept of structural inertia has the most potential to make links with other perspectives on organizational change, this line of research is only taken up, in the early 1990s, in a few empirical studies on rates of change in organizational forms and on the relationship of organizational change with age, size, and failure (Amburgey, Dawn, & Barnett, 1993; Dawn & Amburgey, 1991; Singh, House, & Tucker, 1986).

In one interesting study, Amburgey et al. (1993) extend Hannan and Freeman's model by incorporating elements from theories of learning and innovation, as well as from the strategic change literature. Their argument is that change can be both disruptive and adaptive and that inertia can also explain the likelihood of an organization repeating a type of change it has experienced previously (i.e., an organization learns to change by changing). For example, they use the concept of momentum (i.e., repetitive inertia) to capture the effect of the sequence and history of changes on organizations' risk of failure.

As discussed by Baum (1996) in his review, these rare studies give mixed results and offer inconclusive evidence for structural inertia theory: "Organizations change frequently in response to environmental changes and often without any harmful effects" (p. 106). He agrees with the view of Amburgey et al. (1993) that selection and adaptation are complementary explanations rather than mutually exclusive. But ecological studies, because of their methodology, tell us nothing about why and how organizations change, only that those that are likely to succeed in their change efforts tend to be older and to have experienced change early on.

In fact, as Baum (1996) clearly articulates, one of the main criticisms of the ecological perspective stems from its methodological approach, the "use of large-scale, historical databases in which, by necessity, measures are frequently removed from concepts" (p. 107). One of the major forces of population ecology has been to produce comparable, cumulative results, but this comes at a price. Population ecologists have sacrificed realism and precision for generality. In terms of a theory of change, they develop explanations that infer processes from indirect measures. For example, Amburgey et al. (1993) infer a learning process from measurements of the frequency and timing of types of change over time.

But the interest in organizational-level change that appeared in the early 1990s and the related move toward considering the complementarity between adaptation and selection has produced a shift from a focus on population ecology to an emphasis on organizational evolution (Amburgey & Rao, 1996). The evolutionary perspective (Aldrich, 1999), one of the perspectives presented in the third period of evolution of the field, is characterized by the use of a variety of methodological approaches to understand the process of organizational change.

In summary, population ecology has been mostly concerned with explaining variability in organizational populations that occurs through a process of blind variation, environmental selection, and retention through reproduction and diffusion. This approach focuses on change as the emergence of new organizational forms (i.e., new configurations of goals, structures, and activities). Even if it acknowledges the possibility of organizational transformation, it is more concerned with knowing what the probability is that organizations within a population will attempt and survive a major change than with understanding the process that the few organizations that attempt change go through.

To conclude, the population ecology approach, on top of provoking a general debate over the issue of free will and determinism, has questioned some basic assumptions held by most in the field of organizational change. In contrast with previous perspectives that view change as a natural phenomenon, generally beneficial for organizations, ecologists conceive of change as disruptive and hazardous for organizations. The concept of structural inertia on which such a vision of change is based offers an interesting counterpoint to the assumption in organizational change theories to date that inertia (or resistance to change) is necessarily a bad thing. From their point of view, "real" change, or change in core features, is rare and very difficult to achieve and makes the organization undergoing it quite vulnerable. As Miller, Greenwood, and Hinings (1997) suggest, this vision of change, while it is less appealing to managers, may be more realistic. And, as we will see later, this conception of change influences the transformational perspectives on change, which characterize the 1980s. These approaches popularize the conception of change as rare and difficult by giving it a managerial point of view, organizational transformation becoming the main challenge facing heroic managers.

However, population ecology itself remains basically aprocessual and acontextual, at the organizational level of analysis. Therefore, like the other perspectives presented so far, it has little to say about how organizations achieve change, except that change takes time and is costly.

The "New" Institutionalism

In 1977, the same year Hannan and Freeman's article on population ecology comes out, Meyer and Rowan publish their classic article establishing the bases of the new institutional perspective in sociology.[1] This "new" institutionalism (DiMaggio & Powell, 1991), as it is later labeled to distinguish it from the work of Selznick (1949, 1957) and others who study institutionalization as an organizational-level process,[2] is a reaction to the rationalistic explanations of contingency theory (see Table 2.2).

The new institutionalism, according to Meyer and Rowan (1977), is based on the idea that organizations adopt new structures not because they are necessarily more efficient, but for symbolic purposes, "to increase their legitimacy and their survival prospects, independent of the immediate efficacy of the acquired practices and procedures" (p. 340). Furthermore, Meyer and Rowan question the assumption of tight coupling between structures and organizational activities,

Table 2.2   Neo-institutionalism

NEO-INSTITUTIONALISM
General model of change: ISOMORPHISM Imitation of legitimated practices Focus: Organizational change as the result of social processes such as coercion, mimetism, and normative pressures Antecedents: Sociology

Organization:	Flexible, loosely coupled (nonrational) symbolic system
Process of change:	Organizations change gradually, adopting newly institutionalized practices and norms in their organizational field, to achieve legitimacy
Authors:	DiMaggio & Powell (1983); Tolbert & Zucker (1996)

arguing that structures reflect the myths embedded in the institutional environment and that their adoption by organizations is often ritualistic. Expanding on Meyer and Rowan's work, DiMaggio and Powell (1983) develop the notion of institutional isomorphism to account for what they see as the tendency for organizations to become more similar as the environment of which they are a part becomes established. These authors explain organizational change not by competitive selection like the ecologists, but by the quest for legitimacy. Emphasizing cognitive and cultural controls, they further argue that organizational adaptation is not necessarily purposeful, claiming it often results from "taken-for-granted assumptions rather than consciously strategic choices" (p. 149).

The institutional perspective, like contingency theory and population ecology, conceives organizations as open systems, and thus as strongly constrained by the environment. But, unlike them, this approach emphasizes the socially constructed nature of the environment and the impact that belief systems and normative and cultural constraints, as opposed to techno-economic ones, have on organizations. DiMaggio and Powell (1983) view the environment as an organizational field, which they describe as "those organizations that, in the aggregate, constitute a recognized area of institutional life: key suppliers, resource and product consumers, regulatory agencies, and other organizations that produce similar products" (p. 148).

The concept of organizational field, as Scott (1998) mentions, draws attention to a group of organizations in terms of the system of interaction that they constitute, as well as the cultural rules and meaning systems that they share. Therefore, organizations are not viewed as atomistic entities living in a jungle where only the strongest survive, but as members of a social network in which they are embedded.

Like population ecologists, the new institutionalists are interested in changes in organizational forms, for example, the spread of the bureaucratic model of organization (DiMaggio & Powell, 1983). But they don't share population ecology's hierarchical view of organizations, or its dramatic conception of organizational change, because they view organizations as loosely coupled systems. DiMaggio and Powell's definition of organizational change, relegated to a footnote, refers to "change in formal structure, organizational culture, and goals, program, or mission" (p. 149).

By presenting change as mimetic and, particularly in the case of Meyer and Rowan (1977), as largely ceremonial (i.e., decoupled from organizational behavior), new institutionalists de-emphasize the internal dynamics of change and give a view of change as a mostly gradual and incremental process. In fact, they aren't really concerned with how change is implemented; rather, their focus is on organizational change as a *result* of the processes that drive the institutionalization of a field.

THE PROCESS OF INSTITUTIONALIZATION

Broadly speaking, institutional analysis seeks to understand "the basis of social meaning and social stability" (Scott, 1998, p. 117). In that spirit, the new institutionalism focuses on environments or organizational fields that become structured, in other words, that are stabilizing. DiMaggio and Powell's major contribution is in spelling out the mechanisms underlying this institutionalization. They go further than Meyer and Rowan's (1977) classic article by drawing attention to the process of organizational homogenization by which a field becomes institutionalized. In so doing, they develop a theory of institutional isomorphic change.

This theory explains the formation of an organizational field, or its structuration, as consisting of the interplay between increased interaction, the appearance of regulating bodies, and information sharing that leads to mutual awareness (DiMaggio & Powell, 1983, p. 148). DiMaggio and Powell derive from the unfolding of this process the existence of three mechanisms that drive institutional change: coercive isomorphism, mimetic isomorphism, and normative isomorphism. Coercive isomorphism explains organizational change by the existence of "formal and informal pressures exerted . . . by other organizations . . . and by cultural expectations" (p. 150). Political pressures that can be enforced by regulating bodies (e.g., environmental protection standards, gender equity programs) are examples of coercive isomorphism. Mimetic isomorphism refers to the tendency of organizations to adopt standard practices in the face of uncertainty. The rapid diffusion of practices such as Total Quality Management (TQM) and reengineering and the various waves of mergers and acquisitions can be attributed to the fact that managers faced with uncertainty prefer copying what is seen as legitimate. They would rather take the risk of being wrong with everybody else. Finally, normative isomorphism is associated with professionalization. Particularly, the development of formal education (that accompanies the establishment of a recognized cognitive base) and the emergence of organized professional networks are viewed as producing pressures for organizations to conform to legitimated professional practices. DiMaggio and Powell (1983) argue that "the professionalization of management tends to proceed in tandem with the structuration of organizational fields" (p. 153).

While the theory they develop is framed in terms of the process of institutionalization, the empirical work done within that perspective focuses on institutionalization as a state, an outcome of the process itself (Tolbert & Zucker, 1996). As stated by Tolbert (1988), most of this research analyzes "the effects of the institutionalization process at the field level . . . examining the diffusion of structural changes across sets of organizations" (p. 101). Apart from a few early case studies, such as the description of the evolution of American college textbook publishing by Coser, Kadushin, and Powell (1982), most of the research is quantitative. A good example of this work is Tolbert and Zucker's (1983) investigation of reform in the U.S. civil service. Using a regression model to assess the effects of city characteristics on adoption of the reform, they show that organizational variables, such as city size, socioeconomic characteristics, and total expenditures, are related to early adoption of the new structure, but don't predict later adoption. From these findings, they infer that it is the increasing legitimacy of the new structure that explains later adoption.

Other research based on case studies (Powell, 1988) focuses on the effects, at one point in time, of specific institutional environments on organizations' structures and practices. It analyzes particular organizations in more depth to understand what factors influence decision making, but it studies established, ongoing practices, not situations of change.

Finally, the new institutional perspective, although it is introduced as a theory of institutional change, in terms of the research it inspires is really a theory of stability (DiMaggio & Powell, 1991). But as will be seen, in the following years it becomes an influential school of thought in the field of organizational change (Greenwood & Hinings, 1996).

DISCUSSION

Unlike population ecology, whose dominance in the 1980s derives from the coherence of its research program (Baum, 1996), institutional theory owes its popularity in the field of organization theory to its rapid diffusion among scholars (Zucker, 1988b). As a consequence, very diverse points of view share the label of institutional theory (Hirsch & Lounsbury, 1997; Zucker, 1988b). Like population ecology, it has sparked a lot of controversy, but within the boundaries of organization theory. Nonetheless, some of this discussion is particularly relevant to a discussion of organizational change.

Broadly speaking, one of the main criticisms leveled at the new institutionalism is its neglect of interest and agency (DiMaggio, 1988; Oliver, 1991). Because of this neglect, this perspective has relatively little to say about change (Hirsch & Lounsbury, 1997). Even DiMaggio (1988) admits that "institutional theory tells us relatively little about "institutionalization" as an unfinished process (as opposed to an achieved state), about where institutions come from, why some organizational innovations diffuse while others do not" (p. 12).

As well, the new institutional theory, because it reduces action to cognition in the form of macro-level scripts, norms, and rules, appears as abstracted and disembodied, with "inexorable social processes" determining organizational evolution.

Starting in the late 1980s, some scholars, reacting to the passive view of organizations inherent in such an account, develop explanations integrating institutional analysis with political (Covaleski & Dirsmith, 1988) and resource dependency (Oliver, 1991) perspectives. For example, Covaleski and Dirsmith, in their naturalistic qualitative study of a university budgeting process, show that political pressures predominate when the organization fails to comply with social expectations. Oliver, for her part, discusses the range of strategic responses available to organizations depending on the characteristics of the institutional environment facing them.

However, Goodrick and Salancik (1996) argue that such views "risk discounting the social-fact quality of institutions, much as earlier theorists discounted the role of agents" (p. 1). As well, Tolbert and Zucker (1996) comment that such revisions lead to a confounding of institutional and resource dependency theory. They suggest that the idea of decoupling between behavior and structure, introduced by Meyer and Rowan (1977), opened the door to such a reinterpretation of institutionalization in terms of manipulation (a strategic response) rather than unconscious adoption of taken-for-granted practices. They question whether structures lacking in normative and cognitive legitimacy (i.e., adopted for ceremonial value) really are appropriately described as institutional. Furthermore, they react to the notion implicit in such a view that structural change is largely costless and has a negligible impact on day-to-day activities.

However, Tolbert and Zucker (1996) also lament the fact that a process-based approach to institutionalization (Zucker, 1977) has not given rise to more research. Arguing that the distinctive focus of institutional theory on cultural determinants of behavior should be maintained, they propose a model of the process of institutionalization, at the field level, comprising three stages: habitualization (generation of new structural arrangements), objectification (consensus development accompanying diffusion), and sedimentation (perpetuation of structure). According to them, it is the process of innovation propelling habitualization that the literature on organizational innovation and change is most appropriate to explain. It is at that stage that the creation of new organizational forms is an independent activity (i.e., an organization-level phenomenon) rather than a process of imitation (i.e., a field-level activity). This process approach has gained momentum in recent years, as witnessed by the special issue of the *Academy of Management Journal* devoted to institutionalization in 2002.

A related stream of research inspired by neo-institutionalism is the work on the diffusion of managerial innovations (Abrahamson, 1991, 1996). The reflection on the process by which "managerial fads and fashions," such as TQM or benchmarking, are adopted in organizations through the influence, notably, of consultants and business schools is particularly relevant to an understanding of organizational change in recent decades. As the label suggests, fads and fashions follow relatively short cycles of propagation, and as such, this topic addresses issues of change more explicitly than early neo-institutional analysis. This issue is also of interest to the Scandinavian school of institutionalism (Czarniawska & Sevon, 1996b).

Concurrently with the development of institutional theory in the United States, in Scandinavia, a related approach, with its origins in the work of Olsen and Brunsson, emerges. These scholars influenced by authors such as March and Meyer develop an institutional approach concerned with the ambiguity of organizational change. Brunsson (1989), for example, drawing on Meyer's notion of decoupling between structure and behavior, explores what he terms organizational "hypocrisy." Research done within that framework shows that faced with conflicting norms and values, organizations adopt decoupled structures that contradict each other, say one thing and do another, and attend sequentially to conflicting demands (Demers & Barral, 1999). As described by Czarniawska and Sevon (1996b), this "Scandinavian" institutionalism embraces the paradoxicality of stability and change that, as will be seen, is specific to the third period of evolution of the field of organizational change.

While institutional theory tends to treat change as largely incremental and convergent, in contrast, Greenwood and Hinings (1996) develop a model of radical organizational change that connects old and new institutional theory within the configurational approach. This development is in agreement with Hirsch and Lounsbury's (1997) exhortations for a reconciliation between old and new institutionalism, calling for a dialogue "across levels of abstraction and analysis as well as research methods" and the "study of process and mechanisms of change and the actions between equilibrium states" (p. 86). Greenwood and Hinings's contribution is discussed later as it relates to the transformational approaches to organizational change.

To sum up, at its birth, new institutionalism has little ascendancy in the field of organizational change. This is not surprising when one considers that even its most representative authors describe it as a theory explaining the dynamics of stability and providing a vision of organizations that emphasizes passivity and inertia. However, by challenging the assumptions of functional rationality dominant in most theories of adaptation at the time, neo-institutionalists offer an interesting account of organizational change as the result of social processes. In keeping with the cognitive turn in the social sciences, to which I will come back later, they direct attention to the impact of shared frames of reference on managerial action, arguing that managerial decisions are often the result of taken-for-granted assumptions rather than rational analysis. They also emphasize the search for legitimacy as opposed to the quest for efficiency as the motive behind organizational change. Moreover, through its wide diffusion in organization theory in the United States, Europe, and Scandinavia, the new institutionalism evolves to become, in the 1990s, one of the most influential theories in the field of organizational change.

Conclusion

The selection and imitation points of view on change in organizational forms emerge in the late 1970s but come into prominence in the 1980s and 1990s in organization theory. In contrast, growth and rational adaptation approaches, such as life-cycle and contingency theory, reach their peak in the 1970s and early 1980s.

In a sense, population ecology and neo-institutionalism are the turning point between the first and second periods, because their arrival coincides with the beginning of a period of turbulence that continues well into the 1980s. They belong in the first period because their point of departure, the questioning of the assumptions behind rational adaptation, sparks a debate that culminates in the early 1980s. More important, from the point of view of the field of organizational change (as opposed to organization theory), their impact is rather limited in the second period because they are not perceived, due in part to the type of research they inspire, as theories of organizational change. It is only later with the convergence of perspectives that leads to a broadening of the conception of change that their contributions are integrated into the mainstream of organizational change.

Notes

1. Institutional analysis, as mentioned by Scott (1998), is not restricted to sociology. Economists, political scientists, and anthropologists, for example, have also been concerned with understanding the role of belief systems and rule-based systems in

maintaining social order and stability. Economists tend to focus on regulative systems and have an instrumental vision of institutions, and early sociologists draw attention to the normative aspects of institutions, while recent developments in sociology and anthropology emphasize the cognitive and cultural bases of institutional systems. (For a more detailed presentation see Scott, 1995.)

2. Selznick (1957) defined institutionalization as a process of instilling values, of defining the character of an organization. He emphasized the normative aspects of institutionalization, giving precedence to moral beliefs and internalized standards of conduct. He saw the role of the leader as purposefully driving this process, but also emphasized the sometimes unforeseen results of his actions due to the political nature of organizations. He viewed institutionalization, in the functionalist tradition, as an important means of contributing to environmental adaptation by showing an organization's coherence with society's main values (Tolbert & Zucker, 1996).

CONCLUSION TO PART I

Looking at Change From the Outside

So what do we retain from this period of emergence of the field of organizational change? One thing is sure; the ferment in the domain of organization studies is reflected in the literature on change. The interaction between authors espousing a number of diverse theoretical approaches frames that period of evolution in terms of a debate between voluntarism and determinism, based on different explanations of organizational growth and development. The main approaches are summarized in Table I.1. They range from visions of organizations as flexible, technical tools in the hands of omniscient managers, designed to pursue predetermined goals or react to environmental constraints, to living organisms that evolve through prescribed stages, to non-rational social systems changing through drift (because of politics in old institutionalism) or imitation (in search of legitimacy in new institutionalism) or inertial entities selected by the environment.

But despite the differences in how they explain adaptation, in terms of the conception of organizational change they adopt, there are striking commonalities. Most look at change as an outcome (i.e., stage of development in life-cycle theory, structural change in contingency theory, strategic response in resource dependency, new organizational form in population ecology and neo-institutionalism) and infer a causal relationship to explain it (Van de Ven, 1992). By studying change as a difference in a variable and not directly observing the process leading to that difference, they look at change from the outside and treat the organization as a black box. By focusing on what changes rather than on how change occurs, they develop explanations of change in terms of antecedents and consequences, rather than in terms of a sequence of events and activities.

They also take an outsider view in the sense that they adopt an objective stance, using externally observable measures of the variables they study. For example, they conceive the environment as a given, a set of tangible features.

Table I.1 Adaptation or Selection: An Overview

	Rational Adaptation	Organic Adaptation	Life Cycle	Population Ecology	New Institutionalism
Organization	Unitary vision Technical instrument	Pluralist social vision Political arena (nonrational)	Unitary vision Living organism	Unitary vision Tightly coupled, inertial system	Unitary vision Loosely coupled social system (nonrational)
Environment	Task UNCERTAINTY	Ignored or constraint	Ignored or catalyst	Economic—JUNGLE	Institutional—RULES, NORMS
Model of change	Environmental change ← Organizational change	Environmental change → Organizational change	Passage of time → Stage change	Environmental change → Population change	Environmental change → Field change
Reason for change	=	=	=	=	=
Nature	FUNCTIONAL ADAPTATION	ADAPTATION OR DRIFT	ORGANIZATIONAL TRANSITION	DEATH and REPLACEMENT	ISOMORPHISM
Process	COHERENCE = FIT	PRESSURES (internal and external)	IMMANENT PROGRAM	SURVIVAL	LEGITIMACY
	STRATEGIC CHANGE Frequent and gradual	ALL CHANGES Frequent and gradual	STRUCTURAL CHANGE Rare but natural	STRATEGIC CHANGE Rare and radical	ALL CHANGES Frequent and gradual
	PLANNED, DELIBERATE, REACTIVE or PROACTIVE	LARGELY UNPLANNED, EMERGENT (bargaining, negotiation)	SEQUENCE OF 4 STAGES (entrepreneurial, specialization, multidivisional, matrix)	MAJOR REORGANIZATION Implementation problems (not studied empirically)	COERCION IMITATION NORMATIVE PRESSURE
Change agent	Rational top managers	Divergent coalitions	Rational top managers (implicit)	Rational top managers (implicit)	Top managers (implicit)
Outcomes	NEW INTERNAL/ EXTERNAL EQUILIBRIUM	FUNCTIONAL OR DYSFUNCTIONAL	NEW INTERNAL EQUILIBRIUM	Increased probability of DEATH (short term) Increased probability of SURVIVAL (long term)	SOCIAL STABILITY
Determinism/ Voluntarism	From constrained managerial voluntarism to "pure" voluntarism	Internal determinism, (behavioral or system determinism)	Internal determinism	Environmental Determinism	Environmental determinism

41

Moreover, they assume that managers are rational decision makers and never try to study what goes on inside the manager's mind. There are a few exceptions, notably the old institutionalists such as Selznick (1949, 1957) and authors within the strategic choice perspective (Child, 1972), who discuss the process of change and are concerned with subjective aspects of change. Child, for instance, argues that it is the way that top managers perceive and conceive the environment that determines the changes they will decide upon. While these scholars become more influential in the second period of evolution of the field, they share with most researchers of the first era a definition of change as a gradual, cumulative, and convergent process.

On the whole, it is this assumption of order and stability, making of change a normal, generally positive, and expansive process, an incremental adjustment designed to maintain equilibrium, which best characterizes the conception of change of that epoch. While population ecology's concept of organizational inertia makes it a theory of stability, it also includes the notion of change in core features, defining it as crisis, possibly leading to mortality. From that point of view, the ecologists are at the forefront of the mutation in the conception of change that characterizes the second period of evolution of the field.

Up to that point, the theme of change has been more or less subordinated to that of adaptation. To some extent, change is seen as an almost self-evident concept (i.e., adaptation is defined as change), and conceptions of change are often implicit rather than explicit.[1] As we will see, this second period involves a major rupture to a context where change becomes the central concept and emerges as a domain of inquiry in its own right.

Note

1. The OD literature focuses on organizational change. However, it is concerned with prescriptions for how to achieve change that derive from action research, rather than with theoretical discussions of the concept of change.

PART II

Transformation or Evolution?

> One paradigm that has heavily influenced our thinking about change
> processes is Darwin's model of evolution as a slow stream of small
> mutations, gradually shaped by environmental selection into novel
> forms. This concept of incremental, cumulative change has become
> pervasive. . . . Within the field of evolutionary biology, however,
> Darwinian gradualism has been challenged. Natural historians Niles
> Eldredge and Stephen Gould (1972) postulate a very different view of
> evolution as punctuated equilibrium. They propose that lineages exist
> in essentially static form (equilibrium) over most of their histories, and
> new species arise abruptly, through sudden, revolutionary "punctua-
> tions" of rapid change.
>
> (Gersick, 1991, p. 11)

Is Transformation Always Revolutionary?

The 1980s constitute a new era with a more dramatic view of change emerging
in the literature. "Real" change is now seen as a period of discontinuity, of disruption; it is talked about in terms of transformation and revolution. Whether
one sees this as a good thing or as something to be avoided, there is recognition that change does not always follow a path of cumulative, gradual adaptation; episodes of transformation or radical change now take center stage. During
this period, more attention is given to defining what a transformation or radical change is, as opposed to an incremental or gradual change, and to examining the process by which such a change is realized (Miller & Friesen, 1984;
Tushman & Romanelli, 1985).

This shift in tone occurs while the environmental uncertainty and turbulence initiated by the 1970s oil crisis are exacerbated due to the success
of new foreign players in the competitive arena. For the first time since the
Second World War, the United States sees its economic dominance challenged.

The precarious situation in which some of the largest American and European companies now find themselves is reflected in the shift in emphasis of the organizational change literature.

The brutal shock caused by the recession and by the success of East Asian competition provokes a reexamination of the American model and awakens interest in the Japanese style of management. Simultaneously, in other countries in the West, such as Canada and Great Britain, the recession has built up significant government deficits, and economic questions top the political agenda. Governments are forced to question their policies and operating methods. The ensuing philosophy of market liberalization leads to, among other consequences, the privatization of state-owned enterprises and a restructuring of governmental infrastructure in an attempt to reduce costs and increase competitiveness. For example, during the 1980s, the proceeds of privatization ranged from 0.6% of GDP in Canada to 11.9% of GDP in New Zealand and 14.1% of GDP in the U.K.[1] Whereas the postwar years saw the flourishing of the counterculture movement and of human rights, this is the era of glory of economic discourse favoring the rule of the market (Clarke & Pitelis, 1993).

Not surprisingly, the focus gradually shifts from a concern with internal functioning and structural adjustment to a preoccupation with external fit and strategic reorientation, concurrently with the rise in popularity of the field of strategy. In organization studies, cognitive and cultural perspectives on organizations reinforce the conception of change as a frame-breaking, revolutionary event. Change is talked about in terms of reversal (Miller & Friesen, 1984), strategic reorientation (Tushman & Romanelli, 1985), reframing (Bartunek, 1984), and cultural revolution (Allaire & Firsirotu, 1985). The image that stands out is of change as a period of crisis in the life of an organization.

While, up until now, radical change has been viewed in a negative light, as a sign of failure, in the 1980s things start to change. Until then, scholars had typically portrayed radical change as something to be avoided by gradual and continuous adjustments (Miller, 1982). Even authors in the life-cycle tradition, like Greiner (1972), who adopt a metamorphic perspective and see development occurring in abrupt, discrete changes, see revolutions as something to be avoided by good management. However, starting in the 1980s, some authors start questioning the idea that incremental change is necessarily better for organizations or even that fundamental change can be brought about by other means than a revolution (Allaire & Firsirotu, 1985; Miller & Friesen, 1984; Tushman & Romanelli, 1985).

Indeed, this period starts with a debate over whether organizations should be conceived as loosely coupled aggregations of elements that change incrementally, as implicit in the contingency perspective, or rather as configurations or gestalts, that is to say highly integrated systems of interdependent elements that have to change in a concerted way to remain coherent. The new transformational perspective, as it is sometimes called, views change as a period of mutation, initiated by top managers who act simultaneously on the strategy, structure, and culture of an organization. This radical change or transformation, aimed at repositioning the organization in an environment that has often altered suddenly and unpredictably, is seen as very costly and difficult to achieve. But it is viewed as less costly and more efficient than the long period of misalignment between organizational elements inherent in gradual, incremental change.

Although it starts with the configurational approach, the debate over whether change is evolutionary or revolutionary is reinforced and broadened by the cognitive, cultural, and political perspectives, which also become influential in the 1980s. The controversy on the nature of change to a large extent (but not completely) overlaps with the dispute between the managerialist–functionalist and organizational–interpretive perspectives on change.

For instance, authors within the cognitive and cultural approaches who adopt a managerial stance share with scholars of the configuration school a vision of organizations as archetypes[2] or integrated wholes. This conception reinforces a monolithic top-down view of change as a radical transformation. Thus, the cognitive school draws attention to the importance of transforming the worldview of organizational members, starting with top management, to achieve profound change. According to the cultural approach, fundamental change involves a deliberate attempt by management to change the basic, taken-for-granted assumptions and values that guide collective action.

Even authors of the political school, who adopt a managerial point of view, regard managers as capable of deliberately transforming an organization. However, because they consider that organizations are pluralist entities, they conceive the change process leading to radical change as piecemeal and incremental.

Within each school, the most serious challenges to the dominant transformational perspective on change come from those who oppose its managerialist stance. In particular, authors in the cultural and the political schools who adopt an organizational stance (i.e., who view change as an organizational phenomenon, not only in terms of management's point of view and action) call attention to the transformational perspective's neglect of implementation issues and question its assumption that top management is capable of controlling the change process (Crozier & Friedberg, 1977; Meyerson & Martin, 1987).

Each of these four approaches—configurational, cognitive, cultural, and political—is presented in the following chapters, focusing on the specificities of its conception of change (see Figure II.1). Both the mainstream and the more marginal variants of each school will be discussed in terms of their contribution to the debate and reflection about the nature of change. As we will see, these controversies are rooted in different epistemological traditions (for example, functionalist or interpretive) and methodological choices (in terms of considerations such as level of analysis and time period).

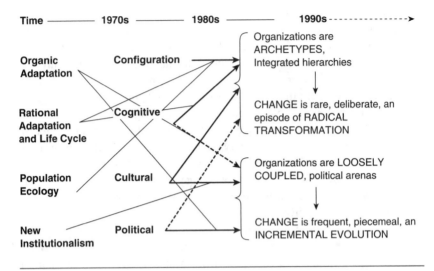

Figure II.1   Second Period: Transformation or Evolution?

However, regardless of the approaches, change is now studied as an *episode,* a series of actions and events, rather than as a difference or an outcome, as in the previous period. Questions relating to both the nature of change (its content, scope, magnitude, and direction) and the dynamics of change (its pace, timing, and the sequencing of actions) come to the forefront. Researchers are asking if organizational transformation is, by definition, revolutionary or if it mainly occurs through a cumulative and gradual process, and, increasingly, how much control managers (and other organizational actors) have over that process.

Notes

1. Clarke and Pitelis (1993, p. 8)
2. In the social sciences, the work of Kuhn (1970) on scientific revolutions popularized the concept of paradigm as a set of taken-for-granted theories and methods that constitute the accepted way to do research in a discipline. Authors in the field of organization theory and strategy have used the term to refer to the strategic orientation or theory of action that is developed by a firm over time and comes to be viewed as the only way to do things (Gersick, 1991; Miller, 1982).

3

The Configurational Approach

The configurational approach displaced contingency theory as the dominant perspective in the literature on change in the 1980s. This perspective is characterized by its "holistic" view of organizations, which are conceived as "composed of tightly interdependent and mutually supportive elements such that the importance of each element can best be understood by making reference to the whole configuration" (Miller & Friesen, 1984, p. 1).

This perspective is developed in reaction to what Miller (1981) calls contingency theory's "partist" approach, which implicitly views organizations as a set of loosely coupled elements. Although it has its roots in contingency theory, sharing with it a functionalist point of view and an emphasis on the notion of "fit," the configurational approach is a significant break with the past. As discussed by Meyer, Tsui, and Hinings (1993), while contingency analysis adopts an essentially reductionist mode of inquiry, configurational analysis is synthetic: "Rather than trying to explain how order is designed into the parts of an organization, configurational theorists try to explain how order emerges from the interaction of those parts as a whole" (p. 1178).

According to configurational theorists, while in theory an infinite number of possible combinations exists due to the number of relevant attributes, in reality only a few coherent patterns are viable. At the end of his book on structures, Mintzberg (1979) asserts,

> How many configurations do we need to describe all organizational structures? . . . With our nine parameters, that number would grow rather large. . . . But there is order in the world . . . a sense of union or harmony that grows out of the natural clustering of elements, whether they be stars, ants or the characteristics of organizations. (p. 300)

This new school of thought evolves in two directions. The first, reviving a long tradition in organization theory dating back to Weber (1947), is concerned with classifying organizations into types, both conceptually derived ideal types and empirically induced taxonomies. The second axis is the development of a model of organizational dynamics based on the idea of organizations as archetypes.

The first stream has given rise to a wide array of typologies. Different types of configurations are developed, among them Mintzberg's pioneering work on types of strategy-making process (Mintzberg, 1973) and types of structure (Mintzberg, 1979). Other well-known contributions include the strategic types of Miles and Snow (1978), Porter's competitive strategies (1980), and Miller and Friesen's archetypes of strategy formulation (1978). The relationship between change in the environment and change in generic strategies is also explored (Meyer, 1982; Zajac & Shortell, 1989).

However, it is the second stream, focusing on the dynamics of organizational transformation (Greenwood & Hinings, 1988; Miller & Friesen, 1984; Tushman & Romanelli, 1985), that is of most interest in this book. Clearly the two are related, "two sides of the same coin," as Mintzberg, Ahlstrand, and Lampel (1998, p. 302) argue. It is because configuration theorists, like population ecologists, conceive organizations as gestalts (i.e., tightly coupled wholes) that they view change as rare and revolutionary: a process of destroying one configuration and replacing it with another. Relationships between elements can only be stretched to a certain extent before active resistance is provoked. Therefore, it is necessary to break down these links to permit new linkages to be formed and a new configuration to emerge. Influenced by Mintzberg's work, Miller (1982), with his colleague Friesen (Miller & Friesen, 1982, 1984), develops the implications of the configurational perspective for a theory of change.

Miller (1982) is one of the first to explicitly challenge the widely held assumption that structural change is, or should be, incremental and gradual. Miller takes issue on that matter, not only with contingency theorists, but also with policy and strategy researchers, such as Braybrooke and Lindblom (1963), Wildavsky (1968), Hedberg, Nystrom, and Starbuck (1976), and Quinn (1980), as well as other major organization theorists who depict organizations as loosely coupled systems (Aldrich, 1979; Weick, 1969).

At the time, most scholars view radical change as something to be avoided. Among the first to systematically study radical change are a group of Swedish scholars who focus on stagnating and declining organizations and their transformation (Hedberg, 1974; Normann, 1977).[1] They observe that organizations have a tendency to repeat the behaviors they have learned and to become imprisoned by the rules and procedures they have developed. Because of this tendency toward inertia, they resist change, do not adapt gradually to environmental evolution, and eventually require radical change.[2] They conclude from that empirical work that radical change occurs due to organizational sluggishness and is to be avoided (Hedberg & Jönsson, 1977; Hedberg et al., 1976). In an article written with Starbuck, one of the first to discuss change in terms of metamorphosis, Hedberg and Nystrom (Hedberg et al., 1976) assert that organizations should be avoiding "drastic revolutions," arguing that "costs such as hostilities, demotivation, wasted energies, ill-founded rationalities, and foolish risks can be lowered by nurturing small disruptions and incremental reorientations—by substituting evolution for revolution" (pp. 60–61).

These scholars contend that organizations should avoid becoming inertial, proposing that managers should maintain a flexible, organic design that allows them to be responsive to environmental changes.

Noting that, for most authors, more responsive organic structures are to be preferred as a way to avoid the need for revolutionary change, Miller (1982) counters:

> Firms that are structured for a dynamic environment must, when their markets stabilize, face an adaptive task that is every bit as difficult as that which confronts mechanistic or bureaucratic firms whose environments are becoming more dynamic. No type of structure can remove the need for periodic restructuring. (p. 132)

From a configurational perspective, an organic structure, like a mechanistic or a bureaucratic one, is a gestalt and is just as inertial to fundamental change.

Furthermore, Miller (1982) contends that "functional aspects of resistance to change are generally ignored" (p. 132). Miller shares with population ecology theorists the view that organizational inertia can be positive. The large-scale empirical studies done by Miller and Friesen (1982, 1984) suggest that radical change, as opposed to incremental change, is associated with better performance. In their well-known book *Organizations: A Quantum View* (1984), they argue that radical or quantum change—that is to say, concerted and dramatic change (as opposed to a gradual piecemeal approach)—is not only necessary to break out of the inertia that is characteristic of a particular archetype, but also minimizes the risks of incoherence and reduces the costs incurred by moving from one archetype to another.

Building on the concept of configuration or, as they also label it, archetype, they distinguish two types of change periods: momentum and revolution (which they later call reversal). Momentum is defined as a long period of incremental adjustments that maintain or reinforce the existing configuration, while revolution is defined as a rare and short period of extensive reversal that gives rise to a new configuration.

This line of reasoning is pursued by Tushman and Romanelli (1985), who propose a "punctuated equilibrium" framework of organizational change. They elaborate on Miller and Friesen's main insights by articulating the dynamics characterizing periods of convergence (momentum) and revolution (reversal).

Drawing on a broad range of literature on organizational behavior, organization theory, and strategy, Tushman and Romanelli systematically discuss the determinants of change (i.e., the forces pushing toward convergence and those behind reorientation), as well as the process dynamics associated with both types of change.

Also building on the contribution of Miller and Friesen, but parting with their functionalist stance, Greenwood and Hinings (1988) propose the concept of organizational tracks to account for different patterns of movement between archetypes.

To better understand what is implied by this perspective on organizational change, the punctuated equilibrium model and the framework elaborated by Greenwood and Hinings (1988) are presented (see Table 3.1).

Momentum and Revolution: The Punctuated Equilibrium Model

As already mentioned, scholars taking a configurational approach adopt a holistic view of organizations, which are conceived as multidimensional constellations of elements forming a coherent pattern, generally attributed to the influence of a dominant coalition. But this holistic stance gives rise to different conceptions of organizational configurations.[3]

For example, Miller and Friesen's (1980) archetypes are clusters that are empirically derived by statistical analysis of relationships among structural and strategic variables from a large sample of organizations over long periods. In the same vein, these authors define quantum (i.e., radical) structural change as concerted and dramatic change, which they operationalize as a high correlation between changes in a significant number of variables (concerted) and a large proportion of extreme change scores (dramatic) in a short period of time (5 years) (Miller & Friesen, 1982). In another study (Miller & Friesen, 1984, chap. 10), they define quantum change as a reversal, that is, as "flips in the direction of change across a significantly large number of variables of strategy and structure" (1984, p. 251) within a short period of time. As will be discussed later, it is with data collected mostly about the nature (content, magnitude, direction, and scope) and sequencing of change that they test their momentum and revolution theory of change.

In Miller and Friesen (1984), the nature of the interrelatedness among the components of the configuration is not really specified (Greenwood & Hinings, 1988). Functional relationships among components, as well as aesthetic, perceptual, and cognitive considerations, are inferred to explain the existence of the archetypes derived by statistical manipulation (Miller, 1981). For example, in

Table 3.1   Configurational Approach

CONFIGURATIONAL APPROACH
General model of change: CONVERGENCE   –   REORIENTATION Incremental change   Radical transformation
Focus: Defining radical change and understanding its dynamics
Antecedents: RATIONAL ADAPTATION   – Strategic choice (Child, 1972) – Contingency theory (Pugh, Hickson, Hinings, & Turner, 1971) – Life cycle (Starbuck, 1965) – Population ecology (Hannan & Freeman, 1984)
<div align="center">Momentum and revolution—Functionalist view</div>
Organization: System of tightly coupled structural elements; unitary view
Process of change: Punctuated equilibrium as long periods of convergent change interrupted by short periods of abrupt divergent change
Authors: Miller & Friesen (1984); Tushman & Romanelli (1985)
<div align="center">Design archetypes—Interpretive view</div>
Organization: Clusters of structures, systems, and interpretive scheme; unitary view
Process of change: Sequences of interpretive decoupling and recoupling following different tracks (e.g., inertia, linear, oscillating, aborted)
Authors: Greenwood & Hinings (1988)

some studies, the environment is part of the configuration, and it is assumed to be a major force behind the existence and change of configurations. The limited number of such configurations leads Miller and Friesen (1980) to argue for a limited number of patterns of transition.

Tushman and Romanelli (1985), for their part, develop a theoretical model in which the concept of strategic orientation is critical to explaining organizational convergence. While Miller and Friesen's notion of archetype applies to groups of organizations sharing similar characteristics, the concept of strategic orientation explains, from a single organization's point of view, how a coherent pattern emerges from a hierarchically organized set of activity domains, ranging from core values through strategy, distribution of power, structure, and controls. High performance is predicated on achieving consistencies among activity domains that support the strategic orientation and on adopting a strategic orientation that is coherent with environmental demands (Tushman & Romanelli, 1985). Reorientations are described as simultaneous and discontinuous shifts in strategy, distribution of power, structure, and control in a cascading effect, while the more radical form of reorientation, including discontinuities in core values, is termed a re-creation. These shifts, although they can be triggered by internal forces, are mostly assumed to occur due to external pressures. While a stable environment is a force for convergence through the constraining effect of industry structure, it can exert strong pressures for reorientation if changes in demand, technological, and institutional factors affecting product class evolution occur.

Extending Miller and Friesen's (1984) ideas on momentum and revolution, Tushman and Romanelli (1985) develop a two-phase model of evolution where long periods of momentum or convergence are punctuated by brief periods of revolution or reorientation. However, in contrast to Miller and Friesen (1980), the authors suggest that there are multiple paths in terms of the nature and direction of change, each organization following its own path (Romanelli & Tushman, 1994).

Despite these differences among the authors, the punctuated equilibrium model is characterized by its focus on various aspects of change in terms of its nature, that is, its content, direction, magnitude, and scope, as well as its dynamic, that is, its pace and duration. Is a change mainly structural, or does it affect the organization's strategy and values? Does a change maintain a tendency or is it a break with the past?—for example, an increase in centralization in an already centralized firm, as opposed to moving toward decentralization. Is the change a minor step or a dramatic jump?—for example, hiring an R&D specialist to develop new products, as opposed to merging with a firm recognized for its new product development competence. Is the change an isolated initiative or part of a program including numerous change projects?—for example, ordering an across-the-board 10% cut in costs, as opposed to adopting a turnaround strategy. These questions help researchers define what is being converged upon, that is, the archetype or strategic orientation.

Periods of momentum are characterized by convergent, small, and piecemeal changes. Such changes are adjustments that reinforce the existing configuration or strategic orientation. In a sense, during momentum, organizations change to remain the same; they do more of the same thing or do the same thing more efficiently. They become more coherent, refining their strategic orientation. During periods of momentum, as the name suggests, organizations are highly inertial, changing at a very slow pace. In contrast, periods of reorientation imply divergent, large, and concerted changes. Such changes destroy the old configuration and aim to create a new strategic orientation. Here, organizations go in the opposite direction of where they were heading or do something totally different. In periods of reorientation, numerous changes occur at a very rapid pace.

In terms of dynamics, Miller and Friesen are limited to considering issues of timing and pacing (the sequencing of changes and the degree of simultaneity with which different changes occur). Their empirical studies don't allow them to elaborate further on the process associated with the passage from one archetype to another. Because they rely on measures of change in content variables over a period of time, they study radical change as an outcome in terms of co-occurrence and pacing. For their part, Tushman and Romanelli (1985), drawing on the literature, theorize about some aspects of the process associated with the different change periods. They argue that reorientation is a deliberate top-down process most often initiated by a new top management team. Momentum, on the other hand, is characterized by a stable executive team assisted by middle management responsible for implementing incremental adjustments that fine-tune the existing strategic orientation. But only a few empirical studies were done within the punctuated equilibrium framework (Romanelli & Tushman, 1994). And these rare studies (Romanelli & Tushman, 1994; Virany, Tushman, & Romanelli, 1992) don't analyze the processes of convergence and revolution within the organization. Like previous studies by Miller and Friesen (1984), they only measure the content, direction, and pacing of changes.

To sum up, the punctuated equilibrium model is a generic model of organizational evolution that shows some kinship with life-cycle theory. It specifies two distinct phases where change is described as a totally different phenomenon in terms of both its nature and process. In this model, the organization remains an instrument in the hands of managers who, through decisions about factors such as values, strategy, structure, and control, have powerful levers to adjust or transform the organization according to their objectives. It is a top-down view of change.

Miller and Friesen (1984) and Tushman and Romanelli (1985) adopt an objective approach and a predominantly functionalist explanation for the existence of configurations. Although they reframe the reflection on change, they remain in continuity with the dominant managerialist view of the previous period. As we will see in the next section, Greenwood and Hinings (1988), while retaining the holistic point of view characteristic of the configurational approach, develop a different conception of configuration that influences the framework they evolve for studying change.

Design Archetypes: From Punctuated Equilibrium to Theories of Stability and Change

Drawing on Giddens's (1976, 1984) and Bourdieu's (1977) ideas,[4] Greenwood, Hinings, and their colleagues (Greenwood & Hinings, 1988, 1993; Hinings & Greenwood, 1988; Ranson, Hinings, & Greenwood, 1980) challenge the dominant view of organizations as formal structural entities, constrained by internal and external pressures, articulated by, among others, the contingency and punctuated equilibrium theorists. According to these British authors, this view, which they label the "prescribed framework," must be completed by the "interaction perspective," which conceives organizations as emergent patterns resulting from collective meaning creation processes.

They define design archetypes as "clusters of prescribed and emergent structures and systems given order or coherence by an underpinning set of ideas, values and beliefs, i.e., an interpretive scheme" (Hinings, Greenwood, Ranson, & Walsh, 1988, p. 22). The interpretive scheme defines what is appropriate in terms of purpose and mission, organizing principles, and criteria used for evaluation; it is embodied in the set of structures and systems that constitute the organization's design. This conception of archetypes leads them to extend, and, to a certain extent, depart from the punctuated equilibrium model in two ways.

Like Tushman and Romanelli (1985), Greenwood, Hinings, and their colleagues view structures and systems as secondary to values and beliefs. However, while the former emphasize the role of top management in instilling the values and beliefs underpinning the strategic orientation, Greenwood and Hinings (1988), adopting a neo-institutionalist explanation, draw attention to the sectoral origins of interpretive schemes. In their view, organizations are embedded in an institutional setting that legitimates only a restricted number of design archetypes and, thus, interpretive schemes. In terms of change, they suggest that the existence of competing archetypes in a sector furnishes the alternative configuration toward which individual organizations might move. This conception of design archetypes leads the authors to distinguish between sectoral archetypes, which act as ideal types, and their more or less coherent embodiment in specific organizations.

Second, the emphasis these authors place on the emergent processes in organizations leads them to develop a more complex framework for organizational evolution: a theory of organizational tracks. They argue that the dynamic of power relations and the evolving pattern of commitments to existing and alternative interpretive schemes, as much as the alignment of internal and external contingencies, influence the pattern of evolution—that is, the particular track an organization will follow. Rather then seeing organizations following a generic cycle of momentum followed by revolution led by a visionary leader, they suggest that movement between archetypes can best be described as following different paths. These include, apart from the dominant track of inertia, a range of possibilities of more or less successful (linear, oscillating, delayed, abortive, unresolved) attempts at reorientation, success being defined as achievement of archetypal coherence. According to them, the movement between archetypes should be conceived as sequences of interpretive decoupling and recoupling. Therefore, elements of different archetypes could coexist in organizations, leading to archetypal incoherence. Studies done since the 1990s by these authors (for example, Greenwood & Hinings, 1993; Greenwood, Hinings, & Brown, 1990) and others (Denis, Lamothe, & Langley, 1996; Pinnington & Morris, 2002), mostly in professional and public organizations, are framed within the archetype change model, but the empirical work on organizational tracks has remained scarce to date.

Other process researchers, such as Pettigrew (1985a) and Child and Smith (1987), can also be viewed as contributing to process theories of punctuated change, theories in which "stability and change are inextricably linked as an organization moves through time" (Hinings et al., 1988, p. 193). Their empirical work on the well-known British firms ICI (Pettigrew, 1985a) and Cadbury (Child & Smith, 1987) supports the idea of complex patterns of evolution. As well, Child and Smith's (1987) sector-specific approach[5] to the study of radical change has some commonalities with the idea of Greenwood and Hinings (1988) that archetypes are related to specific institutional settings. However, as these scholars study the intraorganizational dynamics in a single organization in its context over a long period of time, an effort to build cumulatively from these separate findings would be needed for the identification of different tracks of change.

To summarize, Greenwood, Hinings, and their colleagues contribute to the configurational perspective by elaborating a richer model of the dynamics of radical change. Their framework includes the possibility of failed attempts at change, while most of the literature focuses exclusively on successful attempts.[6] Also, by integrating the social construction point of view with the formal structural perspective on organizational change, they highlight the role of meaning creation processes and of politics in organizational change. In this sense, they are clearly in tune with new developments in organization theory (Reed, 1992) that bring to the forefront cognitive and cultural as well as political approaches to change that are presented in the next sections. Finally, although their focus on radical change places them firmly in the second period, their conception of organizations and of the dynamics of organizational evolution previews the third era with its emphasis on emergent change.

Discussion and Conclusion

As stated at the outset, the configurational approach to change developed as a challenge to the incremental conception of change shared by contingency theorists and most early organization and policy researchers. Not surprisingly, this point of view also draws its share of criticism.

The most common is a refutation of the essentially revolutionary nature of organizational change. One of the most vocal critics of the configurational school is Donaldson (1996a), a staunch advocate of the structural contingency school, who finds configurations to be "simplistic caricature" (p. 127). He argues that most real organizations don't fit neatly into these types; they almost always lie somewhere in the middle between types. And, if configurations don't exist, it follows that quantum change is a flawed concept. Donaldson maintains that "most organizations, most of the time, are changing incrementally" (p. 122). He disagrees with the idea that organizations that change incrementally hover between archetypes in a state of disequilibrium, contending that it leaves the management of the transition between archetypes to be accounted for. Donaldson (1996a) asks,

> How can the machine bureaucracy come into existence? How can an organization exist at all which is large in size if it has not been able to grow incrementally from the small, simple structure through medium size to large size? (p. 113)

On a less radical note, some authors argue that long periods of momentum followed by a quick revolution might not be the only trajectory followed by organizations. Mintzberg et al. (1998, p. 314), for example, suggest that it might apply particularly well to one type of configuration, namely, large, established mass-production organizations, while innovative organizations would follow a more balanced pattern between stability and change. This line of reasoning is echoed by research on new organizational forms that suggests that punctuated equilibrium might not be an appropriate model for describing the evolution of organizations in hyperturbulent environments, which go through "continuous morphing" (Rindova & Kotha, 2001).

In fact, one of the main limits of the configurational approach to change is the lack of empirical research on the actual processes of convergence and transformation (Sastry, 1997). Most studies done within that perspective are based on archival data and official documents and identify what changes occurred and when, not how changes were realized. As Romanelli and Tushman state in a 1994 article, still very little research has been done within the punctuated equilibrium perspective on the underlying "patterns of influence among substantial changes over different domains for both revolutionary and non-revolutionary transformations" (p. 1160). For example, the announcement of a major reorganization can be the beginning of a period of radical change, as described by Biggart (1977) in the case of the U.S. Post Office or the officialization of a change that has long been under way, as in the story of the religious order told by Bartunek (1984). But both would be defined the same way in the type of analysis done by Miller and Friesen (1984) and Romanelli and Tushman (1994).

In fact, some in-depth case studies of strategic change processes, such as those by Burgelman (1983), Mintzberg and McHugh (1985), Quinn (1980), Pettigrew (1985a), and Johnson (1988), show more complex patterns of change. Local strategic initiatives leading to "nonrevolutionary" radical change are described in the first two of these, and long periods of experimentation and/or aborted attempts preceding a transformation in the last three. This process research gives credence to Pettigrew's warning: "Beware of the myth of the singular theory of social or organizational change" (p. 1).

Some of the preceding criticisms are partly avoided by Greenwood and Hinings (1988), who define an archetype in terms of the interpretive scheme from which strategy, structure, and systems emerge. From their point of view, what determines radical change is not so much the change in structural form but of the interpretive scheme underlying it. For example, a continuously morphing organization would not be changing radically if its interpretive scheme remained stable (i.e., "We are an innovative organization that changes all the time."). Hinings and Greenwood (1988) also propose a theory of tracks that allows for multiple possibilities of evolution, but very little empirical work has been done on the concept of tracks itself. In fact, this part of their theory, because it departs from the punctuated equilibrium model to extend into a theory of stability and change, blurs the boundaries between the configurational perspective and other more evolutionary perspectives on change. One of the main challenges of their quest is to reconcile the demands of contextualized process research with the essentially typological objective of configurational research.

Despite the limits mentioned, the configurational approach in its various forms continues to be influential, as reflected in the special issue of the *Academy of Management Journal* devoted to it (Meyer, Tsui, & Hinings, 1993). Since the 1990s, it has been applied to the study of radical organizational change in different sectors such as health (Denis et al., 1996; Meyer, Goes, & Brooks, 1990), architecture (Pinnington & Morris, 2002), municipal government (Greenwood & Hinings, 1993), and the cement industry (Keck & Tushman, 1993). Some authors have extended its use to the study of radical change at the industry level (Meyer et al., 1990). Finally, recently, Whittington and Pettigrew (2003) propose using Milgrom and Roberts's (1990) economic theory of complementarities, which provides the operational means for measuring the benefits of holistic configurations. Complementarities theory lends support to the configurational approach's thinking on change as a centralized, transformational process.

To conclude, one of the main contributions of the configurational perspective on change is to bring to the forefront the idea of radical change or transformation. Starting from the premise that organizations can be conceived as configurations or archetypes—constellations of tightly integrated elements—its proponents define radical change as a change of configuration. The differences in their conception of configuration should not be underestimated. For Miller and Friesen (1984), a few generic archetypes can be distinguished across the whole population of organizations, while for Tushman and Romanelli (1985), each organization develops its own particular configuration or strategic orientation. Greenwood and Hinings (1988), for their part, suggest that a few design archetypes or templates exist in each institutionalized setting. In terms of the dynamics of change, they all agree that discontinuous change is difficult. But while Miller and Friesen (1984) and Tushman and Romanelli (1985) propose a punctuated equilibrium model to describe the overall dynamics, Greenwood and Hinings (1988) suggest a theory of multiple tracks in which punctuated equilibrium is only one possibility. In many ways, Greenwood and Hinings, because they extend the reflection on punctuated change to a theory of stability and change, provide a bridge between the second and the third periods of evolution of the field.

Finally, the configurational perspective explores the concept of radical change, in terms of both its content and dynamics. But, because it views change from above, it is still largely aprocessual and acontextual.

Notes

1. These Swedish scholars, although influenced by Anglo-Saxon literature, develop an original stream of research by integrating into their analysis concepts borrowed from various perspectives such as contingency and life-cycle theories, Selznick's institutionalism, cognitive theory, and OD. They belong to the strategy process research tradition discussed in the introduction.

2. As mentioned in the previous chapter, population ecologists (Hannan & Freeman, 1977, 1984) also see radical change as a result of organizational inertia. As well, they view the transition to a new organizational form as dangerous, leading more often to organizational mortality than to its transformation. However, as these researchers are interested in populations of organizations, they do not study individual organizations that attempt transformation. In contrast, these cases of radical change are particularly interesting to scholars who are interested in structural and strategic change and who typically adopt a managerial viewpoint.

3. As mentioned by Greenwood and Hinings (1988) as well as Meyer, Tsui, and Hinings (1993), the configurational approach can include the study of any number of dimensions that combine into overall patterns, whether they are at the individual (type of leader), organizational (structural, strategic, cultural), or environmental (turbulence, connectedness) level. In the study of organizational change, organizational configurations are most often analyzed separately from environmental dimensions.

4. Giddens and Bourdieu, one a British and the other a French sociologist, separately develop theories that argue that the traditional opposition between structure and agency (or determinism and voluntarism) is inaccurate and unproductive. They propose a new perspective that, while retaining the analytical differences between the structure and action perspectives, sees them as involved in a relationship that is both constitutive and constituting. Emergent patterns of interaction are both constrained by

and constitutive of structural frameworks. In other words, structural frameworks only exist because they are constantly produced and reproduced through interaction. Therefore, action is not prescribed by structural frameworks, although structures are used as resources in interaction and are both maintained and transformed through day-to-day action. Giddens's structuration theory, particularly, has become influential in the literature on change in the 1990s, as will be seen in Part III.

5. Pettigrew's (1985a) contextualist methodological framework for doing process research on strategic change will be presented in Chapter 6 at the same time as his political–cultural approach to organizational change. Contextualism emphasizes the importance of studying organizations over their history and taking into account the evolution of the inner and outer context, the content of strategy, and of their interaction in multilevel processes of decision making and change. While adhering to Pettigrew's contextualist vision, Child and Smith (1987) focus on the relevance of studying the sector in terms of objective dimensions, industry recipes (shared strategic frameworks), and networks in order to understand the processes of strategic change.

6. How many of the underperforming firms in large-scale studies, categorized as going through incremental changes, were in fact attempting reorientations but were incapable of realizing them? How much of a momentum period is made up, in fact, of failed attempts at undermining the old archetype?

4

The Cognitive Approach[1]

W hile neo-institutionalism focused on how taken-for-granted norms and ideas at the field level increased isomorphism, in the 1980s, it is the role of managers' cognition in transforming organizations that takes center stage. Already previewed in the work of authors such as Weick (1979b), with his concept of enactment, and Child (1972), with his notion of strategic choice, the study of managerial and organizational cognition as well as of cognitive processes in organizations becomes an increasingly popular topic.

Two major approaches can be identified in the emerging field, which we label the objective-functionalist perspective and the subjective-interpretive perspective, in keeping with the way the debate is framed at the time (Burrell & Morgan, 1979). The functionalist perspective emphasizes cognition as, essentially, an information processing function yielding a more or less accurate picture of the world "out there." Walsh (1995, p. 280) suggests that interest in cognitive research is a reaction to the rise in the 1970s of theoretical explanations for organizational behavior that de-emphasized the role of managers in organizational adaptation. Research on managerial cognition, in particular, offers the possibility to examine the link between the way managers interpret information, the resulting mental frames, and organizational adaptation. The second perspective, on the other hand, sees cognition as a meaning creation process that constructs organizational reality.[2] What is sometimes called the interpretive turn in organization studies parallels an earlier movement in the social sciences (Reed, 1992). The interpretive perspective on cognition shares many similarities with some of the work on organizational culture[3] going on at the time, which is presented in the next section. Organizations that were traditionally viewed as objective, concrete entities are now conceived as intersubjective, symbolic constructions. Within this perspective, the study of the way in which individuals and groups make sense of their world becomes central to understanding organizational change.

It is not surprising, in this context, to find an interest in cognition permeating most research on organizational change from the 1980s onward. In terms of organizational change, the cognitive approach is characterized by two lines of studies. The first is concerned with studying changes in cognitive structures (the products of cognition). Most of this research, whether functionalist or interpretive, is focused on top management's cognitive schemes, starting from the premise that managers' mental frameworks must change for radical organizational change to occur (Barr, Stimpert, & Huff, 1992; Hedberg & Jönsson, 1977, 1978; Kiesler & Sproull, 1982; Sheldon, 1980). Reframing, or frame-breaking, as it is sometimes called, is essentially described as a mental process that occurs in the mind of managers. The second stream of research, which is essentially interpretive, sees organizational sense-making as a social construction process and seeks to understand how reframing as a collective process occurs or, in other words, how collective interpretations change. It focuses on the interaction between the meaning-creation processes and action that produces radical change (Bartunek, 1984; Gioia & Chittipeddi, 1991). In the next section, organizational change as a cognitive process will be briefly described, comparing the functionalist and interpretive perspectives. Then, the two research streams on reframing will be presented (see Table 4.1).

Organizational Change as Reframing

Starting in the late 1970s, more and more scholars start viewing organizational change as a change of interpretive schemes (i.e., the mental frameworks that individuals use to understand events). As mentioned in the discussion of the configurational perspective, changes in values and beliefs that guide action (Tushman & Romanelli, 1985) or interpretive schemes (Greenwood & Hinings, 1988) are presumed to be an integral part of organizational transformation. In this sense, there is overlap between the configurational and cognitive perspectives on change. But while the researchers adopting the former approach develop general models of change dealing with interpretive schemes, strategy, and structure, scholars in the cognitive perspective specifically focus on major change as reframing, that is, the construction or adoption of a new frame of reference.

This approach, which originates in psychology, starts with an individual-level model, that of human cognition. While some scholars focus on understanding individual cognition in organizational settings, others extend this framework to include cognition at the group and organizational levels (Walsh, 1995). We will see some implications of these different levels of analysis in the literature on organizational change. In this approach, organizations can be viewed as bodies of thought (Weick, 1979b) and/or as interpretation systems (Daft & Weick, 1984). In the first definition, the emphasis is on the knowledge structures or mental maps

Table 4.1   Cognitive Approach

COGNITIVE APPROACH	
General model of change:	UNFRAMING – REFRAMING Destruction of old Creation of new interpretive scheme interpretive scheme
Focus: Radical change from the actors' point of view	
Antecedents: Cognitive psychology, social psychology, social psychology of organizing (Weick, 1969)	
	A change of knowledge structure—Functionalist or interpretive view
Organization:	Set of schemata
Process of change:	Punctuated equilibrium as a conversion process; the substitution of one mental model for another
Authors:	Dutton & Jackson (1987); Barr et al. (1992); Huff (1990b); Isabella (1990)
	A collective interpretation process—Interpretive view
Organization:	Interpretation system
Process of change:	Social process of sense-making and sense-giving
Authors:	Bartunek (1984); Gioia & Chittipeddi (1991)

themselves, the products of cognitive processes. The second definition focuses on the processes through which organizations develop mental representations of their world. In the objectivist-functional perspective, organizations are viewed as information processing systems; some call it the computer metaphor (Tenkasi & Boland, 1993). Managers notice changes in the information environment, select the relevant elements, and modify their mental schemes so they, hopefully, become more accurate representations of reality. On the other hand, according to interpretivists such as Weick (1979a), organizations actively construct their reality, and they do this through processes of sense-making that involve enacting.[4] Whereas noticing puts the emphasis on perception of the world "out there," the concept of enactment brings to the forefront the idea that cognition is an active process. As we experience the world through our acts, we construct it.

For the most part, the cognitive approach is a top-down view of organizations (Neilsen & Rao, 1987), which sees top management as being the only ones to develop a global understanding of the organization in its context (Daft & Weick, 1984, p. 285). Managers' knowledge structures and organizational knowledge structures are therefore often treated as equivalent (Barr et al., 1992). While many authors view organizations as socially constructed realities, few actually study organizational change as a collective sense-making process that includes all organizational members.

In the cognitive approach, the environment, as represented or enacted in the cognitions of organizational members, is of most interest. It is assumed that managers' interpretation of the evolving environment influences organizational action and change, not the environment itself. For example, some theoretical and empirical articles discuss the link between changes in the environment and change in knowledge structures of managers (Barr et al., 1992; Fahey & Narayanan, 1989; Kiesler & Sproull, 1982). Scholars working within the functionalist perspective are interested, for example, in studying how valid managers' interpretive schemes are, as the accuracy of their representations is assumed to be the key to successful adaptation. Researchers within the interpretive perspective, for their part, are interested in studying how organization and environment are simultaneously enacted in periods of radical change.

In terms of types of change, authors distinguish between first-order change, which is a modification of the existing interpretive scheme, and second-order change, which is the adoption of a new frame of reference[5] (Bartunek, 1984; Hedberg, 1974). First-order change is incremental, convergent change, the refinement of the existing frame that comes with experience. Second-order change or reframing, to use the term borrowed from Watzlawick, Weakland, and Fisch (1974), is described as divergent change, "a radical, discontinuous shift in interpretive schemes" (Bartunek, 1984, p. 356).

In terms of the dynamics of change, most of the theoretical and empirical work within the cognitive perspective gives support to the thesis of punctuated change. This literature suggests that interpretive schemes are very difficult to change significantly. First, because they are organizing devices allowing us to categorize information, they constrain thinking in novel ways about situations (Weick, 1979b). Furthermore, they focus our attention on certain elements at the expense of others, thereby neglecting information that could challenge our worldview (Kiesler & Sproull, 1982). Second, mental frameworks allow us to economize on time and effort and reduce our anxiety by providing us with a way to make sense of the world. Therefore, a lot of effort goes into trying to incrementally modify our mental structures to avoid having to discard them (Hedberg & Jönsson, 1977). Finally, even when we are aware that our present frame of reference doesn't allow us to understand what is occurring and act efficiently, we are not necessarily able to construct a new one (Hedberg, 1974).

Trying to think outside our mental frame is like trying to lift ourselves by our own bootstraps. The preceding arguments suggest that reframing is rare, painful, and, by definition, discontinuous change (Gersick, 1988, 1991).

Researchers who conceive cognitive change as an essentially individual mental process focus their attention on cognitive maps, studying their content as well as their structure. On the other hand, those who see it as a social process are more interested in the efforts at the management of meaning that accompany strategic change. In the next few pages, we will present the first line of research as it relates to organizational change.

REFRAMING AS A CHANGE OF KNOWLEDGE STRUCTURE

Change in the frames of reference and knowledge structures of managers are the main theme of these studies. As Walsh (1995) mentions in his review of the cognitive literature in organizational studies, authors use a variety of labels, such as cognitive maps or frameworks, templates, mental or cause maps, frames of reference, knowledge structures, and schemata, to talk about managerial and organizational cognitions. These terms all refer to a similar construct, which Walsh (1995) calls a knowledge structure and defines as "a mental template consisting of organized knowledge about an information environment that enables interpretation and action in that environment" (p. 286).

Schwenk (1988), for his part, distinguishes between the more general schemata (or knowledge structures) and a particular type of schema, cognitive maps (or causal maps). The first are "representations of attributes and the relationships between them that constitute common-sense social theories" (Rumelhart & Ortony, 1977, cited in Schwenk, 1988, p. 46), and the second are "concepts about aspects of the decision environment and beliefs about cause-and-effect relationships between them" (Schwenk, 1988, p. 45). Both kinds of schema are studied in organizational research on change.

The study of knowledge structures and their change poses particular methodological problems. Cognitive mapping refers to the methodological tool used to graphically represent a knowledge structure or schema. While some researchers talk of cognitive or mental maps as if they were synonymous with knowledge structure or schemata, others argue that maps should not be confused with knowledge structures. According to them, maps are more or less accurate pictorial representations of cognitions (Huff, 1990b).

In *Mapping Strategic Thought*, Huff (1990b), who has done extensive work on strategic change from a cognitive perspective, identifies a variety of mapping methods that are used. One of their main differences is the degree of interpretation they require on the part of the researcher. For example, concept mapping only requires the analysis of interview or written material to identify the most important concepts used by a manager (or an organization) and the associations between them. On the other hand, causal mapping involves the construction of maps describing the cause-and-effect relationships between concepts relating to some aspects of reality (Barr et al., 1992), and argument mapping integrates the logic behind the chains of reasoning (Fletcher & Huff, 1990). Whatever the method used, change in cognitive maps (and knowledge structures) is usually measured in terms of the proportion of concepts changed (either through addition, deletion, or substitution) and/or the proportion of changes in the links (either through addition, deletion, or change in the type of link, its direction, or its value); for more details, see Huff (1990b).

Although a number of scholars insist that knowledge structures are strictly individual-level phenomena, others argue for the existence of group-level, organizational-level, and industrial-level knowledge structures. For some, these supra-individual frameworks refer to shared worldviews that emerge from socialization (for example, the dominant logic of Prahalad & Bettis, 1986); others believe that such a thing as a collective mind exists, and that it transcends the sum of individual cognitions (Daft & Weick, 1984; Levitt & March, 1988).[6] In most cognitive studies, group-level knowledge structures are constructed through aggregation of individual knowledge structures, while organizational knowledge structures are assumed to be those of the dominant coalition (often obtained by analysis of top management's discourse or official documents).

In his extensive review of the literature on managerial and organizational cognition, Walsh (1995) shows that most of the research on the development and change of knowledge structures over time deals with the refinement of schemata through experience (i.e., incremental change) and the stability of established schemata (i.e., how they resist change). The main conclusion that can be drawn from this work is that the development of knowledge structures over time leads to tunnel vision and groupthink.

The literature dealing specifically with change in knowledge structures explores a variety of topics, which can be clustered around two themes, the first studying the link between the content and structure of managers' mental frameworks and their propensity to change, and the second examining changes in mental structures and the linkage of such change with environmental change and/or strategic change.

In the first group, some studies on the mental schemes of managers focus on generic content dimensions relating to change (Dutton & Jackson, 1987; Ford & Baucus, 1987). Adopting an interpretive perspective, Dutton and her colleagues, for example, discuss the link between the categorization of a new strategic issue (i.e., a new development, an event, or a trend) and organizational change (Dutton & Duncan, 1987; Dutton & Jackson, 1987; Jackson & Dutton, 1988). They argue that different ways of labeling an issue, for example as a threat or an opportunity, will lead to different conceptions of change (Dutton & Jackson, 1987). This work underscores the subjective nature of issue categorization, highlighting the meaning creation process inherent in understanding new situations and its impact on change actions.

In terms of the structure of cognitive maps, the main concern is with the complexity of the schema, the degree of relatedness of its elements, and their impact on the ability to change. Some authors argue that only managers with sufficiently complex maps can be effective change agents (Bartunek, Gordon, & Weathersby, 1983). Lyles and Schwenk (1992) further develop this idea and hypothesize that organizations having complex and loosely coupled knowledge structures are more adaptable than those having simple and tightly coupled ones. This argument is reminiscent of the debate between the incremental and transformational perspectives on change reported earlier.

The second body of work, most of it done within an information processing perspective, focuses on the change of mental models in the context of strategy formulation (Schwenk, 1988). For example, researchers explore the link between changes in the information environment and changes in the content of knowledge structures over time (Barr et al., 1992; Fahey & Narayanan, 1989; Fletcher & Huff, 1990; Isenberg, 1987). Most studies find that changes in the information environment lead to changes in mental structures, but there are mixed results in terms of the accuracy of these cognitive changes (Fahey & Narayanan, 1989), and few studies look at the link with changes in the strategy itself (Rajagopalan & Spreitzer, 1997).

The work of Barr et al. (1992) is an exception. These authors are among the first to study the relationship between changes in causal maps and organizational action and performance. In a study of one failing and one surviving railroad company over 25 years, they construct causal maps from managers' letters to shareholders. They find that both firms change their representations of the environment at the same time. But it is the firm that changes its representation of the organization's strategy first and modifies it over time that survives. The second firm, which abruptly changes its representation of its strategy much later, fails. From this, they conclude that strategic renewal can be achieved by an incremental approach. Their findings show that, although a major reframing occurs the year top management is changed, it is preceded by 6 years of minor changes and is followed by years of further incremental change.

Gersick (1991), drawing on her own studies of change in work teams and on theories from different fields, comes to different conclusions from similar findings. She is one of the rare researchers to explicitly discuss the process behind reframing as a mental activity. Most scholars just infer that reframing has occurred from looking at changes in mental maps. Gersick believes that what she calls the dynamics of insight drive punctuated change. According to her, in a situation of radical change, after a period of confusion and questioning, individuals or groups can suddenly develop a new vision. Citing Kuhn and Gould, she says that in larger systems "the new direction does not emerge all at once; instead, a catalytic change opens the door to it" (Gersick, 1991, p. 29). She also contends that the uncertainty inherent in periods of transition fosters divergent thinking around which a new cognitive structure can crystallize; after a while "things fall into place" (pp. 28–29). Afterward, this new cognitive structure must take over the rest of the organization; the whole system must be converted. Isabella (1990), in her well-known study of managers' changing cognitive models as a change unfolds, supports that view. She finds that managers evolve through a four-stage model of interpretation, going from a disorganized frame or "unframe" at the beginning of the change process to a well-constructed evaluative frame at the end of the change period. This research shows the unsettling effect of major change on individuals who are subjected to it and lends support to the idea that major change is frame-breaking. As we will see next, studies of reframing as a social process present a similar picture.

One of the main conclusions that can be drawn from this stream of research is that the stability of managers' cognitive structures is one of the major obstacles to organizational adaptation and eventually leads to radical change. The studies on cognitive structure development show the prevalence of convergent change (i.e., the tendency to modify and refine the existing frame) over discontinuous change. While some authors theorize about what managers need to do to facilitate cognitive reframing, this approach views most managers as incapable of undergoing second-order change in cognitive schemes without outside help. It thus supports the notion that radical change is usually the result of the adoption by the organization of a cognitive framework developed or imported by a new management team.

Finally, this stream of work tends to separate thinking from acting in organizations. In a sense, by emphasizing cognition as something managers do, these researchers imply that other organizational members are doers, not thinkers. They equate change in top management's mental frame with organizational reframing. As we will see, the second line of research, which emphasizes reframing as a social interaction process, although it still focuses on top management, sees managers' role not only as strategic thinkers but also as symbolic actors or managers of meaning.

REFRAMING AS A SOCIAL INTERACTION PROCESS

Some authors, while adhering to the view that cognitive reorientation is necessary for radical change to occur, emphasize the social nature of reframing at the organizational level. These scholars focus on cognition as sense-making as opposed to information processing. Weick (1969, 1979b, 1995), one of the main contributors to the sense-making approach through his concept of enactment, focuses attention on interpretation as creating reality. He argues that interpretation is an active process: We enact or create our world by selecting what we pay attention to and then acting in ways that are consistent with the world we have created. These actions, in turn, influence what we pay attention to. In this view, cognition and action are inseparable: Action drives cognition as much as the other way around.

In this perspective, interpretation becomes not a question of accurately assessing an objective environment, but of reducing the ambiguity and equivocality inherent in organizational life. The assumption is that "facts do not speak for themselves" (Ford & Baucus, 1987, p. 367) and that each actor (whether manager or employee) actively constructs organizational reality from his or her own point of view. A multiplicity of perspectives is therefore inevitable in an organizational setting, and the problem of organizational change becomes one of creating a common understanding. Furthermore, in the case of radical change, what is needed is a shared framework or ideology, that is, a set of ideas and beliefs that "describe how things are and prescribe how things should be" (Brunsson, 1985, p. 28) to generate enthusiasm and commitment to change actions. This suggests that the role of managers as change agents is not so much to develop an accurate vision as to create one that will lead to action.

An important part of the theoretical and empirical work done from this perspective explores the process through which top managers try to build consensus around a new cognitive frame (Gioia & Chittipeddi, 1991; Huff, 1983; Poole, Gioia, & Gray, 1989). The empirical studies are in-depth case studies that record organization members' interpretations and actions in context, often using ethnographic methodology.

Some studies, for example, have focused on the processes by which this adhesion is gained. Poole et al. (1989) suggest that influence modes such as coercion and manipulation that provoke strong emotional reactions are most effective in eliciting schema changes. Gioia and Chittipeddi (1991), studying a top-down strategic change (which they define as a cognitive reorientation), analyze in detail the process through which the new strategic vision is communicated to the rest of the organization. Although they focus on a leader-driven change, their analysis shows that interpretation of the leader's vision is not a passive reproduction process but an active process of meaning creation that modifies the initial vision. They use the concepts of sense-making and sense-giving to describe this reciprocal process involving both cognition and action.

These studies also discuss how the management of meaning, through the framing of the situation, influences this collective meaning creation process in a top-down change. For example, Gioia and Chittipeddi (1991) describe what they call "ambiguity by design" as an effective framing approach. According to them, this approach leads to uncertainty regarding the existing frame, thereby encouraging reframing, while giving organization members some leeway in articulating the change, thus reducing their resistance to change. In contrast, Brunsson (1985) argues that clear and narrow organizational ideologies are more conducive to change, because they avoid lengthy analysis and discussion. However, he adds that narrow ideologies, because they can easily be challenged and displaced, make an organization "changeable." On the other hand, complex ideologies make an organization "changeful," because they allow more potential for adaptation within the frame. Other studies show how top managers create a sense either of urgency or of opposition by framing a change as radical (Demers, 1992; Reger, Gustafson, & Mullane, 1994) or routinize it by defining it as business as usual (Pondy & Huff, 1985).

But despite the fact that sense-making is viewed as a collective process, so far most studies on change have looked at top-down change and have focused on management's attempts to propagate their vision of change. One exception is Bartunek's (1984) well-known study of reframing in a religious order. Her research is particularly interesting because it describes a collective process of reframing rather than the more usual top management–driven one. She analyzes how the order's members, through a dialectical process leading to a synthesis, develop over time a new interpretive scheme from two divergent visions. The author also shows the importance of action in creating shared meanings around the order's mission. Other research (Demers & Barral, 1999; Schön, 1979; Sheldon, 1980) points to various types of collective sense-making processes leading to different outcomes, such as synthesis, substitution, compromise, and reinterpretation (giving a new meaning to an existing scheme), that suppose different types of power dynamics. For example, even in the case of a top management driven radical change, an empirical study shows how the transformation is reinterpreted by organization members as a destruction of the organization and is thus delegitimated (Demers, 1990). As Neilsen and Rao argue (1987), strategic change implies a collective legitimation process "in which leaders, followers, and stakeholders alike participate in the making of meaning" (p. 523).

In short, this second stream of research, rather than focusing only on top managers' interpretive schemes, emphasizes the processes through which a cognitive reorientation spreads in an organization, usually after the arrival of new management. Drawing attention to reframing as the management of meaning, it highlights the role of managers in bringing the organization to a new understanding of its situation.

Although some research, particularly later studies, points to the fact that organizational reframing involves a process of collective sense-making, the emphasis is still on change defined from the point of view of top managers, that is, a period of planned intervention largely managed from the top. However, an important contribution of this work is to highlight different aspects of what constitutes radical change. Because of its subjectivist perspective, it suggests that a radical change is one that is defined as such by the people who initiate it or live it; it also gives prominence to the emotional and political dimensions associated with change as a social interaction process. As will be shown later, the cultural perspective also draws attention to the collective dimension of organizational change.

Discussion and Conclusion

While it is very popular and has influenced most of the literature on change since the 1980s, the cognitive approach has also been the target of some criticism. Some challenges come from those who belong to different epistemological traditions, both within and outside the cognitive perspective. Those who favor an objectivist-functionalist approach to research find that the case-based studies of change done from an interpretive perspective do not lead to valid comparison and cumulative knowledge. They also argue that such studies "provide little useful guidance for managers" (Rajagopalan & Spreitzer, 1997, p. 66).

On the other hand, from an interpretive perspective, much work on cognitive structures is criticized for neglecting to take into account the social context. A holistic approach requiring in-depth longitudinal case studies of changing organizations is deemed necessary to understand cognition in organizational settings. Interpretivists also believe that the main objective of research in management is understanding, not prescribing (Gioia, 1986). Moreover, they are "wary of recipes and routines," because they believe that sense-making involves improvisation and spontaneity (Weick, 1995).

But despite these traditionally irreconcilable differences as to the nature and aims of inquiry in the social sciences, recently some authors have argued for an integration of objectivist and interpretive perspectives to study change (Aldrich, 1999; Huff, Huff, & Barr, 2000). Huff, Huff, and Barr even contend that it is because the cognitive approach can be a bridge between interpretive and objectivist perspectives that it should be given more prominence in the study of change (2000, p. 29). As we will see later, the debate over a possible convergence, whichever form it might take, is one of the characteristics of the third period of evolution of the field.

More specifically related to the study of change, questions have been raised regarding the focus of cognitive research. One of the weaknesses of studies on cognitive structures, particularly, is that they give the impression that organizational change is a disincarnated process occurring in the mind of managers (Demers, 1990). Neilsen and Rao (1987), for their part, challenge the way even the interpretive literature portrays top managers. They argue, "The implicit message seems to be that organizational leaders have near monopolistic control over the interpretive process and that they determine the limits to their control" (p. 524).

In fact, when the interpretive process is examined, it is to the actions and reactions of managers that attention is given. Rarely are the interpretations and actions of other organizational members studied systematically to explore the change process from their point of view (Demers, 1993). Neilsen and Rao (1987) suggest that the study of legitimation as a collective sense-making process is an important topic for future research on change. This call foretells the evolution of the field of change in the 1990s toward a view of change as a multilevel phenomenon (Aldrich, 1999; Huff, Huff, & Barr, 2000; Pettigrew, Woodman, & Cameron, 2001; Van de Ven & Poole, 1995).

Another comment concerns the neglect of most cognitive studies to explore the link between changes in cognitive structures and actions and changes in strategy content and outcomes (Rajagopalan & Spreitzer, 1997). As mentioned by Walsh (1995), this type of research poses methodological challenges. In fact, it more or less implies the use of historical data (gathered either through retrospective interviews or documents) to reconstruct knowledge structures after strategic change has occurred (and the outcome is known). However, reliance on retrospective accounts is criticized because of poor recollection or rationalization (Rajagopalan & Spreitzer, 1997), and there are questions about the validity of documents as a way to access knowledge structures (Walsh, 1995). The few ethnographic studies of organizational changes, done in the 1980s and early 1990s, concentrate on the processes underlying reframing and rarely link them to organizational outcomes.

In fact, since the 1980s, most process researchers who have studied major change have taken into account cognitive, as well as structural, cultural, political, and strategic aspects of change (Brown, 1995; Doz & Prahalad, 1988; Johnson, 1988; Pettigrew, 1985a). However, their aim usually is to better understand a particular type of change by exploring the relationships between strategic, cultural, political, and cognitive processes. As a result, they don't really contribute to the development of the cognitive perspective directly. Finally, despite the fact that most researchers conceive change as involving a cognitive dimension, there is still a dearth of empirical research that specifically theorizes about the cognitive processes of change at both the managerial and organizational levels (Huff, Huff, & Barr, 2000; Walsh, 1995).

Research on change from the cognitive perspective in the 1990s has tended to move in two directions. In recent years, there has been a growing interest in emotion, a dimension closely connected to cognition[7] (Gioia, 1986; Park, Sims, & Motowidlo, 1986). For example, some scholars have turned to the study of the emotional dynamics in radical change (Huy, 1999), as well as the clash between emotion and cognition in radical change (Fiol & O'Connor, 2002). Another increasingly important stream of research on cognitive change is associated with the learning approach (Glynn, Lant, & Milliken, 1994; Baumard, 1996), which becomes very popular in the 1990s and will be presented in the third part of this book.

To conclude, the main body of cognitive research provides a psychological explanation for the occurrence of radical change in organizations. This approach supports and elaborates the model of punctuated equilibrium. The incapacity of existing managers to change their cognitive schemes is stressed. Changes within the frame are therefore attempted until there is a crisis, and radical change occurs only with the arrival of a top manager with a different frame of reference. This new manager is usually described in heroic terms as the leader of the ensuing cognitive reorientation. Change is thus portrayed as revolutionary and as having high human costs. The view of change as a momentous event, a period of crisis in the life of an organization, is reinforced. Once again the image of the organization that emerges is of a unitary entity, an instrument in the hands of top managers. But this time they are information processors and visionaries, rather than objective strategists and designers of new organizational forms.

A second group of studies brings to our awareness the social nature of the interpretation process. Our vision of the manager as a change agent is thus altered; his or her role is to manage meaning, to lead a legitimating process. While, as we have discussed, it falls short of its promise to explore the collective process of sense-making, this approach still adds to our knowledge about how organizational change is managed. In this case, sense-making for oneself and for others is heralded as the new skill to be mastered in managing radical change.

Finally, the main contribution of the cognitive approach is to draw attention to the idea that organizational change has a subjective dimension and that the way actors interpret issues influences how they change. Even those who adopt an objectivist perspective on reality acknowledge that human subjectivity is important to take into account when studying organizational change.

Notes

1. One might ask why we don't talk of the learning approach instead of the cognitive approach, as numerous authors write on learning at the same period (Argyris & Schön, 1978; Duncan & Weiss, 1979; Hedberg, 1981). During the 1980s it is the psychological view, emphasizing cognitive and, sometimes, emotional aspects of change, that is at the forefront. The literature on organizational learning, in my reading of the field of change, takes center stage in the 1990s when behavioral learning becomes popular and starts linking with the cognitive approach (Glynn, Lant, & Milliken, 1994).

2. While objectivist research seeks to better understand a reality that is assumed to exist "out there," the subjectivist-interpretive perspective argues that what matters is socially constructed reality. Because it is impossible to have a direct experience of the reality "out there" (i.e., without the mediation of cognition), it is our cognitive frameworks that determine our action and ultimately enact our world (Weick, 1979b).

3. The simultaneous rise in popularity of both the cognitive and cultural schools and the importance in both approaches of concepts such as interpretive schemes, ideologies, provinces of meaning, frames of reference, worldviews, assumptions, and belief structures sometimes makes the work difficult to classify. Furthermore, the tendency of organization scholars to borrow freely from different domains and theoretical perspectives without

clearly positioning themselves creates some confusion. However, there are sufficient differences between the two approaches to warrant separate treatment, as will be discussed in the next section.

4. Although some researchers view the interpretive perspective as a primarily methodological approach focusing on the actor's point of view, most, including Weick (1979a), associate it with a social constructionist ontology (see Hatch & Yanow, 2003, for a thorough discussion of that perspective).

5. At about the same time, Argyris and Schön (1974) introduce a similar idea with their concept of single-loop and double-loop learning. But most of Argyris's work is devoted to showing the individual defense mechanisms that make double-loop learning so difficult (Argyris, 1982). Therefore, it is more a theory about individual resistance to change and organizational stability than a theory of organizational change.

6. Some authors within that perspective view organizational knowledge as embedded in structures, routines, and organizational systems and not mainly in mental schemes. This conception will be further explored under the organizational learning approach.

7. As argued by Park et al. (1986), although one could question whether affect (feeling) should be considered part of a theory of cognition (thought), research on that topic emanates from the field of cognitive psychology. Furthermore, they are interdependent: "Their relationship might best be understood as a *cognitive basis of affect* and/or an *affective basis of cognition*" (p. 220).

5

The Cultural Approach

On both sides of the Atlantic, the cultural approach to organizational change becomes highly visible during the 1980s, even in the popular press (for example, *BusinessWeek,* October 27, 1980; *Fortune,* October 17, 1983). A phenomenal number of both academic and prescriptive writings on the topic of cultural change are published in the early 1980s.[1] The interest in the concept of culture is largely linked to the now fashionable view that the management of change requires particular attention to cultural phenomena in organizations and, particularly, that radical change implies a cultural revolution (Allaire & Firsirotu, 1985). In fact, this approach is characterized by a lively debate over the extent to which culture can be managed and changed (Frost, Moore, Louis, Lundberg, & Martin, 1985).

Although the interest in culture is sometimes described as a fad, for some scholars it represents a way to study organizations that offers a counterpoint to the dominant rationalistic view (Pondy & Mitroff, 1979; Smircich, 1983a). According to this group, the cultural perspective directs attention away from the technical and instrumental aspects of organizations, toward their social and symbolic dimensions (Morgan, Frost, & Pondy, 1983; Pettigrew, 1979). However, by the mid-1980s, the majority of writings associated with the cultural approach to change present an instrumental vision of culture (Barley, Meyer, & Gash, 1988; Frost, Moore, Louis, Lundberg, & Martin, 1991). Culture, often defined as the shared values that hold the organization together, is seen as a critical element in the management of change because of its persistency (in other words, its resistance to change). However, it is also believed that managing a cultural revolution, that is, a management-driven change in core values, will lead to successful organizational transformation. In this dominant functionalist stream, culture thus becomes a tool, like strategy and structure, a powerful (although, for some, difficult to manipulate) lever to reorient organizational action. The objective is to align culture with strategy and structure (Schwartz & Davis, 1980; Tichy, 1982). In this spirit, management is redefined by some authors as symbolic action (Pfeffer, 1981).

This dominant point of view is challenged by an influential group of researchers who adopt an interpretive perspective (Barley et al., 1988; Smircich, 1983a). For these scholars, what makes the cultural perspective interesting is that it allows us to conceive organizations as cultures, that is, as socially constructed systems of meanings. As a consequence, strategy, structure, and power relations are seen as expressions of this culture. While, in the preceding view, culture is one organizational element among others, here it becomes the overarching concept.

Culture is conceived as emerging from a group's history. Thus, while culture is viewed as a form of social control, it is seen as impossible for managers (or any other group) to control the culture unilaterally and to change it in a predetermined way (Barley et al., 1988). Because culture is the result of collective sense-making and action over time, there is always an unpredictable side to cultural evolution. Moreover, managers are considered to be inside the culture (not above or outside it). Cultural change is, therefore, conceived more as a natural, ongoing structuring process than as an episodic intervention by managers.

In the following pages, we will briefly discuss some of the issues involved in defining culture. Then, the conceptions of cultural change and processes of change underlying the two views will be presented, starting with the orthodox view, labeled the cultural change management perspective, and ending with the alternative view, the cultural dynamics perspective (see Table 5.1).

Culture and Change: Functionalist and Interpretive Perspectives

Although the study of organizational culture reaches a peak in the 1980s—in part, some suggest, because of the crisis many major corporations are now facing (Barley et al., 1988, p. 42)—the interest in cultural change is not new. In the 1950s, authors such as Jaques (1952) and Selznick (1949, 1957) develop a "cultural" view of organizational change. For example, Jaques, a psychologist, in his book *The Changing Culture of a Factory*, is one of the first to explicitly refer to organizational culture. Selznick (1957), a sociologist and founder of the institutional school, is included as a precursor in most discussions of the cultural approach. Writers in organizational development, starting in the 1960s, also define organizational development as cultural change, arguing that "the only viable way to change organizations is to change their 'culture'" (Bennis, 1969, p. v).

Part of the appeal of the concept of culture is that everyone intuitively knows what culture is: "the way we do things around here." In most definitions, one will

Table 5.1   Cultural Approach

CULTURAL APPROACH

General model of change: REVOLUTION   OR   INCREMENTALISM
                            Destruction and   Gradual renewal
                            reconstruction

Focus: Cultural change management versus cultural dynamics

Antecedents: Anthropology, sociology

	Cultural change management—Functionalist view
Organization:	Tribe with shared assumptions, values, and norms
Process of change:	Punctuated equilibrium as a radical process of undermining of old culture and conversion to a new one
Authors:	Hedberg & Jönsson (1977, 1978); Gagliardi (1986); Schein (1985)
	Cultural dynamics—Interpretive view
Organization:	Tribe with shared patterns of thinking and behavior
Process of change:	Gradual and emergent evolution of cultural patterns
Authors:	Meyerson & Martin (1987); Hatch (1993)

find a common core referring to a shared frame of reference, including, among other elements, beliefs, values, and norms, expressed in symbols and artifacts, through which organizational members make sense of their world and by which their action is guided.[2] From the preceding, one could argue that there is no significant difference between the cognitive and the cultural perspectives. In fact, some authors talk of a cognitive school within the cultural tradition (Alvesson, 2002; Eisenberg & Riley, 2001; Smircich, 1983a). Others include the study of culture within the cognitive perspective (Huff, Huff, & Barr, 2000; Walsh, 1995). This is not surprising, because there are numerous points of convergence between scholars who adopt an interpretive epistemology, whether they define themselves as belonging to the cognitive or the cultural school. Aldrich (1992), for example, includes both the cognitive and the cultural perspectives within what he calls the interpretive approach. However, a large number of researchers within each of these two schools are not interpretivists. Furthermore, the cultural approach does not reduce itself to the cognitive school. Most of all, I have chosen to present the cultural and the cognitive schools separately because the cultural approach has its roots in anthropology and in sociology, as opposed to psychology in the case of the cognitive school. It thus offers a somewhat different vantage point from which to explore the topic of organizational change.

The one element that is inherent in the notion of culture is that it applies to a group, a collective. In contrast to cognition, a psychological concept first developed to account for individual mental activity, the notion of culture is used to explain the existence of collective patterns of thinking and behavior. In the cultural perspective, organizations are compared to tribes or societies. While culture is conceived to be a property of a human group, it has been used at different levels of analysis to study small groups, such as a work unit in an organization, as well as large ones, such as a multinational corporation, a profession, or even a nation, in the case of cross-cultural study. As will be seen later, the fact that culture can be used as a multilevel concept, or a concept "without scale," opens up interesting possibilities for the explanation of organizational change from a pluralistic perspective.

Apart from these common underpinnings, when one scratches the surface there is a diversity of definitions of culture and an even greater disparity in uses of the term in organization studies. Some authors have developed typologies linking these different definitions to relevant theories in anthropology (Allaire & Firsirotu, 1984; Smircich, 1983a). One often cited basic distinction is the one made by Smircich (1983a, p. 347) between those who view culture as a variable, "something an organization has," and those who view it as a root metaphor, "something an organization is." It closely parallels the one already alluded to between functionalists and interpretivists. At one extreme are those authors who view culture as a managerial tool. According to them, building a "strong" culture, one that is coherent with the strategy pursued, is seen as an important role of managers. At the other extreme are those scholars who see culture as a collective sense-making process over which managers have very little control. Another interesting distinction is between those researchers who study "organizational culture" and those who study "culture(s) in organizational settings." The former tend to view culture as an integrating mechanism, while the latter look at cultural diversity, even fragmentation, within organizations (Meyerson, 1991; Meyerson & Martin, 1987).

But those distinctions are difficult to apply, as mentioned by several authors (Alvesson, 2002; Frost et al., 1991; Nord, 1985), because many researchers do not fit neatly into one or the other of these categories. For example, although some functionalists view culture as a variable, not all of them do. As well, not all of those who study cultural differentiation adopt an interpretive stance; some, for example, adopt a critical stance. This is all the more confusing because writers use broad definitions of culture that are very similar, but depending on their epistemological assumptions their interpretations and conclusions are totally different. As mentioned by Alvesson (2002), there are "very different understandings of culture that are only to a limited extent reflected in differences in its formal definition" (p. 15).[3]

Furthermore, there is often an important difference between the definition of culture used and its application to empirical material. For example, authors will adopt a definition of culture as a shared set of values and beliefs, but will study cultural change in terms of logos, mission statements, ceremonies, and the like, which are relatively superficial changes. Finally, researchers differ a lot as to what they analyze when they study cultural changes. Some studies of cultural change focus mainly on symbolic forms, such as myths, stories, dramas, and rituals (Pettigrew, 1979; Trice & Beyer, 1984). Others emphasize what is sometimes called the deep structure of culture: basic assumptions (Schein, 1985) or shared understandings (Smircich, 1983b). For the purposes of this book, I will distinguish between the functionalist and the interpretive perspectives because they form the basis of two different approaches to change. Furthermore, they will allow us to more easily compare the cultural perspective to the other approaches.

A FUNCTIONALIST FRAMEWORK

The most popular writings on corporate culture at the time (Deal & Kennedy, 1982; Peters & Waterman, 1982), although they advocate change in order to develop a "strong" culture, don't really address cultural change in any detail. Actually, they more or less take the feasibility of cultural change for granted and focus on the outcome, that is, the kind of culture aimed at. They don't define culture very precisely either. Instead, they identify a list of values (e.g., being close to the customer, quality) and of behaviors (participation, risk-taking) that, according to them, make up a strong and successful culture, that is, one that is dominant and coherent.

One of the best-known definitions of culture is given by Schein (1985, p. 9). He develops a framework for explaining culture in management that is more sophisticated than most and representative of the functionalist approach. As assessed by Hatch (1993), "Schein's formulation remains one of the only conceptual models ever offered" (p. 658). Schein defines the culture of a group as "the collective or shared learning of that unit as it develops its capacity to survive in its external environment and to manage its own internal affairs" (Schein, 1990, p. 58).

Schein shares with other functionalists an integrative view of organizational culture that is in accord with their unitary conception of organizations. A culture has to be shared, consensual, and aligned with management's objectives to fulfill its many functions; among those mentioned in the literature are integration, commitment, and control. Many authors, such as Pettigrew (1979) and Lodahl and Mitchell (1980), also emphasize the uniqueness of the culture as a key to members' identification with the organization.

For functionalists (e.g., Gagliardi, 1986; Schein, 1985; Lundberg, 1985), the leader plays an important role in the development of those shared values that over time become the basic assumptions guiding organizational action. Schein (1990), more than others, emphasizes the fact that a group must have existed long enough, with a stable enough membership, and have had the occasion to develop shared assumptions (i.e., values and beliefs that have acquired a taken-for-granted status) for a culture to develop. For example, he asserts, "One cannot simply *create* a strong culture by executive action. Such a culture can evolve only through shared history and a consistent pattern of leadership over a long period of time" (p. 64).

In his view, some organizations have a culture, but others don't. As Schein reminds us (1990), the concept of culture was originally developed to explain permanence, not change: "Cultural assumptions are the things that survive through successive generations" (p. 57). In anthropology, the construct was used to explain the stability of traditional communities. Schein, like Pettigrew (1979), is as interested in understanding the origins of culture and the dynamics behind the persistence of culture as in studying cultural change (Schein, 1991, p. 246). In a sense, the ideas of culture and change stand in an ambiguous relationship for this author and other functionalists. Once a culture is created, it is difficult to change because it is taken for granted, but it must also be managed if it is to retain its vitality. In that regard, Schein's position is very close to that of Selznick (1957). Schein, like all functionalists, acknowledges cultural change and the possibility of managing it. However, his works contain more moderate claims of managerial control than do most of the managerial writings on cultural change in the 1980s (e.g., Kilmann, Saxton, and Serpa, 1985).

In the functionalist view, the environment is viewed as an important catalyst for change. It provides a test for the functionality of the culture (i.e., "Is the culture effective as a solution to the group's survival challenge?"). If the organization succeeds in its environment, then the culture is reinforced; if not, the culture is undermined, and change can occur.

Change, as in the configurational and cognitive approaches, is typified as superficial or profound, and as incremental or revolutionary (Gagliardi, 1986; Schein, 1985). This follows from the definition of culture as hierarchical. According to many authors (Gagliardi, 1986; Lundberg, 1985; Schein, 1985), a culture comprises multiple levels, from the most visible to the most intangible. Schein distinguishes three levels from the superficial to the profound: artifacts (technology, symbols and rituals, shared behavior patterns) and values (discussable beliefs about why things are the way they are) are the observable manifestations of an underlying pattern of assumptions (implicit, taken-for-granted ideas about the nature of reality and truth, of human nature and activity, and of human relationships). He insists (1990) that the integration of these basic assumptions into a coherent pattern is what makes up the organization's paradigm, the deep structure, "the most important layer of organizational culture" (p. 62).[4]

A cultural transformation requires a change in basic assumptions, while a change in artifacts, even values and beliefs, is seen as superficial cultural change. However, cultural change is viewed differently by functionalists according to what cultural elements they study. Those who view the management of cultural change as evident tend to equate organizational culture with more superficial and easy-to-control manifestations of culture, such as the espoused values of top management and symbolic artifacts (Tunstall, 1985). For others, who consider it as something risky and difficult to achieve, a cultural revolution is a modification of deep taken-for-granted assumptions and understandings (Schein, 1990). However, even those who consider cultural change difficult to manage advocate that managers should strive to achieve cultural control (Martin, 1985). In fact, what characterizes most the functionalist discourse on cultural change is its managerialism (Barley et al., 1988, pp. 53–54).

As we will see in the next section, Schein (1990) and other functionalists describe the process of cultural change as leader-driven within a life-cycle model. But first, the definitions of culture and cultural change from the interpretive perspective are presented.

AN INTERPRETIVE DEFINITION OF CULTURE

From an interpretive point of view, organizations are cultures. Most interpretivists define the concept of culture as dealing essentially with shared symbols and meanings. Frost et al., in the allegorical introduction to their now-famous book *Organizational Culture* (1985), propose that culture means "talking about the importance for people of symbolism—of rituals, myths, stories and legends—and about the interpretation of events, ideas, and experiences . . ." (p. 17). While some interpretivists also explicitly include patterns of behavior and practices as an important part of culture (Meyerson & Martin, 1987; Van Maanen & Barley, 1985), symbols and meanings are considered the "quintessential" content of any culture by Van Maanen and Barley. For some, symbols, meanings, and cultural patterns of behavior are considered more useful for cultural analysis than are assumptions and values, because it is through its enactment that culture exists and can be deciphered (Van Maanen & Barley, 1985, p. 35; see Schein, 1991, pp. 244–245 for a critique of this view). Ethnographic methods, borrowed from anthropology and sociology, are often used to study cultural change.

While symbols and interpretations are also part of the functionalist definition of culture, they are understood differently by interpretivists. As already mentioned, functionalists view shared interpretations as "solutions," that is, as ideas put forward by the leader and accepted by the group because they work.

On the other hand, interpretivists consider meanings to be continually (re)created collectively and to be "fundamental to the very existence of organization" (Smircich, 1983a, p. 353). As for symbols,[5] functionalists view them as artifacts, that is, as observable manifestations of culture, and as means to maintain social order. In contrast, within the interpretive perspective, symbols are of interest as "generative processes that yield and shape meanings" (Smircich, 1983a, p. 353). As stated by Morgan et al. (1983), this point of view "takes the existence of all aspects of the culture as problematic, and seeks to understand the methods and practices by which its elements are created and sustained" (p. 19).

Discussing symbolism and organizational change, Gioia (1986) contends that culture "is both expressed and learned through symbolic processes" (p. 67). In the same vein, Hatch (1993) contends that what is neglected in Schein's (1985) framework is the place of symbols, which Schein equates with artifacts, the most superficial manifestation of culture. While there are divergences as to the relationship between symbols and artifacts in this literature (Hatch, 1993), a symbol is defined (Gioia, 1986) as "a sign (for example, a concept, event, or action) that serves as a meaningful representation of some significant element of the organizational experience" (p. 52). In other words, a symbol is a sign that derives its significance from its association to some other concept or entity that gives it added meaning (Gioia, 1986; Morgan et al., 1983). For example, the resignation of an experienced manager becomes the symbol for the beginning of a new era, rather than just the decision of one executive to benefit from retirement. For this event to be an organizational symbol, it must have the same meaning for most organizational members. In this view, the creation and emergence of new organizational symbols thus becomes a crucial aspect of organizational change.

This conception of culture suggests a vision of organization and change that can be quite different from the one adopted by functionalists. In contrast to the functionalist tradition, the interpretive perspective views the development of a culture as problematic, as something to be explained. Scholars within that stream are more sensitive to the existence of multiple interpretations of reality within an organization and, as a result, of the difficulty of developing shared symbols and meanings.

However, very few authors within the interpretive tradition develop an explicit conception of change. And those who do, such as Scandinavian scholars Hedberg and Jönsson (1977, 1978) and Berg (1985), tend to have an integrative vision of culture and a managerial focus. Berg, for example, articulates an explicit cultural-symbolic model of organizational change based on the idea of a unitary culture. He views organizations as symbolic fields and considers that organizational change is a transformation of the form and content of the symbolic field that makes up the organization. He develops an interesting definition of culture incorporating both dynamic and static elements. He distinguishes between symbols and sagas (described as points of reference, which allow an organization to adapt by redefining past experiences and creating new collective experiences) and root metaphors and myths (the stable pattern of underlying assumptions that provides the code for interpreting the different points of reference). And although he rejects planned change, arguing that "a serious strategic change program is . . . an exploration of the unknown" (p. 297), he advocates symbolic management, particularly through the development of a corporate identity (the significant properties of a culture in a given context), as a way to promote collective understanding. As can be seen, the definition of culture as unitary pushes these authors into the same ambiguous position as the functionalists with regard to the management of cultural change.

On the other hand, the possibility of an organization being constituted not of one integrated culture but of a mix of differentiated cultures, particularly in the case of large, complex organizations, is acknowledged by several researchers (Meyerson & Martin, 1987; Nord, 1985; Van Maanen & Barley, 1985). For some, these subcultures can be embedded within a dominant organizational culture, while others view the existence of a homogeneous organizational culture as a rare phenomenon. For example, occupational groups, functional units, and hierarchical groupings can all be sources of differentiated, even antagonistic, cultures within an organization.[6] In contrast to the functionalist point of view, which tends to see culture as an integrating force and assume the existence of harmonious values, an interpretive point of view doesn't necessarily equate culture with consensus and harmony. Although few interpretive accounts of cultural change describe such organizational culture, shared meanings and symbols could emphasize diversity, individualism, and competition, for example.[7]

Moreover, this conception of culture allows for the possibility of cultural change having multiple sources, both internal and external, and for a view of change as continuous, rather than as an episodic event. For example, organizational subcultures are seen as possible sources of change. Changes in the group's composition and dynamics can alter the organizational culture. As explained by Nord (1985), "The existence of the larger entity depends as much on a dynamic tension among the parts as it does on their similarity" (p. 195).

Furthermore, as argued by Meyerson and Martin (1987), pluralist views of culture "emphasize environmental (or external) catalysts for change that have localized impact on many facets of organizational functioning" (p. 634). Thus, the environmental context as construed by organization members is considered as a potential source of change, through, for example, new ideas and practices. However, it is not an important part of most studies on cultural change.

In this approach, cultural changes are conceived to be incremental and local. Therefore, organization-wide cultural changes are viewed as almost impossible to realize according to managerial intentions. Expressions such as "riding the wave" and "exploration into the unknown" are used to suggest that cultural change is about making the most of what is already there and being open to changing one's objectives as the process unfolds (Berg, 1985; Turner, as cited in Hassard, 1999). Indeed, the existence of differentiating forces within an organization means that cultural dynamics are, by definition, more or less unpredictable, unstable, and subject to constant revision. However, as will be seen in the section on the process of cultural change, few empirical studies of cultural change explore the possibilities that this conception offers.

Cultural Change Processes

As mentioned before, in the 1980s, the study of cultural change processes is generally framed around the question of whether culture can be managed or not, that is, whether it can be changed by managerial action. The orthodox point of view, or cultural management discourse, emphasizes issues related to radical change, while the interpretive perspective, or cultural dynamics discourse, depicts change as incremental.

As will be seen, the picture of organizational change that emerges from both these perspectives on cultural change shows similarities, as well as interesting differences, with the configurational and cognitive perspectives.

MANAGING CULTURAL CHANGE: REVOLUTION OR EVOLUTION?

The most popular model of cultural change in the 1980s is based on the idea that organizational transformation implies a cultural revolution (Allaire & Firsirotu, 1985; Gagliardi, 1986). It is the work of writers who adhere to a functionalist perspective and a managerial point of view. This work has spanned a number of empirical studies of cultural change, most of them qualitative case studies (for typical examples, see Frost et al., 1985; Kilmann et al., 1985).

As described by Meyerson and Martin (1987), in this perspective, change is viewed as "a monolithic process, as an organization-wide phenomenon" (p. 628). As such, it describes cultural change as the destruction of a shared worldview that is then, if change is well managed, replaced by a new one. This process is assumed to be under the control of top managers, although many authors suggest more or less important constraints on their action.

Schein (1985, 1990), for example, develops a life-cycle model to identify the conditions that make cultural change more likely and the methods to be used according to circumstances and stages of development. He describes the birth of an organizational culture as a process of collective learning driven by the founder. The leader's beliefs and values, which guide the behavior of group members, become their own as they are validated through shared experiences of success. Over time, these values and beliefs are idealized and take on a "sacred" quality (Gagliardi, 1986, p. 124), that is, they are transformed into assumptions. Both scholars stress the importance of success in the development of shared assumptions, an argument similar to the one made by Tushman and Romanelli (1985) in their discussion of punctuated equilibrium, where they suggest that convergence is strengthened by success.

Schein also suggests that in the growth period, culture is usually a positive force, and if change is required, it usually is in the form of managed evolutionary change. This type of change is convergent, enhancing the existing culture. In midlife, however, because of cultural erosion or fragmentation, and at maturity, due to cultural stagnation, more substantial changes might be needed, ranging from incrementalism to turnaround and rebirth.

Schein (1990) proposes a general three-stage model of cultural change that is an extension of Lewin's popular unfreezing-moving-refreezing model (Burke, 2002). Lewin's three-step model has been very influential, particularly, in the Organization Development movement. Developed from action research projects with groups, it is based on the idea that individuals will resist a change that deviates from the group's behavioral norms. To achieve change, therefore, one must change the values of the group—normally, through discussions where individuals can experience others' views and come to question their own. To "refreeze" or fix the change, ways must be found to make the new behavior "relatively secure against change" (Lewin, 1947, p. 344, cited in Burke, 2002, p. 151).

Schein (1990) elaborates Lewin's model, expanding each of the three stages and adapting it to the organizational context. First, he develops the unfreezing stage into three elements: (1) disconfirming evidence, which (2) produces guilt, which must be combined with (3) psychological safety to allow people to move to the next phase. The second phase, cognitive redefinition, allows the development of new assumptions. Finally, a refreezing phase at both the individual and interpersonal level is necessary to stabilize the new learning. Schein cautions, however, against wholesale cultural changes because of their traumatic impact, warning that one of the most difficult aspects facing managers is the choice of what to change and what to preserve.

In the same vein, Gagliardi (1986), whose vision of culture is very close to that of Schein (1985, 1990), proposes that the culture, which he calls a symbolic field, can be compared to a fan of options. The base of the fan comprises the assumptions (for Gagliardi, they are sacred and not open to discussion), which can be manifested in a number of primary and secondary strategies. Some assumptions permit a wider range of options than others. Gagliardi views the primary strategy of the firm as preserving the culture and makes the point that a "firm must change to remain the same" (p. 127). He labels this apparent cultural change a change in cultural manifestations that leave the assumptions and values untouched. In talking of cultural revolution (i.e., real cultural change), which according to him can only be brought about by new leadership, he claims that only if the new values are not antagonistic to the old values will cultural change be possible. If the new values are perceived to be opposed to the old ones, the culture must be destroyed and rebuilt anew. On the other hand, if the new values are perceived as different, then a broadening of the range of options can be accomplished and cultural change can ensue. Tunstall's (1985) story of the divestiture of AT&T offers an interesting description of the cultural change process as conceived by these authors. He stresses the role of leadership in promoting new values and the positive effect of advertising successful actions reflecting such values. But Tunstall also talks of the importance of highlighting continuity with the past through the affirmation and reinterpretation of traditional values.

As mentioned by Meyerson and Martin (1987), the process described by those who adopt a managerialist perspective is often very similar to models of individual cognitive change. Because their model focuses on cognitive redefinition as the basis for cultural change,[8] it blurs the differences between the cognitive and the cultural approaches. In fact, it is the cognitive change, viewed as the first step in cultural change, which is conceived as manageable.[9] This conception reaffirms both the vision of change as radical and the model of punctuated equilibrium. However, it should be noted that cultural theorists are more cautious than configuration theorists with regard to the likelihood and benefits of cultural revolution.

Furthermore, there is another side to the cultural process as described by some of these authors, which distinguishes it from the cognitive approach and challenges the punctuated equilibrium model. Schein (1990), Lodahl and Mitchell (1980), and Martin, Sitkin, and Boehm (1985), for example, distinguish between the process of cultural change itself and the deliberate management of that process. While these authors stress the influence of the leader on culture, they also acknowledge that the cultural process left to its own will lead to differentiation (the birth of subcultures) or drift (the erosion of the dominant culture). In a later article, Schein (1996) argues that organizations are made up of a number of subcultures (i.e., the engineering, operational, and executive subcultures), which makes global cultural change very difficult to achieve. A study by Lodahl and Mitchell (1980), for example, shows evidence of cultural drift in an innovative university. However, few studies actually document this process because they focus exclusively on management's actions.

In contrast, the process of cognitive development is generally described as leading to a reinforcement and refinement of cognitive frames. From a cognitive point of view, "natural" evolution leads to convergence, which is coherent with individual development. On the other hand, from a cultural point of view, such unmanaged evolution can lead to divergence, which reflects the fact that modern organizations, unlike traditional societies, are subject to numerous influences.

While the functionalist school, with the metaphor of culture as glue, tends to view these competing influences as problems to overcome, Nord (1985, p. 195) suggests viewing culture as a magnetic field to develop a more dynamic vision of culture. The latter metaphor is more in tune with the interpretive view of cultural change processes, which we discuss next.

CULTURAL DYNAMICS: FROM INTEGRATION TO FRAGMENTATION

The interpretive perspective on organizational culture, as discussed previously, allows for a more differentiated and dynamic view of culture. However, as mentioned by Nord (1985) and Meyerson and Martin (1987), very few authors pursue such a path in the 1980s. Nord, for example, comments, "Current views of organizational culture underemphasize the tensions and dynamism of organizations" (p. 194). Meyerson and Martin, for their part, who develop models of cultural change based on nonintegrative views of culture, note that few researchers "have attempted to articulate a systematically dynamic view of culture" (p. 633).

In fact, as discussed previously, a number of authors within the interpretive tradition have an integrative vision of culture and focus on managers' concerns. For example, Swedish scholars Hedberg and Jönsson (1977, 1978) are among the first to develop a framework explaining the dynamics of discontinuous strategic change in terms of a cultural analysis. They explain that when the organization's ruling myth (i.e., the theory of the world of the dominant group) is undermined by anomalous information, a cognitive crisis ensues. According to Hedberg and Jönsson, the replacement of a myth is not a mental process based on a rational assessment of the situation. Instead, the acceptance of a new myth is described as a leap of faith. It is based on emotional and speculative arguments, because the new myth still has to prove itself in action. When organizational members adhere to a new myth, anxiety and confusion are replaced by enthusiasm and wishful thinking. It is only in the development of the new myth that the existence of different cultures within the organization is alluded to, as the new myth is either imported by an outside group of managers or developed within the organization by a group challenging top management. As can be seen, such a model of cultural change is not very different from the ones elaborated by functionalists.

As a pluralist theory of organizational change, this approach is therefore less systematically developed, but two streams of work will be presented here. The earliest one, the differentiation studies (Meyerson & Martin, 1987), is characterized by work that elaborates a view of organizational change based on the study of the continuous interplay of cultures within organizations. The second and later group, labeled the fragmentation perspective (Meyerson & Martin, 1987), includes the writings of authors that present culture as inconsistent, in a state of constant flux.

Differentiation Studies

According to Meyerson and Martin (1987), the picture of the cultural change process that characterizes differentiation studies emphasizes "fluctuations in the content and composition of subcultures, variations in the structural and inter-personal relations among subcultures, and changes in the connections between subcultures and the dominant culture" (p. 634).

Such a vision draws attention to the emergent nature of change because it highlights diffuse and unintentional sources of change, as opposed to studies that concentrate only on deliberate attempts by management to influence cul-ture. As a consequence, organizational change is viewed not as an organization-wide, monolithic process but as the more or less loosely coupled interaction of multiple local processes. While a change can be revolutionary for some subcul-tures, its effects on the whole are likely to be incremental.

Empirical research on cultural change done from this perspective stresses the impact on the change process of different cultures in organizations. Some, which are very close to integration studies, focus on organization-wide cultural change but take into account the impact of different subcultures on the process. The longitudinal study by Dent (1991) of the cultural transformation of a railway company through the emergence of a counterculture falls within this category. Others examine the way subcultures influence change interven-tions. Bartunek and Moch (1991), for example, describe the often negative reactions of different subcultures to a Quality of Working Life intervention.

But overall, there is little empirical work on cultural change done during the 1980s from the differentiation perspective. It remains marginal compared to the functionalist studies. Furthermore, in the late 1980s, some scholars begin to put forward a conception of cultural change that is even more marginal than the preceding: the fragmentation perspective.

Fragmentation Studies

Meyerson and Martin (1987) present the fragmentation perspective as a third way that has yet to be explored in cultural studies. From this point of view, ambiguity is a way of life and culture is continuously changing. In fact, "any change among and between individuals, among the patterns of connections and interpretations, *is* cultural change (at the organizational or sub-organizational level)" (p. 639).

In a sense, culture is thus seen not as stable and permanent but as constantly being enacted and changed. Change is not viewed as a period of transition between periods of stability but as constant flux. It goes without saying that in such a view, cultural change is uncontrollable, the result of simultaneous inter-locking local processes.

In the early 1990s, a few empirical studies, including one by Feldman (1991) and another by Meyerson (1991), show among other things that cultural fragmentation is experienced by organizational members as everything always changing yet remaining the same. As well, Hatch, in the early 1990s, proposes a fine-grained theoretical description of the dynamics of organizational culture that is compatible with the fragmentation view. She develops a complex model of cultural dynamics that articulates the processes of manifestation, realization, symbolization, and interpretation, linking assumptions, values, artifacts, and symbols (Hatch, 1993).

Actually, the view of cultural change put forward by these latter scholars remains a very marginal part of cultural change studies of that period, but it echoes the conception of change that is prevalent in the third period and that we will discuss later. It emphasizes the fact that organizational life is complex and dynamic and that ambiguity and contradictions are important dimensions in the study of change.

Discussion and Conclusion

Despite its popularity (or because of it), the cultural school is the subject of a lot of debates in the late 1980s, most notably concerning the conception of cultural change. Many of the attacks come from within the field itself, researchers from different traditions being the most vocal in their comments (see Martin & Frost, 1996, for an historical account of "the organizational culture war games").

For example, advocates of the interpretive perspective accuse some functionalists of having too superficial a view of cultural change, focusing on easy-to-change variables such as symbols, logos, and espoused values, and reducing culture to the level of a managerial tool (Berg, 1985; Meyerson & Martin, 1987). Wilkins and Dyer (1988) argue that, except for Schein (1985), researchers develop generic models of cultural change that are not sensitive to differences in culture. Smircich (1983a), an influential cultural researcher, states, "The notion of 'corporate culture' runs the risk of being as disappointing a managerial tool as the more technical and quantitative tools that were faddish in the 1970s" (p. 346). Smircich, with her colleague Calás, questions the future of the field in the late 1980s, arguing that the culture concept is in danger of being dominant but dead (cited in Frost et al., 1991).

Those who defend a differentiation perspective disapprove of functionalists and those interpretivists who assume an overly homogeneous view of cultural evolution (Alvesson, 2002; Martin et al., 1985; Nord, 1985; Turner, cited in Hassard, 1999). Martin et al., for example, comment, "Unfortunately, the social construction of reality is generally used as a descriptive phrase, a synonym for assumed consensus, rather than as a topic for systematic empirical investigation" (1985, p. 103). On the other hand, Schein (1991, pp. 244–245), a functionalist, berates interpretive scholars (practitioners of what he labels the ethnographic approach) for their poor conceptualization and definition of culture and the limits of their empirical work with regard to the holistic nature of culture. He also argues for culture being consensual, by definition: "The concept of sharing or consensus is core to the definition, not something about which we have an empirical choice" (p. 248). Others, among them Alvesson, a scholar in the critical tradition, discuss the limits of the fragmentation perspective: "Conceptually, even though ambiguity may well be an important aspect of culture, it is hardly the dominating one" (2002, p. 164). Trice and Beyer (1993, p. 14), for example, argue that ambiguity, fragmentation, and constant changes are the opposite of culture as it is commonly defined.

Another line of criticism comes from those who find that the cultural literature concentrates too much on ideational aspects of culture such as visions, slogans, and ceremonies, neglecting its material dimensions related to the organization of work and the development of procedures (Gregory, 1983; Meyerson & Martin, 1987). For example, Alvesson (2002, p. 147) argues that the interest in symbolic activities, as opposed to "substantive" activities, comes from their appeal to managers who view them "as inexpensive means" to realize their preferred outcomes. More important, critical theorists (Alvesson & Deetz, 1996; Willmott, 1993) disapprove of the neglect of power issues and conflict of interests even in pluralist accounts of culture. Adding to this criticism, Martin and Frost (1996) write, "It is surprising to note that few differentiation studies go beyond the delineation of subcultural differences to examine processes of organizational change that might . . . benefit those who are at the bottom of the hierarchy" (p. 605).

This challenge to the cultural approach, as will be seen in Chapter 8, is taken up by scholars within the critical tradition who emphasize issues of power and domination associated with culture and change.

In short, from the standpoint of a theory of organizational change, one of the main critiques that can be addressed to the cultural approach is that very little systematic conceptual and empirical work is done on cultural change as a collective process in the 1980s. Despite its promise of looking at change from the point of view of different organizational stakeholders, for all intents and purposes the cultural approach remains a top-down view of change.

After its period of glory in the 1980s, cultural change as it is represented in the work of most scholars in "mainstream" functionalist and interpretive approaches ceases to dominate the literature on organizational change.

However, cultural analysis becomes the preferred approach of scholars adopting critical and postmodern perspectives to organizational change (Alvesson, 2002;

Martin & Frost, 1996). Moreover, a preoccupation with cultural processes, in general, is pervasive in all organizational change literature since then, as researchers and practitioners move from a concern with change as an episodic radical transformation to an interest in change as an ongoing process of learning, innovating, evolving, and becoming. In this context, a growing number of authors (Chreim, 2005; Dutton & Dukerich, 1991; Eisenhardt et al., 2000; Gioia & Thomas, 1996) turn to the concept of organizational identity, which is closely intertwined with organizational culture, to explain change. The impact of change on organizational identity, which is traditionally defined as what is enduring and central in the organizational self-concept, is increasingly analyzed. For example, Hatch and Schultz (2002) discuss the interplay among organizational identity, organizational culture (internal context of identity definition), and image (external context of identity definition) in terms of ongoing dynamics. At the same time, as will be discussed in Chapter 8, critical authors become concerned with issues of individual identities as (re)constructed by new managerial practices that attempt to transform the existing organizational culture.

In conclusion, the cultural approach to organizational change is the success story of the 1980s. As a top-down approach to organizational change, its appeal comes from its focus on the symbolic, emotional, and expressive facets of organizational change, as opposed to rational and technical ones. As such, it contributes to a richer understanding of change. An attention to culture highlights the importance of symbolic management in the context of change and, more so than the cognitive approach, it underlines the collective nature of change in an organizational context. The less "mainstream" work, by addressing the issue of diversity in organizations, challenges monolithic, organization-wide revolutionary models of organizational change. However, its potential is not fully realized in the 1980s in terms of a theory of change. Most empirical studies are still accounts of radical top-down changes. Yet the literature on cultural change, particularly the debates on the limits to managerial control over the change process, opens the door to a challenge of the dominant view. Finally, the more incremental vision of change put forward by differentiation theorists finds a stronger voice in the political approach that will be presented next.

Notes

1. On the academic side, a good example is *Organizational Symbolism*, a volume edited by Pondy, Frost, Morgan, and Dandridge (1983). A well-known practitioner-oriented book is *Gaining Control of the Corporate Culture*, edited by Kilmann, Saxton, and Serpa (1985).

2. As will be seen later, scholars in the functionalist school emphasize assumptions and values, while those in the interpretive school tend to focus more on symbols and meanings (Frost et al., 1985; Hatch, 1993; Pondy et al., 1983).

3. I agree with Martin and Frost (1996), who distinguish between a critical and an interpretive orientation in differentiation studies. However, I have chosen to include authors who are concerned with politics and domination in the political and critical approaches rather than the cultural approach. In a sense, for them, culture is a context in which to uncover conflicts of interest and/or expose exploitation and oppression, rather than a core concept. In contrast, for interpretivists, culture defined as meanings and sense-making is central as both concept and object of study.

4. This view of culture raises important methodological issues. If the most important cultural layer is inaccessible to observation, how can it be studied? Schein (1991) favors the use of clinical methods through which insiders surface their own assumptions, guided by an outsider using the above framework.

5. Actually, one could say that it is the importance given to symbolism in the cultural perspective (Hatch, 1993) that differentiates it most from the cognitive approach to change. Another difference, which will be discussed later, is the existence within the cultural school of a small stream of work emphasizing cultural differentiation, and even fragmentation, while the cognitive school focuses only on dominant frames of reference.

6. Van Maanen and Barley (1985) argue that the concept of culture can more usefully be applied to workgroups within organizations than to the whole. But this view is by no means shared by all interpretivists. In fact, in the 1980s, most study culture at the organizational level and explain the existence of organizations by the constitution of common systems of meanings, even though this is viewed as problematic and an ongoing process (Smircich, 1983b).

7. Members of an organization could all agree that they disagree about many things, that they compete with one another, and so on. They would have a conflictual culture, but a culture just the same.

8. This is not surprising, because the author who developed the most popular model of cultural change, Schein (1990), is a psychologist who was himself inspired by another psychologist, Kurt Lewin.

9. For instance, these authors emphasize the management of meaning through the creation of ambiguity and the development of a vision that inspires action to bring about organizational members' cognitive redefinition. That is why I include authors such as Brunsson (1982) and Gioia and colleagues (Gioia & Chittipeddi, 1991; Gioia, Thomas, Clark, & Chittipeddi, 1994) in the cognitive school, even though they are included in the cultural school by other writers. It is important to note that Gioia himself positions his work in the cognitive school (see Gioia, 1986; Gioia & Chittipeddi, 1991; Gioia et al., 1994).

6

The Political Approach

I s there really an approach to organizational change that takes as its focus power and political action and, if so, where does it fit? This is a legitimate question because the issue of power has always been a sensitive and, some say, neglected one in organizational studies, as witnessed by the title of the review article "Some Dare Call It Power" by Hardy and Clegg (1996). Moreover, this is particularly the case in the organizational change literature (Buchanan & Badham, 1999; Hardy, 1995). In fact, the literature on change that deals with power can be divided into two schools: the political approach, with its largely functional and managerial orientation, and the critical approach, with its macrosociological point of view inspired by the work of Marx and Weber (Hardy, 1995). In contrast to the other approaches presented thus far, it is in Europe, rather than America, that the political and, in particular, the critical (particularly the radical and postmodern) approaches to change seem to have acquired the most visibility over time.[1]

At the start of the 1980s, while the transformational model of change, popularized by the mainstream configurational, cognitive, and cultural approaches, occupies center stage, a small body of work addressing the political dimension of change provides an alternative viewpoint that emphasizes incrementalism (see Table 6.1). Later, the critical school emerges as a fundamental departure from traditional conceptions of organizational change. Putting concepts such as domination and hegemony at the forefront, these authors, more or less explicitly, challenge mainstream organizational change literature (including most work done within the political school) for being concerned only with apparent change, in other words, change that reinforces the existing system of domination. As we will see in Chapter 8, this critical approach becomes an increasingly noticed point of view in the 1990s and onward, by proposing an alternative reading of organizational change and by provoking a strong debate on its nature and ethics.

Table 6.1   Political Approach

POLITICAL APPROACH
General model of change: INCREMENTALISM Step-by-step planned or emergent gradual change
Focus: Realization of change intentions in terms of power both overt and covert

Antecedents: ORGANIC ADAPTATION   – Disjoint incrementalism (Braybrooke & Lindblom, 1963)
                                                   – Behavioral theory of the firm (Cyert & March, 1963)
              RATIONAL ADAPTATION   – Resource dependency theory (Pfeffer & Salancik, 1978)

	Politics in deliberate change
Organization:	System of structured power relations
Process of change:	Political activity of top-management or lower-level employees drives a gradual, cumulative change process
Authors:	Hardy (1995); Kanter (1983); Quinn (1980)

	Political dynamics
Organization:	Context-specific system of collective action based on evolving power relations
Process of change:	Continuous process of negotiation and competition with indeterminate outcomes
Authors:	Crozier & Friedberg (1977); Pettigrew (1985a)

In the 1980s, the political approach, characteristic of the management literature, portrays organizational change as a dialectical process, where groups of divergent interests compete more or less openly. While the dominant transformational model of change presents a unitary, more or less consensual view of organizations, the political approach is based on a pluralist vision of organizations, where power struggles and conflicts are part and parcel of the change process.

In this literature, power is generally defined as "the potential capacity to get others to do things they might otherwise not want to do and/or to resist others' effort to get one to do what they want one to do" (Frost & Egri, 1991, p. 236).

While the use of power is acknowledged, it is often described as "illegitimate," that is, as behavior occurring outside the formal channels of authority (Buchanan & Badham, 1999; Hardy, 1995). In the change literature, the term *politics* is used to refer either to resistance against management-driven change or to clandestine change initiatives, both usually leading to incremental change. According to Frost and Egri (1991), this is the realm of surface power, which deals with "the day-to-day contests and struggles for collaboration" (p. 236) occurring within the existing rules of the game.

Although it is never at the forefront, the political literature constitutes an undercurrent that creates a bridge between the first and third periods in the field of organizational change. Its origins are in the marginal organic adaptation perspective of the first period with its vision of change as a largely emergent phenomenon. In the second period, it remains an alternative yet increasingly influential point of view that previews the conception of change typical of the 1990s.

Power and Change: From Resistance to Renewal

As noted in the first part of this book, starting in the 1950s, a variety of authors from different theoretical perspectives (for example, Braybrooke & Lindblom, 1963; Child, 1972; Cyert & March, 1963; Pettigrew, 1973; Selznick, 1957) view political activity as an important element in understanding organizational adaptation. In the 1970s, however, it is the concept of power developed in strategic contingency theory (Hickson, Hinings, Lee, & Schneck, 1971) and resource dependency theory (Pfeffer, 1981; Pfeffer & Salancik, 1978), based on a hierarchical view of structure, that becomes particularly influential (Hardy & Clegg, 1996; Mumby, 2001). As stated by Pfeffer (1981), "power is first and foremost a structural phenomenon, and should be understood as such" (p. x). In these theories, power is understood as resulting from the possession of resources such as information, expertise, and control of sanctions and rewards. Particularly, the skillful use by individuals or groups of resources that enable them to control an important source of organizational uncertainty (either internal or external) is believed to create interdependencies that structure power relationships (Crozier, 1964). However, the numerous empirical studies of power done at the time are not concerned with organizational change; most are cross-sectional analyses examining, for example, the relative power of subunits in relation to their control of strategic contingencies (Hinings, Hickson, Pennings, & Schneck, 1974) or to their impact on resource allocation decisions (Pfeffer & Salancik, 1974).

In the late 1970s, with the shift in interest from structural to strategic issues, some authors begin to look at strategy making as a political process and to incorporate discussions of power in their reflections on organizational change. As is also the case with the literature on cultural change, the political approach is a reaction to the rational approaches that dominate the field at the time. For example, Quinn (1978), in his famous article on strategic change, states, "When well-managed major organizations make significant changes in strategy, the approaches they use frequently bear little resemblance to the rational-analytical systems so often touted in the planning literature" (p. 7).

As mentioned by Hardy (1995), most of these early writers adopt a managerial point of view on change, and talk of power and politics in opposition to authority, which is conceived as the legitimate form of power. Political activity is often described as a form of resistance to change or as an illegitimate or clandestine change strategy. The use of power is thus seen as making organizations inertial or unpredictable and as a major factor in the success or failure of change programs.

The political school can be divided into three streams of research related to change. The first focuses on the impact of politics in shaping organizational change as a top-down incremental process, as opposed to a "revolutionary" one (Johnson, 1988; Quinn, 1978, 1980). The second stream highlights political action as a source of bottom-up, "emergent" change (Kanter, 1983; Mintzberg, 1983; Zald & Berger, 1978). The third stream views change as a multilevel political process, producing emergent and deliberate as well as incremental and transformational changes (Crozier & Friedberg, 1977; Pettigrew, 1977, 1985a).

TOP-DOWN INCREMENTAL CHANGE: POLITICS VIEWED AS A FORCE AGAINST CHANGE

Quite a few authors of functionalist orientation who focus on politics discuss it mainly in terms of resistance to management-driven change (Hardy, 1995). They conceive organizations as political arenas held together by a dominant coalition, that is, by top management. They contend that change programs, because they challenge the status quo, awaken latent forces of opposition and give rise to a lot of political activity (see, for example, Markus and Pfeffer's [1983] discussion of the problems associated with MIS implementation). From their point of view, the role of top managers is to unify these diverging groups of interest. Therefore, for them, one of the major objectives of change management is to defeat or to prevent political activity so that the organization can continue to function as a unitary entity.

Logical incrementalism is one of the best known theories of strategic change of the early 1980s to deal explicitly with political issues[2] from that point of view. Quinn (1978, 1980), following a study of strategic change processes in 10 major corporations including IBM, Xerox, and General Mills, develops a model in which the rational approach is confronted by what he calls the power-behavioral dimension of organizations. Influenced by the work of Braybrooke and Lindblom (1963), already discussed as part of the organic adaptation stream, Quinn coins the term "logical" incrementalism to distinguish his model from their "disjointed" incrementalism or "muddling through" approach. Although he agrees that change evolves in a step-by-step, flexible (some would say opportunistic), and continuous fashion, he disagrees about the disjointedness, insisting (1978) that the process is "conscious, purposeful, proactive management" (p. 19).

Quinn shares with Braybrooke and Lindblom (1963) and Cyert and March (1963) a view of organizations as political arenas, with multiple goal structures and coalitions, where bargaining and negotiation are an integral part of decision making and change. In keeping with the reasoning of the time, Quinn (1980) defines power as a personal resource, stating, "Each player has a different level of power determined by his or her information base, organizational position, and personal credibility" (p. 11). He describes organizations as composed of a set of strategic subsystems that function relatively autonomously to tackle specific issues. For instance, the diversification subsystem is concerned with acquisition decisions, while the government–external relations subsystem articulates the posture to adopt regarding external stakeholders. Each subsystem has its own people, its goals and set of issues, and its own logic and timeframe. The role of top management is to articulate a consistent pattern of decisions and actions among the various subsystems. Quinn's major concern is with these internal dynamics of strategic change. For him, the environment is a largely unpredictable context that must be attended to proactively, as well as a source of precipitating events over which management has little control.

Quinn (1978) argues that those precipitating events, both internal and external, lead top executives to act in an incremental fashion, rather than use a formal planning approach leading to dramatic change, because of both cognitive (learning) and process (political–behavioral) constraints. An incremental logic allows top managers "to test assumptions and learn from and adapt to the others' response" (p. 9) and to manage decision processes in a way that is sensitive to "the power bases and needs of their key constituents" (p. 10). As mentioned by Mintzberg, Ahlstrand, and Lampel (1998), top managers led by the CEO remain the architects of strategic change, but "the organization is less obedient; it has a mind of its own" (p. 181). In fact, it is when he details the management of strategic change that Quinn's political orientation becomes clearest. Reitter, Chevalier, Laroche, Mendoza, and Pulicani (1991) describe his logical incrementalism as "the art of political action, which increases the quality of relevant information emanating from each subsystem, but more importantly helps define the critical elements for sustaining the legitimacy of top management's power . . ." (p. 43).[3]

For instance, Quinn (1980) outlines two broad process stages that, according to him, generally occur in well-managed companies: creating awareness and commitment, and solidifying progress. Each broad stage is further divided into a series of steps. What is striking in this description is the importance of power issues, both in terms of building a power base for certain decisions and actions and in terms of preventing or defeating opposition. Activities such as "building credibility," "legitimizing viewpoints," "broadening political support," "creating pockets of commitment," and "focusing the organization" are basically aimed at preventing opposition by building the power base of those in authority. Through such actions, top management encourages new thrusts and channels these local initiatives to maintain control of the overall direction. Other steps, including "tactical shifts and partial solutions," "overcoming opposition," "managing coalitions," and "eroding consensus," are mostly designed to reduce political opposition. These moves are meant to defeat those who resist the change that top management has converged upon. Incrementalism is thus defined by Quinn as the logical solution to the political problems caused by change. An incremental approach to change is adopted as a strategy to prevent or defeat political activity aimed at opposing management-driven change.

As can be seen, for Quinn, then, organizational change does not mean a change in power relations at the top. Power structure changes are those decided by top management as it incrementally develops a new strategic thrust. In contrast, theorists who adopt a transformational view describe radical change as coinciding with the arrival of a new top management team and thus as implying a change of those in power. While proponents of the cognitive and cultural schools argue that the current managers can't significantly change the strategic direction of their organization because of cognitive and cultural limits, Quinn (1980) suggests that this is not always the case. The major corporations he has studied are, according to him, examples of organizations that have managed major strategic redirection incrementally over long periods of time. While Quinn's work is widely referred to in the literature on change, few empirical studies in the 1980s describe major top-down change as mainly incremental. One exception is the study by Pondy and Huff (1985), which describes a significant change being routinized—that is, by integrating it into existing routines, it is defined as normal, incremental change.

Quinn (1980), with his focus on top managers' behavior, shows how they use their power to control locally driven change initiatives and implement top-down change. In contrast, the authors featured in the next section focus on the use of power by lower-level participants to effect change.

BOTTOM-UP INCREMENTAL CHANGE: POLITICS VIEWED AS A FORCE FOR CHANGE

The literature dealing with bottom-up change (i.e., change that is considered emergent from the point of view of top management) is rather modest. It can be divided into two strands, with some authors attaching a somewhat negative connotation to politics (Mintzberg, 1983, 1984; Zald & Berger, 1978) and others presenting it more positively (Huff, 1988; Kanter, 1983). The first group tends to emphasize the conflictual and parochial side of bottom-up change, while the second explores its positive influence on innovation and strategic change.

Zald and Berger (1978), comparing organizations to nation-states and organizational politics to social movements, describe politics as "unconventional opposition" (i.e., occurring outside the legitimized channels). They stress the conflictual nature of politics and discuss them in terms of "coup d'Etat, insurgency and mass movements" (pp. 824–825). They discuss both the goals and the possible outcomes of these forms of rebellion, arguing that while the last two sometimes aim for major change, incremental change is a more likely result. In a similar vein, Mintzberg (1983) defines politics as "individual or group behavior that is informal, ostensibly parochial, typically divisive, and above all, in the technical sense, illegitimate" (p. 172). He views politics as a force for change, describing the numerous games played to achieve change, for example, the insurgency games, the strategic candidates games, and the young Turks games. However, he emphasizes the irrational, dysfunctional, and destructive side of politics. For instance, he suggests that the power dynamics underlying the organizational life cycle naturally push the various organizational configurations toward a more politicized form, the Political Arena, a dysfunctional configuration. Yet he also acknowledges that politics can be a positive force, noting that it "is often needed to promote necessary organizational change blocked by the Systems of Authority, Ideology and/or Expertise" (p. 229).

This latter point of view is the one emphasized by authors who adopt a positive or neutral approach to power and politics in organizations. Huff (1988), for instance, asserts that "natural political systems often have important and positive side effects, and . . . management can channel political interactions to improve the balance of impact still further towards the good of the organization" (p. 80).

While Quinn (1980) acknowledges the existence of politics as part of organizational reality, his logical incrementalism model is more a discussion of how to avoid political resistance to top-management-driven change. In contrast, Huff (1988) stresses the positive role of politics in the strategic change process, claiming, for instance, that it "provides an arena for identifying and assessing new strategic alternatives" (p. 80) and "challenges organizational leaders to clarify and modify their thinking" (p. 80), and that political diversity enhances organizational adaptation by allowing the coexistence of different ready-made solutions and a pool of potential new leaders. She further describes routinized decision cycles, such as planning and budgeting, as useful vehicles for channeling the expression of dissent and allowing opposition to develop into well-articulated bottom-up change programs.

However, it is Kanter (1983), reporting an in-depth study of 10 large companies in her famous book *The Change Masters*, who describes most explicitly the role of politics in successful bottom-up innovation and change. She believes that what she calls "macro-change" is often the result of the accumulation of "micro-changes," that is, small-scale innovations initiated by individuals (p. 18). She asserts that "the degree to which the opportunity to use power effectively is granted to individuals" (p. 18) explains the difference between organizations that stagnate and those that innovate. She argues that these power dynamics are linked to different modes of organizing, which she labels segmentalism and integrative thinking (pp. 27–35).

Segmentalism characterizes companies where everything is compartmentalized and problems are cut into small pieces that are attended to separately. These companies avoid movement of people and resources between functions and departments and emphasize hierarchy and tradition. She describes such companies as anti-change because they are designed to repeat what they already know. In such an environment, innovators emerge *despite* the organization. In contrast, other organizations have an integrative approach that, according to Kanter, fosters innovation. These companies encourage the treatment of problems as "wholes," recognize differences, and ensure that they are taken into account. They also develop mechanisms to transcend these differences and develop a common solution. Such environments, in her view, encourage the entrepreneurial spirit in all their employees by giving each individual who has a project the power and resources to test his or her ideas.

Kanter (1983) defines innovation as "the generation, acceptance, and implementation of new ideas, processes, products, or services" (p. 20), stating that all innovations require change, that is, the disruption of existing routines and the redirection of energy to other purposes.[4] As a consequence, she argues that innovation is linked to the use of power, which she defines, in a neutral fashion, as "the capacity to mobilize people and resources to get things done" (p. 213). According to Kanter, in order to innovate, employees need access to more power (than their status grants them) and the skills to acquire it. From her detailed studies of more than a hundred innovations, she develops a process model of bottom-up change focusing on the actions of employees, often middle managers, as champions of change.

She describes the innovation process in terms of three sequences of activities through which the power necessary to get things done is acquired: problem definition, coalition building, and mobilization. The first sequence, problem definition, involves gathering organizational, technical, and political information to use in shaping a "salable" project, one that is formulated to attract support, and for use as a power resource, by becoming more knowledgeable than anyone else on the issue. She emphasizes the liberties champions take even with the assignments they are given by top management, stressing the emergent nature of the process. The second and third sequences, coalition building and mobilization, are essentially described in political terms, with such steps as "clearing the investment," "making cheerleaders," "horse-trading," securing blessings," "handling opposition," and "rule changing, bending, and breaking," suggesting the specificities of power dynamics when looked at from the bottom rather than the top of the organization. Finally, Kanter (1983) concludes this description by reiterating the importance of the organizational context for the success of innovation:

> The extent to which "heroes" emerge, of course, is a function not only of the skills of the manager . . . but also of the quality of the corporate environment: whether the company makes power tools easily obtainable or less obtainable. . . . (p. 236)

She ends her presentation of the innovation process by linking it to strategic change and discussing the role of top management in the change process. She views it mainly as ex post rationalization of emergent "grassroots" initiatives.

In short, Kanter, like Huff (1988), proposes a political model of innovation in which power is defined as a neutral tool, and political activity is viewed as a positive force for realizing organizational change. However, while Huff (1988) suggests that top managers use routine activities to foster such bottom-up changes, Kanter emphasizes the entrepreneurial actions of middle managers that are encouraged by integrative structural contexts. Change is here again defined as incremental, with small steps leading over time through accumulation to major change.

Like Quinn (1980), who focuses on the behavior of the CEO and his team as political actors in the change process, Kanter (1983) offers a description of change emphasizing the political actions of lower-level employees, particularly middle managers and their teams. Because they focus on specific change agents, these authors describe the organizational change process from a particular point of view and develop a generic model from the comparison of numerous examples taken from different organizations. In fact, they offer complementary views of organizational change framed as the deliberate project of two categories of actors: top managers and employees. In contrast, the authors discussed in the next section conceive change as a context-specific, emergent process, as well as an actor-driven one.

FROM CHANGE TO CHANGING: POLITICS
AS A REPRODUCTION AND TRANSFORMATION PROCESS

In this section, the contribution of two European researchers is highlighted: Crozier, a French sociologist of organizations, and Pettigrew, a British management and strategy scholar. While both Crozier (1964) and Pettigrew (1973) are identified with the early studies of structural sources of power, in their later work (Crozier & Friedberg, 1977, 1980; Pettigrew, 1985a), they develop a view of change as a multilevel political process, stressing both the actor, or micro level, and the organizational, or macro level, of analysis.

For instance, Crozier and Friedberg (1980), in their book *Actors and Systems*,[5] conceive organizations as local and contingent (i.e., fundamentally indeterminate and arbitrary) systems of collective action based on power relations between actors, either individuals or groups. They call these socially constructed systems of interaction "structured games," to call attention to the rules that govern them and the types of individual or group-level strategies[6] that they make possible. They insist that, although actors are constrained by the system of action they themselves have created and that they reproduce through their actions, they are not passive agents determined by the system, but always retain a certain degree of freedom. Crozier and Friedberg's (1977) basic postulate is that "the actor doesn't exist outside the system which defines his freedom and the rationality that guides his action. However, the system exists only through the actor who alone can give it life, and who alone can change it" (p. 9).[7]

Although Crozier and Friedberg (1980) explain the institutionalization of a particular system as the result of political and cultural processes, their analysis places the political dimension at the center. They define power in relational terms as "implying that certain individuals or groups are able to act on other individuals or groups" (p. 30). In their view, power is neither simply the product of an authority structure nor an attribute of actors, but an exchange relationship that is often unequal but always reciprocal.[8] As a consequence, organizations are continuously changing because the rules of the game that holds them together are always subject to negotiation as different groups of actors engage in contests to maintain or improve their position. For instance, Crozier and Friedberg define formal structure as "a provisional codification of a state of equilibrium among opposing strategies of power" (p. 61). Theirs is a dynamic view of organizations, not as fixed entities, but as more or less stable patterns of interaction.

These patterns of interaction are the emergent product of strategies that are rational from the point of view of the actors involved but often produce unintended results that can be irrational from the point of view of the organization. Organizations are thus context-specific indeterminate systems, changing incrementally as the result of power games, bargaining, conflict, and cooperation, which no group of actors can control unilaterally. According to Crozier and Friedberg, such patterns of interaction may sometimes lead to the discovery of new practices that can change certain rules of the game and even the nature of the game itself (Sztompka, 1993, p. 196).

As is clear from the preceding, Crozier and Friedberg view change as a transformation of the nature and the rules of the power game that regulates the system. They distinguish such change, which they say always involves a "rupture," a crisis, from a reversal of power, which might only mean replacing one elite by another (1980, p. 221). Change, in their view, "can only be understood as a collective creation process through which members of a given collectivity learn together, that is, invent and crystallize new ways of playing the social game of cooperation and conflict" (1977, p. 30).[9] Thus, while organizations change all the time, most often incrementally but sometimes radically, "planned" change is always problematic, because of systemic effects. Although all actors have some power, none can unilaterally control the organization, because the cumulative effect of their interactions is impossible to foresee.

Paradoxically, because Crozier and Friedberg (1977) develop a dynamic view of organizations conceiving organizations as fragile and unstable, their own empirical studies are more concerned with how stability is maintained in organizations. However, their perspective on change as a political process is very influential in France, where it is viewed as a complement to new perspectives on change and innovation, such as actor-network theory (Callon & Latour, 1991), typical of the third era in the field of organizational change (Amblard, Bernoux, Herreros, & Livian, 1996).

Crozier and Friedberg's dynamic conception of organizations as recurrent patterns of interaction leading to both reproduction and change is labeled by Dow (1988) the coactivational view. He opposes it to what he calls the configurational view, a more static conception of organizations that emphasizes formal systems of authority.[10] Dow underscores the similarities between Crozier and Friedberg's framework and Giddens's (1979) structuration theory, which inspires, in part, Pettigrew's (1985a, 1985b) vision of organizational change.

Following Giddens (1979), Pettigrew (1985b) conceives "structure and context not just as a barrier to action but as essentially involved in its production" (p. 288). He argues that action processes are constrained by structures but also constitute them, "either in the direction of preserving them or in that of altering them" (p. 288). Like Crozier and Friedberg (1977), Pettigrew develops a process view of change that focuses on both the actor and the system, or what he calls action and structure. He asserts that the field must move from studies of particular changes to the dynamics of changing, from the language of being to that of becoming; in short, to the study "of actors and systems in motion" (1985b, p. 287).

As well, like Crozier and Friedberg (1977) and Giddens (1984, chap. 5), Pettigrew puts power at the center of his explanation of the change process. He argues that change processes can be understood as resulting from "processes of competition" between interest groups adhering to different rationalities (e.g., goals, timeframes, values). For him, the micropolitics associated with these intra-organizational forces are also inextricably linked to the macropolitics involved in environmental changes.

However, unlike Crozier and Friedberg (1977), who only briefly discuss the importance of cultural processes for understanding power dynamics, Pettigrew (1985a) emphasizes the link between political and cultural processes of change. Combining an interpretive explanation with the traditional functional one, he describes politics not only in terms of a contest for resources but also as a legitimacy-creation process. He defines the management of meaning as "a process of symbol construction and value use designed both to create legitimacy for one's actions, ideas and demands, and to delegitimize the demands of one's opponents" (p. 44).

Using Hardy's (1985) distinction between overt power used to defeat opposition and covert power used to suppress or avoid it altogether, Pettigrew (1985a) discusses how this political–cultural view of change implies that one looks at both the front-stage and back-stage uses of power. He insists that explanations of change processes in terms of both "unobtrusive systems of power derived . . . from culture creation" and the "more public face of power expressed through the possession, control and tactical use of overt sources of power" (p. 45) are necessary.

Pettigrew (1985a, 1985b) further elaborates a methodological framework that he labels contextualism. This approach requires that the researcher study an organization in context over a long period of time to uncover the various processes of legitimation and delegitimation through which change occurs. He emphasizes the multilevel and processual character of this approach, which implies analysis of both vertical (from the actor to the social context level) and horizontal (interactions between levels through time) dimensions.

Pettigrew applies this approach in his well-known study (1985a) of ICI, a giant British chemical company. While it gives some support to the punctuated equilibrium thesis, this study extends it by describing in more detail the process issues associated with periods of relative continuity and change. Pettigrew shows how cognitive-cultural and political processes are involved in changing structures and strategies over time and discusses issues of timing and the links with the economic and social contexts. For instance, in accord with the punctuated equilibrium model, he describes revolutionary periods as catalyzed by "real or constructed crisis" often triggered by environmental disturbances. These "packages" of radical change start with major ideological (or cognitive) and quick structural transformations and are followed by business strategy changes. Moreover, he portrays periods of continuity as being either of a convergent nature ("absorbing the impact of revolutionary action") or a divergent nature ("coming to terms with the fact that further changes are eventually necessary") (p. 447). However, regardless of his model's potential, he concentrates his analysis on top management's activities and does not elaborate further conceptually on the political–cultural aspects of his perspective on change as a result of this study. And although Pettigrew and his colleagues continue to do extensive empirical work in different sectors (e.g., automobiles, healthcare) using the contextualist approach (Pettigrew, Ferlie, & McKee, 1992; Whipp, Rosenfeld, & Pettigrew, 1987), these later studies do not explicitly elaborate on the political–cultural framework presented here.

One scholar who pursues this work is Johnson (1988), a strategy process researcher, who, 10 years after the publication of Quinn's first article on the subject, revisits incrementalism. After doing an in-depth study of three retail clothing companies operating in the United Kingdom, he concludes that the pattern of strategic change that he observed more closely resembles incrementalism in the form of strategic drift than the logical incrementalism described by Quinn (1978, 1980). Johnson describes how, in these cases, it was top managers who resisted all attempts at change that explicitly challenged the existing paradigm. For example, he tells the story of a young marketing manager whose market research report was discredited because it questioned the strategy followed by the organization. In this instance, incrementalism is again explained as the result of both cognitive and political factors, but this time resistance comes from the top, not the bottom.

Adopting an interpretive perspective, Johnson (1988) explains top managers' behavior as the result of their being caught in a "cultural web" through which they define all problems. Furthermore, like Pettigrew (1985a), he stresses the political dimension of such resistance, emphasizing the links between core beliefs and the power structures of the organization. The change process he describes follows an incremental path, but it does not lead to a change of direction that realigns the organization with its environment, as described by Quinn. Here, top-down change is a case of "more of the same," or changing to remain the same, which leads eventually to the company being taken over. Consequently, Johnson's study supports the thesis of punctuated equilibrium; it suggests long periods of convergent incremental change eventually leading to radical transformation, following the replacement of top management (p. 88). However, in contrast to others who offer a functional explanation for this process, Johnson emphasizes a symbolic-political explanation. Furthermore, he suggests that this pattern is particularly likely in organizations whose culture has a strong operational basis.[11]

Since then, with the exception of Hardy's (1995) theoretical paper on strategic change as a political process and a few empirical studies such as those of Brown (1995) and Hislop, Newell, Scarborough, and Swan (2000) that deal explicitly with the political process surrounding the adoption of new information technology, few authors have done work in the same vein. In fact, according to Hardy and Clegg (1996), Pettigrew's political–cultural approach, while it offered a bridge between the managerial approach to power and change and the critical school, has not really been pursued in that direction, particularly in the United States. Instead, the critical school, including both radical studies and postmodernist literature, has developed separately from the political approach, to become increasingly visible in the field of organizational change in the third period. On the other hand, contextualism, the methodological approach proposed by Pettigrew, is widely referred to in strategy process studies. It shows many similarities with the coevolutionary perspective, which has recently become a significant trend in the study of change (Pettigrew, Woodman, & Cameron, 2001).

Finally, because of their political view of organizations emphasizing ongoing processes of negotiation, bargaining, and competition, Crozier and Friedberg (1977) as well as Pettigrew (1977, 1985a, 1985b) are among those at the forefront of the development of a conception of change as a continuous, emergent (i.e., largely indeterminate) process, a widely spread view in the following era. According to these scholars, organizations, because of their essentially political nature, are socially constructed systems that evolve a local, contingent order that is always subject to change. In that sense, they depart from the more generic point of view of Kanter (1983) and Quinn (1980).

To conclude, Crozier and Friedberg (1977) and Pettigrew (1985a, 1985b) draw attention to the way in which power is embedded in the rules of the game (or the strategies, structures, and processes) of the organization. In so doing, they help explain processes of both stability and change over time by acknowledging the multiple ways in which actors can not only overtly but also unobtrusively exert control over others. While Crozier and Friedberg (1977), in their studies, illustrate the freedom of action and use of power of lower-level employees, Pettigrew (1985a) emphasizes the use of power by top management.

Discussion and Conclusion

Naturally, much of the criticism of the political school comes from those who espouse a radical view of power and change. As mentioned previously, they blame authors of the political school for adopting a managerialist point of view. As argued by Hardy and Clegg (1996), "Rather than delve into the power hidden in and mobilized through apparently neutral structures, cultures, and technologies, the vast majority of researchers preferred to . . . view these constructs as apolitical management tools" (p. 631).

This approach is not only criticized on theoretical grounds for not representing organizational power in an accurate way, but also on moral grounds for downplaying the ethical considerations involved in change efforts and for being "ideologically conservative" (Hardy, 1995). According to critical authors, this approach assumes that managerial objectives are legitimate, although they can also be self-serving (Watson, 1982), and it de-emphasizes conflicts of interest among workers and managers. Hardy, for instance, asserts that "the managerialist perspective assumes (implicitly or explicitly) that managers use power responsibly to achieve organizational objectives; while other groups use it irresponsibly to resist those objectives" (1995, p. 13).

For those who adopt a critical point of view, authors such as Crozier and Friedberg (1977) overestimate employees' power to resist and, for the most part, illustrate the dysfunctional impact of this resistive power from an organizational point of view, thereby emphasizing its negative side. Pettigrew, who, as we showed, develops a vision of power that, in many ways, is coherent with the radical point of view, is criticized for, finally, concentrating on top management and neglecting other constituencies' perspectives (Starkey, 1987, p. 418).

Another line of criticism comes from others who assert that the political perspective is not sufficient because change cannot be explained by relying exclusively on dynamics of competition and interests. For example, Amblard et al. (1996) contend that one of the limits of Crozier and Friedberg's work, with its emphasis on power games, is its incapacity to explain the production of the stable agreements among actors that are necessary for change and innovation to occur. As Amblard et al. argue,

> From this point of view, an agreement . . . always conceals a power struggle and, therefore, constitutes, as a figure of stability, a quasi-artifice; as a consequence, it becomes difficult to assign to it a real theoretical status, in contrast to the concept of power. (p. 128)

They also suggest that such political approaches to change, by discussing forms of regulation only in terms of power and control, neglect their importance in the construction of actors' identity (Amblard et al., 1996, p. 46). For these critics, the political approach must be completed by other perspectives, particularly the cultural.

As a matter of fact, from the late 1980s on, there are very few empirical studies that adopt a primarily political perspective on change—apart from the work of critical scholars, to which we will come back in the third part of our synthesis. A few exceptions are the work of Buchanan and Badham (1999), which examines the role of change agents as political operators, and that of Bacharach, Bamberger, and Sonnenstuhl (1996), who explain multilevel political dynamics, in the context of organizational transformation, as a process of cognitive dissonance reduction, thus associating political and cognitive approaches.

However, most other studies of organizational change that attend to the political dimension are done in the contextual–processual tradition. They treat the political dimension as one among others and concentrate on managers' actions. Such research aims at a better understanding of patterns of deliberate or planned change in particular contexts or types of organizations, which is one major trend in recent years in the area of change studies.

This work on strategic change, for example, explores the relationship between power shifts and cognitive and strategic activities (Doz & Prahalad, 1988) or examines, among other things, the impact of intervention style on power dynamics (Greiner & Bhambri, 1989). One group of scholars focuses on change in professional organizations, because of the specificities of their power structure, and discusses its impact on the change process, particularly on the nature of leadership (Hinings, Brown, & Greenwood, 1991; Denis, Lamothe, & Langley, 1996).

These studies, while they focus on radical changes, tend to emphasize the incremental and precarious nature of the transition process itself. Doz and Prahalad (1988), for example, distinguish between the radical cognitive shift and its implementation into concrete strategic change, which they define as an incremental learning process. In fact, quite a few authors in the political school (for example, Crozier & Friedberg, 1977; Kanter, 1983; Quinn, 1980) also explain incrementalism both as a consequence of power dynamics and in terms of the need for organizational learning in situations of change. They emphasize the idea that change takes time to achieve, particularly when it is radical, not only because of people's resistance to changing their behavior, but also because new behaviors must be learned. However, they don't really theorize about how such learning occurs. In a sense, the political perspective can be seen as a complement to the organizational learning perspective that takes center stage in the 1990s.

In conclusion, scholars who are attentive to the political dimension of change, even when they adopt a managerial standpoint, pay more attention to the implementation of change within the organization, that is, to the challenges involved in getting managers' decisions accepted and realized, than do most mainstream approaches at the time. In the 1980s, the political approach is the counterpoint to the radical or transformational perspective on change. Its main contribution is to show that the process of change is more complex and precarious than the one presented by the dominant perspective. Rather than concentrating only on the most visible means of action of top managers—the widely publicized strategic, structural, and symbolic changes—they pay attention to the less-visible, day-to-day actions that help make these changes reality. They also highlight the conflicts and contradictions that are brought to life by change efforts.

Furthermore, scholars within the political school are among the pioneers in drawing attention to the role of lower-level participants in the change process, although more often in a negative than a positive way. In so doing, they open the way for the surfacing of the emergent conception of change that develops in the 1990s. Crozier and Friedberg (1977) and Pettigrew (1985a), for instance, who introduce a process perspective on organizations that redefines change not as a rare event but as a core feature of organizations, are at the forefront of this movement.

Notes

1. In fact, in France, the influence of Crozier and Friedberg (1977) on organization theory has led to the widespread acknowledgment of power issues in organizational change since the 1970s (see Amblard et al., 1996; Bernoux, 1985; Reitter et al., 1991). But there is a strong cleavage in France between the political perspective adopted in organization studies and the critical perspective on power, which is mainly associated

with the study of social change, while in Great Britain, for instance, the radical point of view becomes more prominent in the 1980s and 1990s in discussions of organizational change.

2.   Incrementalism is also closely associated with the learning school in the field of strategy (Johnson, 1988; Mintzberg et al., 1998). Here, incrementalism is included in the political school because, in the 1980s, when it comes out, its focus on the political dimension sets it apart in the literature on change. Also, it is in the 1990s that learning becomes a very popular topic in the field of change.

3.   My translation from the French.

4.   This assertion can be questioned. For instance, new product or service development in a firm that pursues an innovation-driven strategy doesn't necessarily lead to organizational change; it may be part of business as usual. While Kanter (1983) does not distinguish between administrative and other types of innovation, they differ on at least one count: Administrative innovations are meant to be adopted internally, while product and service innovations are meant to be adopted by the customer. This point will be discussed further in the third part of this book, because innovation literature is more and more integrated with the literature on change in the 1990s, due to the importance of innovations in information technologies.

5.   In French, the book was first published in 1977, under the title *L'acteur et le système*. It was translated in 1980 and published by the University of Chicago Press. Although it is rarely cited in the Anglo-Saxon world, it is very influential in the French-speaking academic milieu.

6.   Crozier and Friedberg (1977) label their framework for understanding organizations "strategic analysis." However, in this case, strategy is not used in the sense of organizational or business strategy, but to refer to the strategies that actors and groups use in their interaction with each other, that is, the moves they make to win in the game.

7.   This is my translation, because the introductions to the French and English editions are different. In this instance, *actor* is used in the singular as a generic term and refers to both individual and collective actors.

8.   In their view, an actor, no matter how vulnerable, has some power—that is, as long as he exists as an autonomous actor; otherwise, he becomes simply a means to an end (Crozier & Friedberg, 1977, p. 27). In this sense, conceptually, they don't treat managers differently from other actors. They believe that "strategic analysis" requires the careful identification of all groups of actors, their resources and skills, and the way their interests are maintained through the rules of the game they have contributed to create.

9.   This is my translation, because the introductions to the French and English editions are different.

10.   One exception is the work of Greenwood and Hinings (1988), who, although they define themselves as being part of the configurational school, try to integrate the dynamic and static views of structure (see Chapter 3).

11.   It is interesting to note that, in contrast, Quinn's (1978, 1980) corporations had more "abstract" cultures. Their core beliefs were linked to broad mission statements rather than operational goals.

CONCLUSION TO PART II

Looking at Change From Above

From this presentation of the literature on change in the 1980s, a number of observations can be made. A first series relates to the dominant depiction of organizational change in this period, the managerial–functionalist viewpoint, and its difference with the organizational–interpretive point of view. The second series concerns the nature of the debates that mark the period and the resulting evolution of our understanding of the concept of change.

First, the transformational perspective on change is a challenge to the incremental vision of change that was characteristic of the first era. This challenge is in large part a reaction against the vision of managers as objective and omniscient change agents implicit in the previous approaches. It is manifested most explicitly in the divergence between the objectivist and the subjectivist perspectives, which more or less overlap with the managerial and organizational viewpoints on organizational change. As summarized in Table II.1, mainstream research from the various approaches adopts a managerial focus and paints a picture of change from the top. These writers share a unitary vision of the organization as either an archetype, an information processing system, an interpretation system, or a tribe. Even the political theorists, who conceive the organization as a political arena, believe that managers have the means to make it function as a unified entity. Most view the environment as an objective reality that must be assessed by managers. However, even though the majority adhere to an objectivist perspective on reality, they acknowledge the importance of taking managers' subjectivity into account for understanding organizational change.

While most criticize the rationalist vision of managers presented in the first period, they are still interested in explaining how change is accomplished, essentially in terms of the major tools of change available to top management. Their studies are concerned with the strategic, structural, cognitive, cultural, and political levers of change used by managers. As a consequence, in the transformational

Table II.1   Transformation or Evolution: The Managerial Viewpoint

	Configurational Approach	Cognitive Approach	Cultural Approach	Political Approach
Organization	Unitary vision Form, structural entity	Unitary vision Set of schemata	Unitary vision Tribe	Pluralist vision Political arena, but functions as a single entity
Environment	Constraint, source of pressure for change (objectivist)	Represented (objectivist)	More or less ignored	Constraint, source of pressure for change (objectivist)
Model of change	Punctuated equilibrium (reorientation and convergence)	Punctuated equilibrium	Revolution and/or incrementalism	Incrementalism
Reason for change	Internal/external fit	Internal/external fit	Internal/external fit	Internal/external fit
Change as intended	SECOND ORDER Strategy and structure	SECOND ORDER Cognitive schemes which determine strategy and structure	SECOND ORDER Values and norms which are incarnated in strategy and structure	FIRST OR SECOND ORDER Strategy and structure in a series of steps
Process of change	RAPID DESTRUCTION/ RECONSTRUCTION	ABRUPT CONVERSION	RAPID DESTRUCTION/ RECONSTRUCTION or GRADUAL RENEWAL	GRADUAL RENEWAL
Change agent	TOP-DOWN Top manager as architect	TOP-DOWN Top manager as visionary	TOP-DOWN Top manager as exemplar	TOP-DOWN AND BOTTOM-UP Top and middle managers as political actors
Change actions	Design and implement new strategy and structure	Create and diffuse new worldview	Develop new symbols	Manage power relations and resources
Effects of change	SECOND ORDER Global transformation	SECOND ORDER Global transformation	SECOND ORDER Global or cumulative transformation	SECOND ORDER Cumulative transformation as learning occurs
Change outcomes	NEW EQUILIBRIUM	NEW EQUILIBRIUM	NEW EQUILIBRIUM	CONTINUOUS ADAPTATION

model, the top manager is a hero who embarks on a difficult mission: an architect, a visionary, an exemplar, or an astute politician.

Change is portrayed as an episode, having a specific starting point defined by dramatic actions taken by top management and an end defined as a return to business as usual. Change viewed from above is a short period of upheaval followed by a return to equilibrium. Strategy process researchers contribute a lot to that view by combining in their analyses concepts from the different theoretical approaches to develop top-down models of change.

In contrast, those who adhere to an interpretive-subjectivist perspective tend to adopt an organizational point of view (Table II.2). Although, some (mainly the configurational and cognitive researchers) still adopt a unitary vision of organizations, they view organizational change as a more reciprocal (top-down and bottom-up) process. All actors are viewed as potential contributors to change, as creators of meaning, symbolic actors, and political operators. Therefore, for change to be organizational, a new vision must be shared, and this is viewed as a major challenge. Because they conceive change as a collective process, they allow for the possibility of multiple trajectories. Therefore the process tends to be more incremental, continuous, and emergent, and the outcome is always uncertain. Even though a number of scholars call for research on change that considers multiple points of view and different levels of analysis, such studies are very rare. The focus is still mostly on managers, and studies look at other actors from the point of view of managers, as targets of change efforts.

The second set of observations that can be drawn from the literature is an outcome of the controversy around the evolutionary or revolutionary nature of change. By making the concept of change the center of inquiry, it draws attention to the need for a better definition of what is meant by change. Indeed, the various approaches to change, which are, in some variants, complementary and, in others, mutually exclusive, emphasize different dimensions and/or definitions of change. While adding to the confusion, they also broaden the range of questions addressed by scholars interested in change.

Here are some examples. The debate over the transformational perspective directs attention to the distinction between change as content or difference (i.e., what is changed) and change as process (i.e., how it changes); in other words, between change and changing (Pettigrew, 1985a; Van de Ven & Poole, 1988). In terms of content, the notion of radical change, or transformation, is at the forefront. Some define it simply as major or strategic, while others outline a number of criteria that should be met in terms of scope, direction, and amplitude.

There is also the question of what is studied as instances of radical change: statements and actions of managers (e.g., new mission statement, announcement of a major reorganization), organizational effects (e.g., actual changes in relationships and behavior), and/or organizational outcomes (e.g., increase in productivity, satisfaction). Some researchers focus on managers' discourse and actions, assuming that organizational effects and outcomes will follow, while

Table II.2 Transformation or Evolution: The Organizational Viewpoint

	Configurational Approach	Cognitive Approach	Cultural Approach	Political Approach
Organization	Unitary vision Design archetype	Unitary vision Interpretation system	Unitary or pluralist vision Tribe or tribes	Pluralist vision Political arena
Environment	Enacted (subjectivist)	Enacted (subjectivist)	More or less ignored	Objective, constraint, and enacted (subjectivist)
Model of change	Multiple dynamics: evolution and revolution	Punctuated equilibrium	Incrementalism	Multiple dynamics: evolution and revolution
Reason for change	Internal/external pressures	Internal/external pressures	Internal/external pressures	Internal/external pressures
Change as intended	SECOND ORDER Interpretive scheme as manifested in strategy and structure	SECOND ORDER Cognitive schemes	SECOND ORDER Values and norms	FIRST OR SECOND ORDER Rules of the game
Process	MULTIPLE TRACKS OR TRAJECTORIES	COLLECTIVE SENSE-MAKING	GRADUAL AND EMERGENT	GRADUAL AND EMERGENT
Change agent	TOP-DOWN	RECIPROCAL: TOP-DOWN, THEN BOTTOM-UP	TOP-DOWN AND BOTTOM-UP	TOP-DOWN AND BOTTOM-UP
Change actions	Manager as architect	Manager and other actors as creators of meaning	All actors as symbolic agents	All actors as political operators
Effects of change	Design and implement new strategy and structure	Sense-making and sense-giving in reciprocal process	Symbolic activity	Manage power relations and resources
Change outcomes	FIRST OR SECOND ORDER Successful or failed transformation	FIRST OR SECOND ORDER New cognitive scheme shared or not	FIRST OR SECOND ORDER New symbols take root or not	FIRST OR SECOND ORDER Power structure maintained or transformed
	EQUILIBRIUM OR NOT	NEW EQUILIBRIUM OR REGRESSION	ADAPTATION OR FRAGMENTATION	ADAPTATION OR PARALYSIS

for others "real" organizational change is measured by concrete modifications in organizational functioning. Whereas the first and third elements, managers' discourse and actions and organizational outcomes, can be measured through cross-sectional analysis, in-depth case studies are required to take into account all three and explore the links between them. This brings us to process issues and the need to consider the sequence of events and actions, the pacing, and the links between them to study the dynamics of changing. Terms such as *revolutionary* and *incremental, deliberate* and *emergent,* are used differently from one study to the next without much systematic effort at defining them. In fact, one of the problems is that words like *radical, incremental, evolution,* and *revolution* bundle up issues of content and process that need to be unpacked for analytical purposes.

In a sense, the debate between the radical and incremental view of change is between those who view evolution as occurring through major changes, defined as concerted and dramatic actions by managers, which are required for important results to ensue, and those who believe that minor changes, whether coming from managers or employees, can, through accumulation, have dramatic effects. Finally, interpretive research also raises the question: "Radical or incremental from whose point of view?"—that of the observer, the manager, or the employee, drawing attention to the fact that change is also a social construction. As we will see, these questions become even more important in the third period. Despite these difficulties, there is no question that change is emerging in the 1980s as a major concept and an important area of inquiry. Moreover, there is no doubt that the transformational model dominates the agenda during that period, even among those who question the picture of change it presents.

To conclude, after being subordinated to the concept of adaptation, the concept of change becomes the focus of attention during the second period. In a sense, during the 1980s, the different streams of research on change start to form a field of study in its own right. This work coalesces around the transformational perspective on change and its associated punctuated equilibrium model of organizational evolution. In a way, the punctuated equilibrium framework is the umbrella notion that research in the cognitive, cultural, and political traditions, partly through the influence of strategy process studies, supports and enriches by describing the different processes involved and seeking to explain their patterns of interaction in cases of punctuated change (Johnson, 1987). Therefore, at the end of the 1980s, there is a sense of convergence around a dominant model of change.

However, at the same time, the marginal voices within each approach stressing the continuous, emergent, and organizational (as opposed to the discontinuous, planned, and managerial) view of change are becoming increasingly influential and prepare the way for the third wave in the history of the literature on change.

PART III

Natural Evolution
or Social Dynamics?

*Evolutionary theory does not deny that organizations are constructed
by people who have strong interests in understanding what they are
doing, and who invest much of what they do with symbolic meaning. . . .
But opportunities to construct new worlds are limited because of the
historical accumulation represented by existing organizations, populations and social structures.*

(Aldrich, 1999, p. 41)

*We described how path dependence highlights the role played by
history in the genesis of novelty. We also noted how it falls short of conceptualizing the roles of actors in creating history in real time. . . . With
path creation, attention is focused on the efforts of entrepreneurs who
seek ways to shape history in the making.*

(Garud & Karnoe, 2001, pp. 27–28)

How Do Organizations Renew Themselves?

Unlike the arrival of the second period, which marks a clean break with the first
one, the passage from the second to the third period is more gradual. At the end
of the 1980s, alongside the dominant conception of change as an episode, a rare
and dramatic event, a view of change as process, without clear beginning or end,
becomes increasingly prevalent. In fact, the opposition between continuity and
change itself starts to be questioned (Sztompka, 1993, p. 202). Giving life to
Pettigrew's insightful formulation, an increasing number of scholars frame their
research as studying "the dynamics of changing" (Pettigrew, 1985b, p. 272),
rather than specific change episodes. This processual turn draws attention to

issues such as the relative weight of history and agency, the identification of various change motors (or generative mechanisms), the relevant levels of analysis, and the nature of links between processes at different levels. All of these give rise to lively debates within the field. This process perspective on organizational change now appears under a variety of labels. For example, the dynamics of changing are defined in terms of evolution, learning, emergence, structuration, translation, and improvisation, to name a few.

The gradual crystallization of this new conception of change occurs at a time when the turbulence characterizing the 1980s is starting to be perceived as more than a momentary disruption. There is a growing impression that this is not a period of crisis that will soon be replaced by stability, but that turmoil and unpredictability are here to stay. With globalization, due among other factors to the advent of new information technologies, there comes an acceleration of economic cycles driven by fierce competition. The transformation of the world economy, as witnessed, for example, in the increasing delocalization of jobs to Third World countries, results in layoffs and increasing insecurity in the Western world. New organizational forms, labeled the virtual, modular, or postmodern organization, are heralded as providing the flexibility required to succeed in this new era.

It is in this context that the process view of organizational change takes center stage. While a preoccupation with the link between strategy and environment remains strong, strategic change starts being viewed less as a matter of radical transformation than as a long-term process of organizational renewal, often defined in terms of learning and associated with innovation. Indeed, the writings on learning and innovation, particularly technological innovation, which, up to then, constituted largely distinct bodies of work, are now integrated in the literature on change. Attention is once again focused on internal functioning, as represented in strategy by the popularity of the resource-based view and in organization theory by the interest in new organizational forms. The development of knowledge and competencies enhanced by the adoption of new information technologies and a flexible work organization are seen as the new challenge. New change programs, such as Business Process Reengineering and Knowledge Management, are promoted as enabling organizations to produce innovation by tapping into the vast reservoir of know-how and creativity hidden within the organization. The dominant discourse shifts from a concern with the management of change to an interest in increasing an organization's capacity to change (Demers, 1999; Hafsi & Demers, 1997). The idea promoted is that change is not only something that is done to the organization by visionary managers; rather, it is something that the organization does itself, in which all members are involved. The sensation of crisis that prevailed in the 1980s gives way to an impression of cautious optimism. Change is no longer to be seen as a rare and disruptive event, but as a daily given.

The resemblance to the definition of change as a gradual and cumulative sequence of adjustments, characteristic of the 1950s and 1960s, is misleading. While theories of order focusing on stability and equilibrium prevailed in the first two periods, the third period challenges that view. New conceptual frameworks emphasizing unstable equilibrium and emergence come to the fore. The field moves from viewing organizational change as an anomaly or a crisis, a temporary lapse followed by a return to stability, to conceiving change as a never-ending, indeterminate process. Routine (or continuity) and innovation (or transformation), order and disorder, result from the same processes; attention is now focused on continuity in change, as well as change in continuity. In this process view, actions intended to produce change can, in fact, lead to reproduction (i.e., maintenance of what already exists), while routine actions can unintentionally spark a change, even a revolution. Furthermore, in contrast to the first period's definition of change as adaptation to the environment, change is now increasingly conceived as coevolution of organization and environment. The question is no longer limited to the issue of how to adapt to the environment and/or react to a crisis situation; rather, it brings to the fore the idea that the future is created through organizational renewal, a more proactive perspective. This relatively positive account of changing, however, is tempered by the emphasis on indeterminacy that also typifies this period. Organizational dynamics are viewed as largely unpredictable—just as likely to be destructive as creative.

From the 1990s on, the writings on organizational change present an interesting challenge (or a daunting task!) for anyone attempting to write a synthetic overview of the field. On the one hand, there is an apparent fragmentation. The topic of change, now including anything concerned with organizational processes, is subsumed under a variety of labels, such as learning (Glynn, Lant, & Milliken, 1994), evolving (Aldrich, 1999), innovating (Cheng & Van de Ven, 1996), narrating (Tenkasi & Boland, 1993), translating (Czarniawska & Sevon, 1996b), organizing (Demers & Giroux, 1993), improvising (Orlikowski, 1996), and becoming (Tsoukas & Chia, 2002).[1] On the other hand, there is a sense of convergence (often mixed with confusion), as the same terms appear again and again in the writings of authors from different traditions. One finds that the same words (when they are not employed metaphorically or commonsensically) sometimes refer to conceptual frameworks and at other times to objects of study, and they are used at different levels of analysis. Learning and evolution are particularly good examples. For instance, some scholars study learning as an evolutionary process (Leroy & Ramanantsoa, 1996; Miner, 1990), while others explain organizational evolution as a learning process (Doz, 1996; Mezias & Glynn, 1993). As well, a number of scholars call for a combination of other theories or some of their concepts with their favored generic or meta-framework: for example, the evolutionary approach (Aldrich, 1999), complexity theory (Stacey, 1995; Van de Ven & Poole, 1995), or structuration theory (Jones, 1999; Weaver & Gioia, 1994).

Yet despite these calls for convergence and the widespread adoption of a "process" view of change, there are significant differences among the various literatures gaining momentum in the 1990s. Notably, they differ on the weight or role they give to structure/system and actors, the change mechanisms or generative motors they posit, the timeframe they adopt, the levels of analysis they take into account, and how they address links between levels.

To show both the convergence and the diversity, this large and dispersed literature is here divided into two broad streams, labeled the natural evolution and the social dynamics perspectives, on the basis of the nature and origins of the frameworks that researchers adhere to. Within each stream, approaches characterized by different change mechanisms or types of explanation are distinguished[2] (see Figure III.1). The first stream includes research broadly based on frameworks inspired by the natural sciences and mathematics, most notably the behavioral learning, the evolutionary, and the complexity perspectives. Authors within this natural evolution stream, who are predominantly American, argue that models developed to explain change in biological and physical systems, for example, can also be useful for explaining the evolution of social systems such as organizations. For the most part (but with some notable exceptions), this branch of studies tends to favor formal modeling, simulations, and quantitative methods. Its explanations of change tend to put more weight on structural dynamics and path dependence. Under this label, approaches are presented that look at organizational change as behavioral learning, evolving, and emerging.

The second group of work is composed of research drawing on social studies and the humanities, which is split between the radical and postmodern approaches and the discursive and practice-centered approaches. In contrast to the natural evolution perspective, the social dynamics stream is very strong in Europe (although it includes a number of prominent American scholars). One of its premises is that social systems are irreducible to other types of systems because they are made up of human beings who are purposeful and reflexive, and who make history as well as are constrained by it. Therefore, in this view, taking agency into account is critical for understanding organizational dynamics. This research emphasizes narrative accounts that give precedence to actors making sense of events and acting in specific historical and social contexts. Its aim is to develop conceptual and theoretical frameworks that help us understand, rather than to discover laws (even probabilistic ones). Here, approaches are discussed that define change as emancipating, narrating, translating, and improvising.

In a sense, because of their different origins, these two streams of work come to the study of organizational change from opposite directions. The natural evolution literature, borrowing from the natural sciences and mathematics, for example, starts from an objective point of view that conceives organizations as quasi-natural entities. However, recently some authors within

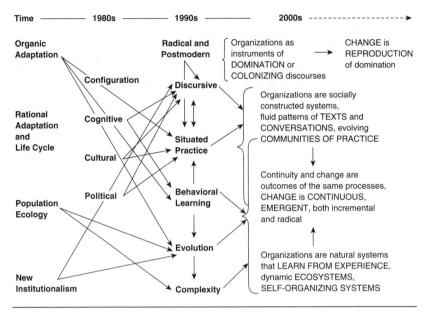

Figure III.1   Third Period: Natural Evolution or Social Dynamics?

that stream have argued that a meta-framework such as the evolutionary approach can accommodate the social construction or interpretive point of view and take into account human agency as a force to explain change (Aldrich, 1999). For its part, the literature anchored in the social dynamics perspective is, as mentioned previously, part of a long tradition of debate between explanations of change based on agency and those based on structure, and between subjectivist and objectivist perspectives. However, starting in the 1980s and culminating in the 1990s, authors have developed conceptions of change based on frameworks that attempt to bridge these oppositions. For instance, the structuration framework, which explains change as the mutual constitution of agency and structure (Jones, 1999; Pettigrew, 1985a; Weaver & Gioia, 1994), although controversial (Mutch, 2003; Reed, 2003), is one of the major influences on newer approaches to change. As well, an increasing number of researchers from both streams are turning to conceptual frameworks built on recent developments in realist epistemologies[3] (Baum, 2002; McKelvey, 1997; Reed, 2003; Whittington, 1988) that bridge subjectivist and objectivist points of view. One notable exception is the postmodernist perspective, an increasingly strong influence in the literature on change, which seeks not to bridge but to eradicate these dualisms (Knights, 1997). Furthermore, while many question the traditional dichotomies, most (but by no means all) scholars belonging to the natural evolution school argue for a "quasi-natural" organization science aiming at the discovery of general laws (Baum, 2002; McKelvey, 1997), whereas those of the social dynamics school promote a view of organization studies that is concerned with contextual "history in the making" (Garud & Karnoe, 2001; Reed, 2003). In part because of these divergent trajectories, despite some similarities and the fact that they often refer to and borrow from each other, they present different portraits of changing.

As a consequence, an overview of the current literature is presented in two chapters. Chapter 7, covering the natural evolution stream of work, is divided in three sections introducing the behavioral learning, evolutionary, and complexity approaches. Chapter 8, focusing on the social dynamics body of work, distinguishes between the radical and postmodern approaches and the discursive and practice-centered approaches.

Notes

1. It is interesting to note that, in contrast to previous periods when handbooks on organizations featured change as one of their topics, recent ones, such as those by Clegg, Hardy, and Nord (1996) or Baum (2002), do not treat change as a specific theme. Does this mean that change is not an issue anymore? My reading of these texts rather suggests that it is because change is pervasive everywhere. It is the explicit overall organizing scheme for Baum's collection of chapters, and it is implicit in the process view adopted (symbolized by the use of verbs, rather than nouns) in most of the current issues chapters in the volume by Clegg et al.

2. For instance, some scholars discuss learning as a behavioral process (March, 1981, 1991), others as an evolutionary process (Leroy & Ramanantsoa, 1996; Miner, 1990) or as an emergent process in complex systems (Cheng & Van de Ven, 1996); still others explain organizational learning as situated practice (Orlikowski, 1996). We will classify researchers in different approaches on the basis of the generative mechanism or causal logic they adopt to explain change, rather than as different variants of the learning approach.

3. It is beyond the purview of this book to discuss these different realist epistemologies, except to say that researchers in the first stream (e.g., Baum, 2002; McKelvey, 1997) adopt a scientific realism inspired by authors such as Campbell (1969), while scholars of the second stream refer mostly to Bhaskar's critical realist epistemology (1986).

7

The Natural Evolution Perspective

The behavioral learning, evolutionary, and complexity approaches, which are part of what I have labeled the natural evolution perspective, have gained increased popularity since the 1990s, and there have been some explicit attempts to highlight their convergence (Baum, 2002; McKelvey, 1997). The first two of these approaches have been around for some time, but it is in the 1990s that they come to prominence.

In the behavioral or adaptive learning approach developed by March and his colleagues (Cyert & March, 1963; Levinthal & March, 1993; March, 1981, 1991), the generative mechanism is behavior modification as a result of experience. In contrast to the cognitive approach, presented earlier, which describes organizational learning as a change in the dominant coalition's mental frameworks, organizations are conceived as adaptive systems that learn from trial and error and that encode and retain that learning in routines (Holmqvist, 2003). But as we will see in the next section, there is a call to integrate these two perspectives in current organizational learning literature.

For its part, the research on organizational evolution has strong links to the work of Nelson and Winter (1982) explaining innovation as the result of mechanisms of inheritance (reproduction), selection, and survival of routines. Unlike the early population ecologists (Hannan & Freeman, 1984) presented in Chapter 2, these authors emphasize that organizations are capable of changing—that is, of learning and adapting—but, more important, of causing change through innovation (Winter, 1990). Some evolutionary studies focus on the internal process of variation-selection-retention, which produces novelty and change (Burgelman, 1983, 1991; Miner, 1990); others have given special attention to the processes of "genetic" reproduction (i.e., the production of new entities from old ones) that drive organizational evolution (Baum & Singh, 1994b). It is interesting to note that both the adaptive learning and the evolutionary approaches are, in large part, a reaction against classic economic theory and its highly rationalistic assumptions, and incorporate behavioral concepts in their frameworks. For instance, both approaches make a central concept of organizational routines, although, as we will see, they use it differently in their analysis of the change process. Furthermore, March (1981, 1994), a pillar of the adaptive learning approach, has an "evolutionary bent of mind" (Aldrich, 1999, p. 20), while Nelson and Winter's (1982) evolutionary theory of economic change was influenced by the behavioral theory of the firm developed by Cyert and March (1963).

Finally, the complexity approach has only been introduced relatively recently into organization research.[1] However, it is well developed in physics, chemistry, and biology, and in mathematics, where advances in the study of dynamic systems have produced an array of sophisticated statistical tools and formal modeling techniques (Carley, 2002; McKelvey, 1997). In organization theory, it is, in large part, an outgrowth of the evolutionary approach. This approach is based on the premise that organizations, as complex systems, display chaotic behavior or stand at the edge of chaos. In complex systems, nonlinear dynamics produce endogenous change, that is, the unpredictable emergence of innovative outcomes (e.g., new routines, new products) due to interaction among loosely coupled elements (Eisenhardt & Bhatia, 2002). Although complexity theory is often used metaphorically, some researchers employ mathematical tools to test the existence of complexity and its effects on the evolution of various organizational systems (Cheng & Van de Ven, 1996; Thiétart & Forgues, 1997). In particular, there are an increasing number of simulation studies based on modeling techniques borrowed from dynamic systems theory used to test aspects of the adaptive learning and evolutionary theories, creating increasing overlap among the three perspectives.[2]

In the following pages, each approach's conception of organization, of the force or motor driving the change process, of the levels involved, and of the interaction among levels, will be discussed.

The Behavioral Learning Approach

Organizational learning is without doubt the success story of the 1990s. It replaces organizational culture as the approach to change that stimulates practitioners and scholars alike. As with the cultural approach, there are a number of different theoretical approaches to organizational learning. For example, the knowledge development approach (Glynn, Lant, & Milliken, 1994), an extension of the cognitive approach, is treated later in this chapter. Other approaches, such as situated learning theory, which are social constructionist, are presented in Chapter 8. However, the rise to prominence of the topic of organizational learning in the late 1980s coincides with the increased influence of the behavioral or adaptive learning perspective. With its focus on organizational routines and "learning by doing," it offers an alternative to the cognitive approach popular in the 1980s. Routines, including formal rules, are viewed as both the repository of past learning and the setting of new learning. According to Schulz (2002), being "independent from the individual actors who make and execute them" (p. 415), they provide a supraindividual basis for learning that makes it truly organizational. Routine-based learning, which is conceived as an experiential (i.e., trial and error) process, emphasizes both stability and change, because success leads to a reinforcement of existing routines, while failure leads to their incremental updating. In contrast, the cognitive approach (see Chapter 4), which defines organizational change as the modification of knowledge structures or mental frames, raises questions as to what constitutes organizational-level learning (Walsh, 1995; Yanow, 2000). This view of learning as an essentially mental activity also emphasizes a radical vision of change linked to top management action or outside intervention (Argyris, 1996; Hedberg, 1981), while the experiential or "learning by doing" point of view portrays change as an organization-wide incremental process (Glynn et al., 1994). In this approach, learning is generally defined as a relatively permanent change, produced by experience, in organizational knowledge (and thereby, in the organization's potential range of behavior).

Widely credited to March (Glynn et al., 1994; Holmqvist, 2003; Schulz, 2002), the adaptive learning approach originates with the behavioral theory of the firm, mentioned in Chapter 1. In this view, organizations are "adaptively rational systems" directed toward the attainment of goals, whose behavior is governed by rules and procedures that allow them to react to performance feedback (Cyert & March, 1963). Performance feedback rules—problem-driven search and choice (or change) rules—are the basic building blocks of organizations as experiential learning systems. Consequently, organizational change is described as the result of "relatively stable, routine processes that relate organizations to their environment" (March, 1981, p. 564). In other words, experience leads organizations to develop relatively fixed rules of functioning that allow for considerable change in behavior. For instance, search rules that are activated primarily in response to negative performance feedback are routines designed to introduce change. Moreover, rules themselves change as the result of learning (for example, search behavior that has been successful in the past becomes encoded in current rules). Cyert and March (1963) envision a hierarchy of rules with lower-level (i.e., more specific) rules changing more easily than higher-level ones. However, as will be discussed later, very little empirical research done within this tradition studies the process by which rules are created and change.

Most empirical studies use simulation methodology, mainly computer simulations and some lab experiments with simulated organizations. Indeed, Cyert and March (1963) remarked that their theory was particularly suited to representation in the language of computer programming or flowcharts. Computer simulations are particularly adapted to describing the evolution of organizational learning over a very long period of time. Levinthal and March (1981) develop such a simulation of organizational learning as adaptive search, inspired in large part by Nelson and Winter's evolutionary theory. This model is the basis of most simulation studies of adaptive learning done later. As mentioned by Glynn et al. (1994), these studies model learning in terms of simple goals and decision rules and "tend to treat the organization as a homogeneous unit or unitary actor" (p. 47). Indeed, in contrast with the behavioral theory of the firm, which views organizations as political arenas, this research ignores issues of intergroup conflict inherent in organizational learning. In the following pages, the process theory of change underlying the behavioral learning approach is introduced (see Table 7.1). Then the research on cross-level learning is presented, leading to a discussion of the links between behavioral and cognitive approaches to organizational learning. This section concludes with a discussion of the limits and contributions of the behavioral approach.

ROUTINE-BASED CHANGE

It should be noted that while learning is described as intendedly rational and adaptive, in later work, the problematic nature of learning under ambiguity (March & Olsen, 1976) and the complexities of experience-driven change, such as the unanticipated consequences of action, are acknowledged (March, 1981).

As noted by March (1981), most rules in organizations specify ways of responding to a context. When the context changes, behavior will change, but not necessarily at the right pace or in the right direction, because performance feedback is not always interpreted correctly and the environment can be unpredictable or change too fast. Echoing Weick (1979a), March (1991) remarks that "exogenous environmental change makes adaptation essential, but it also makes learning from experience difficult" (p. 80). In addition, parallel processes in organizations may combine to produce outcomes that were unintended by anyone. Therefore, in certain situations, minor changes can produce large effects that eventually lead to major changes through routine processes. The adaptive learning approach, thus, emphasizes day-to-day changes that are the result of responding routinely, even conservatively, to a changing and confusing world in which chance plays a significant role.

Of particular interest to the reflection on stability and change is the work done on search rules, that is, routines for introducing change. These routines influence the degree of innovativeness and the type of change that organizations display, by determining what range of alternatives are available for choice. Adaptive learning theorists are particularly concerned with the trade-off between efficiency and flexibility occurring as a result of investing in refinement search,

Table 7.1   Behavioral Learning

BEHAVIORAL LEARNING

General model of change: EXPERIMENTATION – TRANSFER/APPROPRIATION
Trial and Error   Codification/Socialization
Externalization/Internalization

Focus: Combining behavioral learning and knowledge development models to integrate organizational- and individual-level tacit and explicit knowledge. Balancing knowledge creation and preservation.

Antecedents: BEHAVIORISM—Behavioral theory of the firm (Cyert & March, 1963)
COGNITIVE APPROACH—Argyris (1982); Weick (1969, 1979a)

	Behavioral tradition
Organization:	Adaptive learning system, unitary view
Process of change:	Routine-based incremental change (feedback rules, search and choice routines) at the organizational level combined with cognitive and behavioral change at the individual level
Authors:	Glynn et al. (1994); March (1981, 1991); Levinthal & March (1981); Lant & Mezias (1990, 1992)
	Knowledge development (cognitive) tradition
Organization:	Interpretation systems, pluralist view
Process of change:	Knowledge destruction (unlearning) and creation (learning) as mental individual and collective processes
Authors:	Baumard (1996); Crossan et al. (1999); Nonaka (1994)

---

which improves existing knowledge, as opposed to innovative search, which creates new knowledge (Levinthal & March, 1981). For instance, March (1991) argues that there is a tendency, in the short run, for exploitation (i.e., refinements to existing technology or competences) to drive out exploration (i.e., invention of new technology or development of new competences) because exploitation is more efficient and its results less uncertain.

Several studies done since the late 1980s, pursuing Levinthal and March's lead (1981), model organizations following different search rules or strategies and simulate the impact of these strategies on organizational evolution and performance (Lant & Mezias, 1990, 1992; Mezias & Glynn, 1993). For example,

Lant and Mezias (1992) argue that, in contrast to the punctuated equilibrium thesis of Tushman and Romanelli (1985), their study shows that fixed learning routines (modeled as adaptive, imitative, or garbage-can strategies of search)[3] can produce both convergence (few changes) and reorientation (major core changes). Another typical example is a study by Mezias and Glynn (1993), which integrates research on adaptive learning with literature on change and innovation. This simulation examines the impact on renewal and performance of three different innovation strategies in organizations modeled to represent established bureaucracies. From the literature, they identify two intentional strategies to manage innovation and change.[4] The institutional strategy aims to produce innovation through formal programs, while the revolutionary strategy uses informal structures to increase radical innovation. In contrast, the evolutionary strategy is not intentional. In this case, innovation emerges in a random manner because of loose controls.[5] They find that neither of the intentional strategies produces more innovation in relationship to the resources used. Rather, they tend to produce more refinements. The evolutionary strategy is the most efficient, producing more radical innovation and using up fewer resources. To summarize, these simulation studies highlight the role of routine and chance in organizational innovation and renewal and de-emphasize the role of deliberate strategies.

This line of research shows the organization's potential for considerable change over a long period of time, even with simple, stable rules governing the system. These scholars call attention to the important role that the formal encoding of knowledge in rules plays in organizational-level learning, both for stabilizing behavior and for allowing change. However, they don't have much to tell us about the dynamics of learning—for example, about how organizational rules are created and changed.

CROSS-LEVEL LEARNING

In their review article on organizational learning, Glynn et al. (1994) assert that very few researchers look at the links between the individual and the organizational levels of analysis. They argue that the behavioral learning literature focuses on the organizational level, while cognitive research concentrates on individual-level learning.

While recent syntheses show that research within the experiential tradition now focuses on intraorganizational (Argote & Ophir, 2002) and interorganizational (Ingram, 2002) learning, very little of this work studies learning across levels. The more microexperiential learning research typically explores individual and group behavior in laboratory settings without linking it explicitly to organization-level learning.[6] Even the recent research done on interorganizational learning within the experiential learning tradition tends to equate learning with increased performance (and/or productivity) and to look at focal organizations (either partners or competitors) from the outside. It therefore has little to say about the organizational processes involved in learning between organizations (Ingram, 2002). Holmqvist (2003) laments the lack of integration between the literature on intraorganizational and interorganizational learning.

At this point, it should be noted that for some authors intraorganizational learning is synonymous with organizational learning. For example, Huber (1991) adopts this point of view when he states that "*an organization learns if any of its units acquires knowledge that it recognizes as potentially useful to the organization*" (p. 89, italics in original). In this case, organizational learning is, therefore, viewed as the sum of individuals' learning. Cohen and Bacdayan (1994), for instance, study groups who learn together different aspects of an interactive task. They equate organizational learning with the patterned sequences of learned behavior distributed among individuals and stored in their memory. They compare organizational learning to parallel processing in computing.

Yet it is plausible to think that an organization can know both more and less than the cumulated knowledge of its individual members (Glynn et al., 1994). For example, rules, procedures, and structures encode organizational knowledge beyond what is known by individual members. At the same time, individuals and groups develop new knowledge that is not yet available to the whole organization and might never be. Therefore, it can be interesting to distinguish between the two levels and examine the interaction between them. As argued by Epple, Argote, and Devadas (1991), empirically, one should find a range between the extreme of "learning entirely embodied in the organization" and the other extreme where "learning is embodied entirely in workers" (p. 59).

In this vein, the rare authors who explicitly consider cross-level learning define it as the diffusion or transfer of knowledge between individuals (or units) within the organization or between individuals (or units) and the organization (Argote, Beckman, & Epple, 1990; Carley, 1992; Madsen, Mosakowski, & Zaheer, 2002; March, 1991). In coherence with an information processing view of learning[7] (Huber, 1991), organizational-level learning is conceived as either the horizontal or hierarchical transmission (for example, through imitation or codification) of the learning of individuals or units within the organization.

In summary, the first line of research views organizational learning as created by and residing in individuals, that is, as the sum of individuals' knowledge. Moreover, in keeping with the emphasis on routines, studies such as the one by Cohen and Bacdayan (1994) focus on knowledge stored as procedural memory (i.e., tacit knowledge of how things are done), as opposed to the declarative knowledge considered by cognitive theorists. The second group of studies, on the other hand, draws attention to supra-individual-level-learning, embedded in a hierarchical structure (Carley, 1992), in technology (Epple et al., 1991), or in codes of beliefs (March, 1991), and to its role in the retention of knowledge and in the stability of organizations. Both Carley, who studies organizational learning as a bottom-up diffusion process,[8] and March, who models it as a reciprocal process of diffusion leading to convergence between individuals and the organization[9], point to the stabilizing force of organizational-level learning.

In all of these studies, the acquisition of knowledge through one's own experience or the experience of others (often inferred from performance improvement) and its retention in diverse repositories (e.g., procedural memories, formal rules, production systems) replace the search and change routines of simulation studies. On the whole, they are still primarily concerned with the retention of knowledge across levels, rather than with the creation of new knowledge. Indeed, knowledge acquisition in these studies implies the development of simple routines to deal with repetitive tasks. Finally, the behavioral view of organizational learning has more to say about learning as exploitation of existing knowledge than with learning as an innovative change process. Very few researchers working on innovation have used the behavioral learning approach. One exception is a study by Garud and Van de Ven (1992), which shows that trial-and-error learning only explains the ending phase of the innovation process. It is when behavioral learning research and the cognitive approach are brought together that the processes of knowledge creation and development that occur within organizations and between organizations find the most elaboration.

LINKING THE BEHAVIORAL AND COGNITIVE APPROACHES TO LEARNING

While few have studied explicitly the links between individual and organizational learning, it is clear that behavioral learning theorists have always recognized that individual and organizational learning are a mix of behavioral and cognitive learning. March and Olsen (1976), for example, view learning as a continuous cycle between individual beliefs, individual action, organizational action, and environmental response. This model explains behavioral learning at the organizational level as the result of cognitive and behavioral learning at the individual or intraorganizational level. Nevertheless, up until recently, as mentioned by Glynn et al. (1994), the two have been studied separately. As we saw previously, in the 1980s, cognitive theorists focused on intraorganizational learning, emphasizing knowledge creation and development and radical change as individual or group-level mental processes. Behavioral learning theorists, for their part, have concentrated on organizational-level, routine-driven learning, highlighting incremental changes resulting from learning by doing.

But a growing number of theoretical papers and empirical studies, inspired in large part by issues of cross-level learning, have started to examine the relationship between learning as behavioral change and learning as cognitive change (Doz, 1996; Fiol & Lyles, 1985; Glynn et al., 1994; Inkpen & Crossan,

1995; Leroy & Ramanantsoa, 1997; Nonaka, 1994). For instance, these authors observe that cognitive learning does not necessarily lead to visible organizational change (i.e., change in behavior), while new behavior can be random and is not necessarily accompanied by learning (at the cognitive level). This literature suggests that organizational learning is a multilevel process involving both cognitive and behavioral learning, thus leading to a multitude of possible interrelationships. The term *collective learning* sometimes refers to organizational-level, other times to group-level learning, depending on the authors.

Such a view of the organizational learning process raises a number of questions and debates, such as the following: Is there such a thing as organizational cognition? Or should we talk instead of organizational knowledge, which is the aggregated result of individual cognition (Baumard, 1996)? Stated differently, is organizational-level learning simply about individuals learning in an organizational context (Weick & Westley, 1996)? If organizations learn, are the same processes involved as in individual learning? How do cognitive and behavioral learning interact, both within and between levels? What are the types of linkage between levels (direct or indirect, loose or tight)? A few conceptual frameworks attempt to answer some of these questions.

Glynn et al. (1994), for example, develop a model of the processes linking the individual and the organizational levels, as well as the context, in organizational learning. According to them, the learning cycle is a diffusion-and-institutionalization (i.e., transmission-and-codification) process from individual to organizational learning, followed by an enablement (i.e., reproduction or change) process leading to the organization taking actions, which enact (i.e., influence/ structure) the context. This cycle is finally completed through interpretation of the context, resulting in individual learning. The authors also briefly present a reversed cycle in which an organization learns by doing and influences individual learning through socialization. Although they mention in passing the situated or practice-based (i.e., social constructionist) view of learning that we will discuss in the next chapter, most of their discussion focuses on linkages that are consistent with an information-processing view of learning. Their model also emphasizes exploitation rather than exploration (i.e., routine change rather than innovation). Their treatment, although it presents an interesting discussion of learning as a cycle of subprocesses, does not systematically address the relationship between behavioral and cognitive learning both within and between the individual and the organizational levels.

As noted by Leroy and Ramanantsoa (1997), behavioral change has generally been conceived as a consequence of cognitive change by cognitivists. Moreover, only major cognitive change (i.e., change in frame of reference) is considered real or deep learning (i.e., second-order change) from that perspective. In contrast, a number of authors have argued that behavioral change often precedes and leads to cognitive change. Weick (1979b) makes that argument for individual-level learning, while Starbuck (1983), defining organizations as action generators, makes the same case for the organizational level. Furthermore, while cognitivists refer to inferential and generative (i.e., experimental) learning processes where thinking precedes doing, behaviorists focus on trial and error and vicarious learning, where the individual acts first and reflects on what he or she has done, or simply repeats what works. Since the mid-1990s, there has been a growing interest in articulating more explicitly the linkage between both modes of learning as multilevel processes leading to the creation of new knowledge (Inkpen & Crossan, 1995; Leroy & Ramanantsoa, 1997; Nonaka, 1994). This is largely the work of authors doing qualitative field research who start from a cognitive standpoint and integrate aspects of behavioral learning theory into their conceptual frameworks.

In that context, one of the dimensions of knowledge that has drawn the most attention is its tacitness (Baumard, 1996; Leroy & Ramanantsoa, 1997; Nonaka, 1994). These authors, drawing on Polanyi (1966), pay attention to the taken-for-granted knowledge and the informal routines that play an important role in organizations. They highlight the fact that even the execution of explicit, formal rules is partially based on practical skills that are difficult to apprehend and codify. For example, Nonaka, in his well-known model, explains the knowledge-creation process as involving both tacit and explicit knowledge. Tacit knowledge of a procedural (Cohen & Bacdayan, 1994) or operational (Kim, 1993) nature is most often associated with "know-how" and learning by doing, and is difficult to articulate and communicate. Explicit knowledge of a declarative or conceptual form (Kim, 1993) is associated with "knowing what and why," or cognitive learning. Unlike "know-how," it can be transmitted verbally and tends to be easier to codify. Nonaka describes the processes of conversion or transition between the two modes of knowledge creation, arguing that externalization (the transition from tacit to explicit knowledge) and internalization (the passage from explicit to tacit knowledge) are particularly critical for organizational innovation.[10] He illustrates how, in the innovation process, some tacit knowledge derived from personal experience must be articulated and communicated to others to be transformed into an object (i.e., a material artifact or a procedure) that must then be appropriated by users through experience (i.e., practice).

Building on his work, Leroy and Ramanantsoa (1997) show that in the successful implementation of a merger the conversion from cognitive to behavioral learning and vice versa (i.e., the processes of internalization and externalization) is critical and is an occasion for further learning. For instance, they describe a process of cognitive learning in merger implementation workshops where decisions were made regarding the choice of routines for the new entity, followed by a behavioral learning process that either blocked further learning (i.e., adoption was resisted), corroborated previous cognitive learning, or produced new knowledge, both tacit and explicit (through experience or formalization). These authors describe the organizational change process as the interplay between behavioral and cognitive learning, arguing that one without the other results in blocked learning and failed organizational change. Also following Nonaka's lead, Baumard (1996) builds a two-by-two framework in which he specifies reciprocal modes of conversion between tacit and explicit knowledge, and between individual and collective levels. He uses this matrix to study the learning trajectories of four organizations facing ambiguity. Baumard's in-depth case studies show that an over-reliance on the explicit mode of knowledge can be detrimental to the creation of new knowledge and that it is the capacity to quickly switch between modes of knowledge, particularly to allow individual and collective tacit learning to develop, that best explains an organization's recovery.

In brief, Nonaka (1994) and his followers reveal the knowledge creation process as an interplay between behavioral and cognitive learning and show how each is involved in both allowing change to emerge and making it stick. While they acknowledge the importance of both individual and collective levels in organizational knowledge creation, they still are not very clear about the cross-level links, particularly the distinction between the group and the organizational level (Crossan, Lane, & White, 1999). For example, Nonaka (1994) and Leroy and Ramanantsoa (1997) really address the individual–group linkage, while Baumard (1996) distinguishes between the individual and the organizational, neglecting the group level.

Crossan et al. (1999) develop a three-level cyclical framework to account for the tension between continuity and change in organizational learning. Starting from the premise that cognition and action are in an interactive relationship and cannot be divorced from one another, they distinguish four sequentially interrelated learning subprocesses: intuiting (individual/tacit), interpreting (from individual to group/explicit), integrating (from group to organization/explicit and tacit), and institutionalizing (organizational/explicit and tacit). These processes operate in concurrent forward and backward cycles, linking together the individual, group, and organization levels. According to Crossan et al., the relationships between interpreting and integrating (from the individual to the group) and from institutionalizing to intuiting (from the organization back to the individual) are particularly critical in explaining the creation of new knowledge. In the first case, the challenge is to go from individual cognitive maps to collective action to effect change. In the second case, the danger is that institutionalization may impede intuition and new knowledge development. In the same vein, Holmqvist (2003) develops a framework where exploration and exploitation are presented as sequential processes that link interorganizational to intraorganizational learning.

To conclude, these authors, by attending more explicitly to the trade-off between exploration (knowledge creation/innovation) and exploitation (knowledge development/refinement), present a long-term view of organizational learning as a multilevel process leading to both stability and change at the organizational level.

DISCUSSION

As mentioned at the outset, the rise in popularity of the topic of organizational learning in the 1990s is due in large part to the rise in influence of the behavioral learning approach, which becomes as popular as the cognitive approach. The behaviorists have stimulated a lot of research that has drawn attention to the idea that organizations learn from experience and that such learning is embedded in routines, particularly formal rules that specify the structure and the procedures that must be followed.

The main limits of the adaptive or behavioral learning approach are the ones generally attributed to behavioral theories of learning in psychology. For example, because this approach wants to avoid the difficulty of accessing unobservable mental phenomena (Holmqvist, 2003), it neglects the importance of internal mental states for understanding human action and tends to emphasize external regulation at the expense of human agency (Leroy & Ramanantsoa, 1997). In contrast, as discussed in Chapter 4, the cognitive approach is faulted for being too centered on individuals' mental structures (Glynn et al., 1994).

Another criticism that has been addressed to the behavioral learning approach is its focus on incremental learning and change at the expense of radical learning and change (Argyris, 1996). Miner and Mezias (1996), responding to Argyris, argue that this primarily reflects early work, and suggest that, among other reasons, modeling priorities and a concern for model simplicity, as well as theoretical preferences, might explain this emphasis. Aldrich (1999), for example, discussing March (1991), argues that the computer simulations were built on "assumptions that implicitly ruled out radical learning under the most plausible scenarios" (Aldrich, 1999, p. 60). These arguments lead us to another limit of the behavioral approach related to its methodology (Glynn et al., 1994): The use of computer simulations particularly has tended to promote a view of organizations as unitary entities, which does not reflect internal dynamics, particularly the conflicts that are part of organizational life (Glynn et al., 1994).

Indeed, one of the main criticisms addressed to the organizational learning literature in the 1990s is the separation between behavioral and cognitive learning theories (Argyris, 1996; Glynn et al., 1994; Miner & Mezias, 1996). Yet even with the convergence between the behavioral and cognitive approaches and the development of multilevel frameworks in recent years, there is a tendency for organizational learning literature to "sanitize emotional and political processes" (Miner & Mezias, 1996, p. 97).

This is not surprising, since behavioral and cognitive learning theories, classified as teleological by Van de Van and Poole (1995), explain change as occurring within a single entity. They posit an integrative motor of change: a channeling process within a homogeneous focal entity. For example, in trial-and-error learning and vicarious learning, two key processes associated with the behavioral approach, the entity as a whole reacts to external stimuli by changing its behavior. Similarly, in inferential and generative (or experimental) learning, typical of the cognitive approach, a single entity does the inferring and the creative thinking. This means that multilevel frameworks developed from these theories must specify the movement across boundaries between one entity and another (i.e., learning is not something that happens among or between entities). Consequently, in organizational learning, the leap from individual to group or organization is most often described as a transfer mechanism, the passage of knowledge from one entity (the individual or the group) to another (the organization), or as the simple aggregation of individual learning. Learning does not emerge from the interaction between entities but within one entity, and is then transmitted to the other; hence the widespread use of the information processing model of learning as acquisition, transmission, and interpretation.

Consequently, when scholars want to account for the fact that organizational learning is not unitary and can be more (or less) than the sum of individuals' learning, they have difficulty describing the cross-level effects. Crossan et al. (1999), for example, to clarify the relationships between the processes of intuiting, interpreting, integrating, and institutionalizing, linearize organizational learning. One could argue that intuiting also occurs at the integrating phase, for example, when a number of individuals coordinate their actions around a project. Therefore, novelty can enter at different phases in the process. Furthermore, in an organization, different ideas and initiatives circulate simultaneously, and there must be some iterations and cycles within cycles in the learning process. In a sense, because change occurs within a single entity in behavioral and cognitive theories of learning, multilevel frameworks tend to present the linking processes as linear, that is, as a chain of processes. They are not well suited to explaining nonlinear system dynamics with simultaneous nested cycles. To circumvent these limits, some researchers integrate the learning motor within evolutionary (Doz, 1996) or complexity (Cheng & Van de Ven, 1996) approaches that can better account for the complex multilevel dynamics of learning.

Lately, the traditional approaches to learning have been increasingly challenged by a group of scholars who describe learning as occurring not within a single entity but as a result of systems interactions (i.e., learning emerges from and resides in patterns of interrelations). Although it is alluded to by some of the previous authors (Crossan et al., 1999; Glynn et al., 1994; Nonaka, 1994), this social constructionist perspective on learning, because it is based on a different epistemology, cannot really be integrated within their frameworks. It includes approaches such as situated learning (Brown & Duguid, 1991), distributed cognition (Hutchins, 1991), and the cultural view of learning (Weick & Westley, 1996; Yanow, 2000). This point of view is presented in the next chapter within the broadly labeled practice-based approach, which becomes increasingly popular by the end of the 1990s.

To summarize, most recent models present organizational learning as a multilevel behavioral and cognitive process. Some highlight organizational learning as an incremental change process and emphasize the stabilizing quality of behavioral learning as embedded in routines both tacit and explicit, while others focus on its innovative force as intuitive and skill-based knowledge. However, they all call attention to the paradox between knowledge creation and preservation in organizational evolution (Weick & Westley, 1996) and the important role that both behavioral and cognitive learning play in maintaining a balance between the two. The cognitive approach of the 1990s tended to present a view of change as a radical process of unlearning (destruction of the old frame) followed by new learning (the construction of a new frame). In contrast, the organizational learning approach, because of the influence of the behavioral perspective, presents a view of learning as a process of sedimentation where new learning must take hold and slowly transform or replace old learning that is forgotten for lack of use.

So far, however, conceptual frameworks far outweigh empirical applications. Further research is needed to validate and contribute to the evolution of the organizational learning approach in the future. For example, questions regarding the balance between stability and change have increased interest in exploring the key learning processes and, particularly, generative learning. Following Nonaka (1994), understanding learning processes involving intuition and creativity has become one important challenge (Miner & Mezias, 1996) to which many scholars are turning. Moreover, as the emphasis moves from considering learning as occurring in the heads of individuals (particularly top managers) to learning as a multilevel process, more attention is focused on the relationships between actors, their activities, and their tools and on the nested networks in which they are involved (Argote & Ophir, 2002). However, so far, more attention has been focused on the characteristics of these networks than on their emergence and evolution. Researchers who are going in that direction, for example Lee and Cole (2003) in their study of the Linux network, rely on other approaches such as the evolutionary framework, which we present in the next section, to explain learning.

To conclude, organizational learning as a process theory of change has greatly benefited from the contribution of the behavioral learning approach. One of its main contributions is to bring to the fore the idea of change as a natural phenomenon that occurs in the course of day-to-day interactions. As well, by focusing on routines and rules, this approach centers the study of change on concrete activities going on inside the evolving organization.

The Evolutionary Approach

In the late 1990s, the evolutionary perspective gains increasing recognition, due to the combined efforts of a number of scholars in organization theory and in strategy (Aldrich, 1999; Barnett & Burgelman, 1996; Baum, 2002; Baum & Singh, 1994b; Lewin & Volberda, 1999; Volberda & Lewin, 2003). The evolutionary approach seeks to explain organizational change as the result of variation, selection, and retention processes occurring at different hierarchically nested levels, from the intraorganizational to the interorganizational level (Baum, 2002).

As already mentioned, some authors view the evolutionary perspective as an overarching framework within which other organizational theories, including the neoinstitutional, cultural-interpretive, and learning schools, can be included (Aldrich, 1999; Barnett & Burgelman, 1996; Miner, 1994). Others, however, use the term *evolution* more broadly as a synonym for long-term organizational change. Most authors situate the evolutionary perspective as an extension of the debate between selection and adaptation that started in the 1960s (see Part I).

This section will focus on the conceptual and empirical work that explicitly uses a variation-selection-retention framework incorporating both adaptation and selection as explanations of organizational survival and change (Amburgey & Singh, 2002). While evolutionists acknowledge that organizations do change and adapt, they argue that this is not necessarily the result of deliberate managerial actions. In the evolutionary framework, variations (i.e., departures from current ways of doing things) can be intentional or unintentional, and, as noted by Aldrich (1999, p. 23), "Blind variations can be as effective as deliberate ones. Selection of variations follows from their consequences, not from the intentions of those who generated the variations (Langton, 1979)." Therefore, evolutionists originally focused on emergent organizational changes as an alternative to top-down planned organizational change theories (Burgelman, 1983, 1991; Miner, 1990). In this view, planned change theories explain only part of the story (i.e., a particular variation and internal selection process), but it is the external selective retention process that ultimately determines whether such change is adaptive or not. Like population ecology, the evolutionary approach, by looking at selection mechanisms, takes into account both successes and failures to explain evolution, but, this time, at the intraorganizational level, as well as at the organizational and interorganizational levels.

Baum and Singh (1994b) propose that a general theory of organizational evolution should be concerned both with ecological processes of interaction (i.e., competition, cooperation) that occur within populations at different organizational levels, and with genealogical processes of reproduction (i.e., replication, imitation) that occur within and between generations. The origins of the evolutionary approach in organization studies can be traced back to Campbell's model of sociocultural evolution (1969), which inspired Weick's

(1979b) conception of organizing and Aldrich's (1979, 1999) perspective on organizational change and spanned two streams of research. The first branch consists of a string of works on intraorganizational ecology. This research, in contrast to the work of population ecologists, is concerned with intraoganizational change dynamics, that is, how internal variations in populations of competing entities such as projects or jobs, combined with internal and external selection mechanisms, drive continuity and change from the point of view of the individual organization.

However, the evolutionary approach is particularly associated with the "genealogical" tradition[11] represented by the work of, among others, Nelson and Winter (1978, 1982) and their followers, on technological innovations (Bassanini & Dosi, 2001) and, particularly, on an evolutionary theory of the firm in economics (Coriat & Weinstein, 1995). It is also an extension of the work of McKelvey (1982) on organizational systematics[12] (Aldrich, 1999; Baum & Singh, 1994b). These authors argue, in contrast to population ecologists, that the most suitable unit of analysis in an evolutionary perspective is not the organization as a whole but the competencies (McKelvey, 1982) or routines that are embedded within organizations (Aldrich, 1999; Galunic & Weeks, 2002). Comparing routines to genes in biological evolution, Nelson and Winter propose that it is their reproduction and modification both within and between organizations over time that drive organizational, industrial, and economic continuity and change (Winter, 1990).

In short, in an evolutionary theory of organizational change, the ecological stream is concerned with how internal variations are selected through competition among entities, while the genealogical stream focuses on reproduction processes that produce new entities from old ones (Baum & Singh, 1994b). While the evolutionary approach does not preclude discontinuous, revolutionary change (for example, as a result of recombination or mutation of routines), ecological and genealogical processes are assumed to generally produce small, incremental changes. However, because evolutionary processes occur in nested hierarchies, discontinuous change at the organizational level can be the cumulative result of gradual changes at lower levels (Burgelman, 1991; Aldrich, 1999; Warglien, 2002).

From this point of view, organizational continuity and change are the result of the complex interplay between ecological and genealogical processes that are hierarchically nested. However, up to now, the two streams of work have developed separately and the work on cross-level interactions is still sparse (Baum & Singh, 1994b; Warglien, 2002). Therefore, in the following pages, the ecological and the genealogical points of view are presented separately, starting with the latter as it is more generally associated with the origins of the evolutionary approach at the organizational level[13] (see Table 7.2). Each model's particular portrayal of the variation-selection-retention mechanisms driving organizational stability and change will be presented, focusing on internal dynamics. Then, the passage from

Table 7.2   Evolutionary Theory

EVOLUTIONARY THEORY

General model of change: VARIATION – SELECTION – RETENTION
                                       Intentional/   Top-down   Reproduction/
                                       Spontaneous   Codification
 	
Focus: Balancing exploration (innovation) and exploitation (refinement), studying multilevel coevolutionary processes
 	
Antecedents: BIOLOGY
                     Behavioral theory of the firm (Cyert & March, 1963)
                     Evolutionary economics (Nelson & Winter, 1982)
                     Sociocultural evolution (Campbell, 1969)

	Genealogical tradition
Organization:	Bundle of routines, self-replicating system, pluralist view
Process of change:	Combination and reproduction of routines continuously produces incremental changes that can be retained over time
Authors:	Baum & Singh (1994a); Lovas & Ghoshal (2000); Zollo & Winter (2002)
	Ecological tradition
Organization:	Ecosystem of competing entities (e.g., rules, projects)
Process of change:	Process of micro-level variation and macro-level selection and retention
Authors:	Aldrich (1999); Baum & Singh (1994a); Burgelman (1991); Miner (1990); Lewin & Volberda (1999)

an evolutionary to a coevolutionary framework will be discussed, with particular attention to how it links with complexity theory.

ORGANIZATIONAL GENEALOGY: PRODUCING THE NEW FROM THE OLD

The study of organizational genealogy starts from the premise that organizations, like biological organisms, are self-replicating systems. Therefore, to understand their evolution it is necessary to understand their process of reproduction and to identify the units or "genes" that are at the basis of this replication. Baum and Singh (1994b) define those units as "components of institutional memory engaged in the preservation and dissemination of production and organizing information" (p. 9). So far, routines have been most widely used as the basic units in organizational genetics, although more recently other scholars have proposed the use of human and social capital (Lovas & Ghoshal, 2000) and memes, that is, cultural elements such as ideas, assumptions, values, beliefs, and know-how (Weeks & Galunic, 2003, p. 1320), as replicators in organizational evolution.

At the outset, routines are defined by Nelson and Winter (1982), in very broad terms, as "all regular and predictable behavioral patterns of firms"[14] (p. 14). Organizations are therefore viewed as the carriers of bundles of operational and administrative routines that are "held by their members and embedded in their technologies, material artifacts, and other structures" (Aldrich, 1999, p. 36). These routines must reproduce themselves if organizations are to persist. They allow organizations to function economically, and they reduce the disturbance caused by personnel turnover. It is through their expression in organizational actions and outcomes that an organization's survival and growth (i.e., its fitness in a particular selection environment) is determined. In other words, from a genealogical point of view, routines (like genes in biological organisms) are selected indirectly, through the differential survival and reproduction[15] of organizations that are the vehicles for specific configurations of routines (Aldrich, 1999).

The focus on routines (or, more broadly, on components of institutional memory) as genealogical entities draws attention to the process of retention. Routines are, by definition, patterns of behavior that have become institutionalized or automatized. Retention, that is, the persistence of routines through time and space, is the result of reproduction processes that, as mentioned by Warglien (2002), can take different forms and occur at different levels. In biological systems, reproduction is generational (from parents to offspring). In social systems, the processes of replication are much faster and can be intraorganizational (diffusion of routines within an organization) and interorganizational (imitation or transfer of routines between organizations). The emphasis on retention highlights the importance of routines as a stabilizing force within organizations. As argued by Baum and Singh (1994b), "organizational routines not only record history, they shape its future course" (p. 11). Because "practice makes perfect," the more an organization reproduces a routine, the more competent it becomes in using it, and the more likely it is to depend on that routine in the future and to generalize its use. In that sense, routines drive organizational inertia.

However, evolutionists also point out that each instance of reproduction is at the same time an occasion for routine change, whether intentional or not. Variations can occur as a result of mistakes (a distracted or inexperienced employee), of personnel transfer, or imperfect imitation by other units or competitors, but they can also be the result of individual initiative or of institutionalized attempts at innovation. The process of replication is therefore viewed as costly and time-consuming. As reported by Nelson and Winter (1982),

> The replication assumption in evolutionary models is intended primarily to reflect the advantages that favor the going concern attempting to do more of the same, as contrasted with the difficulties it would encounter in doing something else or that others would encounter in trying to copy its success. (p. 119)

Indeed, Nelson and Winter (1977, 1982) develop the notion of routines in the role of genes as part of a theory of innovation. According to Winter (1990), the question they attempt to answer is "how the various (functional and dysfunctional) sources of continuity in behavior affect the rate and character of change" (p. 277). Following their lead, a number of scholars explain technical change as a deliberate but inherently stochastic process (i.e., with indeterminate outcomes) where the development of "new" routines is the source of technological innovation.

Borrowing from the behavioral theory of the firm, Nelson and Winter (1982) posit a hierarchy of routines. Some routines concern current operations, while others (e.g., the search routines) determine medium-term changes in operations. Over the long term, the search routines themselves are modified. Evolutionary theorists, like the adaptive learning theorists we presented in the preceding section, are particularly interested in search routines (also called dynamic routines), which drive innovation. Nelson and Winter (1977, 1982) define the process of routine replication as a cumulative learning process. Following Schumpeter (1942), they explain the creation of new routines as resulting primarily from a recombination of old routines (i.e., a different way of putting together current skills and resources that leads to the development of new skills and resources). Apart from adaptive learning theory, Nelson and Winter's influence has been felt most strongly in two other streams of research: a series of studies on technological trajectories, which adopt a macro point of view, and a more micro stream of work on organizational dynamic capabilities.

The literature on technological trajectories focuses more on the development and diffusion of a specific innovation than on the innovating firm. This work explores how new technologies come to replace old ones (Anderson & Tushman, 1990), and it stresses, among other factors, the role of exogenous conditions and luck (as opposed to technological superiority) in a technology's success. While it focuses on the emergence of new industries, this research highlights the role of path dependence,[16] that is, the constraining effects of initial conditions and past events on present and future development (Bassanini & Dosi, 2001). As well, it shows that incumbents have great difficulty adapting to technological breakthroughs that are labeled competence-destroying

(Tushman & Anderson, 1986). As a consequence, it is not concerned so much with organizational change as with interorganizational dynamics within and between industrial sectors.

On the other hand, the work on dynamic capabilities, done by a group of scholars taking an economic perspective on the study of strategy, is clearly concerned with issues of strategic adaptation. In this view (Teece, Pisano, & Shuen, 1997), the competitive advantage of firms is seen as resulting from "a firm's ability to integrate, build, and reconfigure internal and external competences to address rapidly changing environments . . . given path dependencies and market positions" (p. 516). Until recently, this literature has mostly consisted of theoretical developments (Galunic & Rodan, 1998; Kogut & Zander, 1992; Mahnke, 2001; Teece et al., 1997; Winter, 2003; Zollo & Winter, 2002). Authors explore different characteristics of organizational capabilities, such as tacitness, specificity, imitability (Kogut & Zander, 1992; Winter, 2003), and dispersion, and propose different modes of capability-building such as recombination, synthesis, reconfiguration, and transformation (Galunic & Rodan, 1998; Teece et al., 1997). They emphasize that an organization's past learning, its repertoire of routines, restricts the scope of future learning; that is, evolution is path-dependent (Teece et al., 1997).

These theoretical writings refer to empirical process studies, not done explicitly within an evolutionary framework, which cover different topics such as new product development (Dougherty, 1992; Henderson & Clark, 1990; Iansiti & Clark, 1994; Nonaka, 1994) and technology transfer (Leonard-Barton, 1988) within established organizations, as well as strategy process research on strategic renewal and alliances (Hamel, 1991; Prahalad & Hamel, 1990). Apart from a few studies of the adoption and implementation of an existing new technology by an organization, this research is more concerned with identifying the appropriate way to manage the innovation process than with processes of organizational change per se. Apart from a few exceptions (such as Iansiti, 2000), this research attempts to evaluate the efficacy of different innovation practices and not the evolution of such practices over time or their link to organizational change over time (i.e., product development routines are studied at one point in time). Most of this literature concentrates on technological or product innovations developed by firms (alone or as part of alliances) for sale to (i.e., adoption by) other firms.[17]

As interpreted by evolutionists, these internal innovation processes are conceived as routines for changing. For example, the launch of a new product is defined as an instance of change possibly leading to better organizational adaptation. Such variations in product–market strategy entail, for the most part, organizational change of a continuous kind, that is, doing more of the same thing. For example, product innovation is the output of stable organizational routines, and new product development routines most often function in a gradual, additive manner (i.e., most new products are added to, rather than replace, existing ones). Yet the field studies show the disruptive effect of such incremental change and the difficulties involved in integrating novelty, even when it is routinely produced by the organization (Dougherty, 1992). In the same vein, the work on technology transfer (i.e., the adoption or imitation by a firm of an existing innovation) highlights the difficulty facing a firm that wants to integrate routines developed elsewhere without adapting them first to fit its routines (Leonard-Barton, 1988). This research is discussed by evolutionary theorists to illustrate, among other things, how complementarities among routines drive organizational inertia (Teece et al., 1997). Although, in evolutionary theory, continuous change of this nature can lead to major (and sometimes disruptive) organizational change in the long run, such issues are not addressed by this empirical literature because it studies the innovation process as an event—that is, as an episode with a clear beginning and ending.

One exception is a study by Salvato (2003) of the process of strategic innovation in two successful Italian firms. Adopting a genealogical point of view, he focuses on the description of "core micro-strategies," which are "recurring action patterns acting as replicators within organizations" (p. 85). These core microstrategies, which Salvato views as dynamic capabilities, are tightly coupled bundles of routines and resources intentionally developed by top management to recombine previously existing operational routines and resources with new resources and competencies. His "engineering of strategic evolution model" suggests that dynamic capabilities "operate more through repeated recombination patterns of stable organizational factors, than through disruption of existing practices" (p. 83). Like other scholars contributing to the dynamic capabilities theory, he concentrates on the process of strategic variation, which he describes as guided by top management, and does not explicitly model the process of internal selection except to mention that it is also induced by top management. Lately, the work on dynamic capabilities has increasingly moved to the study of coevolution between organization and environment, which we discuss later on in this chapter.

In short, the genealogical perspective as it evolves into the dynamic capabilities theory focuses increasingly on the stable patterns through which old skills and resources are recombined or synthesized with new ones to produce novelty. While Nelson and Winter (1982) stress the indeterminate nature of the evolutionary process (i.e., whether innovations are successful or not is viewed as largely outside of management's control), the dynamic capabilities approach increasingly emphasizes the role of top management in guiding successful innovation. From the perspective of organizational change, evolutionists paint a picture of organizations staying more or less the same while producing a variety of new outputs. To an external observer, these organizations are rapidly changing (i.e., launching new businesses and moving into new markets), but to an insider they are just repeating (and improving) well-known routines. In fact, as will be argued in the discussion, the change process they are looking at is different from the one scholars within the configurationist or cognitive approaches had in mind. According to the latter, such evolution does not constitute organizational change: These organizations basically maintain the same configuration, the same way of doing things.

Finally, the genealogical tradition is really an evolutionary learning approach (Aldrich, 1999). With its growing emphasis on dynamic capabilities, it moves even closer to the organizational learning literature in terms of its contribution to our understanding of organizational continuity and change. For example, in a recent article, Zollo and Winter (2002) elaborate a model of knowledge evolution that is influenced by Nonaka's (1994) model of knowledge creation, but couched in evolutionary terms (i.e., as a cycle of variation, selection, and retention). They argue that the "dynamic capability-building" process involves "adopting an opportune mix of behavioral and cognitive processes" (p. 345). Their model treats replication (diffusion) and retention (routinization)[18] as separate processes in organizational systems to reflect the fact that learning is spatially dispersed. Surprisingly, it also specifies an internal selection process, something that had not been developed so far by evolutionary theorists because of their conception of selection as indirect.[19]

However, there is still much confusion and divergence in the genealogical literature, particularly with regard to the links with the ecological processes, in terms of both the level at which selection occurs and the appropriate unit of selection. For example, recently a few scholars (Weeks & Galunic, 2003; Taylor & Giroux, 2004) have proposed genealogical models of organizational evolution emphasizing a cultural reproduction process. It should be noted in passing that, like Weick's (1979b) model of organizing as a process of multiple interacting cycles of enactment (i.e., proactive variation), selective interpretation, and retention,[20] these models present organizations as social constructions (i.e., as the enactment of memes in cultural patterns or in narrative structures). However, because of their high level of abstraction and their generality, they differ from the contextualized, subject-oriented research typical of social constructionist approaches presented in the next chapter.

These scholars choose memes as the unit of reproduction, unlike authors such as Nelson and Winter (1982), who focus on routines as observable replicators, which are easier to study formally (Holmqvist, 2003; Leroy & Ramanantsoa, 1997). Conceiving them either as cultural elements (Weeks & Galunic, 2003) or language components (Taylor & Giroux, 2004), they argue that such genealogical entities allow for a better distinction between genotype and phenotype. They clearly separate the genetic material (the memes), that is, the organizational "blueprint" or what Aldrich (1999) and others refer to as the representations of routines and competencies, from its phenotypic expression in a particular organization, conceived as a combination of cultural or discourse patterns. Even though Weeks and Galunic (2003) speak of an intraorganizational ecology of memes and identify them as the cultural unit of selection, they agree with authors such as Aldrich (1999), Warglien (2002), and Taylor and Giroux (2004), that it is the phenotype (i.e., the organization or firm) in its interaction with the environment that is selected and drives the memes' reproduction and diffusion. Moreover, all agree that these "genes," no matter how they are defined, are fairly stable replicators that, when combined, enact a variety of related but unique interactors (i.e., populations of organizations).

As we will see next, in the second stream of work of the evolutionary approach, which is concerned with ecological entities within organizations, there is also no agreed-upon definition and hierarchy of organizational inter-actors (for example, populations of rules or projects). However, in this case, the internal selection process, as opposed to the retention process, plays a particu-larly crucial role, reflecting the competitive struggle going on within the orga-nization among lower-level interactors.

INTRAORGANIZATIONAL ECOLOGY: A BOTTOM-UP PROCESS OF CHANGE

Intraorganizational ecology[21] starts from the premise (Warglien, 2002) that "an organization can be seen as an ecosystem that hosts an amazing variety of populations" (p. 99). Strategic initiatives (Burgelman, 1983, 1991), development projects (Warglien, 1995), jobs (Miner, 1990, 1991), functional routines (Leroy & Ramanantsoa, 1996), and formal rules (March, Schulz, & Zhou, 2000) are among the populations of entities that have been studied. These entities are called inter-actors, in contrast to replicators that participate in the genealogical process. To function as ecologies, these populations of interactors must be subjected to a scarcity of resources that makes competition among individuals and selection of some over others inevitable. Although empirical studies of intraorganizational ecology are still rare, two trends can be distinguished: The first is anchored in the strategy literature and is mostly based on intensive field studies of a single or a few organizations (Burgelman, 1983, 1991; Leroy & Ramanantsoa, 1996; Lovas & Ghoshal, 2000; Noda & Bower, 1996); the second originates in organization theory and tends toward quantification and formal modeling (March et al., 2000; Miner, 1991; Schulz, 1998).

Also taking as its focus the new product development process, Burgelman (1983, p. 1991) is one of the first to link the innovation process to long-term organizational change in an explicit evolutionary model. He provides us with a rich description of strategic continuity and change over time as the result of two interrelated ecological processes. Building on his early work on internal corpo-rate venturing (Burgelman, 1983), his study of Intel's transformation from a computer memory company to a microprocessor company (Burgelman, 1991) offers a detailed explanation of organizational survival and renewal as long-term "balancing of variation-reduction and variation-increasing mechanisms" (p. 257). Viewing organizations as ecologies of strategic initiatives, Burgelman describes the induced strategy-making process as a variety-reduction mechanism that leads to exploitation and refinement of existing knowledge and the autonomous strategy-making process as a variety-increasing mechanism resulting in major change from new learning or exploration. The variation process is described as the emergence of strategic initiatives, which originate at the operational level influenced by career advancement incentives. These various initiatives compete for resources (e.g., money, people, top management attention) and are subjected to a selection process. In the case of projects exploiting the current strategic competences, the selection criteria are embedded in the corporate structural context (administrative mechanisms such as strategic planning, formal roles, and incentive programs, as well as cultural influences) built by top management. They are meant to preserve a tight coupling to existing strategy. On the other hand, the projects that are exploratory (outside the current strategy) are selected through a less formal set of criteria labeled the strategic determination context (which involves both informal relational mechanisms and market simulation experiments), also ultimately controlled by top management. Finally, retention involves either reinforcement of existing strategic bases (distinctive competences, goals, activity domains) or formal changes to strategic vision (e.g., inclusion of a new competence or activity domain). This is where induced and autonomous ecological processes interact.

In contrast with the punctuated equilibrium model, which views exploitation and exploration as sequential processes (Tushman & Romanelli, 1985), induced and autonomous strategy making are parallel processes that occasionally intersect when new learning expressed in innovative activities is officially recognized and becomes selected into the induced process, thus provoking a major change. However, such a change, labeled strategic renewal, is the officialization, following internal experimentation and selection, of a new strategic vision, rather than an ex ante top-down decision to realize a new strategic orientation.[22]

Finally, Burgelman (1991) is one of the few to explicitly link intraorganizational ecology to organizational-level selection, arguing that when internal selection criteria are aligned to external selection pressures, the induced process promotes survival and adaptation. On the other hand, autonomous strategic activities emphasize that internal variation and selection mechanisms can anticipate adaptation to external selection pressures (but can also lead to dissipating internal resources and diluting distinctive competence).

As Warglien (2002) underlines, Burgelman (1983), in his study of internal corporate venturing, describes the multiple hierarchically nested processes involved in the autonomous evolutionary process, from team unit to division to corporate level, showing that selection mechanisms linked to internal criteria (e.g., a champion's reputation) are stronger at the lower level but become more tightly linked to market forces (e.g., marketing studies, growth in sales) at the later stages, as the initiative moves from idea to product to line of business.

Like previous strategy process researchers such as Bower (1970), Quinn (1980), and Mintzberg and McHugh (1985), Burgelman (1991, 1996) emphasizes the emergent nature of strategic evolution. In this evolutionary framework, top management's role in strategic change is restricted to being "willing enough to recognize strategically bottom-up initiatives and capitalize on them rather than pass them by" (Noda & Bower, 1996, p. 188). However, recently some researchers have suggested that top management can play a more active role in strategic evolution (Galunic & Eisenhardt, 2001; Lovas & Ghoshal, 2000; Salvato, 2003). Also focusing on new product development, Lovas and Ghoshal's "guided evolution" model, like Salvato's "engineering of evolution" model, describes a different process of internal variation and selection.[23]

Following Baum and Singh (1994a), Lovas and Ghoshal (2000) propose an integrated genealogical and ecological model of evolution. Based on a case study of Oticon, a firm that has completed a successful reorientation, their model explains the concurrent development (or coevolution) of human and social capital (the genealogical entities) and strategic initiatives (the ecological entities). They argue that the variation, selection, and retention of social and human capital are partly determined by the variation, selection, and retention of strategic initiatives (and vice versa). In contrast to Burgelman's model, in which internal selection is top management's role, in Lovas & Ghoshal's model, both variation and internal selection of strategic initiatives are collective processes, the project-based design of the firm acting as a replication of a natural selection environment. However, these collective processes are driven by the strategic intent defined by top management. In their "guided evolution" model, there is no autonomous process functioning in parallel.[24] As a by-product of this ecological process, human and social capital embedded in individuals are selected, retained, and developed, providing the foundations for future innovation.

These models, despite their differences, describe how strategic initiatives that can emerge anywhere in the organization compete to be selected internally and, once retained, can lead to major organizational change that is potentially adaptive (i.e., that will increase the organization's fitness in its selection environment). Finally, they both define organizational change as a by-product of experimentation.

Unlike the strategy process research presented above, the second group of studies, rooted in organization theory, focuses on administrative changes, that is, variations in populations of jobs or rules. Like population ecology research, this work is interested in the demographics of the population under study. Miner (1991), for example, defining organizations as bundles of routines, studies the ecology of formal jobs in a university over 6 years. She considers jobs as a specific type of routine and looks at the attributes of jobs (job age, types of jobs created) related to job deaths. Based on her research on jobs, Miner (1990) also proposes an evolutionary model of structural change as the selective retention of idiosyncratic jobs, arguing that "this type of change can operate in addition to a top-down planned organizational change, providing 'another engine' of organizational transformation over time" (p. 195). Viewing the emergence of idiosyncratic jobs as a source of unplanned variations, she discusses their adaptive potential, arguing that while they can undermine survival potential, they can also act as experiments leading to "undirected" adaptation.

March and his colleagues (March et al., 2000; Schulz, 1998; Zhou, 1993), for their part, concentrate their efforts on the dynamics of formal rules. Following in the footsteps of population ecologists, they use demographic measures such as density dependence, rate of births and deaths, age, timing, and frequency counts of changes, to study the long-term evolution of populations of rules. Their studies demonstrate that rules are density-dependent: Their birthrates are affected by the number of existing rules and the rate of rules death in a rule niche. Their extensive study of the dynamics of rules at Stanford University over a hundred years shows that patterns of rule births and patterns of rule changes have different dynamics (March et al., 2000). Rule births seem to be primarily related to external changes, while rule changes seem to be more strongly linked to internal dynamics. In terms of impact on organizational stability and change, their research suggests that changes in rules are destabilizing and have a contagion effect (i.e., revision of one rule increases the likelihood of changes in other rules). However, there are factors that stabilize the system of rules, for example, responsibility barriers and limits in attention, energy, and time. These contain rule changes "within relatively narrow domains and within relatively brief periods of time" (p. 195).

Baum and Singh (1994a) suggest that ecological entities structure and integrate organizational systems and the interactions (i.e., resource exchange and transformation) between them. They state that "the dynamic interactions at each level hold the entities at the next-higher level of the nested ecological hierarchy together" (p. 10). In this sense, the fast-rising domain of intraorganizational ecology provides an interesting framework to look at change as a bottom-up process rather than a top-down one. Because it focuses on internal selection mechanisms, it is better equipped than the genealogical tradition to articulate the processes of internal competition.

In contrast to traditional adaptation theories, where top management reacts to a changing environment by implementing a deliberate top-down intervention process, this framework reverses the directionality of organizational change propagation, seeing it as a bottom-up process. In the classical evolutionary framework, selection is conceived as happening at the next-higher level, but it selects from variations that have emerged from the lower level. This means that a number of lower-level variations must struggle (compete and cooperate) for attention and resources so that the internal selection process can act as a filter.

The result of that selection is expressed in actions that affect the fitness of the organization in its selection environment. It is in this sense that in the evolutionary framework change is always indeterminate, that is, the outcome of both internal and external selection mechanisms is never totally predictable.

However, as Lovas and Ghoshal's (2000) model describes and other scholars (Baum & Singh, 1994b; Lewin & Volberda, 1999; March et al., 2000) have noted, organizational stability and change are the result not of one but of a number of interacting evolutionary processes. This observation has led to a call for systematic investigation of coevolution, which is discussed next.

FROM EVOLUTION TO COEVOLUTION

One of the major recent developments in evolutionary thinking is the acknowledgment of processes of mutual adaptation, both within levels and across levels (Lewin & Volberda, 1999; McKelvey, 1997; Volberda & Lewin, 2003). Most evolutionary research so far has focused on the evolution of one population (e.g., of strategic initiatives, jobs, organizations, routines) in an exogenous, and most often stable, selection environment. However, this approach is being challenged in two ways: first, by recognizing the existence of coevolutionary processes within organizations or communities, for example, between ecological and genealogical populations; and second, by emphasizing coevolution as a cross-level process of mutual causation, arguing that because units of adaptation are nested (routines embedded in organizations that are embedded in populations), the interaction among levels impacts evolutionary dynamics.

In the first case, authors argue that if the organization is conceived as an ecosystem encompassing a number of coexisting populations, the study of the mutual influence of these populations is of interest. For example, as March et al. (2000) conclude following their study of formal rules, there are numerous populations of rules in an organization, and the evolution of any rule system is dependent on the evolution of other neighboring systems of rules.

As well, in Baum and Singh's (1994a) dual-hierarchy framework, ecological and genealogical processes are conceived as interacting and influencing each other. The variation and reproduction of genes (whether they are routines, human and social capital, or memes) constrains the variation and selection of ecological entities (whether they are jobs, projects, division charters, or organizations) and vice versa. However, apart from Baum and Singh's (1994a) own conceptual effort and Lovas and Ghoshal's (2000) empirical study described earlier, there has been little work that systematically ties ecological to genealogical processes.[25] Although some scholars more or less explicitly link learning processes to ecological processes (Bruderer & Singh, 1996; Lampel & Shamsie, 2003; Miner, 1994), few have modeled the learning processes in ways that allow their systematic analysis as genealogical processes interacting with ecological processes. Furthermore, as stated by Warglien (2002), "a coherent joint definition of ecological units and genetic entities is still to a large extent missing" (p. 112) and is necessary for such coevolutionary research to proceed.

The second argument driving coevolutionary thinking is the acknowledgment that environments are not exogenous. They are largely constituted of organizations (competitors, suppliers, customers, government agencies, professional associations) that interact and are influenced by each other. While there is a long tradition of scholars, in both organization theory (Weick, 1979b) and strategy (Child, 1972), that have advanced this view, until recently, most evolutionary research has assumed that selection environments are not influenced by the population of entities they select. In other words, while organizations seek to adapt to the environment, the environment is assumed to evolve independently from their efforts. Now, there is more and more research that views environments as endogenous and attempts to study "the mutual adaptation between the unit of evolution and the environment" (March, 1994, p. 43). This implies that researchers need to devise nested coevolutionary studies to examine organization–environment systems.

McKelvey (1997) has provided one of the most systematic presentations of multilevel coevolutionary thinking that is explicitly linked to Darwinian theory. Like Baum and Singh (1994b), he builds his explanation on the premise that "micro-coevolutionary order within firms emerges in the context of macrocoevolutionary selectionist competitive pressure" (p. 361). In other words, while there is mutual causation over time, current higher-level dynamics produce lower-level order. As noted by Aldrich (1999), intraorganizational (i.e., lower-level) selection processes that are not relevant or connected to environmental (i.e., higher-level) selection processes will raise an organization's risk of failure (i.e., of being unfit with regard to its selection environment).

Furthermore, McKelvey (1997), giving the example of a division manager's initiative that can be selected for or against by both his superiors and his subordinates, suggests that selection of a variation can be explained at either a higher or a lower level of analysis. He adds that to untangle such issues it is helpful to conceive organizations as comprising thousands of nested variation-selection-retention cycles (which he calls Darwin machines) that in a competitive context create changes through systematic selection of certain entities (either components or wholes).

According to Baum and Singh (1994c), "the goal of coevolutionary inquiry is understanding how the structure of direct interactions and feedback within organization–environment systems give rise to their dynamic behavior" (p. 380). In a formal modeling exercise, they show how different growth patterns of two populations in a community are the result of different interaction patterns (competition and cooperation) between them, mediated by feedback effects. In such organization–environment systems, the environment is conceived as being the community, that is, the set of interacting populations, along with contextual variables such as demand and resource availability. This system is coevolution-ary in the sense that, apart from direct interaction between certain populations of entities, there are systems effects due to variation-amplifying or variation-reducing feedback loops, which modify simple cause-and-effect relations.

Because of these cross-level interaction effects, coevolutionary systems often do not reach equilibrium. In that case, the complex feedback processes make the distinction between dependent and independent variables meaningless since changes in any variable can be caused endogenously by changes in other vari-ables (Baum & Singh, 1994c). This circular causality means that such systems are difficult to understand due to counterintuitive effects. Consequently, the formal study of coevolution requires the use of models developed to study non-linear dynamics (McKelvey, 1997; Lewin & Volberda, 1999), and researchers inter-ested in this topic are driven into the burgeoning area of complexity theory, which is introduced in the next section.

However, nested coevolutionary research is still quite rare (Lewin & Volberda, 1999; McKelvey, 1997; Volberda & Lewin, 2003). So far, a number of empirical studies have focused on microcoevolution (linking intraorganizational processes to firm-level evolution)—for example, research by Burgelman (1991, 1996), Galunic and Eisenhardt (1996), and Lovas and Ghoshal (2000) that has already been referred to. Macrocoevolutionary research, associating firm-level and envi-ronmental evolution, is also thriving (Baum & Singh, 1994c; Flier, Van Den Bosch, & Volberda, 2003; Lampel & Shamsie, 2003; Levinthal & Myatt, 1994; Rosenkopf & Tushman, 1994). Most of this work is linked to dynamic capabilities and resource-based theory and is concerned with the emergence of new organizational forms.

Some recent research, based on longitudinal qualitative case studies, illus-trates interactions over time within and/or between different levels, such as the firm, the industry, and the country (Djelic & Ainamo, 1999; Huygens, Baden-Fuller, Van Den Bosch, & Volberda, 2001; Rodrigues & Child, 2003). While it is labeled coevolutionary, this work straddles the natural evolution and social dynamics streams, particularly with regard to its concern with the historical con-text and the role of agency (for example, Djelic & Ainamo, 1999; Huygens et al., 2001; Rodrigues & Child, 2003). This is not surprising, considering that most of these authors cite Giddens's structuration theory (1979) and Pettigrew's (1985a, 1997) contextualism as sources of inspiration, sometimes explicitly drawing out the similarities between these integrative frameworks and coevolutionary think-ing. For example, Huygens et al. (2001), in their historical study of the music industry in Britain, illustrate how capabilities developed over an organization's history both enable and constrain its future development. They also show the role that such capabilities play in the coevolution of competitive regimes, busi-ness models, and organizational forms. They observe that industry incumbents' adaptation seems to be based on strategic renewal processes (Burgelman, 1991) rather than punctuated equilibrium (Tushman & Romanelli, 1985). However, in contrast to other structurationist research, which we will present in the next chapter, this strand of work has little to say about intraorganizational change processes, for example, about how "capabilities are actually generated and refined over time" (Huygens et al., 2001, p. 1005). Their focus is more on the content and sequence of organizational changes (e.g., new capabilities, new structural features) and not on the intraorganizational dynamics from which they emerge. Furthermore, with a few exceptions, they concentrate on economic, competitive, and technological influences in their historical analysis, neglecting the social, the political, and the cultural, and adopt an objective rather than an interpretive point of view.

On the other hand, these empirical studies, which use narrative accounts and historical analysis, are viewed by some, who call for a more formal approach to the study of coevolution (McKelvey, 2002; Volberda & Lewin, 2003), as not systematic enough. As mentioned by March (1994, p. 43), the study of evolution when some adapting units are integral parts of other adapting units, as is the case for organizations, is quite complicated. In fact, an increasing number of studies of coevolution use complexity theory rather than a classical evolutionary approach, based on the belief that, under certain circumstances, endogenous complexity effects might be stronger than exogenous selection effects in explaining organizational stability and change (McKelvey, 1999). They want to explore issues of emergence and self-organization.

DISCUSSION

Ever since sociobiology, the ancestor of actual evolutionary theory, emerged in the 1970s (Wilson, 1975), it has been the subject of ferocious controversy, if not simply treated as taboo, in the social sciences (see Markoczy & Goldberg, 1998, for a sample of the criticisms addressed to evolutionary psychology and a rebuttal). The debate centers on the conception of human nature, particularly the continuity claimed by sociobiologists between genetic processes and social processes, which is manifested, for example, in their explanation of moral values and cooperation in terms of natural selection mechanisms.

In the case of its application to organizational change, biological evolution is used analogically rather than literally, with organizations compared to self-replicating systems subjected to selective competitive environments.[26] Despite its increasing visibility in the field of organization studies in the last few years, the recent evolutionary approach, favoring a "weak" form of the selection argument, seems to be mostly ignored by scholars of other persuasions who still aim their criticism at population ecology.[27] Some of the rare comments by "outsiders," among them Meyer and DiMaggio, pioneers of neo-institutionalism, and Porac, a well-known researcher in the cognitive approach, are included in Baum and Singh's (1994a) landmark book on the evolutionary approach.

The main criticism of evolutionary thinking, which is more specifically addressed to population ecology, is directed to what is perceived as its environmental determinism and to a "logic which subordinates collective and individual action to efficiency and survival imperatives largely beyond human influence" (Reed, 1996). Evolutionists reject the first charge, claiming that indeterminacy of outcomes is a basic principle of the evolutionary approach and that it is probabilistic rather than deterministic (Aldrich, 1999; Baum, 1996). Still, as Meyer (1994, p. 110) argues, while the differences between population ecology and evolutionary theory are significant with regard to the capacity of managers to affect organizational evolution, it remains the case that they both view the selection environment as the driving force and treat organizational change as a random process with regard to its adaptation value, thus giving little weight to managerial action. Therefore, while the environment is nondeterministic in its effects, for most evolutionists, the main causation effect is assumed to be from the environment to the organization. Furthermore, in most organizational evolution research, "managers are prescient yet powerless" (Meyer, 1994, p. 110). This view is deemed unrealistic by a number of authors (Whittington, 1994), even by some who claim to be evolutionists (Lovas & Ghoshal, 2000; Salvato, 2003).

Another criticism aimed at ecologists is that they neglect power dynamics involved in organizational change because they treat organizations as unitary entities (Reed, 1996) and don't take into account, in their explanations, the historical and sociopolitical context in which organizations are embedded (Perrow, 1985). Researchers in intraorganizational ecology who, in contrast to population ecologists, study populations of competing entities within organizations, could take into account the heterogeneous and conflictual nature of organizations. However, their models don't include power dynamics and thus tend to treat all competing entities as equivalent from an analytical point of view. Furthermore, because evolutionary theory is essentially acontextual (Levinthal, cited in Murmann, Aldrich, Levinthal, & Winter, 2003, p. 31), its models, even if they are built from rich historical and background data, paint a picture of the environment as an abstract set of impersonal and neutral objective features (e.g., market forces) where power structures are not theorized or evoked (Reed, 1996).

Indeed, even though this theory's proponents always assert that "history matters" and that knowledge of initial conditions and path dependencies is essential for explaining evolutionary dynamics, they differ from critical theorists and social constructionists in their conception of history. In their studies, they look at history as the chronological sequence of events making up an organization's life. They reduce the various contextual forces (institutional, political, social, economic, technological) that influence organizational and population evolution to a selection environment and, more important, they don't take into account the meaning given to events, which makes history so crucial for understanding human evolution.[28]

In the same vein, Porac (1994) discusses how one of the great advantages of evolutionary theory, its level of generality and abstraction, is also one of its main weaknesses. On the one hand, because it is so general and abstract (i.e., it applies to any system, whether biological, cultural, or organizational), it can develop into what McKelvey (1997) calls a quasi-natural organizational science. Indeed, Levinthal (cited in Murmann et al., 2003) argues that, like the neoclassical economics in reaction to which it was developed, evolutionary theory owes its success both to the fact that it is context-free (and, therefore, can invade many niches) and to its ability to aggregate. On the other hand, according to Porac (1994), it risks being trivial (or neglecting important causal variables) if it remains too generic.

Miner (1994) and Aldrich (1999) are among those who contend that this level of generality makes the evolutionary approach a good candidate as a meta-framework for organizational change theories. While Aldrich (1999) selectively borrows from other theories to better articulate and specify the evolutionary approach, Miner (1994) suggests that rational, political, and learning models be considered "special cases of the more general evolutionary framework" (p. 88). Such an integrative view holds evolutionary models of bottom-up or unplanned change such as those presented by Burgelman (1991) and Miner (1990) as alternatives to traditional change models, special cases rather than generic representations of the evolutionary framework. It also raises interesting questions about the applicability of an evolutionary framework to top-down planned change. In this case, instead of a population of competing variations, variation is mandated by top management and selection is made by lower-level employees, thus inversing the selection hierarchy, as suggested by McKelvey (1997). Such research, framing the study of planned change in terms of the impact of various group-level selection mechanisms on the timing and spatial diffusion of new practices (Demers & Giroux, 1993), has not been done so far.

At the same time, some authors (Greve, 2002) caution that "delineating and defining evolutionary work is the single most important problem of current evolutionary theory" (p. 568). The traditional strength of evolutionary thinking, as represented in population ecology research, has been its formalization, which allowed it to develop a well-defined series of cumulative studies. In the more inclusive evolutionary approach, there is, yet, no agreement between authors as to the appropriate units of analysis and number of levels, in either the genealogical or the ecological hierarchy, and, consequently, on the mechanisms at work and the connections between them (Aldrich, 1999; Warglien, 2002). Aldrich (p. 39), for example, wonders which is the "natural" unit of selection, routines or organizations, adding that we need further empirical evidence before we can answer that question. He further questions the call for adding the community as a unit of selection, suggesting that a whole community is rarely selected. Both the stimulating richness and the confusion are evident in Baum's (2002) recent anthology, where an evolutionary meta-framework serves as a classificatory scheme within which ecology and evolution are included as separate approaches, at three levels of analysis: intraorganizational, organizational, and interorganizational. There is significant overlap yet little clear articulation between approaches and among levels.

In summary, the evolutionary approach, like the behavioral learning approach, explores the tension between continuity and change at the organizational level, but not as an integrative motor within a single entity. In contrast to the learning approach, the evolutionary model has a micro–macro motor of change because each unit of analysis is not conceived as a unified whole, but as a set of components. In this case, organizational change emerges from lower-level dynamics, while in the learning approach the interface between micro and macro has to be specified by calling on other theories, such as diffusion or communication frameworks.

The evolutionary approach describes organizational dynamics as the interplay between ecological and genealogical processes within an ecosystem, the organization, nested within larger ecosystems (Baum & Singh, 1994a). Research on genealogical entities, such as routines and memes, shows how replication processes produce new combinations. Research at the ecological level describes how, from competition between interactors, such as strategic initiatives and jobs, a new organizational profile emerges. Both streams of work link organizational change to innovation and picture change as an essentially incremental process. However, as mentioned before, this work focuses essentially on changes to operational routines as a result of new product development, depicted as a stable search process.

Levinthal (1994) argues that evolutionary theory is concerned with operational or technical change, while transformational theories of change (Tushman & Romanelli, 1985) focus on structural or what he calls managerial change, that is, change of the power structure and control systems, which is more radical or discontinuous. He further suggests that the latter can be conceived as change in the internal selection environment of the firm. One could argue that this can also influence the internal variation and retention processes and, therefore, the balance between continuity and change, or exploitation and exploration (Miner, 1994). While these processes are generally portrayed as stable by evolutionary theorists, it should be noted that, at least in Burgelman's model, an incremental process can lead to radical change of the kind talked about by Levinthal (1994), that is, a major structural and strategic change. But, in this case, because much of the operational change occurs before the structural change, there is no need for a prescient leader with a vision. Still, this is not a reactive view of change; such internal variation involving the combination of the old with the new and expressed in emergent competing initiatives can anticipate and in fact partly create future selection environments, both internal and external. As such, the evolutionary approach offers an alternative to the trajectory implied by the punctuated equilibrium model.

Finally, the evolutionary approach, as it tries to reconcile adaptation and selection as the interplay of multilevel processes, is led to consider the coevolution of organization and environment in terms of nonlinear dynamics, and moves toward complexity theory.

The Complexity Approach

At the end of the 1990s, one of the newest trends in the literature dealing with organizational change is complexity theory. It is described both as a new perspective on organizational change and development (Brown & Eisenhardt, 1998; Brown & Eisenhardt, 1997; Stacey, 1995) and as a broad interdisciplinary paradigm including an array of mathematical and computational procedures and techniques to study and model complex systems such as organizations (Carley, 2002; Dooley & Van de Ven, 1999). These two descriptions are not mutually exclusive but engender different ways of using the complexity approach in organization studies—as a metaphor to generate theoretical models of organizational change processes or as a formal method to analyze complex processes in organizations.

To date, there have been more articles and books describing this approach and its potential for organization and strategy studies (including a large number of prescriptive writings aimed at managers) than actual empirical studies using the complexity approach. This is not surprising, considering that it has its roots in mathematics, computer science, and the natural sciences (particularly biology and physics) and is highly sophisticated technically. While it is presented as a promising trend in future research on organizational evolution (Anderson, 1999; Begun, 1994; Brown & Eisenhardt, 1997; Poole, Van de Ven, Dooley, & Holmes, 2000; Stacey, 1995; Thiétart & Forgues, 1995), some wonder whether it will turn out to be just a fad (Carley, 2002; Cohen, 1999; Baum & Silverman, 2001).

The interest in complex systems in organization studies is not new. As Simon (1996) remarked, complexity theory has a long history; its origins can be traced back to cybernetics (Ashby, 1956) and general systems theory (Forrester, 1961), both of which have had a profound influence on organization theory. Traditionally, complexity was considered in static structural terms (for example, the degree of vertical and horizontal differentiation in an organization). The recent approach highlights processual complexity and studies different types of systems behavior that challenge the classical conception of equilibrium (Anderson, 1999; Stacey, 1995). Until recently, organizational systems were conceived as homeostatic, that is, as self-stabilizing entities, and, accordingly, change was viewed as a transitory disturbance before a return to equilibrium. Stability was associated with persistence and disequilibrium with disintegration (or failure). The complexity approach, on the other hand, views organizations as nonlinear dynamic systems[29] whose behavior can be unpredictable and far from equilibrium, yet adaptive.

Nonlinear systems, depending on the balance between positive (deviation-amplifying) and negative (deviation-reducing) feedback loops over time, can exhibit different types of temporal patterns. Although they can attain stable equilibrium, either fixed (static) or periodic (cyclical), they often develop more complex behavior characterized as edge-of-chaos behavior (self-organized criticality), deterministic chaos (bounded instability) or random noise (explosive instability) (Anderson, 1999; Morel & Ramanujam, 1999; Thiétart & Forgues, 1995).

Chaos theory and complex adaptive system (CAS) theory, two interdisciplinary streams of research, currently make up the dominant branches of the complexity approach[30] in organization studies (Baum & Silverman, 2001; Morel & Ramanujam, 1999) (see Table 7.3). Chaos theory studies deterministic nonlinear systems whose behavior appears random but is, in fact, orderly and bounded. Organizational scholars have used it, so far, to study innovation and crisis situations (Baum & Silverman, 2001; Cheng & Van de Ven, 1996; Koput, 1997; Thiétart & Forgues, 1997), as well as supply chain dynamics (Ginsberg, Larsen, & Lomi, 1996; Levy, 1994). Complex adaptive system theory, on the other hand, focuses on complex nondeterministic systems that are far from equilibrium (at the edge of chaos) but whose random behavior displays interesting patterns, such as emergent order (Morel & Ramanujam, 1999). Researchers such as Brown and Eisenhardt (1998), McKelvey (1999), and Siggelkow and Levinthal (2003), draw on complex systems theory to explore the link between organizational design and firm adaptability and, more generally, coevolutionary dynamics. In a sense, chaos theory and CAS theory are respectively concerned with two different types of complex behavior that will be defined later: chaotic equilibrium and behavior at the edge of chaos. They focus on studying the properties and dynamics of two different potential "states" of organizations viewed as complex systems. Indeed, the far-from-equilibrium behavior called "edge-of-chaos" is often described as preceding chaotic equilibrium (McKelvey, 1999; Morel & Ramanujam, 1999). Thus, a complex system can evolve through different dynamics from stable, to edge-of-chaos, to chaotic or explosive instability[31] and, depending on its dynamics, could be modeled differently (i.e., as a linear system, a complex adaptive system, a deterministic nonlinear system, or a stochastic system), as explained by Dooley and Van de Ven (1999). In the following pages, chaos theory and CAS theory will be briefly compared to highlight the different change models they represent and the kinds of studies they inspire.

CHAOS AND PUNCTUATED CHANGE

Chaotic behavior appears in a system because of the combination of "at least two underlying not-entirely-compatible forces" connected through feedback loops (Koput, 1997, p. 530). In fact, chaotic behavior typically results from the interaction of only a few variables.[32] According to Morel and Ramanujam

Table 7.3   Complexity Theory

COMPLEXITY THEORY		
Model of change:	PUNCTUATED CHANGE Chaotic behavior	OR POWER LAW OF CHANGE Edge of chaos (self- organized criticality)
Focus: Understanding the dynamics of chaos and of self-organization		
Antecedents: Physics, biology, mathematics, computer science		
	Chaos theory	
Organization:	Deterministic nonlinear dynamic system producing chaotic behavior	
Process of change:	Bifurcation between numerous divergent (innovative) and convergent (routine) paths. Small changes, amplified over time, can produce large effects: punctuated change	
Authors:	Cheng & Van de Ven (1996); Thiétart & Forgues (1995)	
	Complex adaptive system (CAS) theory	
Organization:	Self-organizing nondeterministic dynamic systems	
Process of change:	Power law pattern or avalanche (small changes at the micro level through interaction effects can abruptly produce unforeseen macro-level changes: a new emergent order)	
Authors:	Anderson (1999); Brown & Eisenhardt (1997); Stacey (1995)	

(1999), "Mathematical chaos suggests that simple models can have very complex dynamics" (p. 280). In this type of system, positive feedback loops, which reinforce the initial change and push the system toward instability, compete with negative feedback loops, which dampen the change and tend to restore the system's stability. As Thiétart and Forgues (1995) explain, the difference between the system reaching explosive instability, stable equilibrium, or chaotic equilibrium depends "on the dynamic combination and on the relative strength of the relationships" (p. 20) among the variables. They argue that organizations can potentially evolve to chaotic equilibrium (also called deterministic chaos), because they involve a number of opposing forces, most notably between planning, structuring, and controlling, that push for stability, and experimentation, innovation, and initiative, which are pressures for change.

Systems in chaotic equilibrium never follow a repetitive cycle; "they can never pass through the same exact state more than once" (Levy, 1994, p. 170). Their individual trajectories are unpredictable. However, their paths are not totally erratic; when plotted on return maps[33] over a long period of time, the time series displays a pattern, a hidden order. In contrast with truly random time series, which fill all the space and require an almost infinite number of dimensions to plot all the points, they have low dimensionality. They are bounded within a geometric space, often called a strange attractor,[34] which means that the limits of the system's outcomes are known. The system exhibits path dependence (i.e., high sensitivity to initial conditions), which entails that small initial differences "bifurcate or branch out into numerous possible pathways resembling a complex decision tree" (Cheng & Van de Ven, 1996, p. 608). But large initial differences may also converge because of the existence of the attractor. As summarized by Poole et al. (2000), "Without divergence, there is no chaos. Without convergence, there is no attractor. The repetitive occurrence of divergence and convergence can be considered a metamodel of chaos" (p. 328).

As a consequence, the system's behavior is unpredictable over the long term, because small changes, amplified over time, can result in a totally different and unexpected output trajectory (i.e., have monumental effects that are impossible to foresee).

When transposed to organizations, this view of change implies a considerable reduction of the possibility of control that managers can have over an organization's evolution, because the system's behavior can only be predicted in the very short run (Thiétart & Forgues, 1995, 1997). There is no direct relationship between initial actions and their outcomes over time. In contrast, traditional change theories assume that the effects of a change are predictable and proportional to its size (i.e., direct causality rather than the circular causality typical of dynamic nonlinear systems). However, as Dooley and Van de Ven (1999) note, in a discussion of the implications of chaos theory for understanding organizational evolution, this does not imply that such a system is in a state of confusion (in contradiction with the usual sense of the word chaos). Rather, according to them, the presence of chaotic behavior can be explained by "a causal theory that contains few significant factors that act in an interdependent fashion" (p. 367). Furthermore, they suggest that these causal factors are global, rather than local, asserting that only the presence of macro-level constraining forces can explain the "low dimensional behavior in an organizational system that by nature tends to be high dimensional" (p. 365). The authors argue that, in a large system, particularly one that includes a considerable number of interacting individuals, each one having free will, a unique way of interpreting organizational reality, distinctive behavior, and particular goals, the presence of low-dimensional behavior is improbable. Unless, that is, only a small part of the system (a few individuals) is involved in the process or the dimensionality (i.e., the degrees of freedom) of the behavior is reduced "by significant control and/or cooperative mechanisms" that may be "managerial, adaptive, institutional, and/or self-induced" (p. 367). This means that, in organizations in chaotic equilibrium, actors through their previous actions have reduced the system's complexity (i.e., created chaotic order), and future behavior is now deterministically constrained (in a nonlinear fashion) by the current state of the system (Thiétart & Forgues, 1997). However, as Dooley and Van de Ven (1999) point out, actors in the system may not be aware of the configuration of the system (i.e., the variables and of their feedback loops) or its deterministic nature. They add that because of the nonlinear nature of interaction between variables in an organizational system, it is improbable that the control and cooperation mechanisms that exert global pressures are fully planned or even adaptive (conscious) responses.

COMPLEX ADAPTIVE SYSTEM
THEORY AND POWER LAW PATTERNS OF CHANGE

Unlike chaos theory, complex adaptive systems (CAS) theory is concerned with nonlinear dynamic systems that are not deterministic. Such systems are characterized by a large number of interacting adaptive agents following relatively simple rules whose collective behavior spontaneously evolves toward a complex structure (Morel & Ramanujam, 1999, p. 280). As noted by Anderson (1999), "The hallmark of this perspective is the notion that at any level of analysis, order is an emergent property of individual interactions at a lower level of aggregation" (p. 219).

The view of organizations as self-organizing systems is not new. Weick's (1969) pioneering work on organizing is a good example. Drazin and Sandelands (1992), who adhere to what they call the autogenetic perspective, describe organization (or structure) as emerging "through the self-organizing capacities of individuals interacting in a social field" (p. 231). They show that this point of view is also shared by many authors contributing to the social-construction literature we review in the next chapter. But whereas, in the social-construction stream of research, such emergent structure or order is conceived as a mental construct (Drazin & Sandelands, 1992), in CAS theory, it is an empirical fact (Morel & Ramanujam, 1999).[35] Self-organization is conceived as a dynamic process through which "nontrivial, organized configurations of states" arise from the aggregation of several sites (or agents) (Morel & Ramanujam, 1999, p. 283). The level of connectivity (or density of connections among agents) is critical—too few connections and the system is homeostatic; too many and it can either disintegrate or become totally random. According to Morel and Ramanujam (1999), when the system reaches a certain level of connectivity, it "can display self-organizing behavior before becoming chaotic" (p. 283). Anderson (1999) explains this emergent order as the natural result of interaction when feedback loops exist within a system of interconnected agents. Over time, self-reinforcing cycles linking together groups of agents lead to structured collective behavior. Anderson describes complex adaptive systems as nested hierarchies composed of other complex adaptive systems. Both systems and subsystems coevolve, which implies that, in complex adaptive systems, unlike what we find in chaos theory, where the relationships between variables are fixed, every aspect of the system can change over time. For example, agents can enter, exit, or recombine into new agents, and their rules of behavior can change, as can the nature and strength of their connections to other agents. As a consequence, the feedback loops are not fixed; they are changed by agents' actions.

In addition, for self-organization to occur, energy must be constantly imported from the outside. Complex adaptive systems, like other nonlinear dynamic systems, are known as dissipative structures: They are open to the environment and function "far from equilibrium" (Anderson, 1999). As Brown and Eisenhardt (1998) put it, "Order arises from the persistent exchange of matter and energy. Simply, it takes work to maintain order" (p. 29). Such systems have evolved to a dynamical state, known as the edge of chaos, or self-organized criticality (SOC). In contrast to systems in chaotic equilibrium, whose behavior has low dimensionality, systems at the edge of chaos display high-dimensional (or random) behavior. Yet there is a subtle temporal pattern to that randomness. This pattern is labeled "pink noise" to distinguish it from other types of random behavior (Dooley & Van de Ven, 1999).[36] As explained by Morel and Ramanujam (1999), when a system is "self-organized critical," a small change at time t can produce small, medium, or large changes at time $t + 1$, following an inverse power law (i.e., the frequency of occurrence of changes is inversely proportional to their size). Such systems are also said to be "fractal," in reference to the fact that these power laws are independent of scale. The implications of this property for social systems such as organizations are intriguing, but few scholars explore them in any detail (Levy, 1994). Dooley and Van de Ven (1999, p. 362) propose that "a natural 'scale-free' generating mechanism" might be at work. Morel and Ramanujam (1999) suggest that it could be tested on processes such as learning (i.e., is the same mechanism at work in individual, organizational, and interorganizational learning?). Finally, Thiétart and Forgues (1995) mention opposing arguments on the issue of scale invariance in organization theory.

The property known as edge-of-chaos can refer both to the state of dynamic equilibrium and to the dynamics of change of the system (Morel & Ramanujam, 1999). In the first case, the power law represents the probability of different magnitudes of changes occurring as a result of a small variation when the system is far from equilibrium. As in the ubiquitous sandpile example, one additional grain of sand may cause a certain critical threshold to be reached, which, in most cases, will result in a very small avalanche, but occasionally trigger, through a cascading effect, a massive avalanche. These dynamics describe a situation where a global outcome is the result of a single local action whose effect is amplified because of the interconnections between multiple agents. In the second case, the power law corresponds to the punctuated equilibrium model of evolutionary biology, which posits long periods of small evolutionary change interrupted by short bursts of dramatic change. Dooley and Van de Ven (1999), using the example of innovation, explain these dynamics by the fact that a complex series of events must precede the radical outcome. Simply, behavior at the edge of chaos is explained either as the result of an aggregated response to parallel local change processes or by the existence of multiple, interdependent causes (Dooley & Van de Ven, 1999).

Drawing the implications of CAS theory for organizational evolution and change, researchers such as A. D. Brown and Eisenhardt (1998), S. L. Brown and Eisenhardt (1997), and Stacey (1995) contend that organizations that can maintain themselves at the edge of chaos are more competitive. They are more innovative, which is critical in fast-changing environments. These authors build on the work of researchers such as Kauffman (1995), an evolutionary biologist, who argues that all complex adapting systems evolve to the edge of chaos because it gives them a selective advantage. As recounted by Anderson (1999), Kauffman suggests that if small changes in behavior only produce small outcomes, then the organization can't improve much: It is too rigid. On the other hand, if small changes lead to wildly different outcomes, then the organization cannot maintain any improvement it has made (and it can also plunge to its death): It is too erratic. Finally, only at the edge of chaos, where occasionally one small change can trigger a large change in outcome, but most small changes produce only small effects, can the organization potentially attain a really improved position and, once there, maintain its advantage.

This view is very different from the well-known punctuated equilibrium model of the 1980s, which posits that radical change is the result of inertia. For Tushman and Romanelli (1985), long periods of stability, due to organizational inertia, lead to misalignment that eventually makes radical change initiated by top management necessary. This is compatible with a stable equilibrium view of organizations. In contrast, in complex adaptive systems theory, these dynamics of change naturally arise from the coevolution of partially connected adaptive agents. There is no need for a designer or an outside source to direct the change (Anderson, 1999; Stacey, 1995). Radical change can spontaneously arise as the result of the normal interaction between local agents as the system operates far from equilibrium. In other words, when at the edge of chaos, organizations are constantly changing, and no one in the organization controls the change process completely. Managers can act to influence change (by setting the system's parameters), but they cannot know in advance what the outcomes of their actions will be, because feedback produces surprising effects (Anderson, 1999; Brown & Eisenhardt, 1998).

Finally, Dooley and Van de Ven (1999) suggest that behavior at the edge of chaos is the result of numerous local causal factors, in contrast to chaotic behavior that could be explained by a few causal factors that are global. In other words, while in human systems such as organizations, deterministic chaos suggests the presence of system-wide constraints (such as global control or cooperation mechanisms), edge-of-chaos or pink noise implies a system where numerous independent individuals influence the observed outcome. Although the individuals are coupled together by feedback loops that produce a certain pattern in the randomness, the constraints are only partial and local. Furthermore, while in chaotic equilibrium, the constraints are fixed; in complex adaptive systems, the rules evolve.

A number of authors discuss the implications of complexity theory for management (Anderson, 1999; Boisot & Child, 1999; Brown & Eisenhardt, 1998; Dubinskas, 1994; Levy, 1994; Nonaka, 1988; Stacey, 1995; Thiétart & Forgues, 1995), using this approach as a metaphor. Whether they refer to chaos theory, CAS theory, or a mixture of both, most authors make similar claims in terms of organizational change. Most contend that the complexity approach offers a synthetic way to look at management as the tension between opposing forces such as formal and informal networks, execution (exploitation), and innovation (exploration) (Brown & Eisenhardt, 1998; Levy, 1994; Stacey, 1995; Thiétart & Forgues, 1995). These contradictory pressures, which keep the system oscillating between stability and change, mean that periods of stability are the exception rather than the rule for organizations (Dubinskas, 1994). Some, comparing organizations in general to complex systems, emphasize the unpredictable and surprising nature of organizational change and the impossibility for managers to directly control an organization's evolution, because there are no clear links between actions and outcomes (Levy, 1994; Thiétart & Forgues, 1995).

Others argue that, while organizations are drawn to stability,[37] in fast-changing environments or environments that are far from equilibrium, organizations that remain at the edge of chaos are more competitive, because they are more adaptable (Brown & Eisenhardt, 1998; Stacey, 1995). Anderson (1999) further argues that "adaptation must be evolved, not planned" (p. 228), and suggests that managers must act on the system and its constraints rather than try to directly influence the outcomes. These writings tend to define edge-of-chaos as a mode of organizing that favors continuous change and innovation (Brown & Eisenhardt, 1998; Stacey, 1995). As a result, complexity theory as a metaphor is often linked to discussions of new organizational forms, for example, hypertext organization (Nonaka, 1994) and modular organization (Schilling, 2000). Moreover, it should be noted that many authors, such as Dubinskas (1994),

Mathews, White, and Long (1999), and Stacey (1995), discussing the implications of the complexity approach for organization studies, emphasize its similarities with new theoretical developments in the social construction literature, particularly the work influenced by Giddens's (1979) structuration theory.

CHANGE AS AN EMERGENT PHENOMENON

Although articles discussing the implications of chaos theory and CAS theory for organizational evolution and change have multiplied, empirical work that systematically applies the complexity approach to understand organizational change and evolution has remained relatively sparse. The conception of change inherent in the complexity approach requires that empirical data be available for very long periods of time, preferably over the whole life of the organization. Indeed, because of the unpredictability linked to feedback effects between actions and outcomes, the whole process under study must be observed to understand the change dynamics. While chaos research is usually based on case studies of real change processes, most empirical work on complex adaptive system theory uses computer simulations. However, most articles, so far, do not report systematic empirical studies but, rather, use field study data or anecdotal evidence to illustrate theoretical insights derived from chaos theory and CAS theory (Hurst & Zimmerman, 1994; Levinthal & Warglien, 1999; Nonaka, 1988).

To date, chaos theory has been applied most systematically to concrete situations that are typically considered disorderly, such as crisis and innovation[38] (Baum & Silverman, 2001; Cheng & Van de Ven, 1996; Thiétart & Forgues, 1997). These rare empirical studies apply nonlinear dynamical analysis to test for the presence of chaotic patterns in time series derived from longitudinal case studies. A few researchers also develop computer simulations of organizational processes such as supply chain dynamics and innovative search and test their results for the presence of chaotic behavior (Koput, 1997; Levy, 1994).

So far, these studies mostly confirm that chaotic behavior is found in organizational processes that, until now, were often considered random. Innovation projects and crisis situations are depicted as instances of emergent change. In these cases, there usually is a transition from chaotic to stable equilibrium. In contrast, empirical studies, traditionally, portrayed change as a deliberate process involving a transition from one orderly state to another.

The study by Cheng and Van de Ven (1996) of a biomedical innovation provides an interesting example of such work. These authors propose that, contrary to views of learning as sense-making or trial and error in which actions are coupled to outcomes, the process of discovery inherent in the start of an innovation process is characterized by expanding and diverging behavior with "parallel but separate chaotic branching . . . that creates a variety of experiences with alternative courses of action" (p. 608). According to the researchers, such a process, which uncouples actions and outcomes, increases an organization's creative capacity. This chaotic phase is followed by a more stable periodic phase characterized by narrowing and converging behavior (i.e., a coupling between actions and outcomes that signals either sense-making or trial-and-error learning). The dynamics of innovation are thus characterized by a transition between these two types of temporal patterns, whose timing the researchers discuss by referring to the details of their case study. Finally, while they diagnose chaos mathematically, in their explanation of the dynamics of innovation, they use chaos theory mostly as a metaphor, since they are not able to develop a formal model of the system from their data.

Actually, to our knowledge, only a couple of organization scholars have modeled systems based on chaos theory. One of them is Koput (1997), who develops a chaotic model of innovative search and uses it in a computer simulation to compare its results to data from a real innovation. Formal modeling based on chaos theory focuses on a few variables that constrain the system's outcomes and give rise to chaotic order, in change processes that are typically considered random. In contrast, as will be shown in the following pages, empirical work on complex adaptive systems seeks to explore the dynamics of partially connected multiagent systems.

While nonlinear dynamical analysis of event time series data can also be used to identify edge-of-chaos or pink noise (Dooley & Van de Ven, 1999), most empirical research based on complex adaptive systems theory, apart from a couple of qualitative studies,[39] relies on computer-simulated models. In fact, many scholars argue that what makes CAS theory particularly useful is that it allows the behavior of multiple interconnected agents to be formalized through computer simulation (Carley, 2002; McKelvey, 1997; Morel & Ramanujam, 1999). Idiosyncratic human behavior is abstracted into an idealized model where simple rules can apply (McKelvey, 1997, p. 365). In contrast to models of chaotic systems where a set of equations determines a system's moves over time, CAS modeling involves specifying a multiagent network. As explained by Anderson (1999), such models "ask how changes in the agent's decision rules, the interconnections among agents, or the fitness function that agents employ produce different aggregate outcomes" (p. 220).

CAS models are used to examine how higher-level dynamics emerge as a function of the behavior of interconnected lower-level agents. It should be noted that because complex adaptive systems are networks or connected systems (Lomi, Larsen, & van Ackere, 2003), this work has some natural links with organizational research on network analysis. However, traditionally, researchers have focused on the structural characteristics of internal and external networks (Anderson, 1999; McKelvey, 1999). It is only recently, in part with the help of tools borrowed from complexity theory, that scholars such as Carley (2002) have started exploring their dynamics.

So far, the empirical research based on CAS theory is rather sparse and fragmented. It is more or less focused on two broad themes: first, the implications of self-organization on global system dynamics, and second, the impact of organizational design, particularly the degree of internal and/or external interconnectedness, on organizational adaptation and/or selection. In fact, most researchers build adaptive complex systems models to test and extend existing theories of learning, adaptive change, and evolution at different levels of analysis.[40] However, we are only concerned with those that explicitly refer to some of complexity theory's main concepts.

As mentioned before, the focus of CAS modeling is on endogenous change, more specifically on how focal micro-agents (whether individuals, groups, or organizations), which McKelvey (1997) calls microstate events, "self-organize into emergent aggregate structure" (p. 371), for example, organizations or populations. Among the most widely used methods in organization studies are cellular automata[41] and NK[42] models (Anderson, 1999; Sorenson, 2002). For example, Lomi and Larsen (1996) build a cellular automaton to simulate the evolution of populations as the result of the behavior of individual organizations. More specifically, they show how, starting from an initial random positioning of individual organizations, local clusters emerge from simple micro-level interdependence rules. Such work, while it examines the bottom-up evolutionary process between individual organizations and populations, tells us very little about the organizational change process itself, except as a source of emergent local order.

Other studies, while addressing the issue of emergent order, also formalize and extend earlier work on the relative impact of loose or tight coupling on organizational change and adaptation (Eisenhardt & Bhatia, 2002). The most widely used method for this type of research is NK modeling (Levinthal, 1997; McKelvey, 1999; Siggelkow & Levinthal, 2003). NK models were initially developed by Kauffman (1995) to study biological evolution. These models represent a system's evolution as a process of searching for the highest peaks in a simulated landscape, such peaks being associated with higher fitness levels.

In one such study, Levinthal (1997), a pioneer in using this approach, models adaptation as the result of two organizational change processes: incremental, as a result of local search (i.e., by identifying a neighboring superior form, one that varies by a single element), or radical, as the result of innovative search (i.e., the adoption of a new form from a random distribution, only if it is an improvement over the actual one). He finds that, over time, a number of dominant configurations that correspond to local fitness peaks emerge. These results lead him to argue that local adaptation produces an emergent order (i.e., a reduction in the variety of organizational forms), even when selection pressures don't operate. Levinthal then adds a selection process to study evolution at the population level. This global selection process leads to a progressive convergence of the population toward the fittest organizational form. This simulation is a good illustration of the interplay between organizational-level adaptation and selection processes in the evolution of populations of organizations. Here, Levinthal (1997) uses complexity theory to bridge the gap between evolutionary and population ecology approaches.

In terms of organizational change, his results also show that high internal interdependency diminishes an organization's ability to adapt to a changing environment by local adaptation (i.e., changing one attribute at a time). In a changing environment, a tightly coupled organization's survival depends on a successful reorientation (i.e., changing to a new form). Therefore, in contrast to configuration theorists who emphasize tight coupling and radical change, complexity theorists, applying adaptive learning and evolutionary perspectives, demonstrate the advantage of loose coupling for long-term adaptation in changing environments.

In another study, which simulates different levels of both internal and external interdependencies among elements of an organization's value chain, McKelvey (1999) comes to similar conclusions. His results show that high internal interdependency levels reduce the capacity of a population of organizations to attain higher fitness levels. However, he finds that a high level of external independency will counteract the effect of high internal dependency, by keeping the system out of equilibrium longer and allowing organizations to achieve higher fitness levels. Following Kauffman (1995), he argues that, in coevolutionary multilevel systems, complexity effects (i.e., emergent order) can override selection effects (i.e., order as a result of top-down selection forces).

His study also shows that, in a coevolutionary pocket,[43] incremental change is always more advantageous, and particularly at low internal and external interdependency levels. He concludes that, in most cases, an organization is better off having a level of internal and external interdependency just below that of its opponents. McKelvey (1999) contributes to the ongoing discussion over the relative advantages of loose and tight coupling and interorganizational linkages in terms of adaptation by developing a formal approach with which to tackle them. Other NK models, comparing different designs or configurations (Rivkin & Siggelkow, 2003; Siggelkow & Levinthal, 2003) that influence the balance between stability (exploitation) and innovation (exploration), show that a design implying a moderate level of interdependency (as opposed to high or low levels) leads to better adaptation over time in both a fixed and a changing landscape (environment). While these findings raise interesting issues with regard to organizational design, they don't really tell us much about the internal organizational change process itself.

In short, such empirical studies use CAS methodology to study issues of design, change, and adaptation that revisit the debate of the previous era around tight versus loose coupling and radical and incremental change. Their main contribution is to offer a formal method by which to approach them. For example, they provide a way to specify interdependency levels and measure and compare their effects. However, it is mostly when they consider the link between the organizational and interorganizational levels that issues of change are treated in ways that are distinctly associated with complexity theory as a theory of change.

Actually, most empirical studies so far don't really model the microorganizational level and, as a result, treat the internal change process as a black box. The few CAS studies that, to our knowledge, take into account intraorganizational processes are the simulations of Carley and her colleagues (Carley & Lee, 1998; Carley & Svoboda, 1996) and the qualitative work of scholars such as A. D. Brown and Eisenhardt (1998) and S. L. Brown and Eisenhardt (1997).

For instance, Carley and Lee (1998) construct a multiagent model that specifies both an operational and a strategic level. They use it to study the link between task learning at the individual level, structural change at the organizational level, and organizational performance (defined as success in accomplishing the task). The simulation reveals that loose coupling between operational and strategic levels leads to different adaptation patterns for high and low performers. The results show it is the pattern of change (the types of change, such as reengineering or restructuring, and their sequence and timing) rather than the frequency of change that distinguishes high-performing from low-performing organizations over time. For example, the change strategies of low performers tend to decrease operational knowledge. However, the low performers could not use the change strategies of the high performers even if they wanted to, because of the path dependence of strategic change.

Carley and Lee (1998) define their model as descriptive "in the sense that it embodies empirical results and theories about organizational behavior" (p. 293). It provides answers about how organizations are likely to behave if the theories and the way they are formalized in the model are valid. From the point of view of organizational change, this simulation provides an interesting exploration of the nonlinear feedback loops between top-down structural change and aggregated individual changes leading to emergent organizational outcomes. However, the authors explain their findings on organizational change in terms of learning theory and not complex adaptive system theory.

Building on qualitative research, Brown and Eisenhardt (1998) and Brown and Eisenhardt (1997) combine insights from CAS theory and evolutionary theory to develop a theory of organizational-level change. These scholars are probably the ones who exploit CAS theory's concepts most explicitly, albeit in a metaphorical manner, to explain their findings from an in-depth study of organizations in the fast-changing computer industry. Comparing the innovative high performers to their less nimble counterparts, they find that the firms who are more successful innovators have developed a mode of organizing that fosters self-organization. Like Burgelman (1991), they contend that continuous change through product innovation is closely associated with broader organizational change. The project-based organizations they studied rely on what the researchers label "semistructures." In this mode of organizing, which only partially constrains behavior, some features, such as responsibilities, priorities, and timing, are predetermined, but others, such as the actual design process, are not. There are only a few simple rules, which, according to the authors, operate at the system level, not the individual level, to allow the individuals to self-organize. Eisenhardt and Sull (2001) identify five categories of simple rules concerning process issues, priority setting, boundaries, timing, and exit issues.

They argue that these organizations function at the edge of chaos, which they describe as involving processes of dialectic change between forces for structure and chaos. The authors contend that such change processes exhibit a wide range of scale following an inverse power law. Continuously changing organizations make frequent small changes, which occasionally cascade into major strategic reorientation. Eisenhardt and Bhatia (2002), observing that there has been very little empirical research to date on edge-of-chaos in organizations, compare it to improvisation, a topic that has drawn lots of attention recently in the social construction literature and is presented in the next chapter.

On the issue of adaptation, their findings are similar to those of previous complexity theorists concerning the advantages of loose coupling. They contend that modularity (i.e., less interdependency) allows for quicker action in a fast-changing environment. They describe the process of "patching," which involves agents (i.e., organizational units) entering, exiting, splitting, or recombining, as a quick and less risky path to organizational adaptation. Their research shows that smaller and more independent agents are easier to recombine in high-velocity environments (Brown & Eisenhardt, 1998). They also find that long-term adaptation involves time-pacing, a concept inspired by evolutionary theory. Time-pacing involves "links-in-time," by which managers ensure that attention is always focused on different timeframes and the links between them, and sequenced steps that allow the organization to reinvent itself over time. Their study shows that time-pacing puts high performers in a situation where, rather than reacting to the environment, they set the speed of evolution that others will follow. Their work is interesting because it contributes to defining the concepts of complexity theory in terms of concrete organizational practices. However, so far, little qualitative research extending their work on CAS theory and organizational change has been published in major journals.

Finally, what is the contribution of this empirical work to our understanding of organizational change? First, despite its diversity in terms of both methods and objects of study, the main contribution of empirical research done so far has been to confirm the existence of behavior typical of complex systems in organizations, particularly the existence of order in apparent randomness. By establishing that organizations are complex systems, such research validates the general conception of organizations as continuously changing and of organizational change as largely emergent (i.e., largely unintentional) and unpredictable; these the basic tenets of the complexity approach.

Second, by using the formal techniques of the complexity approach, the empirical studies done so far extend and provide empirical support for other related theories, such as the adaptive learning, ecological, and evolutionary approaches. In particular, these methods allow researchers to observe multilevel effects, for example, between individual and organizational learning (Carley & Lee, 1998), organizational adaptation and environmental selection (Levinthal, 1997), or intraorganizational and interorganizational coevolution (McKelvey, 1999). Finally, the complexity approach also revisits questions linked to structural contingency and social network theories by providing the means by which to study them dynamically.

Discussion

As soon as it gained momentum in organization studies, the complexity approach engendered as much skepticism as enthusiasm. Most of the debates are associated with methodological issues, but there are some more basic questions regarding the applicability of this approach to social systems such as organizations, coming mostly from scholars who don't adhere to the approach.

On the methodological front, there is a debate among insiders over whether complexity theory is mainly useful as a set of mathematical and modeling tools that allow formalization or as a metaphor that provides new theoretical insights into organizational change and evolution. For instance, McKelvey (1997) contends that researchers should concentrate on developing formal models and testing them. Carley (2002) and Morel and Ramanujam (1999), among others, also favor the formal modeling approach. These scholars believe that computational methods are required to develop precise understanding of complex systems' properties and nonlinear dynamics. They also fear that complexity theory, if used mainly as a metaphor, will turn out to be just another fad, as happened to catastrophe theory in the 1980s. However, researchers such as Eisenhardt and Bhatia (2002) argue otherwise, claiming that rigorous qualitative case studies have the advantage of being more closely tied to real organizational phenomena. Therefore, they can reveal the nuances behind such concepts as edge-of-chaos or fitness landscape and help specify these concepts for the organizational context. Sorenson (2002), although he rejects as uninteresting most of the metaphorical applications of complexity in management studies, argues that serious historical accounts of the evolution of organizations and industries can usefully complement computational approaches by providing detailed knowledge of complex cross-level dynamics.

Even among those who favor formal computational approaches to complexity theory, some limits of modeling are acknowledged. The most important concerns the realism of computer models (Carley, 2002; Sorenson, 2002). One of the main advantages of computer modeling is that by simplifying it can reveal important and, possibly, counterintuitive effects of nonlinear relationships, but its reductionism[44] is also one of its main weaknesses. To what extent do the simple rules underlying the behavior of agents really capture the essential features of the real context? As is the case with all computer modeling, the validity of the results depends on the assumptions on which the models are built (Carley, 2002). Some complexity theorists question whether models imported from evolutionary biology, physics, or computer science, such as NK models or cellular automata, should be adopted without modification to simulate organizational systems (McKelvey, 1997, 1999; Moldoveanu & Bauer, 2004; Sorenson, 2002). Sorenson (2002), for example, discusses some limitations specific to cellular automata and NK models that restrict realistic representation of organizational behavior. Cohen (1999), commenting about research on complex systems, mentions the difficulty of assessing the validity of such models.

Some authors have fundamental questions regarding the applicability of the complexity approach to organizations. For instance, Johnson and Burton (1994) doubt whether the requirements of chaos theory, such as low dimensionality (i.e., few causal factors) and boundedness (i.e., as opposed to open systems) make it applicable to real social systems. On a more practical level, drawing on Ruelle (1991), they argue that neither the precise structural equations, nor the long time series necessary to reconstruct the attractors, are present in organizational research. Moreover, they caution that it is currently impossible for researchers to know if a social system has really passed through a bifurcation point. While they find complex adaptive system theory less constraining, Johnson and Burton still maintain skepticism as to whether organizations really can be considered self-organizing systems, stating, "Systems of people in organizations are usually the result of conscious, purposive actions taken by individuals with long and phenomenally complex histories and belief systems of their own" (1994, p. 327).

For the same reason, Dubinskas (1994, p. 365), although he argues for integrating the complexity perspective in organization studies, warns against viewing it as "a grand synthetic theory" of organizations. Finally, Tsoukas and Hatch (2001) critique complexity theory for its strict adherence to neutral "logico-scientific" thinking. Arguing that complexity is a matter of interpretation, they propose that it should be complemented by the narrative mode of thinking, which draws attention to the author's position. These authors point here to one fundamental difference, despite the similarities, between the work on complexity and the research based on social constructionist perspectives presented in the next chapter—that is, the importance given to actors' reflexivity and their capacity to enact new paths.

In summary, like adaptive learning and evolutionary theory, the complexity perspective explores the tension between continuity and change, but in this case by focusing on issues of equilibrium between opposing forces. This approach conceives organizational change as an ongoing process involving a number of counteracting forces whose interaction often moves the system to the edge of chaos or drives it to chaotic equilibrium. In such states, behavior appears random, but in fact follows simple causal factors or rules, either multiple local rules or a few global rules. In the first case, the generative motor is multilevel, with organizational change emerging from the interplay of agents responding to local rules: It is self-organizing. On the other hand, if global rules leading to low-dimensional chaos arise, the generative motor operates at the organizational level, constraining lower-level behavior. But whether the system is at the edge of chaos or in chaotic equilibrium, starting conditions and history are influential, sometimes producing self-reinforcing cycles that were unanticipated by any agent. As well, rare events, which can appear insignificant when they occur, can have dramatic consequences over time. Like the adaptive learning and evolutionary perspectives, the complexity approach is a process theory of change that emphasizes emergent change as opposed to intentional change. This is not surprising, because research on complex systems generally involves transforming data on actors' behavior into simplified event time series, or modeling agents' behavior as the result of very simple rules of trial-and-error learning and of local or random search.

In conclusion, the complexity approach is a very abstract framework that can be applied at every level of analysis and to any type of dynamic nonlinear system. It contributes a vision of organizational dynamics as the emergent product of a series of nested self-organizing systems. This perspective allows us to see inside the organization as it continuously evolves, by transforming it into an "idealized" system whose agents adapt by following simple rules.

Conclusion

Although it can be traced back to the 1960s and 1970s, it is in the 1990s that this conception of change based on a biological metaphor comes to the forefront. The three preceding approaches share a common conception of change largely influenced by these common roots; they all depict change as natural, not only in the sense that it is an ongoing and inevitable process in all living systems, but also as an organizational phenomenon that does not necessarily imply foresight and intentionality, that can happen spontaneously. These perspectives tend to be, as expressed by McKelvey (1997), more interested in the "natural" side, not the "intentional" side, of organizational phenomena, that is, in the identification of "invariant background laws."

Therefore, they are fairly abstract frameworks conceiving organizations as emerging from the action of agents (i.e., a force that brings about a result) following routines (i.e., a programmed procedure), or simply as sets of routines, and where context and history are reduced to rudimentary "factual" elements. Organizational change is viewed as a result of error in routine reproduction, of recombination of agents or routines, and of mutations. Although the focus is clearly on bottom-up incremental change, there is a progression from the learning and evolutionary approach to the complexity approach toward more emphasis on its transformational potential.

There are many similarities in the conception of organizational change between the natural evolution and the social construction point of view, most notably as to the latter's emergent and pervasive nature. However, there are also important differences stemming from its conception of organizations as social systems made up of actors (i.e., reflexive and purposive human beings) who engage in social practice (i.e., situated, not acontextual action). As we will see next, in this case, organizational change is the often unanticipated result of the more or less willful actions of reflexive organizational members attempting to make sense of and act on their world.

Notes

1. Although, in the 1980s, there are a few references to complexity theory (e.g., Morgan, 1982, 1986; Ramaprasad, 1982), it's only in the 1990s that this approach gains popularity.

2. It is interesting to note the number of references to the same studies in chapters on these approaches in Baum (2002).

3. Adaptive strategies are defined as those in which organizations adjust to performance feedback, while imitative strategies are operationalized as those in which organizations adopt the behavior of the most successful (in this case the largest) organization in the same group. Finally, the garbage-can strategy is essentially a random response to different stimuli.

4. Like other authors, such as Kanter (1983), Mezias and Glynn define innovation in very broad terms, including both administrative and product innovations. It should be noted that administrative innovations are, by definition, organizational changes, while product or service innovations are oriented to customers and may not entail much organizational change. Although it is true that radical innovations can induce major organizational change by changing the core competencies required, most of the time their development is done within new units and does not, at least in the short run, impact existing operations; see, for example, Burgelman's (1991) discussion of Intel.

5. In the learning model they adopt, the institutional strategy is operationalized as giving more resources to global search (both refinement and innovative), the revolutionary strategy as giving more money to innovative search, and the evolutionary strategy as increasing the variance of the distribution of outcomes of the searches.

6. Research on intraorganizational learning in terms of networks of members, tasks, and tools, for example, is typically static, concerned with network characteristics that correlate with learning. Such studies do not look at the creation or transformation of learning networks or the evolution of knowledge (Schulz, 2002).

7. The information processing approach, like experiential or trial-and-error learning, is derived from behaviorism and views behavior change as the result of a stimulus–response sequence.

8. Carley uses a nested design where individuals learn first and transfer their learning to the organizational level. Individual learning is aggregated differently according to whether the structure is modeled as decentralized or hierarchical. Her study shows that a decentralized team structure learns better and faster, but that a hierarchy retains the learning better in the presence of turnover.

9. One could argue that March's model is cognitive rather than behavioral, as it refers to the mutual process of influence between individuals' beliefs and the organization's code of beliefs. However, because of the simplicity of the learning model described, it functions more like a stimulus–response mechanism than a complex cognitive motor.

10. Nonaka's interpretation of Polanyi's text has been criticized. Some authors argue that, for Polanyi, knowledge is both tacit and explicit, while others claim that it is impossible to make the tacit completely explicit (Giroux & Taylor, 2002).

11. Indeed, for some authors (Warglien, 2002; Weeks & Galunic, 2003), the focus on replication or retention, as opposed to selection, is what distinguishes evolution from ecology. As stated by Warglien (2002), "Defining and analyzing such "genealogical" entities and the processes affecting their reproduction moves us from the domain of ecology into the domain of evolution" (p. 101).

12. McKelvey's ambition was to provide the basis for a systematic classification of organizations that could guide scientific research. Arguing against the conventional vision of organizational forms as monothetic groupings (i.e., organizations sharing the same set of properties), he proposed the concept of comps (or competence elements) as the building blocks of organizations. McKelvey was mostly interested in classifying organizational populations or species, which he defined (1982) as "polythetic groups of competence-sharing populations isolated from each other because their dominant competencies are not easily learned or transmitted" (p. 192).

13. Furthermore, Nelson and Winter's (1982) seminal work is a major influence on some studies in intraorganizational ecology.

14. Later, they narrow their definition to specify that they are repetitive patterns of behavior, embodied in human and physical assets and routines and easily classifiable to facilitate operationalization (Winter, 1990).

15. For example, through internal growth (replication of units) or acquisitions (transfer of routines from the acquirer to the acquired), an organization insures the dissemination of its routines (Winter, 1990).

16. The notion of path dependence has various meanings and is used quite differently depending on authors. See Hirsch and Gillespie (2001) and Bassanini and Dosi (2001) for a discussion and clarification of its usage.

17. As noted by Nelson and Winter (1977, p. 62), in this case, there are two kinds of innovation: one related to new technology or product development, and the other related to its adoption. As we will see in the discussion, although this distinction is not further addressed by evolutionists, the focus on innovation development, as opposed to adoption by the customer firm, influences the conception of change that these scholars develop.

18. As we will see later, the applicability of the notions of reproduction and replication in the case of routines raises questions as to their appropriateness as genealogical units (Warglien, 2002; Weeks & Galunic, 2003).

19. The genealogical tradition, traditionally, emphasizes competition among organizations conceived as carriers of routines, not directly among routines themselves.

20. It also highlights the fragility of organizational order and will be discussed further within the improvising metaphor in the next chapter.

21. We use the term *intraorganizational ecology* to refer to this stream of research, because Hannan and Freeman (1989) started referring to their work on populations of organizations as organizational ecology and Baum and Singh (1994a) use *organizational ecology* as a generic term to refer to the whole set of nested ecological processes going from the intraorganizational to the interorganizational level.

22. It is interesting to note that such a process can resemble punctuated equilibrium from the outside, with major change followed by periods of relative inertia. However, here the periods of inertia are also the occasion for internal experiments that are really small changes that, if they are selected, can grow into big changes.

23. As will be mentioned in the discussion, this more "managerial" point of view on organizational evolution is criticized by other evolutionists as biased because it only looks at successful cases.

24. However, it should be noted that they are describing a firm that has just gone through a major reorientation during which it was reconfigured as a project-based organization by top management. One could argue that the authors are describing a firm that is in a convergence or exploitation mode, not an exploration mode. As well, the absence of a parallel process suggests that top management will be responsible for inducing exploration as part of strategic intent (and therefore for managing the trade-off between exploration and exploitation).

25. For example, Baum and Singh define a dual ecological and genealogical hierarchy in terms of interconnected levels: job, workgroup, organization, population, community, and ecosystem constitute the six nested ecological entities, and routine, organization, species, and polyphyletic groupings make up the four nested genealogical entities. If, following Burgelman (1991, 1994), Galunic and Eisenhardt (1996), Levinthal and Myatt (1994), and Lovas and Ghoshal (2000), we apply the same type of thinking to evolutionary research in strategy, the ecological entities could be strategic initiatives, business unit strategy, corporate strategy, strategic group orientation, and industrial strategy, and the genealogical entities could be human and social capital and organizational and industrial dynamic capabilities.

26. For an exception, see Campbell's (1994) contribution in Baum and Singh (1994a), where he proposes group selection, as opposed to individual selection, and applies it to the organizational context on the basis of research in biological evolution. In this case, he founds his argument on the biological nature of humans and applies it to a social situation.

27. Indeed, it is clear that postmodernists, critical theorists, and social constructionists defend very different points of view, but few directly focus on the evolutionary perspective and the scientific realist epistemology that underlies it. The brunt of their criticism is directed at managerialism and a broadly defined functionalist perspective that includes some evolutionary thinking.

28. For example, while population ecologists often refer to institutional processes such as legitimation to explain population dynamics, they never study them directly and only invoke their existence to analyze otherwise unexplainable empirical findings (Delacroix & Rao, 1994).

29. A dynamic system is one in which variables at a given time are, at least in part, a function of the same variables at a previous time. For example, in organizational settings, actions in one period are partly a function of actions taken in an earlier period. A nonlinear system is one in which there are incompatible forces or sources of variations.

Exploration and exploitation activities, for instance, could be a source of nonlinearity in organizations. See Poole et al. (2000) for a thorough discussion of nonlinear dynamical systems.

30. Catastrophe theory, which is introduced in the field of organizational change in the 1980s, like chaos theory, deals with a form of deterministic nonlinear dynamic systems. It popularized the term *bifurcation* to explain radical change as an abrupt passage from one state of equilibrium to another. Authors such as Gersick (1991), Leifer (1989), and MacIntosh and MacLean (1999) develop models of organizational transformation built on this approach to nonlinear dynamic systems. Their frameworks belong to the second era, with its emphasis on radical change initiated by top management. Polley (1997) offers an extensive comparison of catastrophe theory and chaos theory.

31. Naturally, a system could also remain in a stable equilibrium (either fixed or periodic), and there is no prescribed sequence of dynamics implied here.

32. While, as Thiétart and Forgues (1995) and Baum and Silverman (2001) argue, such systems typically involve a large number of interacting agents or actors, as Dooley and Van de Ven (1999) explain, because chaotic behavior has low dimensionality (as opposed to random behavior, which has high dimensionality), it implies a reduction of individuals' autonomy and the presence of global control or coordination mechanisms (or, in the words of Baum & Silverman, 2001, only a few stable, homogeneous interaction rules).

33. A return map plots the value of x at time t against the value of x at time $t + 1$ to show the temporally related patterns in the data (Dooley & Van de Ven, 1999).

34. As explained by Poole et al. (2000), an attractor is "a recurrent pattern of behavior" (p. 326), and chaotic attractors are often called "strange" because of their complicated geometrical shapes.

35. Morel and Ramanujam (1999) insist, "The emergent properties we refer to are independently observable and empirically verifiable patterns" (p. 279).

36. Recent developments in nonlinear dynamical systems theory have provided tools that identify different patterns in apparently random time series. Apart from chaotic behavior, which is not truly random, there are also different types of random patterns that are called colored noise. For a description of these different types of noise, see Poole et al. (2000).

37. These authors, rather than viewing all organizations as complex adaptive systems, reserve that perspective for a certain type of highly innovative and dynamic organization. They, more or less explicitly, consider that traditional equilibrium theories of change apply to most organizations because they operate in stable equilibrium.

38. Although defining a beginning and ending point is always problematic, such processes usually offer some convenient reference points. However, as noted by Cheng and Van de Ven (1996), they are constrained by the small number of data points for the type of analysis used.

39. For instance, Carley (2002) mentions the work of Perrow (1984) on normal accidents, and Sorenson (2002) presents the historical studies of David (1992), Kirsch (2000), and Karnoe and Garud (2001) as good examples of qualitative research on complex systems. However, these studies describe technological innovation, not organizational change.

40. In fact, as mentioned by McKelvey (1999) and Carley (2002), early computer simulations such as Cohen, March, and Olsen's (1972) Garbage Can model or March's (1991) model of organizational learning are also multiagent networks. However, unlike the studies we present in this section, which explicitly refer to concepts from complexity

theory, these older studies clearly belong to the adaptive learning and evolutionary approaches. It should be noted that not all computer simulations are based on CAS modeling.

41. In cellular automata models, each agent occupies a cell in a lattice whose size and shape is determined by the researcher. The state of the cell depends on the state of neighboring cells, according to a rule specified by the modeler.

42. Each system is composed of N elements (or attributes), which can alternate between two (or more) states or values. The fitness of each system is an average of the fitness value of each element. In addition, if there is interdependence between the system's elements, the value of each element varies according to what other elements it is associated with. The relief (i.e., the smoothness or ruggedness) of the landscape is, therefore, in part, a function of K, the level of interdependency. When K = 0 (i.e., all components are independent), the fitness landscape is smooth, slowly converging toward one peak; as K increases (i.e., the number of connections between components increases), lower peaks emerge (i.e., particular combinations of interdependent elements produce more sharply differing fitness values for adjacent points on the fitness landscape). In other words, a change of one element in an organization can have a large impact on its overall fitness when there is tight coupling (i.e., interdependence) among elements.

43. A coevolutionary pocket is one in which interdependently evolving organizations coproduce their environment. Such an environment is not the one depicted by Levinthal (1997). In his study, organizations are modeled as independent from one another and subjected to a large random exogenous shock.

44. McKelvey (1997) argues that the complexity approach can encompass both reductionist and contextualist explanations and theories (i.e., the complex behavior of multiple agents gives rise to order that can be explained by simple rules). Anderson (1999, p. 220), for his part, describes complex adaptive system studies as being both reductionist and holistic because "they allow investigators to focus on an agent in its local environment" and analyze complex systems "without abstracting away their interdependencies and nonlinear interactions."

8

The Social
Dynamics Perspective

The social dynamics literature is far less convergent than the work done in the natural evolution perspective. Although in both streams a process view of organization that questions the traditional dichotomy between continuity and change becomes more popular over time, the meaning and implications of that conception of change are far more contested (Oswick, Grant, Michelson, & Wailes, 2005; Sturdy & Grey, 2003) in what is here broadly defined as the social dynamics stream. In the natural evolution school, scholars adhere to realist ontology and a conventional definition of scientific practice that is reflected in the quest for cumulative knowledge in that literature on organizational change. In contrast, the social dynamics stream is characterized by ongoing debates between realists and social constructionists. Furthermore, the view of research as a primarily descriptive and analytical endeavor is challenged by critical scholars whose aim is to denounce the status quo and to stimulate social change.

As a result, another basis of distinction between perspectives becomes increasingly prevalent in addition to the traditional ones founded on ontological, epistemological, and theoretical differences. Now the managerial/prescriptive, organizational/analytical, or critical/revolutionary orientation of authors becomes a particularly relevant feature when addressing organizational change issues (Doolin, 2003; Heracleous & Barrett, 2001). To reflect that evolution in the field, the chapter on the social dynamics stream is divided into two sections; the first presents the radical (Weberian and neo-Marxist) and postmodern (mainly poststructuralist) perspectives on change and the second, the discursive and practice-centered approaches. This division highlights the main differences in the conception of organizational change, while being relevant from an historical point of view.

Culminating in the 1990s, critical scholars adopting a radical or a postmodern perspective each in their own way dispute the legitimacy of other research perspectives on organizational change. These critical scholars confront those who conceive research on organizational change as a neutral and detached undertaking, accusing them of contributing to practices of domination and exclusion (Collins, 1996; Hardy, 1995; Sturdy & Grey, 2003). They bring to the fore issues of power and control that were up to then neglected in the literature on change, arguing that organizations are structures or discursive arenas that reproduce an oppressive social order. Consequently, these critical studies of organizational change, in contrast to the political approach presented in Chapter 6, tend to expose manager-driven change interventions as reinforcing existing regimes of control (Knights & Willmott, 2000; McCabe, Knights, Kerfoot, Morgan, & Willmott, 1998). Some critical theorists, influenced by postmodern, particularly poststructuralist, conceptions of power, question even the possibility of emancipation. The latter, who equate power with knowledge, argue that all actors, including managers, are constituted by systems of power/knowledge relations from which it is impossible to escape, except to re-create other systems of domination (Hardy, 1995). Despite their differences, radical and early postmodern studies tend to show that most organizational change is superficial; it only serves to reproduce and reinforce the dominant social order and to increase organizational control.

By the late 1990s, however, the growing importance of language and practice studies (Reed, 1997; Hatch & Yanow, 2003; Whittington, 2004), leads to the popularization of a process view of change within the social dynamics perspective. Although inspired in part by postmodernism, this "practice and language turn," which parallels what is happening in the social sciences generally, is referred to by some as "post-postmodern" (Calàs & Smircich, 1999) or "after modernism" (Whittington, 2004). Despite the ongoing debates, this movement, which eschews both the deterministic tone of early critical studies and the radical skepticism of the postmodernists, puts forward a conception of organizational change as a generative process, variously labeled narrating, translating, organizing, and improvising.

Discursive approaches, which also have roots in cultural and cognitive approaches to change, evolve from a concern with messages about change (as vehicles for information or as representations of new worldviews) to an interest in discursive and narrative practices (conversation, rhetorics, storytelling) that construct organizations. Conceiving change as a "discursively constituted object" (Grant, Michelson, Oswick, & Wailes, 2005), this body of work comprises studies that focus on how texts enact change and others that concentrate on the discursive processes, such as narrating and translating, through which organizations are continuously re-created (Boje, 1991; Chreim, 2005; Czarniawska, 1997; Doolin, 2003; O'Connor, 1995, 2000; Skoldberg, 1994). In this view, organizations are texts or a network of evolving conversations.

Practice studies, for their part, emphasize a conception of change as situated action. They focus on concrete work practices, arguing that every performance of an activity in a specific work context is an occasion for change (Feldman, 2000; Feldman & Pentland, 2003; Orlikowski, 1996, 2000). Practice theorists also tend to highlight the physical and material aspects of social practice (Heath, Luff, & Knoblauch, 2004) in explaining organizational change. Organizations are conceived as unstable and context-specific patterns of collective action.

As will be argued, the radical and postmodern perspectives present a view of change that straddles the second and the third period. While these critical scholars become particularly active in the field of organizational change only in the 1990s, they tend to emphasize the stability of existing regimes of control and to downplay the potential of actors to make change happen in organizations. Therefore, by default, they present organizational change as rare and radical. The discursive and practice-centered studies, for their part, represent an increasingly popular view, characteristic of the third period. Even when adopting a critical stance, they can be distinguished from the former group by their increasing focus on organization as an emergent performance and of change as a continuous process where the creative potential of action in specific contexts is highlighted.

In the following pages, the various strands of research included within the social dynamics stream will be presented, starting with the radical and postmodern approaches and ending with the discursive and practice-centered approaches, focusing on each one's conception of the organization, of the forces driving the change process, particularly the meaning given to agency, and on the spatiotemporal context considered.

The Radical and Postmodern Approaches

By the late 1980s, a stream of work influenced by Marxist and Weberian thinking (Hardy & Clegg, 1996) and by the work of Habermas (Alvesson & Willmott, 1992) has already developed in organization theory, particularly in the UK and other European countries.[1] These writings, apart from exposing the limits of orthodox management theory, argue that social structures perpetuating inequalities (on the basis of class or occupational status, for example) are reproduced within organizations. While there are a few early calls to study processes of organizational change from a critical perspective (Benson, 1977; Watson, 1982), they remain largely unheeded.

By the late 1990s, however, these critical approaches, although still marginal, become an increasingly influential voice in the literature on change. One reason is that a growing number of radical theorists have taken interest in the issue of organizational change, particularly in assessing the impacts of certain managerial and technological innovations that are promoted as enabling more egalitarian and participative work structures. By that time, structuration theory (Giddens, 1979, 1984) and postmodern thought, principally through the poststructuralism of Foucault (1973, 1980), have started challenging the Weberian and neo-Marxist[2] perspectives and influencing the reflection on organizational power and change (Mumby, 2001). The introduction of postmodernism, particularly, provokes a strong debate within the critical studies community, ranging from authors who draw on both radical and postmodern writings (Alvesson & Deetz, 2000; Knights, 1997) to others who forcefully reject postmodernism for what they view as its absolute relativism (Reed, 1993, 1997; Thompson, 1993).

It is impossible in the present context to do justice to the diversity of theoretical points of view included under the radical and postmodern labels.[3] This brief presentation, as summarized in Table 8.1, will therefore concentrate on the commonalities and the differences between these perspectives on the basis of their relevance for understanding the evolution of the field of organizational change in recent years.

CHANGE: FROM EMANCIPATION TO LANGUAGE GAMES

The critical perspective is characterized by a social and historical point of view on power and change. More fundamentally, that point of view is informed by a negative assessment of the state and evolution of contemporary society. For example, theorists of neo-Marxist traditions claim that the modernist project of social progress through rational-technical means is fundamentally flawed; by extension, these theorists view organizations, which are powerful instruments in that quest, as inherently suspect. The primary goal of radical theorists, as stated by Alvesson and Deetz (1996), "has been to create societies and workplaces that are free from domination" (p. 198). In other words, according to them, organizational change *should be* a process of emancipation,[4] that is, a reform of the social order oriented by values such as autonomy and responsibility (Willmott, 2003). Radical theorists warn against the destructive consequences of letting instrumental-technical reason, informed by profit motives, rule organizational evolution and plead for the increased influence of practical reason, based on ethical and political criteria (Alvesson & Willmott, 1992, pp. 10–11). In their view, the first step toward realizing emancipation is to "ferret out situations of domination and distortion" (Alvesson & Deetz, 1996, p. 198).

As a consequence, critical research, such as that inspired by labor process theory (Braverman, 1974), focuses on the asymmetry of work relations, examining the games of domination and resistance that occur in the workplace and, more generally, denouncing the extensive control that organizations have over

Table 8.1   Radical and Postmodern Approaches

Radical and Postmodern Approaches		
	Radical approach	
Model of change:	REVOLUTION versus REPRODUCTION Destruction/creation of Reinforcement of existing new democratic regime social order	
Focus:	Expose domination, promote emancipation. Research as political action.	
Antecedents:	Neo-Marxism, Weber	
Organization:	Instrument of domination	
Process of change:	Power relations embedded in structural, economic, and ideological control are reproduced and impede fundamental change (revolution).	
Authors:	Hardy & Clegg (1996); Knights & Willmott (2000)	
	Postmodernism	
Model of change:	LANGUAGE GAMES Confrontation between different discourses	
Focus:	Denounce exclusion, give voice to marginality. Research as political discourse.	
Antecedents:	Poststructuralism (Foucault, 1980)	
Organization:	Locale of competing discourses	
Process of change:	Power/knowledge relations embedded in discourse reproduce the social order. Managerial discourse increases disciplinary control.	
Authors:	Alvesson & Deetz (1996); Boje & Winsor (1993); Townley (1993)	

employees (Hardy & Clegg, 1996). A second approach to emancipation, inspired by Habermas's work (Forester, 1992; Willmott, 2003), emphasizes communicative action that encourages emancipatory dialogue. This has led to studies of actual communication practices in organizations in an attempt "to counteract systematic communicative distortions of jargon, misrepresentation, deceit, and illegitimacy" (Alvesson & Willmott, 1992, p. 11) and, more broadly, to denounce "the general political-ethical agenda of society" (Alvesson & Deetz, 1996, p. 203).

For instance, political strategies, such as treating the existing social order or some of its features as natural and self-evident (naturalization), as value-free (neutralization), or as serving higher purposes (legitimation), are exposed (Frost & Egri, 1991).

On another level, critical theorists condemn the role of "orthodox" organization and management theorists who, in the words of Alvesson and Deetz (1996), "serve dominant groups through socialization in business schools, support managers with ideas and vocabularies for cultural-ideological control . . . and provide an aura of science to . . . managerial domination techniques" (p. 199).

Like political theorists, radical theorists view organizations as political arenas. However, in the political approach, conflicts and politics are analyzed as internal organizational phenomena, and the use of power is described in neutral terms. Radical theorists, on the other hand, expose asymmetrical power relations that serve the interest of specific groups and tend to show how they are embedded in specific historical and sociopolitical contexts. According to them, organizations both express and perpetuate the contradictions of the social world of which they are an important component. Moreover, in contrast to political theorists, they emphasize the asymmetry of power relations and the capacity of managers to dominate and "manufacture consent" (Hardy & Clegg, 1996). They are skeptical of management's goals and tend to view managers as the (sometimes unwitting) guardians of regimes that favor their interests over those of the workers. As a result, they have portrayed organizations as relatively unchanging. Their writings have mostly explored how existing forms of domination are perpetuated and reinforced by current structural arrangements and management practices.

Over time, as radical theorists' conceptions and analysis of power shift from concern with mainly overt and coercive forms of structural and economic control to encompass more unobtrusive forms of cultural-symbolic control, they increasingly focus on how ideological control operating on all organizational members, including management, explains the relative absence of resistance to oppression and, hence, of fundamental change (Alvesson & Deetz, 1996; Hardy & Clegg, 1996). For example, inspired by Giddens's structuration theory, Knights and Willmott (1989) criticize labor process theorists for neglecting "the extent to which workers collude in their own oppression by active acceptance of the identities extended to them by capitalist organizations" (Whittington, 1992, p. 702). According to Jones (1999), Willmott and his colleague (Knights & Willmott, 1989; Willmott, 1987) focus on "the relationship between power and identity, seeking to extend Giddens's dialectic of control to consider how individuals' pursuit of self through social identity may contribute to the reproduction of conditions of subordination" (p. 116).

An influential early interpreter of structuration theory in organization studies, Willmott (1981, 1987) emphasizes the radical dimension in Giddens's writings, in contrast to other authors who also draw on his work. However, while

Giddens's (1979, 1984) dialectic of control implies that actors can exercise autonomy and have the potential to subvert regimes of domination, as noted by Whittington (1992), in practice, Willmott's studies emphasize the overwhelming force of capitalist logic and offer very little insight into how managers, for example, do exercise autonomy.

Another important influence in critical studies is postmodernism, which challenges the dominant ideology thesis,[5] in which "power differences per se are equated with domination and are held to be in opposition to reason" (Deetz, 1992, p. 36). Following Foucault, some scholars (Hardy, 1995) argue that power is present in all relations and that knowledge "simply represents another set of power relations" (pp. 14–15). In this view, power and subjectivity are intimately intertwined, the agent/subject being constituted "through culturally and historically specific power relations" (Coombs, Knights, & Willmott, 1992, p. 58).

This understanding of power and subjectivity derives from the primacy afforded to discourse by postmodernists. They take to its extreme conclusion the idea, first developed by social constructionists and language philosophers, that language is fundamental in the constitution of reality (Lawrence & Phillips, 1998). In this view, discourses do not "represent" some preexisting reality; rather, they temporarily create a stable world out of the fluid, intractable, and changing flux of lived experience (Chia, 2003). Every competing discourse is a different way of ordering the world. Deetz (1992) gives the example of how changes in banking from the old centralized site located in an imposing building to dispersed branches to automated tellers produce a different subject: "the modern person . . . as consumer, even of money" (p. 33). From this point of view, all discourses are arbitrary constructions; there is no basis from which to judge the validity of one discourse over another. Therefore, for postmodern scholars, change becomes a language game or a "play of texts" (Lawrence & Phillips, 1998): The emergence of a new discourse challenges old discourses and, in so doing, reinvents the world.

For Foucault, according to Alvesson and Deetz (1996), discourse is "the combination of a set of linguistic distinctions, ways of reasoning and material practices that together organize social institutions and produce particular forms of subjects" (p. 209). In contrast with other variants of postmodernism, the Foucauldian conception of discourse is more encompassing, producing subjects "not only linguistically, but also practically through particular power techniques" (Alvesson & Deetz, 1996, p. 206). From this point of view, the construction of ourselves as individuals does not precede our experience of language; rather, our experience of the world is structured by discourses that constitute our worlds and construct our identities. In this sense, a discourse provides us with a particular social identity that both empowers us (enables us to act in certain ways) and disempowers us (constrains our action). Foucault develops the notion of "disciplinary power" to refer to techniques of power that structure and normalize individuals' as well as institutions' responses. Disciplinary power refers both to direct forms of surveillance such as supervision, formalization, mechanization, and automation that control from the outside, and to cultural practices such as forms of knowledge and training that function as self-surveillance techniques. Foucault argues that, over time, techniques of self-discipline are replacing more overt forms of coercion.

Foucault developed two analytical approaches, archaeology and genealogy, whose aims are, respectively, to trace the rules that, unknown to the actors involved, govern particular discursive practices and to attend to "the forces and events that shape discursive practices" (Alvesson & Kärreman, 2000b, p. 1128). His intent was to take away the taken-for-granted, commonsense character of such practices, and to show how arbitrarily and unintentionally they were constituted (Calàs & Smircich, 1999). As a consequence, most studies using Foucauldian discourse analysis have focused not on organizational change per se but on the evolution of meta-narratives, that is, on institutional or macro-level organizational discourses. Such studies involve a postmodern reading of texts, written by academics or practitioners, to strip them of their familiar appearance. A good example of that research is Townley's genealogical analysis (1993) of the human resource management (HRM) and literature. As stated by Calàs and Smircich (1999), "Townley defamiliarizes HRM so that it can be observed as a strange set of practices that simply accumulated over time" (p. 656).

In this framework, social reality, including subjects and organizations, is constituted through the constant struggle between heterogeneous discourses. Organizations are viewed (Clegg, 1989) as "discursive locales of competing calculations" (p. 101) that produce types of subjects whose positions carry more or less weight, that is, whose voices are less or more marginalized. Therefore, postmodernists call for studies of organizational change that pay attention to the ways in which identities and organizations are constituted through discourse. Postmodern theorists, like radical theorists, challenge the modernist ideal of progress and rationality; they provide a critical assessment of contemporary organizations, especially in reference to what they consider increasingly pervasive forms of disciplinary control (Boje & Winsor, 1993). Deetz, for example, argues that "worker participation programs, for example, can move the work group from interest solidarity to member self-surveillance. No cohort in resistance exists when everyone/anyone can be a member of the 'management team'" (Deetz, 1992, p. 40). However, unlike radical theorists, whose aim is revolutionary, that is, to transform society, postmodernists, because of their skepticism in the possibility of full emancipation, have a more modest goal. Their objective is to expose the arbitrariness of dominant discourses, to reveal the diversity and fragmentation inherent in organizational life, and to give voice to marginalized and excluded groups (Alvesson & Deetz, 1996).

On a more general level, postmodernism questions the basic claim of scientific discourse to be an objective, "truthful" representation of reality. If social reality is constructed through discourse, then there can be no claim for objective, universal knowledge. This has sparked a revision in the way authorship is conceived in organizational studies (Czarniawska, 1997), calling into question the disengaged style of scientific writing that portrays researchers as objective interpreters of social reality rather than as active creators of that reality. Researchers (and their research subjects) are authors of organizational reality, and are also constituted by their discourse in a contingent, emergent, and recursive process. This radical challenge to the scientific quest for universal truth and objective knowledge has directed attention to the little stories that constitute organizations (Grant et al., 2005) and has contributed to a renewed interest in looking at concrete activity in its specific context (Whittington & Melin, 2003), a development that is often referred to as the language and practice turn.

NEW ORGANIZATIONAL FORMS: TRANSFORMATION OR REPRODUCTION?

As stated above, until recently, radical and postmodern theorists had paid relatively little explicit attention to organizational change per se as an object of study and, therefore, had achieved only modest visibility in that domain of research. However, starting in the 1980s and gaining momentum in the 1990s, a body of work on the theme of new management and work practices has increased their influence in the field of change. This research started with a critical reflection on "cultural engineering" (Deetz, 1985; Willmott, 1993), which is viewed (Willmott, 1993) as a corporate change program aiming toward "the homogenization of norms and values within organizations" (p. 534). It culminates with studies on what can loosely be labeled "new organizational forms"[6] based on managerial and technological innovations (McLoughlin & Badham, 2005), such as Total Quality Management (TQM), just-in-time manufacturing (JIT), and Business Process Reengineering (BPR). These innovations, which are touted by some as favoring transparency, decentralization, empowerment, richer work environments, and increased workers' initiative, can be viewed as enabling emancipation by creating a more egalitarian workplace. The interest in these organizational changes is made all the more salient for critical theorists because they are taking place in a context where discussions of sociopolitical and economic changes (e.g., globalization, demise of the welfare state, the managerialization of public administration, commercialization of the professions, decline of the union movement) abound.

In contrast to most researchers, who focus on the efficiency of these managerial and technological innovations but don't question their legitimacy, radical and postmodern theorists are suspicious of the claims of their proponents and of the motives of practitioners who implement them (Knights & Willmott, 2000). Some of their work is an assessment of these new managerial and work practices based on a critical reading of the discourse of their proponents (Gunge, 2000; Fincham, 2000). However, a growing number of critical theorists conduct empirical studies of the process of implementation and of the effects of managerial innovations, such as self-managing teams (Barker, 1993) and TQM (Knights & McCabe, 1999; McCabe, 1996; Sewell & Wilkinson, 1992), as well as information and communication technology (ICT)-enabled changes, such as Business Process Reengineering (Fincham & Evans, 1999; Frances & Garnsey, 2000; McCabe & Knights, 2000), the implementation of electronic data interchange (EDI) systems (Morris, Tasliyan, & Wood, 2003) and of homeworking (also known as teleworking or telecommuting) (Brocklehurst, 2001), and the emergence of call centers (Bain & Taylor, 2000).

While most "orthodox" research so far has linked failure of such organizational changes to problems of implementation (Davenport, 1993; Reger, Gustafson, & Mullane, 1994), critical theorists claim that these innovations are inherently flawed. The work of Knights, Willmott, and their colleagues on BPR (for example, Knights & McCabe, 1998; Knights & Willmott, 2000; Willmott, 1995) is representative of this trend. For instance, McCabe and Knights (2000) conclude their study of BPR implementation in a bank by saying that the aims of this change (i.e., flattening of the hierarchy, increased employee empowerment, and development of multiskilled teams) are doomed to failure because "its form and content, its process of introduction will be constituted and reconstituted by organizational power relations that are both hierarchical and functional" (p. 84).[7] They show, for example, how team leaders in fact act as managers without having the title and status traditionally accorded to supervisors, thereby retaining hierarchical structure while promoting through the team leader role more subtle forms of control. In fact, most critical theorists argue that BPR and TQM do not represent discontinuous organizational changes, but rather reproduce in more subtle and insidious ways (i.e., through self-discipline) existing forms of domination. Even among those who argue that BPR can result in major change, the new organizational forms are described as resulting in an intensification of control. For instance, Frances and Garnsey (2000) claim that the transformation of grocery retailing in the UK is a "fundamental redesign," leading to an integrated network from growers to consumers controlled by the major retailers. They conclude that rather than favoring free market competition, in accord with its official message, BPR has given these giant corporations control over both suppliers and consumers, in the process eliminating alternatives and constraining potential resistance.

The influence of postmodern thinking can be felt in the increasing attention to the way subjectivity is constituted by such change programs, which are seen as part of broader social discourses. For example, McCabe et al. (1998) discuss quality initiative programs as discourses that constitute the identities of organizational members and have the potential to make them fully committed employees, rather than merely compliant workers. Although they recognize the possibility of employee creativity and innovation, they frame it in the context of the pervasiveness of macroorganizational discourses that exert "hegemonic control" over participants and produce "self-disciplined subjects" (pp. 405–406). Barker (1993) shows how, over time, self-managed teams construct systems of concertive control that are stronger than the previous bureaucratic system of control because workers' identities are invested in being members of the team. He argues that his findings are compatible with the theoretical predictions of both Weber and Foucault to the effect that "organizational life will become increasingly rationalized and controlled" (Barker, 1993, p. 435). In the same vein, Brocklehurst (2001), in his study of teleworking, analyzes how professionals who work at home do not seize the potential gain in power afforded by their new situation. Rather, these self-disciplined teleworkers re-create the same work routines at home to maintain their identities. However, Brocklehurst concludes by stating that the new discourse around teleworking is not yet fully developed and notes that it is too early yet to pass judgment on this new form of organizing.

In conclusion, radical and postmodern studies have tended to present organizational change as an act of domination that reproduces existing power relations both inside and outside the organization or as a discourse that, through self-discipline, creates ever-more-compliant subjects. Most empirical work done so far from those perspectives focuses on the dominant control of social structures or colonizing discourses and portrays organizational members as increasingly subjected through "social technologies of control" (Deetz, 1992). In other words, "Plus ça change, plus c'est pareil."

DISCUSSION

As mentioned at the outset, radical and postmodern studies, even though they provoke strong reactions, remain relatively marginal in the literature on organizational change. Until recently, they had largely been ignored by the mainstream, and most of the debates regarding critical studies have been internal.

Indeed, both radical and postmodern approaches are not theories of change in the traditional sense. They are theories of radical change or dissensus as opposed to theories of regulation or consensus (Alvesson & Deetz, 1996; Burrell & Morgan, 1979). As already mentioned, in contrast with other approaches, which try to understand and explain how change unfolds in organizations, they are more concerned with denouncing the status quo and promoting emancipation.

As a result of this political orientation, one of the main attacks from the outside has been of the nonscientific nature of these critical approaches. For instance, starting in the 1980s, authors such as Donaldson (1985) have condemned radical approaches for being antimanagement ideologies and, therefore, not serious explanations of organizational phenomena. Donaldson (1985, 1996a), a proponent of structural contingency, whose work is discussed in

Part I as part of adaptation theory, has faulted radical theorists for failing, among other things, to provide research that is useful for the advancement of knowledge and therefore the practice of management. More recently, the rising popularity of postmodern thinking has generated accusations of nihilism and absolute or radical relativism, which are denounced not only by mainstream scholars (Moldoveanu & Baum, 2002) but also by critical theorists from other traditions (Reed, 2003).

As mentioned before, postmodernism radically challenges the idea of science as objective, truthful knowledge, claiming that all discourse, including scientific discourse, is historically and socially situated and constitutive of the reality it purports to represent. In this sense, all discourses have the same truth-value, and there are no reliable criteria by which to judge their validity. This view is vigorously denounced by "orthodox" scholars, particularly evolutionary theorists, who accuse postmodern thinkers of adhering to an outdated epistemological position (McKelvey, 1997; Moldoveanu & Baum, 2002) and by critical realists who criticize them for what they consider flawed or ambiguous ontology (Fleetwood, 2005; Reed, 2005). The former contend that only the scientific method based on a realist epistemology can protect organization studies from false theories and charlatans (McKelvey, 2002). The latter's point of view is expressed by Fleetwood (2005), who argues that postmodernists are guilty of confusing entities and discourse, of ontological oscillation (i.e., suggesting both that extra-discursive entities exist and that they do not exist), or of empty realism (i.e., accepting the existence of extra-discursive entities about which nothing can be said except that they exist).

Postmodern relativism is further condemned, by both mainstream and some critical theorists, because it is viewed as weakening the legitimacy and practical relevance of organization studies (Hardy, 1995; McKelvey, 2002; Reed, 1993; Thompson, 1993). For McKelvey, organization "science" must be defended against "the anti-science attacks by postmodernists" (2002, pp. 774–775) if it is to develop more legitimacy among practitioners. Thompson, a radical theorist, considers postmodernism a "fatal distraction," arguing that it retreats from engagement by switching to an ironic mode. He concludes: "I obstinately cling to the idea that knowledge and rational inquiry can be modest aids to illuminating and changing society" (1993, p. 203). Hardy argues that radical and postmodern scholars are more concerned with intellectual debates than with action, and she laments the fact that critical studies offer little conceptual or practical guidance on how emancipatory change might be achieved. In this sense, according to her, critical theory has had little relevance for the field of organizational change, except ideologically. This view is countered, as noted by Fournier and Grey (2000), by postmodern theorists such as Burrell (1996), who are explicitly antimanagement and reject all forms of engagement with managers and mainstream scholars. They fear their work on discourse and power will be transformed into new tools that managers will use to further strengthen their hegemonic control. According to them, the task of critical studies "is not to reform management toward some more humane or ethically minded activity, but to undermine it . . ." (Fournier & Grey, 2000, p. 24).

From a theoretical point of view, both radical and Foucauldian poststructuralist analyses have been charged with being too deterministic. As mentioned before, these analyses tend to downplay the dynamic potential of agency, in favor either of long-term institutional trends or of colonizing discourses. Whittington (1992), for instance, claims that even Willmott, who rejects the determinism of labor process theory, does not succeed in incorporating agency convincingly in his studies. Reed, citing Connolly, argues that Foucauldian-inspired analysis portrays "social actors as artifacts, rather than agents, of power" (Reed, 1996, p. 45). Thomas and Davies (2005), for example, note that most Foucauldian studies of workplace resistance to new management practices have been criticized for offering "a highly deterministic and unidirectional view of worker identity" (pp. 685–686). Alvesson and Kärreman (2000b, p. 1147), for their part, lament the fact that the institutional (macrosystemic) and deterministic ("muscular") nature of discourse is postulated rather than "grounded and shown" in some Foucault-inspired writings.

At the same time, postmodernism is also criticized for its influence on the growing popularity of language and practice studies that focus on the local, contingent, and indeterminate. As already mentioned, underpinning postmodern thought is a conception of social reality based on the primacy of fluidity, indeterminacy, and immanent change that is only momentarily fixed through discourse (Chia, 2003). This process view of organization and change is viewed as dangerous by some radical scholars (Reed, 1996, 1997, 2003; Thompson, 1993), because, according to them, it risks disconnecting organizational analysis from the wider sociohistorical context and neglecting or ignoring the more persistent global social structures and the force of institutional power. In reaction to that perceived imbalance, beginning in the late 1990s, a number of UK writers, such as Clark (2003), Kirkpatrick and Ackroyd (2003), Mutch (2002, 2003, 2005), and Reed (1997, 2003), have turned to the critical realist perspective, as represented mainly by Archer's morphogenetic theory,[8] to explain organizational dynamics.

Following Archer, they argue that Giddens's structuration theory, which emphasizes the mutual constitution of agency and structure and their analytical inseparability, as well as postmodern and other social constructionist views that explain social life solely as the result of discursive or interaction processes, "conflate" structure into agency (Mutch, 2002; Reed, 1997, 2003). By rejecting the existence of a stratified reality where the structural level is conceived as a separate entity, they do not adequately explain, according to critical realists, the dynamic interrelationship between action and structure. Morphogenesis defends the necessity of analytically separating action and structure, to better understand the interrelated processes through which both are mutually constituted (Mutch,

2002; Reed, 2003). However, apart from Clark (2003), whose studies of the globalization of organizational innovations (i.e., new management practices)[9] are inspired by morphogenesis, most writings on the morphogenetic framework have been conceptual (Mutch, 2005; Reed, 2005). They have fueled an ongoing dispute with postmodernists (Contu & Willmott, 2005; Willmott, 2005). The critical realist perspective, so far, has had more influence in the literature on change through Fairclough's critical discourse analysis (Francis & Sinclair, 2003; Hardy & Phillips, 2004), presented in the next section, which adopts a microprocessual view of organization and change while also taking into account broader institutional processes.

To conclude, the radical and postmodern approaches are important to understanding the field of organizational change for two major reasons. First, despite their important differences, both adopt a political orientation and, while adhering by default to the transformational (or radical) conception of change discussed in Part II, they challenge the traditional literature by arguing that most organizational change is not radical change, but instead mostly reproduces and reinforces the dominant capitalist logic.

Through their critique, these scholars have influenced work on organizational change by making researchers more sensitive to power issues even when they adopt a descriptive-analytical rather than a revolutionary orientation. However, the increased attention by mainstream researchers to dialectical approaches to change (Van de Ven & Poole, 1995) often means that conflicting interests and power relationships are treated as impersonal forces, one type of tension or contradiction among others, thereby risking neutralizing them (Cule & Robey, 2004; Robey & Boudreau, 1999; de Rond & Bouchikhi, 2004).[10] At the same time, as a result of more relativist positions and less deterministic visions of power, there is a tendency toward "deradicalization" even in some recent critical change literature, as will be shown in the section on discursive and practice studies of change.

Secondly, postmodernism, with other social constructionist traditions, is a major influence on the process view of change as organizational becoming (Tsoukas & Chia, 2002; Chia, 2003) that is manifested in recent discursive and practice-centered work. These studies, which are more revealing of the creative potential of situated action and of the dynamic nature of organizations, are now increasingly popular and, as I will argue, are contributing to the transformation of the field of organizational change.

The Discursive and Practice-Centered Approaches

As already mentioned, in parallel with what is happening in the social sciences in general, approaches focusing on language and practice become increasingly popular in the field of organization studies during the 1990s (Grant et al., 2005; Whittington & Melin, 2003). In contrast to the radical and postmodern work discussed previously, they tend to emphasize an emergent view of change and the ephemeral nature of organizations that are continuously re-created through evolving discourse and practice.

This stream of work is made up of many interconnected yet distinct strands. Although it is often associated with postmodernism, particularly Foucault's poststructuralism (Caldwell, 2005; Reed, 2003), the body of work presented here is less deterministic than the Foucault-inspired work referred to in the previous section. As will be seen, research in this area of study also draws on other social constructionist traditions in a wide range of disciplines. In this section, I will present authors who, although they may adopt some of Foucault's concepts and pay attention to macro-level discourses, also attend more to the microdynamics of organizational change.

The distinction between discursive and practice-centered studies demands clarification. Following Foucault and others,[11] a number of authors define discourse very broadly, as encompassing social practice. Some dispute the existence of an extra-discursive realm (Fleetwood, 2005). Other discourse theorists define it more narrowly. For instance, Francis and Sinclair (2003), adopting a critical realist perspective on discourse, state, "We eschew the tendency of some analysts to reduce social practice to discourse alone" (pp. 686–687). In the same vein, Heracleous and Hendry (2000, p. 1265), inspired by Giddens's structuration theory, argue for the study of discourse and action as interrelated but separate domains. From this point of view, discursive studies could be considered a subset of practice studies, since discourse can be defined as one aspect of social practice (Hendry, 2000). Discursive and practice-centered approaches are here distinguished by the way the link between language and action is construed or studied, although, as will be seen, some process studies straddle the line between the two groups.

Whether conceiving social practice as subsumed within discourse or not, discourse scholars focus predominantly on discourse (i.e., texts) and on discursive action (i.e., talking and writing) in their analysis. In these studies, "acting" is more or less equated with "talking." Or, rather, it is talking and texts that this research is explicitly interested in. Practice theorists, on the other hand, view discourse as one realm among others, albeit a fundamental one, and, in their view, "acting" cannot be subordinated or reduced to "talking." Although linguistic practices are often analyzed, they are not treated as the main object of study. Concrete work situations and the physical and material aspects of social practice are brought to the forefront (Heath et al., 2004).

Another reason to distinguish discursive approaches from practice-centered approaches is that, although they sometimes draw on the same theoretical and analytical frameworks, they also originate from different disciplines and theoretical traditions. For example, both refer extensively to Foucault (1973, 1980), to Giddens (1979, 1984), to ethnomethodology, and to the pioneering work of Weick (1979b, 1995). However, discursive approaches are also influenced by the philosophy of language, literary theory, linguistics, and semiotics. Practice studies, for their part, draw from the philosophy of everyday life, anthropology, symbolic interactionism, and activity theory, among others.

In discursive approaches, organizations are conceived as texts, networks of conversations, or situated discursive performances, and change is presented as an essentially language-based product and process. Studies focusing on rhetorics, narration, or translation conceive change as a "discursively constructed object" (Grant et al., 2005), as texts that enact change explicitly (i.e., text about change), or as a discursive process that continuously re-creates the organization (i.e., texts changing over time). In practice-centered approaches, organizations are viewed as evolving communities of practice, as inherently temporary, unstable, and context-specific patterns of action and interaction, and as contested activity systems. Practice studies, which are a relatively new addition to the field of change, focus on situated organizational action, emphasizing a conception of change as innovating, organizing, or improvising. They are interested in the microchanges that take place daily as people go about doing their work, including making change.

Authors of both perspectives clearly emphasize the inherently generative potential of action in situational/local context and conceive organizations as social constructions. However, they adhere to more or less radical forms of social constructionism that influence their conception of organization and change. They are all seeking to explain the internal dynamics that produce organizational change (i.e., change from the inside), but come to it from somewhat different directions. The "moderate" social constructionists tend to highlight the organization as a relatively enduring macro "structure" that both constrains and enables action and try to explain how through microorganizational changes it is transformed or reproduced. The more "radical" social constructionists, for their part, reject this duality and propose that organization is reconstituted in every moment. They have to explain how enduring organizational changes (i.e., new organizational patterns) emerge from such ongoing microchanges. While the former seek to explain change in continuity, the latter attempt to explain continuity in change. These recent perspectives expose the paradoxical nature of organization and change (Tsoukas & Chia, 2002). As will be argued, this processual view of change and organization has profound implications for the evolution of the field.

In the following pages, a variety of discursive approaches, including rhetorics (O'Connor, 1995, 2000), narration (Boje, 1991; Tenkasi & Boland, 1993), critical discourse analysis (Francis & Sinclair, 2003), and actor-network theory[12] (Czarniawska & Sevon, 1996b; Doolin, 2003), will be presented. As well, practice-centered approaches, such as situated learning (Brown & Duguid, 1991), situated change theory (Orlikowski, 1996), and activity theory (Blackler, Crump, & McDonald, 2000) will be discussed.

DISCOURSE AND CHANGE: FROM
INTERPRETING TO NARRATING AND TRANSLATING

In the literature on organizational change, studies concerned with language and communication are not new. Communication, particularly the use of language, in both speech and written texts, has long been considered one of the main tools used by managers to implement change. In the cognitive approach, informants' accounts as well as official texts are studied to analyze change in interpretive schemes or causal maps. In the same vein, stories, myths, and other linguistic artifacts have long been central to the study of cultural change. Most of this research is characterized by a view of language as a "medium for the transport of meaning" (Alvesson & Kärreman, 2000a, p. 138) and portrays organizational change as essentially cognitive or cultural.

However, in the last decade, the "linguistic turn" in organizational studies (Alvesson & Kärreman, 2000a) has changed the way an increasing number of scholars conceive language (Doolin, 2003; Grant et al., 2005; Heracleous & Barrett, 2001). Increasingly, discourse analysts of different theoretical traditions emphasize not the representational, but the constructive nature of language (Alvesson & Kärreman, 2000a). They are concerned with how language, a structured system of signs manifested in discourse (i.e., the practices of talking and writing and the texts they produce),[13] constitutes social reality, including organizations. In contrast, previous researchers viewed discourse as reflecting or mirroring informants' views of that social reality. In other words, current discourse studies seek to answer questions about what discourse does, rather than about what it conveys (Alvesson & Kärreman, 2000a).

One of the problems with this literature is that scholars interested in organizational change who adopt a discursive perspective use terms such as *discourse, language, narrative, story,* and *text* in different ways and sometimes interchangeably, without explicitly defining them. The definition of terms such as *narrative* and *stories* also gives rise to debates within the field (Collins & Rainwater, 2005). However, discourse analysts, whether they adopt broader or narrower definitions of discourse, focus explicitly on texts, discursive processes, or both in their studies (Alvesson & Kärreman, 2000b).

Our aim in this section is not to describe in detail the different types of discursive and narrative approaches used to study change; rather, the focus is on examining the different conceptions of change that are brought to light in discursive studies of change (see Table 8.2). While these studies all share a conception of organizational change as inherently discursive (i.e., constructed through the use of oral or written language), one can distinguish between those who mainly study "discourse about change," that is, about organizational change as enacted in discourse, and others who concentrate on "discourse changing over time," in other words, continuity and change in the discursive processes

Table 8.2   Discursive Approaches

DISCURSIVE APPROACHES	
General model of change:	**COCONSTRUCTION OF TEXT/CONVERSATION** Interaction between textualization (abstract/global) and conversation (concrete/local)
Focus: Tension between univocality (single voice) and multivocality (multiple voices) in organizing as a discursive process	
Antecedents: Giddens, Foucault, Weick, ethnomethodology, philosophy of language, semiotics, literary theory	
	DISCOURSE ABOUT CHANGE Speech act theory, rhetorics, narrative analysis
Organization:	Corpus of texts
Process of change:	Change and continuity as discursively constituted objects. Organization and organizational change are continuously enacted through stories using various discursive strategies.
Authors:	Brown & Humphreys (2003); Czarniawska (1997); Ford & Ford (1995); O'Connor (1995); Sillince (2000); Tenkasi & Boland (1993)
	CHANGING DISCOURSES Critical discourse analysis, structurational approach to discourse
Organization:	Fluid pattern of micro- and macro-level discursive activity
Process of change:	Organizing as ongoing construction through multilevel discourses embedded in context
Authors:	Fairclough & Thomas (2004); Francis & Sinclair (2003); Heracleous & Barrett (2001); Phillips et al. (2004)
	Actor-network theory, text-conversation theory
Organization:	Evolving network of heterogeneous relations/conversations temporarily stabilized through the emergence of macro-actors (spokespersons)
Process of change:	Organizing as a process of translation where the interests of heterogeneous actors (both human and nonhuman) are aligned and materially inscribed to solidify an ever-expanding network
Authors:	Czarniawska & Sevon (1996a); Doolin (2003); Robichaud et al. (2004)

that enact the organization. These two lines of studies will be presented in the following pages.

Discourse About Change

Researchers who focus on change as a discursively constructed "object" are interested in texts that constitute certain situations as change, which I call discourse about change. Regardless of the theoretical lens adopted, these scholars are mostly concerned with the various types of discourses and discursive strategies employed in the social construction of organizational change as a meaningful phenomenon. They analyze what kinds of change-related texts are produced and their effects. They study change as a product of discourse and conceive change as "a linguistic accomplishment" (Brown & Humphreys, 2003, p. 123). They view discourse as action, although not necessarily the only kind of action, and aim to understand how texts do what they do or, more specifically, how texts about change enact change.

Some studies draw on speech act theory (Ford, 1999; Sillince, 1999) and rhetorics (O'Connor, 1995; Sillince, 2000; Mueller, Sillince, Harvey, & Howorth, 2004), among other traditions. But a narrative perspective on discourse has become increasingly popular (Brown, 1998; Brown & Humphreys, 2003; Czarniawska, 1997; Demers, Giroux, & Chreim, 2003; Tenkasi & Boland, 1993; O'Connor, 1995; Vaara, 2002).

Discourse analysts who borrow from speech act theory and rhetorics are primarily concerned with the discursive strategies used by authors to produce change. Speech act theory provides a classification to assess the effects of different types of utterance. Ford and Ford (1995), starting from the classification of Searle[14] (1969), propose that "there are four different combinations of speech acts that correspond to four types of interactions in the intentional change process" (p. 546). Adopting a normative perspective, they suggest that "initiative," "understanding," "performance," and "closure" conversations form a sequence in change dynamics and that managing the transitions between these different conversations is necessary to accomplish change. Rhetorical analysis also focuses on the discursive strategies deployed in a text, but taking into account the context and the target audience (O'Connor, 1995).

Narrative analysts, following authors such as Bruner (1990) and Fisher (1987), conceive humans as storytellers and argue that it is through the narrativization of their experience that they make sense of their world and at the same time enact it. White defines narrativization as "a form of comprehension that is productive of meaning by its imposition of a certain formal coherence on a virtual chaos of events" (White, 1981, p. 251, cited in O'Connor, 1995, p. 777). In this view, the making of narratives is the primary mode of cognition. In contrast to the cognitivist approaches (presented in Chapter 4), which define cognition as a mental process based on schemata or cognitive structures, most narrative analysts conceive narration as a form of social practice where meanings are constructed in interaction in an ongoing process of storytelling (Tenkasi & Boland, 1993).

Some discourse analysts who adopt a narrative approach study narratives as a specific form of discourse. They define narratives as more or less elaborated stories (Boje, 2001), characterized by the presence of a plot that gives meaning to a sequence of events and by the assumption of intentionality of human action (Tenkasi & Boland, 1993; Vaara, 2002). Narratives are stories of transformation (Giroux & Marroquin, 2005). They are sometimes contrasted with logo-scientific discourse, whose purpose is to convince of its objectivity, its truth value, and its generalizability, whereas stories aim to be plausible, coherent, and evocative (Boland & Tenkasi, 1995; Tenkasi & Boland, 1993; Tsoukas & Hatch, 2001). These narrative studies analyze how change is constructed in the stories told by organizational members. The questions generally asked are what is changed (the object of the story), when and how (the context and the sequence of events), with what intent (the quest), and who are the main protagonists or characters (the heroes and the villains). Based on the analysis of the stories that are told or written, researchers can identify how the narrators create a new identity for the organization and its members.

Researchers studying organizational change as enacted in texts pursue two main lines of study. A first group of empirical studies focuses on the stories of those, usually managers, trying to produce change (Demers et al., 2003; Mueller et al., 2004; O'Connor, 1995; Tenkasi & Boland, 1993). A second body of work focuses on accounts of change either as a collective story (Feldman, 1990; Skoldberg, 1994) or as competing narratives (Brown & Humphreys, 2003; Vaara, 2002) from the point of view of those who have lived the change. In both lines of study, the researcher analyzes change as a type of text and what it achieves.

In the first group of studies, change is mostly presented as a single-voiced story. These studies construct change as a project or as an achievement from the point of view of those promoting the change. This empirical work is often based on official texts or speeches of managers. For instance, Sillince (1999), associating speech acts to the political language forms elaborated by Edelman (1966), such as ideals, appeals, rules, and deals, analyzes the discursive strategies used by top managers at AT&T and Chrysler and evaluates their change discourses in terms of their coherence (the connectedness of their parts and the progression in the ideas) and their effects. In particular, he examines the sequential use of specific language forms (i.e., speech acts) to explore how language works more or less effectively to create change. In another study, Mueller et al. (2004), for example, show how, through rhetorical strategies, different groups within a hospital board appropriate an institutional change (New Public Management) but in the process redefine it in ways that serve their various interests. They thus reveal the rhetorical strategies actors employ to make their discourse more effective.

To illustrate the potential of the narrative approach, Tenkasi and Boland (1993) analyze the story of change as told in an interview by the new president of Planned Parenthood and show how it constitutes the narrated (health practitioners and patients) in novel ways, thus enacting a new organization. In other studies, stories are analyzed in terms of the way they constitute the identity of the narrator (i.e., change agent) and/or of the narrated (i.e., the organization and its members) (Demers et al., 2003), or in terms of how they include or exclude certain groups (Demers et al., 2003; O'Connor, 1995) or how they legitimate the change (Leonardi & Jackson, 2004). For instance, Leonardi and Jackson examine how leaders use the story of technological determinism as a way to justify mergers to the public, thus performing discursive closure around the change project.

Empirically, these studies are based on the analysis of texts as products that are fixed in time. Although the authors generally refer to the general context in which the narrative was authored and the audience for which it was meant, it is disconnected from the unique temporal and situational circumstances of its production (i.e., its writing and diffusion) and consumption (i.e., its reception and interpretation) (O'Connor, 2000).[15] The temporality of change is therefore considered as it is inscribed within the story itself, within the content and structure of the text recounting the change situation.

In the second group of studies, the focus of the analysis is mostly on how change is constructed in the accounts of organizational members who have lived it. Here, the researcher constructs either a single story or a set of competing narratives of change out of the accounts, or mini-narratives, collected from the informants through interviews or observation. In the first case, a single narrative is put together by the researcher based on the retrospective accounts of different organizational members (Feldman, 1990; Skoldberg, 1994). Although the presence of different voices is often explicit in the narratives, they are not the focus of the analysis. Rather these voices are reconstituted as a single narrative, which can then be analyzed as a particular literary genre, such as a tragedy or a comedy (Skoldberg, 1994), a drama, a serial, or an autobiography (Czarniawska, 1997) and/or in terms of the creative dimension of these stories. For instance, the legitimizing potential of these archetypal genres (Skoldberg, 1994), the capacity of the narrative to reveal paradoxes (Czarniawska, 1997), and the political and practical effects of discourse (Feldman, 1990; Mueller et al., 2004) and how it constitutes identity (Czarniawska, 1997) are discussed.

In the second case, researchers put the emphasis on change as a plurality of divergent narratives. Here, the different narratives constructed by the participants in the change situation are compared, to highlight, among other things, the plurivocal nature of discourse constituting organizational change. Brown and Humphreys (2003) and Vaara (2002), studying merger narratives, identify different types of stories constructed by the groups involved. For example, Brown and Humphreys (2003) discuss how top management tells an epic story of success while subordinates of the two merged entities construct tragic narratives. Focusing on narratives' sense-making and identity-defining effects, they discuss how "all three groups authored narratives that inoculated them from the others' viewpoints" (p. 138).

While these empirical studies present the narratives in their organizational context (as an episode of planned change), here again the temporal dimension of change is included within the stories themselves. These are texts that recount a change episode, not texts changing over time. In the first case, while the tensions that characterize the change are part of the story, it is told as a single narrative authored by the researcher. In the second case, it is the contradictions between the stories authored by different groups that are the focus.

To summarize, these studies provide us with different views on how change is achieved in different types of text. The first body of work usually presents change as the exciting vision or the idealized epic of an author, the manager, who is the main character of the story. In this context, the discourse aims at constructing unilaterally an ideal organization as imagined or achieved by the manager/author. Here the organization is viewed as a single-authored text. The second group of studies is divided between portraits of change as "tales of the field" or as a "contested terrain." In the first case, the narrators, mainly secondary characters, collectively make sense of what happened and (re)constitute their new organizational and individual identities in more or less positive ways, while in the second case, their divergent narratives construct competing organizational and individual realities. The conception of organization that emerges from these studies is either a drama with multiple characters or a collection of competing dramas.

What is common to this strand of work is that the researcher as author recounts the change as told by the organization's members. Although the researcher selects what will be part of the narrative (which manager's text, which part of the accounts), the participants are the narrators and they frame the stories as stories about change. The question these scholars ask is what kind of change (e.g., tragedy, comedy) their discourse creates and how (what strategies are used). They analyze the discourse's structure and content to understand how discourse works to constitute change through its being labeled and narrated as such. For example, applying that lens to the mainstream organizational change literature, some scholars argue that it discursively constructs a world where organizational change is viewed as inevitable and continuous in response to a rapidly changing environment (Sturdy & Grey, 2003). The pervasiveness of this discourse is interpreted as preventing alternative perspectives from emerging (Oswick et al., 2005). In other words, this discourse participates in enacting organizational change as an ongoing and ubiquitous process both in the academic world and in the world of practice.

Discourse Changing Over Time

Researchers who focus on discourse as a process of organizing, rather than studying narratives of change, study the dynamics of discourse. This literature can be characterized as moving along a continuum with, at one end, authors who tend to conceive micro- and macroorganizational-level dynamics as inter-related but different processes, and at the other end, scholars who conceive the macro level only as a provisional outcome of micro-level dynamics. The first group views discursive activity as bridging the gap between micro- and macro-level processes and focuses on the evolution of discourse embedded in context. These researchers tend to separate discourse from extradiscursive activity to better understand how organizational change is performed through discourse and action over time (Hardy, Palmer, & Phillips, 2000; Francis & Sinclair, 2003). The second group is exemplified by researchers who concentrate on the detailed study of language in use in a specific setting, that is, in a microcontext. Whether they view discourse as the structuring principle of organization (Taylor, 1993; Taylor, Cooren, Giroux, & Robichaud, 1996) or focus exclusively on discourse analysis as a matter of method (Alvesson & Kärreman, 2000b), they study how organization and change are performed linguistically in daily interactions (Anderson, 2005). These two groups of studies present us with two different conceptions of changing, either as the evolution of discourse embedded in context or as an ongoing linguistic performance in which context is embedded. Another dimension that distinguishes these two groups is the meaning given to agency, from a more traditional view of constrained agency, to distributed agency and, finally, no agency at all (Caldwell, 2005). The first group is exemplified by critical discourse analysis (Hardy & Phillips, 2004) and some studies inspired by structuration theory (Heracleous & Barrett, 2001), while the second is characterized by actor-network theory (Doolin, 2003) and the communication or text/conversation model of organizing (Robichaud et al., 2004; Taylor, 1993; Taylor & Van Every, 2000).

Studies drawing on critical discourse analysis, in contrast to the radical and postmodern work discussed in the previous chapter, present some of the strongest examples of the discursive process of organizing in terms of conti-nuity and change. Influenced in large part by Fairclough's work[16] (1992), they distinguish micro- and macrodynamics and analyze discourse in context (Francis & Sinclair, 2003; Hardy et al., 2000; Mueller & Carter, 2005). As Fairclough and Thomas (2004) explain,

> If we find it necessary to focus on discourse in exploring how the world is given meaning and is understood, we must nevertheless also interpret discourse, and concrete texts, against the background of the other moments of the social, that is, we must put them in context. (p. 382)

For example, Hardy, Phillips, and colleagues (Hardy et al., 2000; Hardy & Phillips, 2004; Phillips, Lawrence, & Hardy, 2004) develop a discursive model that seeks to explain "organizing and institutionalizing" as two interrelated but separate processes (p. 640). Drawing on Foucault, they view discursive formations (i.e., macrodiscourses) as partly determining social reality, including organizations. Once created, organizations can become somewhat resistant to "discourse-led transformations" (Fairclough & Thomas, 2004, p. 383). Moreover, due to the plurality of discourses, which are always contested to some degree, agency is always possible. Actors can exploit the tensions between multiple discourses creatively by moving between discourses, playing them off one another or combining them in novel ways (Hardy & Phillips, 2004, p. 304). Referring to Fairclough (1992), Phillips et al. (2004) argue that "actors can influence discourses through the production and dissemination of texts" (p. 637) and do so to advance their own interests. Thus, while they look at the more resistant aspects of social reality, they also allow for the creative potential of action in its immediate context. Phillips et al., influenced by the communicational model of organizing (Taylor & Van Every, 2000), explore the relationship between the level of text (situated linguistic performance or conversation) and the level of discourse (structured collection of texts whose meaning is widely shared). While the text, in their model, refers to local conversations that only have meaning in their immediate circumstances of production, discourse is defined as made of texts that are understandable across different contexts, that have trans-situational or global (as opposed to local) meaning. New texts emerge from the microcontextual or situated practices that are only partly determined by the dominant discourses manifested in the broad institutional context. These new texts, when (and if) they become embedded in the existing discourses reconstitute the discourses, and the institutions that they produce.

Like Taylor and Van Every (2000), Phillips et al. (2004) also draw on Weick's model of organizing (1979b, 1995) to explain how actions relate to discourse, defining sense-making as a linguistic process. Weick (1979b, 1995) argues that sense-making is retrospective; it follows action. Actions that are novel or perceived as illegitimate—in other words, difficult to make sense of—are picked up in local conversations and fixed in texts. These texts can, through repetition and diffusion, become standardized (i.e., understood outside of their context of production) and, eventually, transform discourse (Phillips et al., 2004).

Applied specifically to situations of organizational change, critical discourse studies analyze the interplay of different orders of discourse manifested in ongoing organizational conversations involving change over a period of time. They ask how discursive practices contribute to the reproduction or challenge of organizations as systems of power relations (Francis & Sinclair, 2003; Mueller & Carter, 2005). For instance, Francis and Sinclair explore the development of an HRM (human resource management) change project in two organizations.

Taking into account multiple levels of organizational conversations (the strategic, the managerial, and the operational) embedded in wider corporate and economic discursive structures and processes, they show the shift over time from discursive activity controlled by the change agents (managers) to a phase where subordinates deconstruct the dominant language of change. They examine how the local ongoing conversations around the HRM project manifest the tensions between people-centered and control-centered discourses and reveal how, through their experience of practices enacting the HRM discourse, subordinates gain the ability to construct a different text on the HRM project. They show the limits of both a determinist view of discourse and an unconstrained view of managerial agency. Through their study of discursive processes in their immediate setting (including the new workplace practices that enact the managerial text on change) and in the broader economic, political, and social context, they propose a view of change as a discursive struggle, embedded within a fluid and moving context, which both transforms and reproduces the organization. From this point of view, the organization is an always-shifting discursive arena where practices of advocacy, compliance, and resistance that are both linguistic and extralinguistic coexist (Mueller & Carter, 2005).

Other longitudinal case studies, examining the evolution of discourses embedded in context, either from a narratological perspective (Currie & Brown, 2003) or a structurational perspective (Heracleous & Barrett, 2001), come to similar conclusions. In their study, Currie and Brown reveal how attempts at applying the new public management discourse in a UK health sector organization go through phases of narrative imposition, narrative resistance, and, finally, narrative confluence based on a common discourse of "concern for patients." Heracleous and Barrett (2001), elaborating a framework based on Giddens's structurational framework, explore issues of discursive continuity and change in terms of the mutually constitutive structure and action levels of discourse.[17] Their study of the implementation of a new technological platform in the London Insurance Market, like the study by Currie and Brown (2003), describes discursive struggles among stakeholders and suggests that the project failed "because of their diametrically opposed discourses . . . and their lack of common ground on which to base dialogue" (Heracleous & Barrett, 2001, p. 774). Their research shows that, in this situation of intentional change, it is the reproduction of the enduring themes and arguments of each group's narrative (discursive structure) through their mobilization in local conversations (discursive action) with other groups, rather than their transformation, which predominates. In this case, a situation that is discursively constructed as a change is shown to be a discursive process of reproduction. Heracleous and Barrett (2001), in keeping with their structurationist framework, explore how discursive structures are instantiated in action, that is, in local conversations. Analyzing the competing discourses of different strategic groups in the industry (market leaders, brokers and underwriters, multinational brokers) over time, they study transformation at the interorganizational level. Francis and Sinclair (2003) and Mueller and Carter (2005) situate their analysis at both a more macro and a more micro level. They examine how the potentially hegemonic effects of the pervasive new HRM discourse are challenged through local conversations within an organization.

Another small collection of studies also focusing on the evolution of narratives in the study of the dynamics of change can be loosely defined as belonging to the increasingly popular actor-network theory (Calàs & Smircich, 1999). In contrast to the approaches presented thus far, it doesn't distinguish between macro and micro levels because of its particular conception of agency and network. Actor-network theory (ANT) is not a cohesive theoretical framework; it is more an assemblage of concepts and models that are always under debate and revision, even from within (Calàs & Smircich, 1999; Mutch, 2002). It originates from the sociology of science and technology (Flichy, 1995), and, until recently, the majority of studies using this framework focused on innovation processes (Garud & Karnoe, 2001). It is difficult to situate clearly in discursive or practice studies. Some authors position it (or translate it) as part of the discursive stream (Czarniawska & Sevon, 1996a; Gherardi & Nicolini, 2000; Mutch, 2002); others frame it (or use it) as a form of critical practice studies (Brigham & Corbett, 1997; Fox, 2000). Finally, a third body of work tends to describe it as a generic process approach to study organizational change and the implementation of new technology (Amblard, Bernoux, Herreros, & Livian, 1996; Harrisson, Laplante, & St-Cyr, 2001; Walsham & Sahay, 1999). Actually, studies of organizational change that draw on ANT tend to borrow different concepts selectively and use them in different ways.

Doolin (2003), for example, borrows from actor-network theory the concept of ordering narrative (Law, 1994), which differentiates it from preceding studies by concentrating not only on the discursive nature of change and its social effects, but also on its embodiment in material artifacts. For actor-network theorists, the division between the social and the material is just a discursive construction (Latour, 1991), and they reject approaches that exclude or downplay the material (Doolin, 2003). They consider that the social and the technical are inseparable, that they mutually define one another. For instance, Czarniawska and Joerges (1996), also drawing on actor-network theory, explain change as "an ongoing process of materialization of ideas, of turning ideas into objects and actions and again into other ideas" (p. 13). Following Latour (1991) and Joerges and Czarniawska (1998), Doolin (2003) argues that "it is the way that organizational arrangements are intimately bound up with the material and the technical that makes them cohesive and durable" (p. 758). However, he adds that ordering narratives are always incomplete and therefore always more or less fragile.

Doolin (2003) uses the concept of ordering narrative to analyze the change of a New Zealand public hospital that is restructured into a number of semiautonomous business units based on clinical specialties. He shows how a new clinical leadership narrative is performed in a series of organizational arrangements, involving the creation of a new role, that of clinical manager, and embodied (or inscribed) in a number of material objects, most notably, a new information technology system. He finds that the mobilization (or enrollment) of the information technology system in the clinical leadership narrative reinforces the narrative by giving it a material basis and gives some stability to the new organizational practices. However, a few years later, the clinical leadership narrative is transformed into a clinical partnership narrative that incorporates elements of the old and the new practices, demonstrating the always precarious nature of ordering narratives.

One of the most popular contributions of ANT to the literature on organizational change is the concept of translation (Czarniawska & Sevon, 1996b; Gherardi & Nicolini, 2000; Harrisson et al., 2001; Walsham & Sahay, 1999). Elaborated to explain the passage from project (idea) to innovation (new sociotechnical arrangement), the concept of translation is described by Latour as a displacement or mediation of the interests of heterogeneous actors to create a network of allies and keep their various interests aligned (1995, pp. 313–314). The network is not conceived as fixed, like a structure, but as a form of organizing. The project sustains the network through the enrollment of actors who, in aligning their interests, in turn, solidify the network by enlarging it and inscribing it in material forms. For example, in the preceding study by Doolin (2003), the project of restructuring the public hospital as a corporation is translated by managers in terms of clinical specialty units. Thus, they seek to align the interests of clinicians by enrolling (redefining) some of them as clinical managers. To solidify this network, other actors are involved, both human (consultants) and nonhuman (a new information technology system), who materially inscribe the new organizational structure and give durability to both the project and the network constructed around it. In this process of translation, the configuration of the network, the translators, the translated, and the project are transformed; they coevolve. From this point of view, an innovation (or change) project does not succeed because it is good; rather the one that succeeds (i.e., that constructs a sustainable network) becomes good. The translation model is, at its core, a political model of change and innovation (Brigham & Corbett, 1997; Fox, 2000).

Actor-network theory rejects the notion of separate macro and micro levels of reality, or the distinction between agency and structure (Mutch, 2002). It promotes a "flat" ontology where the macro level is nothing more than a network expanded in time and space, that is, an ever-expanding chain of local actors (or actants as they are also called), both human and nonhuman. As explained by Czarniawska and Sevon (1996a), "Micro-actors associate, creating networks. As the network's operation acquires a relative stability, the network begins to be perceived . . . as a macro-actor. . . . They are one and the same, usually at different points in time" (p. 7).

An actant is a network of heterogeneous relations (between humans and nonhumans) or an effect of such a network, both a set of relations and a node in a larger network (Brigham & Corbett, 1997). This is where the notion of the inseparability of the social and the technical takes all its meaning. According to Latour (1991), it is because humans form alliances with the material objects they have created (i.e., they become hybrids) that they have the possibility of forming networks that transcend time and space (Taylor & Van Every, 2000). In this sense, ANT is different from previous approaches; it has a different view of agency. Actants are a product of network relations; one cannot think of an actant's power to act, outside the networks of which it is part. The actant is constituted by the networks as much as they are constituted by it. As organization and society are also the products of networks, the work of the researcher is "to explore networks, providing rich descriptions of their development and operation" (Mutch, 2002, p. 484). There is only an ever-expanding and -contracting local network reconstituted at each moment, and no sense in looking for explanation in the broader social and historical context because it is embedded in the network (i.e., a product of the network). This conception of the dynamics of change and innovation portrays organizations as actor-networks or action nets (Czarniawska, 1997) that are continuously redefined (i.e., translated) through ongoing conversations. Finally, the translation model conceives organizations as self-organizing (Taylor & Van Every, 2000) and has parallels to complexity theory discussed in Chapter 7. Because of its emphasis on materiality and action, ANT overlaps discursive and practice-centered approaches.

Taylor and his colleagues (Robichaud et al., 2004; Taylor, 1993; Taylor & Van Every, 2000) have developed a communicational or text/conversation model of organizing, which is increasingly referred to in discursive studies of change (Anderson, 2005; Hardy & Phillips, 2004; Tsoukas & Chia, 2002). This model, which is complementary with ANT and with Weick's view of organizing (1995), explains organizing as a process of textualization. Through this process, a conversation (i.e., a situated linguistic action) is translated into a text that "may persist as a trace and record of past conversations" (Robichaud et al., 2004, p. 621). The authors argue that it is this recursivity of language, one of its fundamental properties, which makes it the basis of organizing (Robichaud et al., 2004). The cumulative embedding of texts with their context of use within other texts (i.e., metatexts) over time constitutes metaconversations (conversations about conversations). It is from these metaconversations (where "you" and "I" become "we") that the organization emerges as a macro-actor, an entity that is constituted through successive and ever more encompassing narratives. As macro-actors are constituted through conversations, some actors, for example, the CEO or the union steward, are invested with the authority to speak in their name; they speak as macro-actors (e.g., "The Bank wants to become a major player in the global market" or "The Union can't agree to these conditions") and engage in metaconversations that, while they are always local (i.e., occurring in a specific moment), transcend time and space. As Robichaud et al. (2004) argue, once these macro-actors engage in repeated interaction, "new sets of rules and contracts also take shape as part of the metanarrative" (p. 623). To illustrate their model, they analyze a town hall meeting and show, through excerpts of a conversation between the mayor and some citizens, how a macro-actor such as the "city" is constructed by the interaction between two "conversational worlds" and how the mayor is entitled to speak in its name, that is, to manage it.

This communication model presents organizing as a sociosemiotic process that originates in our biological heritage (as the numerous references to Maturana, 1991, and Maturana and Varela, 1987, indicate). It seeks to extend ANT by explaining network creation as a linguistic process. Although it has many similarities with Weick's view of organizing (1979, 1995), it emphasizes language rather than action as the basis of organizing and presents sense-making as social and narrative (Taylor & Van Every, 2000). For Weick (1995), sensemaking punctuates and, thus, organizes the ongoing stream of events. For example, actors enact change by interpreting as change a past (or projected) sequence of events. Taylor and colleagues argue that it is through conversations that such sense-making occurs. It is in the narrativization of experience that action is hierarchically organized, that collective actors are constituted, and that certain actors are allowed to speak for others. This explains how organization can be, at the same time, a set of different communities of practice and a single collective entity (Robichaud et al., 2004).

As a model of change, this approach implies two modes of changing (Giroux, 1998; Taylor, 1993): a declarative or monologic mode where top managers, who speak in the name of the organization, attempt to change the organization as text (i.e., the metanarrative), and a dialogic mode where actors engage in actions and conversations that may be translated into text. In the declarative mode, for the new text to become durable it has to be taken up by the conversations going on in the organization; conversely, in the dialogic mode, for the change to become organizational, it has to become part of the text. This means that to understand change dynamics, organizational change, both as text and as conversation, must be studied. That is, we must look at microchanges in organizations as well as organizational change (Tsoukas & Chia, 2002) to explore the different trajectories of change.

The communication model of organizing formalizes the discursive process of change. Although it promotes a view of organizing as a product of local conversations, it is very abstract and doesn't pay attention to organizing in terms of specific issues of content or context. As stated by Robichaud et al. (2004), "we believe the principle of metaconversation applies to every manifestation of organization, large and small" (p. 631). So far, its influence in the field of change has been mostly conceptual. Other studies concentrating on fine-grained analysis of language in its context of use have tended to be more descriptive. Anderson (2005), for example, whose conception of change as organizing is close to the communication model, studies a meeting of a project team and shows, using Bakhtin's concept of represented voice, how organizational actors discursively construct change in interaction and make it real. His research suggests that it is by representing the voice of organizational members acting out the old and the new practices that the change is translated concretely in mundane conversations. Drawing on ethnography and conversation analysis, Samra-Fredericks (2003) studies strategy making as a micro-level process based mainly on talk. She analyzes the linguistic performance of a strategist, recognized for his influence, to reveal how strategic effectiveness is accomplished in practice. Heracleous and Marshak (2004), for their part, propose a model of discourse as situated symbolic action and illustrate it by analyzing a meeting of senior managers who have to discuss a new business model. Like the previous authors, they attend to the details of linguistic performance, taking into account the richness of the context of interaction.

In contrast with researchers who study texts of change, these last authors are more interested in studying talking in context or as "naturally occurring routines" (Samra-Fredericks, 2003, p. 141). They are concerned, both theoretically and empirically, with explaining in detail the microprocesses of organizing, that is, the discursive and social practices through which the organization is continuously re-created. That is why most of these studies can be considered discursive or practice studies depending on the relative emphasis they give to talk and other forms of action in the analysis. Although most empirical work reviewed in this section focuses mainly on changing (i.e., as a deliberate organizational change process), from this point of view, all organizational processes (e.g., innovating, decision making, strategizing, changing) are instances where change occurs through ongoing conversations (Tsoukas & Chia, 2002).

To summarize, this literature focuses on discursive processes of continuity and change. For these authors, who adhere to an ontology of "becoming," "the world is an ongoing flux," and discourse is involved in fixing or stabilizing reality by creating "permanences" (Fairclough & Thomas, 2004, p. 381), including those change discourses that take hold and become more durable. From this point of view, change discourses organize in a temporal sequence with a clear beginning a reality that is in constant flow. In agreement with this view of change, this group of studies seeks to explain how change and continuity are constituted discursively over time, or in other words, how texts are involved in the generation of a new order or in the maintenance of the old. Some of these studies present a portrait of change as an ongoing contest between discourses manifested in situated conversations. Others picture it as a process of translation of different interests in a narrative, which becomes enacted in new social relations and embodied in new material forms and, thus, achieves a precarious dominance. Finally, change is also studied as ongoing conversations through which organizing occurs.

Finally, this stream of work presents two different conceptions of a process view of change: The first views change as involving interrelated but distinct processes at the micro and macro levels; the second views macro-level change as emerging from interrelated micro-level change processes. This last conception, as will be seen, is the most prevalent in practice studies.

SITUATED CHANGE: FROM STRUCTURING TO IMPROVISING

This stream of work has grown in importance over the last few years, although each of its different variants includes only a small group of studies. The practice turn in the field of organizational change has been attributed, in large part, to the influence of postmodernism (Chia, 1996; Reed, 1997). It has also renewed interest in Weick's work, particularly in the idea of improvisation developed in his early work on organizing (Weick, 1969, 1979a), which was the main theme in a special issue of *Organization Science* in 1998. As mentioned earlier, Weick's perspective (1998) on organizing emphasizes action, "the micro-practices that enact order" (p. 551). Arguing that postmodern theorists have only repackaged this perspective, Weick suggests that the notion of improvisation as "a mixture of the pre-composed and the spontaneous" (p. 551) may help us to understand paradoxes in organizations, for example, of exploitation and exploration, routine and nonroutine, which are at the center of the process view of change. The renewed attention to organizing as improvising also results from the coalescence of two trends: the growing impact of structuration theory and recent developments in practice theory, particularly in the area of workplace studies (Heath et al., 2004).

As stated previously, Giddens's structuration theory has been particularly influential in new developments in organizational change literature since the early 1990s. It has inspired some coevolutionary research (Huygens, Baden-Fuller, Van Den Bosch, & Volberda, 2001; Pettigrew, Woodman, & Cameron, 2001), some critical studies (Willmott, 1987) and some discourse studies (Heracleous & Barrett, 2001) presented earlier. Giddens is also one of the most widely cited authors in practice-centered writings on change (Barley, 1986; Feldman & Pentland, 2003; Orlikowski, 1996, 2000, 2002; Whittington & Melin, 2003).

Many scholars working in that vein apply to different empirical situations the concept of duality of structure, that is, the idea that structure and action are mutually constituted and constitutive and that structure is a "virtual order," having no reality except as it is instantiated in action or retained as "memory traces" (Giddens, 1984). They take seriously Giddens's idea that every repetition of a recurrent social practice is also an occasion for its transformation (Feldman, 2000; Whittington & Melin, 2003).

Furthermore, these researchers argue that structuration theory must be extended or combined with other approaches to fully explore the dynamics of change (Feldman, 2000; Orlikowski, 2000; Whittington & Melin, 2003). Feldman (2000), citing Sewell (1992), contends that theorists such as Giddens (1984) who explore the relationship between action and structure have generally been more concerned with explaining how systems reproduce than how they transform, most often explaining change in exogenous terms. For example, in Giddens's theory, the coexistence (and confrontation) of competing social systems allow social actors to exercise agency in practice, thus making change possible. But even this has rarely been explored empirically in organization studies (Whittington, 1992). As will be shown in the following pages, drawing on situated action and learning and activity theory, practice-based research aims to describe the concrete interaction processes through which organizations are continuously (re)constituted by human agency (see Table 8.3).

Change as Practical and Social Performance

The term *situated*, as it is used in the organizational change literature (Orlikowski, 1996), comes from recent developments in the theory of practice, particularly the work of Suchman (1987) on situated action and of Lave and Wenger (1991) on situated learning.[18] First, the work of Lave and Wenger (1991), as popularized by Brown and Duguid (1991, 2000) in organization studies, contributed to the expanding literature on organizational learning by redefining learning, not as a primarily abstract mental process, nor as a stimulus–response mechanism, but as an embodied process that is dependent on active participation in practice. In contrast to the knowledge development and behavioral learning perspectives presented in Chapter 7, situated learning stresses the importance of practice as a process of social construction through which one becomes a legitimate member of a "community-of-practice." Learning is not construed here as the transfer of generic, abstract knowledge from those who know to those who don't, but as a collective process where understanding depends as much on the specific setting (i.e., the physical, the organizational, the interpersonal, and the personal conditions) in which work is being done as on the task itself. Brown and Duguid (1991), also drawing on Orr's anthropological study of service technicians (1990) inspired by situated action theory (Suchman, 1987), and on Hutchins's (1991) work on distributed cognition in a navigation team, call attention to the improvisational nature of learning as an ongoing process of innovation and change. Because of the highly specific and ever-changing conditions in

Table 8.3   Practice-Centered Approaches

PRACTICE-CENTERED APPROACHES

General model of change: IMPROVISATION
Interaction between routine (continuity) and innovation (change)

Focus: Routine performance as an occasion for change

Antecedents: Giddens, Foucault, Weick, ethnomethodology, philosophy of everyday life, symbolic interactionism

	Situated learning, situated action/change
Organization:	Community of communities of practice
Process of change:	Organizing as the ongoing performance of recurrent social practices in context, leading to both reproduction and innovation (change)
Authors:	Brown & Duguid (1991); Feldman (2000); Orlikowski (1996, 2000); Rouleau (2005); Whittington & Melin (2003)
	Activity Theory
Organization:	Interlocked multilevel activity systems constituted by the interplay between object (aim), subject (actor), tools/signs (cultural forms), and community
Process of change:	Contradictions within and between activity systems drive organizing processes and the emergence of new practices embedded in a broad sociohistorical context
Authors:	Blackler et al., (2000); Engeström (2000); Miettinen & Virkkunen (2005)

which actual practice occurs, work practices are always evolving in spontaneous and unanticipated ways. In Brown and Duguid's work (1991), therefore, communities-of-practice are depicted as inherently creative and, in the performance of their daily activities, as sources of continuous change.

Yanow (2000), in discussing the similarities between situated learning and the cultural-interpretive approach to learning she developed to analyze an ethnographic study of flute-makers (Cook & Yanow, 1993), stresses that they are both action-oriented, situated, and social perspectives on learning. Yanow (2000) also reminds us that, in this perspective, learning is not conceived only as organizational change "but as organizational maintenance or sustenance as well" (p. 256). This is in line with the view that continuity and change are not opposites but are the result of the same processes (Sztompka, 1993). She also draws attention to the fact that as well as focusing on what people actually do, recent work practice studies emphasize the language and the tools (including material artifacts) that they use and the meaning they give to what they do. It should be noted that such research often concerns work that entails the intensive use of physical artifacts (e.g., photocopiers, computers, flutes, navigation systems), thus calling attention to the importance of materiality in change processes.

Following Brown and Duguid (1991), a number of scholars have borrowed from practice theory to bring action to the forefront in a social-constructionist conception of change. Starting with research on information technology (Orlikowski, 1996, 2000), this line of study also includes work that increasingly involves communication rather than interaction with material artifacts (Weick, 1989), administrative routines (Feldman, 2000; Feldman & Pentland, 2003), and strategy (Blackler et al., 2000; Whittington & Melin, 2003). These studies paint a picture of change as endemic to organizational functioning and give human agency a central place as a motor of change. We will briefly present their contributions to a theory of situated change.

While researchers studying the adoption of new technologies have been among the first to adopt a structurationist perspective (Barley, 1986; Bouchikhi, 1990; Orlikowski & Robey, 1991; Poole & De Sanctis, 1990), most have focused on structuring as the stabilization of practices of technology use following implementation. Not surprisingly, authors in the field of information technology have been sensitive to the material aspects of technology in their reflection on implementation and use (Jones, 1999; Orlikowski, 2000). Acknowledging the difficulty of integrating technology in a structurationist framework, they have also borrowed from the literature on the social construction of technology (SCOT), which "examines how interpretations, social interests, and disciplinary conflicts shape the production of a technology through shaping its cultural meanings and the social interactions among relevant social groups" (Orlikowski, 2000, p. 405). One example of this literature, which was presented earlier, actor-network theory (Callon & Latour, 1991; Latour, 1987/1995), is viewed by some as providing concepts that allow a more explicit treatment of technological issues (Jones, 1999; Mutch, 2002).[19]

According to Orlikowski (2000), so far, SCOT-inspired research has mostly examined how technologies stabilize over time as a result of the settlement of rhetorical debates and how dominant interests are "inscribed" in the technology, thus depicting technologies, once developed, "as static and settled artifacts" (p. 406). Lately, some authors have contended that it is the ongoing changes in technology, practices, and organization stemming from people's day-to-day interaction with technology and each other at work that research needs to focus on. Jones (1999), for example, in an incisive critique of the use of structuration theory in information studies, states, "Given that structuration takes place in every instant of action, each of which is a potential moment of transformation, then we need to look at use in much more detail" (p. 129).

At the forefront of these efforts is Orlikowski (1996), who argues for a "perspective that posits change rather than stability as a way of organizational life" (p. 65). She develops a model of situated change where organizational transformation emerges from organizational actors' "accommodations to and experiments with the everyday contingencies, breakdowns, exceptions, opportunities, and unintended consequences that they encounter" (p. 65). Building on Giddens's structuration framework, Weick's (1993) work on improvisation, and practice theory research (Hutchins, 1991; Lave, 1988; Suchman, 1987), she proposes the adoption of what she calls a "practice lens" to study change as emergence and improvisation. In a comparative analysis of four ethnographic studies of implementation of Lotus Notes software (Orlikowski, 2000), she illustrates how the adoption of the same technology can be associated with different outcomes: inertia (status quo), application (refinement), and change (transformation), depending on users' actions and a number of organizational and technological conditions. Based on a structurationist model emphasizing the duality of technology use, Orlikowski discusses the provisional nature of such outcomes. Because structures of "technologies-in-practice (i.e., rules and resources instantiated in use of technology)" are recurrently enacted in the "ongoing situated use of technology," they are constantly subject to change (p. 410).

Orlikowski's studies show that technology is not a cause of organizational change in itself, although it can be a trigger for change in particular circumstances. Especially in her fine-grained analysis of Zeta Corporation (1996), she illustrates the situated and unanticipated nature of such change by carefully documenting how technology use, interaction patterns, and organizational roles and structures coevolve in the day-to-day work activities of a particular group of individuals in a specific institutional context. It should be noted that in Orlikowski's studies (1996, 2000), situatedness is narrowly defined in terms of both time and space, what in Giddens's terminology relates to social integration, that is, micro-level analysis (Jones, 1999). She doesn't take into account the larger historical context, limiting herself to the period covered by the implementation of the technology, and restricts the institutional context to current organizational conditions. This perspective allows her to reveal "the essentially transformational character of all human action, even in its most routinized forms" (Giddens, cited in Orlikowski, 2000, p. 425).

In the same vein, Feldman (2000) examines work routines themselves as sources of change. In her ethnographic study of the management of a university's residences, she describes the tasks (i.e., hiring and training routines, moving-in routines, and intervention routines) that constitute the day-to-day operations in this specific setting. Her fieldwork reveals the endogenous nature of change in routines when looked at from close up and in real time. Conceiving routines as dualities, she develops what she calls a performative model of routine (Feldman, 2000), on which she elaborates with Pentland (Feldman & Pentland, 2003). This model distinguishes the ostentive aspect or the "routine in principle," the abstract, generalized idea of the routine as a formalized repetitive pattern, from the performative aspect or the "routine in practice," the way it is performed by "specific people, in specific places and times" (Feldman & Pentland, 2003, p. 101). While routines are generally viewed as a source of inertia, the authors claim that considering the dual nature of routines helps us see the improvisational aspect of routines. They propose that it is in the movement between the "routine in principle" and the "routine in practice" that change takes place. They argue that their focus on routines as performances, in contrast to other scholars who concentrate on ostentive routines or "routines in principle," highlights the importance of agency, subjectivity, and power in processes of organizational stability and change. For example, paying attention to the active accomplishment of routines rather than assuming automatic, habitual reproduction allows them to show how routines are socially constructed and made into "objective" realities and, thus, to bring to light the power of particular actors to make certain performances of the routine legitimate or not. Furthermore, Feldman and Pentland draw on evolutionary theory to explain endogenous change in routines in terms of both unintentional and intentional variations and "selective retention" of those variations, arguing that "performances are variations that are selectively retained in the ostentive aspect of the routine"[20] (Feldman & Pentland, 2003, p. 112). They contradict evolutionary theory's view of routines as being sources of rigidity and illustrate how change emerges endogenously from the active participation of all organizational actors in daily, mundane activities. In their conception of routines as dualities, by drawing attention to routines as situated practice, they explain how routines can simultaneously be sources of stability and change, because human agents reflexively engage in their accomplishments. Feldman's empirical studies, like those of Orlikowski, mainly take into account the immediate situation. In this view, history is embodied in present-day routines themselves and not analyzed in a longer timeframe. While both Orlikowski (2000) and Feldman (2000) acknowledge the collective nature of practices, their models don't direct attention to the potential conflict between the different groups involved. They emphasize the duality between situated action and structure at a micro level. In the words of Spender and Grinyer (1996), they attend to the dialectic between action and cognition, or more precisely between the "abstract cognitive aspects and the experiential tacit knowledge aspects" (p. 28).

Where Feldman's work differs from Orlikowski's is in studying administrative tasks where material artifacts do not play as central a role. A lot of the action she describes is, in fact, formalized interaction practices. This shift from work practices that involve intensive use of material artifacts to work that is characterized by communicative action (Weick, 1989) culminates with the work on strategy as practice (Hendry, 2000; Whittington, 1996, 2004). A group of European researchers have called for the study of "strategizing," defined very broadly as "an activity-based view of strategy that focuses on the detailed processes and practices which constitute the day-to-day activities of organizational life and which relate to strategic outcomes" (Johnson, Melin, & Whittington, 2003, p. 3). As discussed by Whittington and Melin (2003), such a view makes organizing and strategizing difficult to distinguish: "Organization *is* the strategy" (Whittington, 2002, cited in Whittington & Melin, 2003, p. 37). Strategy scholars who adhere to this view draw from a variety of theoretical sources. Apart from Giddens (1984), they borrow from authors such as Bourdieu (1990), Luhmann (1995), and Engeström (1987), to develop conceptual frameworks that, while they emphasize strategy as daily practice, also take into account the wider sociohistorical context (Whittington & Melin, 2003).

However, this work is only beginning, and much of it consists of conceptual developments that have yet to be applied empirically. In one rare ethnographic study of strategizing, Rouleau (2005) builds on previous work on sense-making and sense-giving (Gioia & Chittipeddi, 1991) to examine the micropractices of middle managers implementing change concretely in their daily work. Focusing on the practical and social aspects of strategic processes, she analyzes conversations and routines of middle managers at work. She identifies a number of practices such as translating, justifying, overcoding,[21] and disciplining, where managers draw on their tacit knowledge and cultural resources to enact strategic change.

A few researchers have also been inspired by Engeström's activity theory[22] in their empirical studies of strategy development practices (Blackler et al., 2000; Jarzabkowski, 2003). Like Lave and Wenger's (1991) situated learning theory, presented earlier, activity theory is based on the work of Vygotsky, the Russian psychologist. It is characterized by a cultural-historical perspective and considers extended temporal and spatial frames. Some parallels can be drawn between activity theory, structuration theory, ANT, and the communication model of organizing (Blackler et al., 2000; Groleau, 2006; Miettinen & Virkkunen, 2005). Engeström (2000), building on Vygotsky's work, has elaborated activity theory to make it more powerful as a framework that can explain change. To the original trio of subject (the actor), object (the enduring purpose driving the activity), and tools and signs (cultural forms that support situated action and link it to the larger historical and cultural context), he adds another level, that of community, with its associated concepts of rules and division of labor, thus reconceptualizing the activity system as multivoiced (Groleau, 2006). The interaction between the subject and the community in the attainment of the object, because of the different points of view and interests present in the community, implies contradictions. Thus activity systems have built-in tensions that drive their transformation (Engeström, 2000). Activity theory, more than structuration theory, builds on the notion of contradiction to explain change. Contradictions are described not only as the result of confrontations between activity systems, but as endogenous to the activity system itself. According to Jarzabkowski (2003), "When interactions with other constituents and shared activity break down due to contradictions and contested interpretations, practices serve as mediators . . . to effect changes" (p. 27). Studies inspired by activity theory, so far, have used this framework very differently. Jarzabkowski (2003), for example, adopts a simplified version to study formal strategy practices such as resource allocation and direction setting. She analyses how such practices mediate contradictions between constituents and make change possible. In contrast to Orlikowski's (2000) and Feldman's (2000) models, activity theory, particularly as it is applied by Engeström,[23] highlights the coexistence of multiple and divergent points of view. By explicitly considering multiple levels, such as the subject and the community, it allows the scholar to explicitly take into consideration the dialectic between the whole and the parts, as well as the dialectic between practice and cognition (Spender & Grinyer, 1996). As Jarzabkowski (2003) describes it, strategy work concretely involves committee members engaging in talk about past and future interpretations of strategy. This is echoed by Miettinen and Virkkunen (2005), who propose the concepts of epistemic objects ("open-ended projections") (p. 438) and retooling ("the shared creation of artifacts used as a means of reflecting and practical transformation of activity") (p. 443) as both theoretical explanation and practical means to effect change. They illustrate these ideas with an action-research study of a change of practices within a public agency responsible for occupational health and safety inspection. They argue that activity theory has more potential than other practice-based approaches, which rely too much on the notion of routine and focus too much on the subject, to explain "how historically new forms of practice emerge" (p. 441).

To summarize, most practice-based approaches, like many discursive approaches, conceive change as the other face of reproduction in organizing processes. But rather than explaining change mostly in terms of discursive practices and their effects, they call attention to other forms of action, most notably work routines. They are also, like actor-network theory, more sensitive to the role of material artifacts in processes of continuity and change, as well as to the physical dimension of action. Most practice studies of change have focused on the emergent nature of change resulting from the always-different conditions of action. They portray organizational change, even if it is in the context of a deliberate major change intervention, as the emergent and relatively indeterminate effect of microchanges that are more or less intentional.

Thus, while human agency is at the center of their conception of change, it is always more or less dispersed and potentially conflictual. However, particularly in empirical work, it is the convergent effect of such agency, rather than its possibly divergent results, that is illustrated in organizational change studies. Situated change theory, thus, bridges transformational and emergent views of change, by showing how deliberate radical change is integrated and translated in the ongoing daily flux of events, that is, the continuous dynamics of change.

DISCUSSION

It is difficult to summarize the reactions to the practice and language turn in the field of organizational change. Because of its relative novelty and the fact that it refers to a collection of approaches that are so varied, aside from a few general observations most discussions relate to specific aspects that only concern a very small number of studies. We will start with the more general critiques that are addressed to these approaches and then summarize the comments directed to specific discursive or practice-centered approaches.

It is clear that one of the main reservations that mainstream organizational scholars and some critical scholars share about discursive and practice-centered approaches is their social constructionist ontology. As mentioned in the discussion of postmodernism, both mainstream and critical scholars who adopt a realist ontology reject the social constructionist position, arguing that it is not sound epistemologically (Fleetwood, 2005; McKelvey, 1997; Moldoveanu & Baum, 2002). Although most of the authors classified in the discursive and practice approaches are less radical in their epistemological stance than postmodernists (Hatch & Yanow, 2003, p. 79), mainstream scholars question the scientific value of this work. Critical scholars, for their part, refuse to see the status of organizations reduced "to an effect of language" or, more generally, structure (i.e., the social and material conditions that constrain agency) relegated to virtual reality (Reed, 2003).

As a result, critical realists, most notably Reed (1996, 1997, 2003), have been particularly vocal in their critique of these approaches' tendency to resolve the theoretical debate between agency and structure in favor of agency and, thus, to neglect the importance of structure. Reed (1996), for example, warns that such approaches with their "seeming obsession with micro-level processes and practices" (p. 42) lose their capacity to take into account the interaction between situated practices and the more enduring social structures when explaining organizational change.

As we have seen, there is a great variety within this stream of work between approaches such as ANT or situated action theory, which totally dismiss the separation between agency and structure, and others, such as critical discourse analysis, structuration theory, and activity theory, which try to reconceptualize their mutual constitution. However, it should be noted that this mutual constitution is very rarely, if ever, studied empirically. Although a few studies of change link the evolution of local practices to the larger historical and social context, they don't analyze the influence of situated action on the broader dynamics beyond, and most times not even on, organizational dynamics.

As Alvesson and Kärreman (2000b), discussing critical discourse analysis, contend, studying the link between the two levels of analysis is very difficult to achieve because of the "inherent tension" between them. The level of discursive practice is interested in interactions studied at close range in all their richness and variety, while distance and time are needed to reveal the structuration of discourse as a more universal macro-level phenomenon.

In terms of agency, some of these approaches have also been criticized for presenting a view of change that, although it emphasizes the creative potential of action, either atomizes agency or treats actors as mere effects of micro-processes of organizing (Reed, 1997).

For instance, Mutch (2002), a critical realist seeking to incorporate elements of actor-network theory in the analysis of information technology (IT), criticizes ANT for its flat conception of the actor. He contends that by treating humans and nonhumans symmetrically, as products of networks, ANT reduces the value of human beings, assimilating them with machines as "centres of calculation" (p. 490) and neglecting their capacity for reflexivity and emotion. Caldwell (2005), for his part, discussing what he labels the distributed or "conjoint" form of agency characterizing approaches such as situated learning theory and self-organizing models, questions their idealized vision of "order without control." He criticizes this conception on the grounds that it excludes the more intangible forms of institutionalized control that channel microchanges into collective action. As a critical realist, he also challenges those constructionist approaches that define the subject as a product or an effect of processual dynamics for their "eclipse of the subject" (p. 110) and their negation of structure and history. He claims, that "change cannot be explained or analyzed in purely processual terms" (p. 104). He further argues that this conception of change without agency and structure risks dissolving the field of organizational change in terms of both its disciplinary object and its empirical research subject (p. 111), an issue that I will come back to later.

This view is echoed by Azevedo (2002), a realist of the natural evolution tradition, who contends that an ontology of becoming (or what she calls a process metaphysics) is compatible with "the coexistence of many relatively autonomous layers of reality" (p. 727). She argues that "*to perceive change at all, we must create a stable background or framework with which to compare it*" (p. 727, italics in original) and claims that the preferred framework is spatiotemporal context (i.e., macro-level context provides the stability against which micro-level change can be assessed).

On the other hand, critical scholars such as Willmott and his colleagues (Contu & Willmott, 2003; Ezzamel & Willmott, 2004; Lok & Willmott, 2006), whose position is inspired by poststructuralism, criticize most discursive and practice frameworks for neglecting power issues. They also disagree with the proponents of these frameworks on their conception of the subject, which is reflected in their focus on agents' intentional action in explaining change. For example, Lok and Willmott (2006) challenge the critical discourse analysis model of Phillips et al. (2004) because of, among other things, what they label as its centered view of agency. Contu and Willmott also criticize situated learning theory as it has been popularized by Brown and Duguid (1991) and Wenger (1998) for failing to take into account the radical and critical aspects of Lave and Wenger's (1991) original contribution. They recommend that more attention be paid to the power relations in which learning practices are embedded in capitalist work organizations.

Finally, Ezzamel and Willmott (2004), in a paper promoting the use of Foucauldian discursive analysis to study strategy, challenge the strategy practice (or strategizing) perspective advocated by Whittington (2003) for what they see as its neglect of culture and politics in favor of skills and tools, as well as its objectivist point of view.

There are also more specific theoretical debates within and between discursive and practice-centered perspectives that were alluded to earlier. For instance, some forms of discourse analysis are accused of emphasizing talk and text to the exclusion of everything else (Alvesson & Kärreman, 2000b; Sturdy & Grey, 2003), while some authors (Miettinen & Virkkunen, 2005; Weick, 1998) challenge the way the concept of routine is used to explain change in some practice studies. Weick (1998), for example, complains that the concept of routine loses its explanatory power when it is stretched to include improvisation, because it becomes less precise conceptually (p. 551). Miettinen and Vikkunen (2005), for their part, argue that the concept of routine cannot explain organizational continuity and change because it tends to omit the evolving historical and cultural context, the role of individuals, their changing purpose, and future-oriented agency.

Finally, as part of the debates surrounding them, the discursive and practice-centered approaches have fueled a reflection on the nature of change that has led to a new conception with radical consequences. Because most of these approaches reflect an ontology of becoming, they reveal the paradoxical nature of change. On one side, changing as organizing is an ongoing process of organizational renewal. Here, nothing is fixed and organization is an emergent discursive and practical performance. On the other side, change is a new order that punctuates an ongoing flux. Whether it is seen as a discursive construction or as institutionalized structures, it is an interruption in the flow of events, a "metachange." Unlike the concept of second-order change that is opposed to first-order change in the previous periods, a metachange, in this view, is both at the same time: a "change of changes."

As a result of this process view of change, discursive and practice-centered approaches have directed increasing attention to the issue of context in organizational change analysis, as well as stimulated a vigorous debate on the question of agency. But perhaps more important, they have contributed to a redefinition of the field, by leading to an increasing dissolution of the boundaries between change studies and organization studies.

Conclusion

This chapter provides an overview of the critical and postmodern approaches, as well as the discursive and practice-centered approaches, which represent very different perspectives on change. However, although they engage in a lively discussion (fueled mainly by the different factions of critical orientation) over the conception of change and the direction the field should take, it should be noted that they tackle research on change with similar questions regarding the nature of organization, structure, and agency.

These approaches all explain organizational change (or the lack of it) in terms of social interaction, whether power struggles, language games, or situated discursive, social, and material practices. They are also interested in exploring more profoundly the nature of agency as it relates to issues of subjectivity and identity, as well as structure and history. In this sense, they are fundamentally different from the natural evolution perspective.

However, all these approaches contribute to the redefinition of the field of change in the 1990s. For example, the radical and postmodern approaches, as a consequence of their relatively determinist stance and political orientation, adopt a transformational view of change, while the discursive and practice-centered approaches develop a more or less "extreme" process view of change. Yet each in its own way challenges the traditional conception of change, arguing that it is an illusion that they explain as a question of either ideology or ontology.

For the critical and postmodern scholars reviewed previously, there is only reproduction; for discourse and practice analysts, there is only change. When their arguments are pushed to their limits, change ultimately disappears as an object of study. For instance, radical and postmodern studies of popular change programs show them to be more or less deliberate attempts at reinforcing existing organizational structures or discourses, which make employees even more compliant. Therefore, to study organizational change is to study reproduction, and the real objective should be to find ways to really effect change, that is, to facilitate emancipation.

Discursive and practice studies, for their part, show that change is everywhere. And, if one agrees with radical social constructionists, change is all there is. What is labeled and viewed as change by organizational members is, paradoxically, a way of stabilizing an ongoing flux of events. Thus, change, as we know it intuitively, is not really change. And if change is all there is, it ceases to be an interesting object of study in its own right, because there is nothing to say about it, if it can't be compared to or distinguished from anything. How we create (the illusion of) stability or continuity, then, becomes the important object of study.

Finally, even if we adopt a more moderate social-constructionist posture, the traditional definition of the field of change is questioned. Once the conception of stability and change as the outcomes of all organizational processes establishes its dominance, the study of change becomes the study of organizing and, in a sense, everyone's object. One can wonder what happens to the field of change as it invades the whole territory. And it is clear that discourse and practice studies of change, together with the natural evolution stream, have contributed to the increased dominance of this process view at the beginning of the 21st century.

Notes

1. For an explanation of why this is so, see Fournier and Grey's interesting account (2000).

2. Neo-Marxism is broadly defined to include labor process theory, the Frankfurt school of critical theory, particularly Habermas's work, and Gramsci's hegemony theory (Fournier & Grey, 2000).

3. See Alvesson and Deetz (1996, 2000), Fournier and Grey (2000), Hardy and Clegg (1996), and Mumby (2001) for reviews of critical approaches in organization studies and discussions of the debates within that subdiscipline.

4. Alvesson and Deetz (1996) rightfully note that organizational theory of the managerialist orientation, which they label normative discourse, also pursues emancipation, but of a progressive kind, consistent with the modernist project.

5. Simply put, critiques based on the dominant ideology thesis explain the consent of the oppressed (for example, the workers) as a result of false consciousness or distorted communication. See Deetz (1992) for a more detailed explanation.

6. For example, this research is a critique of organizational arrangements that are broadly referred to as the postmodern, postindustrial, post-Fordist and post-Taylorist organization.

7. Although these authors refer to Foucault's concept of power in their presentation of BPR, their analysis is more radical than postmodern (i.e., it is more concerned with revealing the way in which existing structural inequalities are reproduced through BPR than in exploring how subjects and objects are created through discourse, how alternative meanings are suppressed and certain voices marginalized).

8. As will be discussed later, while structuration theory emphasizes the mutual constitution of agency and structure and rejects the existence of the structural level as a separate entity, morphogenesis defends its analytical necessity and focuses on the dynamic interrelationship between action and structure.

9. His work analyzes the emergence and diffusion of new organizational practices rather than organizational change.

10. In a sense, these dialectical approaches have much in common with complexity theory, discussed in the preceding chapter, which defines complex systems as involving contradictory forces that can engender both stability/order (reproduction) and instability/disorder (transformation).

11. This view can be traced back to Wittgenstein, as extended by Foucault (see Alvesson & Deetz, 1996; Fox, 2000).

12. As will be discussed later, depending on how it is interpreted and used, translation or actor-network theory could also be included in practice-based approaches (Gherardi, 2000; Mutch, 2002).

13. These elements constitute the basic core of the definition of discourse, although some define it more broadly, as mentioned earlier.

14. Searle (1969) distinguishes five types of speech acts: assertives (e.g., evaluations, opinions, excuses), directives (e.g., requests, orders), commissives (promises), expressives (e.g., apologies, worries, wishes), and declarations (e.g., announcing a promotion, a strike).

15. This research takes advantage of the fact that a story, whether spoken or written, is portable; it can be reproduced and reinterpreted at will. For example, the letter to employees that is analyzed is exactly the same letter that was read by employees (i.e., the same words on the same physical support), but it is read/interpreted in a different context of consumption.

16. In one of his recent texts (Fairclough & Thomas, 2004), Fairclough says that he advocates a "'moderate' version of social constructivism that recognizes both the performative power of discourse, and the intransitivity of the socially constructed world" (p. 383). This is consistent with a critical realist position (Willmott, 2005, p. 773) that accepts the duality between action and structure, in opposition to Willmott and others (Contu & Willmott, 2005; Willmott, 2005) who adopt a more "radical" form of social constructionism and view both agency and structure as "products of particular discursive articulations" (Willmott, 2005, p. 773).

17. As mentioned in Chapter 6, Giddens's structuration theory (1984) argues that action and structure are mutually constituted and constituting. However, in contrast with the position of critical realists, structure in Giddens's theory is virtual and only exists in the minds of actors and as instantiated in action.

18. Suchman (1987) is an anthropologist who studies workplace practices. Adopting ethnomethodology's particular strand of interactionism (Garfinkel, 1967), she rejects structural explanations of action, emphasizing the ephemeral, socially constructed nature of practices. She focuses on sense-making as a process of negotiation and accommodation occurring in the immediate context, in the here-and-now. Lave and Wenger (1991), while they also adopt a social constructionist view, adopt a less restrictive definition of context to include the wider sociocultural and political background. As discussed by Contu and Willmott (2003), their conception of situatedness is not purely interactionist but is also based on a critical stance inspired by Vygotsky's activity theory, to which we will come back later. However, this more critical reading is occulted by organization scholars referring to their work on situated learning and by Wenger (1998, 2000) himself, in his later writings (Contu & Willmott, 2003).

19. Actor-network theory is mobilized by authors in both the situated action and the discursive approaches and contributes to erasing the boundaries between the two streams of work.

20. In a sense, their discussion of the dual nature of routines in terms of evolutionary theory, as variation-selection and retention, gives a feeling of cyclicality as opposed to the simultaneity that is at the heart of Orlikowski's discussion.

21. Overcoding is the reproduction of sociocultural codes in everyday language and actions.

22. Activity theory has its roots in psychology. It has evolved from the work of Vygotsky, a Russian psychologist, and his student Leont'ev, and is influenced by Marxist tradition (Blackler et al., 2000). Activity theory has recently been extended by Engeström (1987), a Finnish scholar, and some of his colleagues. They have done a number of empirical studies using activity theory to examine change in public organizations.

23. Engeström (2000) has also used his conceptual model in a number of empirical studies of change, particularly in the health sector. His studies are much more fine-grained than the work done by Jarzabkowski (2003) and Blackler et al. (2000) and describe in more detail how contradictions are actually played out in concrete day-to-day work situations.

CONCLUSION TO PART III

Looking at Change From the Inside

The vision of change as a pervasive, continuous, emergent, and indeterminate process has increasingly directed attention inside the organization to the organizational processes in which all members participate. In contrast, in the preceding period, change was viewed as dramatic and rare and looked at from above, from the point of view of the top manager. Reflecting on the evolution of the field since the 1990s, two related trends stand out: the parallel development of the natural evolution and the social dynamics perspectives, leading to the increasing dominance of a process view of change, and the apparent fragmentation of the field of organization change.

It is clear from the two preceding chapters that the conception of change as organizational becoming that comes to dominate at the beginning of the 21st century emanates from two very different streams of research. At a fundamental level, the natural evolution and the social dynamics perspectives conceive the nature of research and the role of the researcher very differently. Theoretically, the way they tackle questions of agency, context, and time reveals, not surprisingly, very different worldviews. However, together they bring the field of organizational change to a major turning point. Since they conceive continuity and change not as opposites but as outcomes of the same processes, studying change increasingly becomes equated with studying all organizational processes. The study of change thus becomes the central focus of organization studies, and in overtaking the whole domain, it fragments into a number of subfields based on specific processes such as learning, innovation, decision making, and strategizing. In a sense, its peak of popularity leads to its possible dissolution.

As documented in Chapter 7, the three approaches that make up the natural evolution framework share the same ontological point of view and epistemological stance. They all participate in a cumulative quest for knowledge where the role of the researcher is developing objective knowledge that aims for truth value. They are part of the enterprise of "normal" science. Moreover, theoretically, they all model the organization from a biological perspective, borrowing from the natural sciences both their conceptual frameworks and their methods. They offer complementary explanations and together form a coherent framework for explaining change as an emergent process.

On the other hand, the social dynamics stream is characterized by the diversity of the ontological, epistemological, and political positions held by researchers from the different approaches. Ontologically, positions vary from realism to various shades of social constructionism, and, epistemologically, science is viewed as a contested terrain. Some deny scientific discourse any special claim and view the researcher's voice as one among others. Others accord a scientific status to the "systematic mode of observing and explaining" that characterizes interpretive approaches (Hatch & Yanow, 2003), demanding that they be judged by their own criteria. In terms of theory, the social dynamics stream is much more fragmented, even though, as the preceding chapter has shown, there are a number of converging trends, most notably the language and practice turn. This stream is characterized by vigorous debates between the different approaches rather than by a search for convergence. This is due, apart from the previously mentioned ontological and epistemological differences, to the divergent political orientations of the authors, which influence their view of the role of research as mainly critical or descriptive.

In theoretical terms, however, the similarities and differences between the different social dynamics approaches, as well as with the natural evolution approaches, are very revealing of the richness of the field. In the following paragraphs, they will be discussed taking the concepts of change, agency, context, and history as focal elements (see Tables III.1 and III.2).

The conception of the nature and role of agency in organizational change is probably one of the most significant differences between the two streams. As mentioned earlier, the natural evolution stream depicts change as natural, both in the sense that it is an ongoing and inevitable process in all living systems and, more important, as a phenomenon that does not necessarily imply foresight and intentionality. From a natural evolution point of view, agency is blind. For instance, in evolutionary theory, although variations are often the result of local action, change (as an outcome) is not explained by the intentions of agents, but by selection (i.e., global or macro-level forces). Agency is also distributed, as in evolutionary theory, where a manager's job is to select the most promising projects, or even more in complexity theory, where organizations are viewed as self-organizing systems. In this case, it is the aggregated effect of more or less intentional, local actions, and not the control of a dominant agent, which produces a new temporary order. Here, an agent is defined, generically and in a neutral fashion, as a force that brings about results. This conception of agency, while having the advantage of being very general (i.e., applying to both physical and social systems), is not very sophisticated.

Table III.1   Natural Evolution Perspective

	Behavioral Learning Approach	Evolutionary Approach	Complexity Approach
Vision of organization	Experiential, adaptive learning system Unitary view	Self-replicating system or ecosystem Pluralist view	Complex adaptive system Pluralist view
Model of change	Routine-based change Trial-and-error learning Organizational level (versus cognitive model = individual level)	Combination of routines Creation of the new from the old	Bifurcation or avalanche
Process of change	INCREMENTAL CHANGE CROSS-LEVEL EFFECTS (transfer between levels)	CONTINUOUS BOTTOM-UP CHANGE Process of micro-level variation and macro-level selection	NONLINEAR DYNAMICS, BOTH RADICAL AND INCREMENTAL Process of self-organization
Effects	MAINLY SMALL EFFECTS (indeterminate)	SMALL EFFECTS OR RENEWAL (indeterminate outcomes)	SMALL OR RADICAL EFFECTS (indeterminate effects)
Change agent	Every organizational member functioning in a stimulus–response mode	Every organizational member Intentionally or not Distributed and blind agency	Every organizational member Intentionally or not Distributed and blind agency
Context	Objective, source of stimulus	Objective, selection environment	Objective, coevolution (endogenous)
History	Embedded in routines and procedures	Sequence of events, path dependencies	Sequence of events, path dependencies
Basic tension	Knowledge creation and preservation	Exploration/exploitation	Order/disorder

Table III.2 Social Dynamics Perspective

	Radical Approach	Postmodern Approach	Discursive Approach	Practice-Centered Approach
Vision of organization	Instrument of domination	Locale of competing discourses	Text, drama, or network of conversations	Emergent, temporary patterns of action Communities of practice
Model of change	Revolution but NO CHANGE	New discourse but NO CHANGE	Mutual constitution of text/conversation Translation	Situated action Situated learning Improvisation
Process of change	REPRODUCTION	LANGUAGE GAMES	CONTINUOUS EMERGENT DISCURSIVE CHANGE	CONTINUOUS EMERGENT CHANGE
Effects	Reinforcement of regime of control	Increasing disciplinary control	MOSTLY INCREMENTAL BUT CAN BE RADICAL (indeterminate effects)	MOSTLY INCREMENTAL BUT CAN BE RADICAL (indeterminate effects)
Change agent	Managers as agents of capitalism	No agency, agents as cultural artifacts, as effects of discourse	Individuals or collectives DISTRIBUTED OR DISPERSED AGENCY	Individuals or collectives DISTRIBUTED CONJOINT AGENCY
Context	Macrosocial, global, objective	Macrosocial, global, socially constructed in discourse	Micro (sometimes also macro) Socially constructed in discourse	Micro, local, immediate
History	Objective, long-term, sociopolitical trends	Discursively constructed, long-term	Socially constructed (often embedded in the present)	Socially constructed (embedded in the present)
Basic tension	Contradiction between capital and labor	Consensus/dissensus	Unity/plurality	Routine/improvisation

Without too much exaggeration, one could say that actors in the natural evolution stream tend to be like intelligent robots, programmed to accomplish certain routines, to learn, and to be capable of acting locally to further their own interests (i.e., in a stimulus–response mode). Agents, by reacting to simple rules, participate in processes of organizing but are powerless to willfully alter the organization's destiny because of the unanticipated consequences of action and environmental selection. Agents are portrayed as either asocial or under-socialized: They are atomized actors or, at best, nodes in a network. But more important for a theory of change, in this perspective, agents are not depicted as human beings with emotions, dreams, and imagination. For instance, they don't try to give meaning to their existence by telling stories; they exchange information. They don't make history; they have trajectories.

In contrast, approaches in the social dynamics stream generally present a more sophisticated and diversified picture of agency. Even if, like the natural evolution stream, they present a weak view of agency, as distributed or dispersed agency, they develop a rich, if divergent, reflection on the nature of the agent. The agent is, most often, conceived as a storyteller and as a competent actor who engages in interaction with other people and tools in a reflexive manner. Although his or her action is more or less constrained and even, according to some, determined, the actor's subjectivity and identity are considered important. Even researchers who are inspired by actor-network theory and postmodernism, approaches that negate agency by conceiving the agent as an effect of a network or of discourse, still tend to be concerned with how agents' subjectivities and identities are constituted in such processes.

With regard to context and history, researchers within the natural evolution stream adopt a "factual" definition. Often, context and history are simply discounted because the aim of such research is to construct generic change models that apply in all situations. When they are taken into account, they are conceived as objective dimensions. Context becomes a set of macro-level variables representing environmental or organizational characteristics, while history is operationalized as a sequence of events. They are measured (or included in simulation models) to evaluate their impact on organizational dynamics. For example, when evolutionists claim that history matters, they emphasize, for the most part, the "weight of history." Their concept of path dependency explains today's choices as, more or less, a result of yesterday's decisions and events.

On the other hand, in the social dynamics tradition, context and history are socially constructed, and it is the way they are interpreted and used by actors in the construction of their world that is of interest. For example, it is not the "objective" features of the situation, but the various meanings they are given by the actors, that are important in explaining change. In the case of history, the focus, rather than being on measurable trajectories, is on history making as a narrative process, where the past is revised and reinvented in the present moment to create the future.

What should be noted, however, is that in both streams of work, context and history are increasingly considered not as a set of (whether objective or socially constructed) constraints or resources for action, fixed at one point in time, that is, as a background for action, but in terms of coevolutionary processes. Agent, organization, and spatiotemporal context are viewed as entwined in processes of mutual construction. Therefore, they must be studied as nested systems evolving over time.

In this conception, the traditional debate between agency and structure, as it is transposed in the micro/macro or local/global dilemma, is also treated in processual terms with attempts made to reconcile the two perspectives, rather than choose one or the other. This reconciliation sometimes takes the form of a negation of that dualism, as in ANT, but the most popular resolution of this tension is as mutual constitution where the structural or macro level is conceived as both emerging from and, simultaneously, constituting the agent or micro level. The evolutionary perspective, and particularly complexity theory, like structuration theory and some of the discursive and practice-centered approaches it has inspired, are good examples of this movement. This conception paints the picture of a multilevel emergent process characterized by paradox, contradiction, or dialectics, with the tensions between exploration/exploitation, chaos/order, autonomy/control, innovation/imitation, plurality/unity, divergence/consensus, and improvisation/routine producing both continuity and change. While the natural evolution perspective depicts these tensions as inherent in opposing impersonal forces (i.e., positive and negative feedback loops), the social dynamics tradition treats them as issues of power and social action.

Because they share a similar conception of change in terms of tensions, not as either/or but as both/and propositions, they distinguish themselves mainly by their different ontological explanations of change as a natural, routine-driven process versus a social process driven by creative, purposeful action. As a consequence, despite the important differences between the two perspectives, the main thrust of this work is to present change as a generic process of organizing, and it is this shared conception that produces the apparent fragmentation of the field. When changing becomes synonymous with organizing, the study of change starts invading the whole domain of organization studies. It thus becomes dispersed within all the subfields of organization studies, such as learning, decision making, innovating, strategizing, and transforming. Finally, after emerging as a distinct field in the 1980s, the topic of change takes central stage in organization studies. One can wonder what this will mean for the field of organizational change in terms of the prospects for research and the relevance for practice. I will attempt some answers in the conclusion of this book, as I revisit the evolution of the field.

Conclusion

In retrospect, the history looks more focused, more efficient, and more insightful at every step than it does at the time it was lived. To the extent that history repeats itself, this streamlined account should help people be more efficient and more decisive in the future. Even if people exaggerate the similarity between the streamlined past and the disorderly present, this very exaggeration may make them more confident. Confidence, you will recall, is a crucial determinant of environmental enactment.

(Weick, 1995, p. 184)

In this area, perhaps, interpretations after the event, a better conceptual organization of complex historical experience and some improved orientation in the chaos of events is the most we should expect from so-called "theories of revolution." That in itself would be a great intellectual feat.

(Sztompka, 1993, p. 321)

Looking for an Elusive Object

It is clear that my reconstruction of the evolution of the field over more than 50 years greatly simplifies, as do all narrative accounts, what is a multifaceted and rich history. It goes without saying that my own position in this field[1] and my reading of the present situation are reflected in this historical account. But this is inevitable. Not surprisingly, I see the evolution of the field as a process of both continuity and change, with the new partly emerging from, and coexisting with, the old. The older approaches don't disappear, yet they can be influenced and, sometimes, rejuvenated by their contact with the newer approaches. Through a process of sedimentation, different layers are added and contribute to the vibrancy of the field as we know it today. Even though I have been careful to draw the threads between the different approaches over time, by necessity, the delineation into three separate periods accentuates the discontinuities. In the next paragraphs, I will briefly summarize the previous historical account, emphasizing the most important links between the different approaches over time, as presented in Figure C.1.

When I first encountered the field as a doctoral student in the early 1980s, it was the beginning of the glorious epoch of transformational change. It was an exciting period full of dramatic stories of turnarounds and strategic reorientations. While up till then change had been more or less taken for granted (as synonymous with growth and adaptation), now more researchers were starting to reflect seriously on the nature of change and attempting to define it more systematically. The topic of change as a field of inquiry was coming into its own. At the time, there was a strong sense of a clear break with the past. However, as I have tried to show, the dominant transformational perspective, with its punctuated equilibrium model, particularly as it was represented in the configurational, the cognitive, and the cultural approaches, was an extension of, as well as a reaction to, the rational adaptation perspective, fueled by insights from population ecology.

Starting in the late 1980s, there is increasing dissatisfaction with this dominant model's single focus on the actions of managers, coming from within the cognitive, cultural, and political approaches and drawing on the early work in the organic adaptation tradition. There is a growing tendency to view organizations not as instruments in the hands of managers, but as made up of groups of individuals with more or less compatible visions, values, and interests and, therefore, to view change as a more collective and emergent process.

By the early 1990s, a vision of change, not as a rare and dramatic episode imposed from above, but as a natural and normal process that occurs everywhere in the organization, starts to take hold. This perspective is not only present in the academic world; it is also carried by the media and very popular among practitioners. Continuous learning and innovating take center stage. Rather than being interested only in dramatic action, research is now focused on the daily gestures that make change happen. This movement is reflected in the increasing popularity of the adaptive learning and evolutionary approaches, followed by complexity theory, direct heirs of the behavioral theory of the firm and of population ecology. This trend culminates with the popularity of discourse and practice studies, which become increasingly popular in the late 1990s. While these approaches are inspired by theoretical traditions that are new to the field, as we have seen, they also lead back to the emergent view of change rooted in the organic adaptation perspective, which up to now had been marginal.

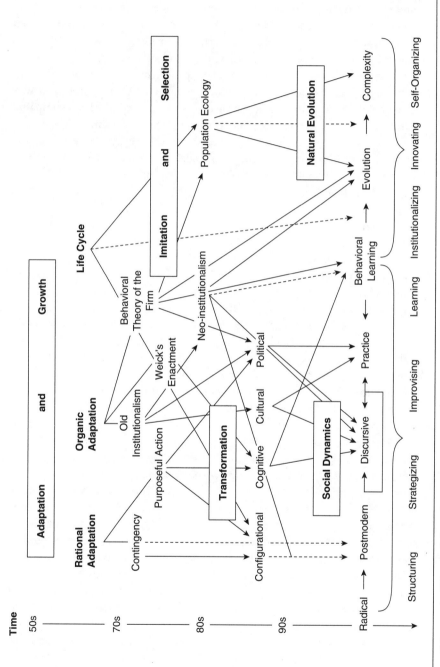

Figure C.1　An Historical Overview

231

However, while the emergent view of change stemming from both the social and the natural traditions starts to dominate the field, it does not replace the transformational model of change. While the notion that organizations alternate between periods of convergence and transformation—between phases of stability, when order reigns, and moments of change, characterized by chaos—has been abandoned, it is now replaced by the idea of chaotic order, a dialectic of stability and change. As I have argued, as this emergent or process view of change takes hold of the field, it evolves into a conception that encompasses rather than opposes transformational change (Langley & Denis, 2006).

In short, these previously divergent visions of change are now seen as dialectically integrated in the same processes. Transformational (or episodic) change and emergent (or continuous) change are not different theories of change but can be studied and explained within the same generic conception of evolution as processes of continuity and change.

However, this convergence around a process view of change is based on two streams of work, the natural evolution and the social dynamics approaches, which can be distinguished by their very different conceptions of agency. This, naturally, is reflected in their models of change. For instance, while, from a natural evolution perspective, an organization learns, evolves, and self-organizes, the organization is narrated, structured, and improvised in the social dynamics framework. In the first case, the emphasis is on the organization doing the changing, on the processes by which it changes. In the second case, the organization is changed; the focus is on the actors and the processes through which they construct the organization, intentionally or not. As a consequence, the natural evolution stream develops a simple view of the agent as a living organism that basically functions in a stimulus–response mode, but develops a rich model of organizing processes. The social dynamics stream, for its part, develops a sophisticated, and contested, view of the agent as a social actor, a conscious and purposeful human being capable of spontaneous, creative action through discourse and practice embedded in context.

It is also interesting to notice, in Figure C.1, how the two streams have evolved differently and mostly separately over time. For example, the contested nature of the social dynamics stream is reflected in its diversity, while the "progressive" development of the natural evolution stream (Baum & Rowley, 2002) is apparent in its relative parsimony. However, there has been some cross-fertilization between the two traditions over time. For instance, lately, the behavioral theory of the firm and complexity theory have influenced thinking in the social dynamics stream, while the cognitive and neoinstitutional approaches are increasingly integrated into the natural evolution framework. Although the two traditions remain separate, lately there have been some tentative attempts at dialogue (Garud & Karnoe, 2001; Tsoukas & Knudsen, 2003).

This book is another such attempt at bringing together these two important traditions in the field, not in the spirit of integrating them, but rather with the view that, by comparison, our understanding of our own position becomes clearer. More important, I think that as change, whether as an object of study, a theoretical issue, or a practical problem, becomes so central in organization studies, students of change cannot afford to ignore these different lenses and the richness of each particular point of view. However, as the field of change becomes increasingly sophisticated and fragmented, keeping up with its evolution becomes more and more challenging. This raises the question of the future of the field.

Culmination or Dissolution?

While I was writing this book, I had the feeling that I was running behind a virus undergoing constant mutation. Thus, I have no intention of trying to predict the future of the field. However, I will address two current issues that I feel will have some bearing on the evolution of this elusive and multiform concept and domain of inquiry: the fragmentation of the field and the debate over agency.

As I mentioned earlier, the field of change has broadened its reach and has fragmented into a number of subfields such as learning, innovating, and strategizing, which are all conceived as processes of change. This can be interpreted as a normal process whereby, as a field develops, it gets splintered into a number of narrower areas of study. In this sense, one can speak of this evolution as a conquest. However, one could also argue that this period of expansion is, in fact, a form of dissolution. As the field of change splinters, it gets engulfed within the wider field of organization studies.

Another way of looking at it is to redefine the field in a narrow sense as only the study of deliberate or programmed change interventions, one of the main organizing processes. However, to better understand these deliberate change processes, the various theoretical lenses developed during the last 10 years must be brought to bear on the subject. Therefore, the study of change implies a participation in the elaboration of theories of organizing as processes of stability and change. The dialectical nature of change means that the reflections on organization and change are now inseparable at least theoretically, if not empirically. This means that to study change will imply getting involved in a multidisciplinary project where defining the boundaries (both theoretically and empirically) becomes an increasingly significant part of the creative act of research. This requires a breadth of outlook and, increasingly, a capacity to cooperate across disciplines and subfields.

Another issue that has drawn attention lately is the question of agency. The debate over the nature of agency, which has always been central in the field, has been reinvigorated with the arrival of postmodernism in the literature on organizational change. The postmodern tradition and some discursive approaches tend to negate agency. Even other approaches in the natural evolution and social dynamics streams, each in its own way, have the tendency to weaken agency. Whether it is by emphasizing how agents are limited by internal and external constraints of different types or by drawing attention to the unanticipated consequences of action and chance events, agency is increasingly viewed as restricted either at the moment of choice or in terms of its results. Furthermore, the increased emphasis on distributed agency and self-organization also raises questions about the possibility of deliberate organizational change.

In short, because change is increasingly portrayed as an indeterminate process where agents are either powerless to act or reduced to gambling, one can question the relevance of the field for practice. Some authors, such as Caldwell (2005), are pessimistic about its future, fearing it will disappear as a result of irrelevance. Others (Sturdy & Grey, 2003), criticizing the current dominant discourse, which portrays change as inevitable and desirable, claim it prevents alternative voices from emerging. They, thus, acknowledge the literature on change as having some practical, if negative, effect.

Whatever the future may hold, it is clear that as long as organizational members see change as a relevant issue in their day-to-day lives, organizational change will remain an important phenomenon and a major object of study, and the interplay between theory and practice will continue to contribute to its constant evolution. Historical analysis combined with the study of history in the making remains, in my view, one of the better ways to understand the interplay between agency and change.

Note

1. Located, as I am, in francophone Quebec, I am at the interface between North America and Europe, which means I participate in the cultural and intellectual traditions of both. I am also a peripheral and eclectic player in this field, which, I believe, explains my interest in tackling this project. Not being a major player in any school, but being interested in all of them, I am in a position where I can be sympathetic to all without having to defend the superiority of any.

References

Abrahamson, E. (1991). Managerial fads and fashion: The diffusion and rejection of innovations. *Academy of Management Review, 16*(3), 586–612.

Abrahamson, E. (1996). Technical and aesthetic fashion. In B. Czarniawska & G. Sevon (Eds.), *Translating organizational change* (pp. 117–138). Berlin, Germany: Walter de Gruyter.

Aldrich, H. (1979). *Organizations and environments.* Toronto, Ontario, Canada: Prentice Hall.

Aldrich, H. (1992). Incommensurable paradigms? Vital signs from three perspectives. In M. Reed & M. Hughes (Eds.), *Rethinking organization: New directions in organization theory and analysis* (pp. 17–45). London: Sage.

Aldrich, H. (1999). *Organizations evolving.* London: Sage.

Allaire, Y., & Firsirotu, M. (1984). Theories of organizational culture. *Organization Studies, 5,* 193–226.

Allaire, Y., & Firsirotu, M. (1985). How to implement radical strategies in large organizations. *Sloan Management Review, 26*(3), 19–34.

Allison, G. T. (1971). *Essence of decision: Explaining the Cuban Missile Crisis.* Boston: Little, Brown.

Alvesson, M. (2002). *Understanding organizational culture.* London: Sage.

Alvesson, M., & Deetz, S. (1996). Critical theory and postmodern approaches to organizational studies. In S. Clegg, C. Hardy, & W. Nord (Eds.), *Handbook of organization studies* (pp. 191–217). London: Sage.

Alvesson, M., & Deetz, S. (2000). *Doing critical management research.* London: Sage.

Alvesson, M., & Kärreman, D. (2000a). Taking the linguistic turn in organizational research. *Journal of Applied Behavioral Science, 36*(2), 136–158.

Alvesson, M., & Kärreman, D. (2000b). Varieties of discourse: On the study of organizations through discourse analysis. *Human Relations, 53*(9), 1125–1149.

Alvesson, M., & Willmott, H. (Eds.). (1992). *Critical management studies.* London: Sage.

Amblard, H., Bernoux, P., Herreros, G., & Livian, Y.-F. (1996). *Les nouvelles approches sociologiques des organisations.* Paris: Éditions du Seuil.

Amburgey, T., Dawn, K., & Barnett, W. (1993). Resetting the clock: The dynamics of organizational change and failure. *Administrative Science Quarterly, 38,* 51–73.

Amburgey, T., & Rao, H. (1996). Organizational ecology: Past, present, and future directions. *Academy of Management Journal, 39*(5), 1265–1286.

Amburgey, T., & Singh, J. (2002). Organizational evolution. In J. Baum (Ed.), *The Blackwell companion to organizations* (pp. 327–343). Oxford, UK: Blackwell.

Anderson, D. L. (2005). "What you'll say is . . . : Represented voice in organizational change discourse. *Journal of Organizational Change Management, 18*(1), 63–77.

Anderson, P. (1999). Complexity theory and organization science. *Organization Science, 10*(3), 216–232.

Anderson, P., & Tushman, M. L. (1990). Technological discontinuities and dominant designs: A cyclical model of technological change. *Administrative Science Quarterly, 35*(4), 604–633.

Archer, M. (1996). *Culture and agency.* Cambridge, UK: Cambridge University Press.

Argote, L., Beckman, S. L., & Epple, D. (1990). The persistence and transfer of learning in industrial settings. *Management Science, 36*(2), 140–154.

Argote, L., & Ophir, R. (2002). Intraorganizational learning. In J. Baum (Ed.), *The Blackwell companion to organizations* (pp. 181–207). Oxford, UK: Blackwell.

Argyris, C. (1982). The executive mind and double-loop learning. *Organizational Dynamics, 11*(2), 5–22.

Argyris, C. (1996). Unrecognized defenses of scholars: Impact on theory and research. *Organization Science, 7*(1), 79–87.

Argyris, C., & Schön, D. (1974). *Theory in practice: Increasing professional effectiveness.* San Francisco: Jossey-Bass.

Argyris, C., & Schön, D. (1978). *Organizational learning.* Reading, MA: Addison-Wesley.

Ashby, W. R. (1956). *An introduction to cybernetics.* London: Chapman and Hall.

Astley, G., & Van de Ven, A. (1983). Central perspectives and debates in organization theory. *Administrative Science Quarterly, 28*(2), 245–273.

Azevedo, J. (2002). Updating organizational epistemology. In J. Baum (Ed.), *The Blackwell companion to organizations* (pp. 715–732). Oxford, UK: Blackwell.

Bacharach, S. B., Bamberger, P., & Sonnenstuhl, W. J. (1996). The organizational transformation process: The micropolitics of dissonance reduction and alignment of logics of action. *Administrative Science Quarterly, 41*(3), 477–506.

Bain, P., & Taylor, P. (2000). Entrapped by the "electronic panopticon"? Worker resistance in the call centre. *New Technology, Work and Employment, 15*(1), 2–30.

Bak, P., & Sneppen, K. (1993). Punctuated equilibrium and criticality in a simple model of evolution. *Physical Review Letters, 71,* 4083–4086.

Barker, J. R. (1993). Tightening the iron cage: Concertive control in self-managing teams. *Administrative Science Quarterly, 38*(3), 408–437.

Barley, S. R. (1986). Technology as an occasion for structuring: Evidence from observations of CT scanners and the social order of radiology departments. *Administrative Science Quarterly, 31*(1), 78–108.

Barley, S. R., Meyer, G., & Gash, D. (1988). Cultures of culture: Academics, practitioners, and the pragmatics of normative control. *Administrative Science Quarterly, 33*(1), 24–60.

Barnett, W., & Burgelman, R. A. (1996). Evolutionary perspectives on strategy. *Strategic Management Journal, 17,* 5–19.

Barney, J. (1991). Firm resources and sustained competitive advantage. *Journal of Management, 17,* 99–120.

Barr, P. S., Stimpert, J. L., & Huff, A. (1992). Cognitive change, strategic action, and organizational renewal. *Strategic Management Journal, 13,* 15–36.

Bartunek, J. (1984). Changing interpretive schemes and organizational restructuring: The example of a religious order. *Administrative Science Quarterly, 29*(3), 355–372.

Bartunek, J. (1994). Editor's introduction. *Journal of Management Inquiry, 3*(4), 336–338.

Bartunek, J., Gordon, J. R., & Weathersby, R. P. (1983). Developing "complicated" understanding in administrators. *Academy of Management Review, 8,* 273–284.

Bartunek, J., & Moch, M. (1991). Multiple constituencies and the quality of working life. In P. Frost, L. Moore, M. Louis, C. Lundberg, & J. Martin (Eds.), *Reframing organizational culture* (pp. 104–114). Newbury Park, CA: Sage.

Bassanini, A. P., & Dosi, G. (2001). When and how chance and human will can twist the arms of Clio: An essay on path-dependence in a world of irreversibilities. In R. Garud & K. P. London (Eds.), *Path dependence and creation* (pp. 41–68). Mahwah, NJ: Lawrence Erlbaum.

Baum, J. (1996). Organizational ecology. In S. Clegg, C. Hardy, & W. Nord (Eds.), *Handbook of organizational studies* (pp. 75–114). London: Sage.

Baum, J. (Ed.). (2002). *The Blackwell companion to organizations.* Oxford, UK: Blackwell.

Baum, J., & Rowley, T. (2002). Companion to Organizations: An introduction. In J. Baum (Ed.), *The Blackwell companion to organizations* (pp. 1–34). Oxford, UK: Blackwell.

Baum, J., & Silverman, B. S. (2001). Complexity, attractors, and path dependence and creation in technological evolution. In R. Garud & K. P. London (Eds.), *Path dependence and creation* (pp. 169–209). Mahwah, NJ: Lawrence Erlbaum.

Baum, J., & Singh, J. (Eds.) (1994a). *Evolutionary dynamics of organizations.* New York: Oxford University Press.

Baum, J., & Singh, J. (1994b). Organizational hierarchies and evolutionary processes: Some reflections on a theory of organizational evolution. *Evolutionary dynamics of organizations* (pp. 3–20). New York: Oxford University Press.

Baum, J., & Singh, J. (1994c). Organization-environment coevolution. In J. Baum & J. Singh (Eds.), *Evolutionary dynamics of organizations* (pp. 379–402). New York: Oxford University Press.

Baumard, P. (1996). *Les organisations déconcertées: La gestion stratégique de la connaissance.* Paris: Masson.

Bégin, L. (2000). *L'allocation des ressources dans une organisation communautaire: Le cas de Centraide du Grand Montréal.* Unpublished doctoral dissertation, HEC-Montréal.

Begun, J. W. (1994). Chaos and complexity: Frontiers of organization science. *Journal of Management Inquiry, 3*(4), 329–335.

Bennis, W. (1969). *Organization development: Its nature, origins, and prospects.* Reading, MA: Addison-Wesley.

Benson, J. K. (1977). Organizations: A dialectical view. *Administrative Science Quarterly, 22*(1), 1–21.

Berends, H., Boersma, K., & Weggerman, M. (2003). The structuration of organizational learning. *Human Relations, 56*(9), 1035–1056.

Berg, P.-O. (1985). Organization change as a symbolic transformation process. In P. Frost, L. Moore, M. Louis, C. Lundberg, & J. Martin (Eds.), *Organizational culture* (pp. 281–299). Beverly Hills, CA: Sage.

Bernoux, P. (1985). *La sociologie des organisations.* Paris: Éditions du Seuil.

Beverland, M., & Lockshin, L. (2001). Organizational life cycles in small New Zealand wineries. *Journal of Small Business Management, 39*(4), 354–362.

Bhaskar, R. (1986). *Scientific realism and human emancipation.* London: Verso.

Biggart, N. W. (1977). The creative-destructive process of organizational change: The case of the post office. *Administrative Science Quarterly, 22*(3), 410–426.

Blackler, F., Crump, N., & McDonald, S. (2000). Organizing processes in complex activity networks. *Organization, 7*(2), 277–300.

Blau, P. (1955). *The dynamics of bureaucracy: A study of interpersonal relations in two government agencies.* Chicago: University of Chicago Press.

Boisot, M., & Child, J. (1999). Organizations as adaptive systems in complex environments: The case of China. *Organization Science, 10*(3), 237–252.

Boje, D. M. (1991). The storytelling organization: A study of story performance. *Administrative Science Quarterly, 36*(1), 106–126.

Boje, D. M. (2001). Corporate writing in the web of postmodern culture and postindustrial capitalism. *Management Communication Quarterly, 14*(3), 507–516.

Boje, D. M., & Winsor, R. D. (1993). The resurrection of Taylorism: Total Quality Management's hidden agenda. *Journal of Organizational Change Management, 6*(4), 57–70.

Boland, R. J., Jr., & Tenkasi, R. V. (1995). Perspective making and perspective taking in communities of knowing. *Organization Science, 6*(4), 350–372.

Boucher, J. P. (1995). *L'évolution de la pratique du changement planifié depuis le début des années 80.* Unpublished master's thesis, HEC-Montréal, Quebec, Canada.

Bouchikhi, H. (1990). *Structuration des organisations.* Paris: Economica.

Bourdieu, P. (1977). *Outline of a theory of practice.* Cambridge, UK: Cambridge University Press.

Bourdieu, P. (1990). *The logic of practice.* Stanford, CA: Stanford University Press.

Bower, J. (1970). *Managing the resource allocation process.* Boston: Harvard Business School Press.

Braverman, H. (1974). *Labor and monopoly capital: The degradation of work in the 20th century.* New York: Monthly Review Press.

Braybrooke, D., & Lindblom, C. E. (1963). *A strategy of decision.* New York: Free Press.

Brigham, M., & Corbett, J. M. (1997). E-mail, power and the constitution of organisational reality. *New Technology, Work and Employment, 12*(1), 25–35.

Brocklehurst, M. (2001). Power, identity and new technology homework: Implications for "new forms" of organizing. *Organization Studies, 22*(3), 445–467.

Brown, A. D. (1995). Managing understandings: Politics, symbolism, niche marketing and the quest for legitimacy in IT implementation. *Organization Studies, 16*(6), 951–969.

Brown, A. D. (1998). Narrative, politics and legitimacy in an IT implementation. *Journal of Management Studies, 35*(1), 35–58.

Brown, A. D., & Eisenhardt, K. M. (1998). *Competing on the edge.* Boston: Harvard Business School Press.

Brown, A. D., & Humphreys, M. (2003). Epic and tragic tales: Making sense of change. *Journal of Applied Behavioral Science, 39*(2), 121–144.

Brown, J. S., & Duguid, P. (1991). Organizational learning and communities of practice: Toward a unified view of working, learning and innovation. *Organizational Science, 2*(1), 40–57.

Brown, J. S., & Duguid, P. (2000). *The social life of information.* Cambridge, MA: Harvard Business School Press.

Brown, S. L., & Eisenhardt, K. M. (1997). The art of continuous change: Linking complexity theory and time-paced evolution in relentlessly shifting organizations. *Administrative Science Quarterly, 42*(1), 1–34.

Bruderer, E., & Singh, J. (1996). Organization evolution, learning, and selection: A genetic-algorithm-based model. *Academy of Management Journal, 39*(5), 1322–1349.

Bruner, J. (1990). *Acts of meaning.* Cambridge, MA: Harvard University Press.

Brunsson, N. (1982). The irrationality of action and action rationality: Decisions, ideologies, and organizational actions. *Journal of Management Studies, 19*(1), 29–34.

Brunsson, N. (1985). *The irrational organization: Irrationality as a basis for organizational action and change.* Chichester, UK: Wiley.

Brunsson, N. (1989). *The organization of hypocrisy: Talk, action and decision in organizations.* London: Wiley.

Buchanan, D., & Badham, R. (1999). Politics and organizational change: The lived experience. *Human Relations, 52*(5), 609–629.

Burgelman, R. A. (1983). A process model of internal corporate venturing in the diversified major firm. *Administrative Science Quarterly, 28*(2), 223–244.

Burgelman, R. A. (1991). Intraorganizational ecology of strategy making and organizational adaptation: Theory and field research. *Organization Science, 2*(3), 239–262.

Burgelman, R. A. (1994). Fading memories: A process theory of strategic business exit in dynamic environments. *Administrative Science Quarterly, 39*(1), 24–56.

Burgelman, R. A. (1996). A process model of strategic business exit: Implications for an evolutionary perspective on strategy. *Strategic Management Journal, 17*, 193–214.

Burke, W. W. (2002). *Organization change: Theory and practice.* Thousand Oaks, CA: Sage.

Burns, T., & Stalker, G. M. (1961). *The management of innovation.* London: Tavistock.

Burrell, G. (1996). Normal science, paradigms, metaphors, discourses and genealogies of analysis. In S. R. Clegg, C. Hardy, & W. R. Nord (Eds.), *Handbook of organization studies* (pp. 642–658). Thousand Oaks, CA: Sage.

Burrell, G., & Morgan, G. (1979). *Sociological paradigms and organisational analysis: Elements of the sociology of corporate life.* London: Heinemann.

Calàs, M. B., & Smircich, L. (1999). Past postmodernism? Reflections and tentative directions. *Academy of Management Review, 24*(4), 649–671.

Caldwell, R. (2005). Things fall apart? Discourses on agency and change in organizations. *Human Relations, 58*(1), 83–114.

Callon, M., & Latour, B. (Eds.). (1991). *La science telle qu'elle se fait.* Paris: La Découverte.

Cameron, K., & Whetten, D. (1993). Models of the organizational life cycle: Applications to higher education. In K. Cameron, R. Sutton, & D. Whetten (Eds.), *Readings in organizational decline: Frameworks, research and prescriptions* (pp. 45–61). Chicago: Ballinger.

Campbell, D. T. (1969). Variation and selective retention in sociocultural evolution. *General Systems, 16*, 69–85.

Campbell, D. T. (1994). How individual and face-to-face group selection undermine firm selection in organizational evolution. In J. Baum & J. Singh (Eds.), *Evolutionary dynamics of organizations* (pp. 23–38). New York: Oxford University Press.

Carley, K. M. (1992). Organizational learning and personnel turnover. *Organization Science, 3*(1), 20–46.

Carley, K. M. (2002). Intraorganizational complexity and computation. In J. Baum (Ed.), *The Blackwell companion to organizations* (pp. 208–232). Oxford, UK: Blackwell.

Carley, K. M., & Lee, J. L. (1998). Dynamic organizations: Organizational adaptation in a changing environment. In J. Baum (Ed.), *Advances in strategic management* (Vol. 15, pp. 269–297). Greenwich, CT: JAI Press.

Carley, K. M., & Svoboda, D. M. (1996). Modeling organizational adaptation as a simulated annealing process. *Sociological Methods & Research, 25*, 138–168.

Carroll, G. R., & Hannan, M. T. (1989). Density delay in the evolution of organizational population: A model and five empirical tests. *Administrative Science Quarterly, 34*, 411–430.

Chandler, A. D. (1962). *Strategy and structure.* Cambridge: MIT Press.

Cheng, Y.-T., & Van de Ven, A. (1996). Learning the innovation journey: Order out of chaos? *Organization Science, 7*(6), 593–614.

Chia, R. (1996). The problem of reflexivity in organizational research: Towards a postmodern science of organization. *Organization, 3*(1), 31–59.

Chia, R. (2003). Organization theory as a postmodern science. In H. Tsoukas & C. Knudsen (Eds.), *The Oxford handbook of organization theory* (pp. 113–140). Oxford, UK: Oxford University Press.

Child, J. (1972). Organization, structure, environment and performance: The role of strategic choice. *Sociology, 6*(1), 1–22.

Child, J. (1997). Strategic choice in the analysis of action, structure, organizations and environment: Retrospect and prospect. *Organization Studies, 18*(1), 43–76.

Child, J., & Kieser, A. (1981). Development of organizations over time. In W. Starbuck & P. Nystrom (Eds.), *Handbook of organizational design: Vol. 1. Adapting organizations to their environments* (pp. 28–64). Oxford, UK: Oxford University Press.

Child, J., & Smith, C. (1987). The context and process of organizational transformation: Cadbury Limited in its sector. *Journal of Management Studies, 24*(6), 565–593.

Chreim, S. (2002). Influencing organizational identification during major change: A communication-based perspective. *Human Relations, 55*(9), 1117–1137.

Chreim, S. (2005). The continuity-change duality in narrative texts of organizational identity. *Journal of Management Studies, 42*(3), 567–593.

Clark, P. (2003). *Organizational innovations.* London: Sage.

Clarke, T., & Pitelis, C. (1993). *The political economy of privatization.* London: Routledge.

Clegg, S. (1989). Radical revisions: Power, discipline and organizations. *Organization Studies, 10*(1), 97–115.

Clegg, S., Hardy, C., & Nord, W. (1996). *Handbook of organizational studies.* London: Sage.

Cohen, M. (1999). Commentary on the *Organization Science* special issue on complexity. *Organization Science, 10*(3), 373–376.

Cohen, M., March, J. G., & Olsen, J. P. (1972). A garbage can model of organizational choice. *Administrative Science Quarterly, 17*(1), 1–25.

Cohen, M. D., & Bacdayan, P. (1994). Organizational routines are stored as procedural memory. *Organization Science, 5*(4), 554–568.

Collins, D. (1996). New paradigms for change? Theories of organization and the organization of theories. *Journal of Organizational Change Management, 9*(4), 9–23.

Collins, D., & Rainwater, K. (2005). Managing change at Sears: A sideways look at a tale of corporate transformation. *Journal of Organizational Change Management, 18*(1), 16–30.

Contu, A., & Willmott, H. (2003). Re-embedding situatedness: The importance of power relations in learning theory. *Organization Science, 14*(3), 283–296.

Contu, A., & Willmott, H. (2005). You spin me round: The realist turn in organization and management studies. *Journal of Management Studies, 42*(8), 1645–1662.

Cook, S. D. N., & Yanow, D. (1993). Culture and organizational learning. *Journal of Management Inquiry, 2*(4), 373–390.

Coombs, R., Knights, D., & Willmott, H. (1992). Culture, control and competition: Towards a conceptual framework for the study of information technology in organizations. *Organization Studies, 13*(1), 51–72.

Coriat, B., & Weinstein, O. (1995). *Les nouvelles théories de l'entreprise.* Paris: Le Livre de Poche.

Corporate culture: The hard to change values that spell success or failure. (1980, October 27). *Business Week*, 148–160.

The corporate culture vultures. (1983, October 17). *Fortune*, 66–72.

Coser, L., Kadushin, C., & Powell, W. (1982). *Books: The culture and commerce of book publishing*. New York: Basic Books.

Covaleski, M., & Dirsmith, M. (1988). An institutional perspective on the rise, social transformation, and fall of a university budget category. *Administrative Science Quarterly, 33*(4), 562–587.

Crossan, M. M., Lane, H. W., & White, R. E. (1999). An organizational learning framework: From intuition to institution. *The Academy of Management Review, 24*(3), 522–537.

Crozier, M. (1964). *The bureaucratic phenomenon*. Chicago: University of Chicago Press.

Crozier, M., & Friedberg, E. (1977). *L'acteur et le système*. Paris: Éditions du Seuil.

Crozier, M., & Friedberg, E. (1980). *Actors and systems: The politics of collective action*. Chicago: University of Chicago Press.

Cule, P. E., & Robey, D. (2004). A dual-motor, constructive process model of organizational transition. *Organization Studies, 25*(2), 229–260.

Currie, G., & Brown, A. D. (2003). A narratological approach to understanding processes of organizing in a UK hospital. *Human Relations, 56*(5), 563–586.

Cyert, R., & March, J. G. (1963). *A behavioral theory of the firm*. Englewood Cliffs, NJ: Prentice Hall.

Czarniawska, B. (1997). *Narrating the organization*. Chicago: University of Chicago Press.

Czarniawska, B., & Joerges, B. (1996). Travels of ideas. In B. Czarniawska & G. Sevon (Eds.), *Translating organizational change* (pp. 11–48). Berlin, Germany: Walter de Gruyter.

Czarniawska, B., & Sevon, G. (1996a). Introduction. In B. Czarniawska & G. Sevon (Eds.), *Translating organizational change* (pp. 1–12). Berlin: Walter de Gruyter.

Czarniawska, B., & Sevon, G. (Eds.). (1996b). *Translating organizational change*. Berlin, Germany: Walter de Gruyter.

Daft, R., & Weick, K. (1984). Toward a model of organizations as interpretation systems. *Academy of Management Review, 9*, 284–295.

Davenport, T. (1993). *Process innnovation: Reengineering work through information technology*. Boston:Harvard Business School Press.

David, P. (1992). Heroes, herds and hysteresis in technological history: Thomas Edison and "the battle of the systems" reconsidered. *Industrial and Corporate Change*, 1, 129–180.

Dawn, K., & Amburgey, T. (1991). Organizational inertia and momentum: A dynamic model of strategic change. *Academy of Management Journal, 34*, 591–612.

Deal, T., & Kennedy, A. (1982). *Corporate cultures : The rites and rituals of corporate life*. Reading, MA: Addison-Wesley.

Deetz, S. (1985). Critical-cultural research: New sensibilities and old realities. *Journal of Management Inquiry, 11*(2), 121–136.

Deetz, S. (1992). Disciplinary power in the modern corporation. In M. Alvesson & H. Willmott (Eds.), *Critical management studies* (pp. 21–45). London: Sage.

Delacroix, J., & Carroll, G. R. (1983). Organizational foundings: An ecological study of the newspaper industry of Argentina and Ireland. *Administrative Science Quarterly, 28*(2), 274–291.

Delacroix, J., & Rao, H. (1994). Externalities and ecological theory: Unbundling density dependence. In J. Baum & J. Singh (Eds.), *Evolutionary dynamics of organizations* (pp. 255–268). New York: Oxford University Press.

Demers, C. (1990). *La diffusion stratégique en situation de complexité.* Unpublished doctoral thesis, HEC-Montréal, Quebec, Canada.

Demers, C. (1991). Le changement vu de l'intérieur: La diffusion stratégique dans les organisations complexes. *Gestion, 16*(2), 22–31.

Demers, C. (1992). Redressement et transformation: Une comparaison du point de vue de la diffusion. In A. Noël (Ed.), *Perspectives en management stratégique,* 27–59. Paris: Economica.

Demers, C. (1993). La diffusion d'un changement radical: Un processus de redéfinition et de restructuration de l'organisation. *Communication & Organisation, 3,* 51–93.

Demers, C. (1999). De la gestion du changement à la capacité à changer. *Gestion, 24*(3), 131–139.

Demers, C., & Barral, H. (1999, May). *Managing contradiction in strategic discourse: Three Canadian electric utilities and sustainable development.* Paper presented at the International Conference on Language in Organizational Change and Transformation, Columbus, OH.

Demers, C., & Giroux, N. (1993). A look at the messy middle: From changing to organizing. *Cahiers de recherche HEC Montréal* (Working Paper No. 93–16).

Demers, C., Giroux, N., & Chreim, S. (2003). Merger and acquisition announcements as corporate wedding narratives. *Journal of Organizational Change Management, 16*(2), 223–242.

Denis, J.-L., Lamothe, L., & Langley, A. (1996). The dynamics of collective leadership and strategic change in pluralistic organizations. *Academy of Management Journal, 44*(4), 809–838.

Dent, J. F. (1991). Reality in the making: A study of organizational transformation. *International Studies of Management & Organization, 21*(4), 23–36.

de Rond, M., & Bouchikhi, H. (2004). On the dialectics of strategic alliances. *Organization Science, 15*(1), 56–69.

DiMaggio, P. (1988). Interest and agency in institutional theory. In L. Zucker (Ed.), *Institutional patterns and organizations* (pp. 3–21). Cambridge, MA: Ballinger.

DiMaggio, P., & Powell, W. (1983). The iron cage revisited: Institutional isomorphism and collective rationality in organizational fields. *American Sociological Review, 48,* 147–160.

DiMaggio, P., & Powell, W. (1991). *The new institutionalism in organizational analysis.* Chicago: University of Chicago Press.

Djelic, M. L., & Ainamo, A. (1999). The coevolution of new organizational forms in the fashion industry: A historical and comparative study of France, Italy and the United States. *Organization Science, 10*(5), 622–637.

Dodge, R., & Robbins, J. (1992). An empirical investigation of the organizational life cycle model for small business development and survival. *Journal of Small Business Management, 30*(1), 27–38.

Donaldson, L. (1985). *In defence of organization theory: A reply to the critics.* Cambridge, UK: Cambridge University Press.

Donaldson, L. (1996a). *For positivist organization theory: Proving the hard core.* London: Sage.

Donaldson, L. (1996b). The normal science of structural contingency theory. In S. Clegg, C. Hardy, & W. Nord (Eds.), *Handbook of organization studies* (pp. 57–76). London: Sage.

Dooley, K., & Van de Ven, A. (1999). Explaining complex organizational dynamics. *Organization Science, 10*(3), 358–372.

Doolin, B. (2003). Narratives of change: Discourse, technology and organization. *Organization, 10*(4), 751–770.

Dougherty, D. (1992). Interpretive barriers to successful product innovation in large firms. *Organization Science, 3*(2), 179–202.

Dow, G. (1988). Configurational and coactivational views of organizational structure. *Academy of Management Review, 13*(1), 53–64.

Doz, Y. (1996). The evolution of cooperation in strategic alliances: Initial conditions or learning processes? *Strategic Management Journal, 17,* 55–83.

Doz, Y., & Prahalad, C. K. (1988). A process model of strategic redirection in large complex firms. In A. Pettigrew (Ed.), *The management of strategic change* (pp. 63–89). London: Basil Blackwell.

Drazin, R., & Sandelands, L. E. (1992). Autogenesis: A perspective on the process of organizing. *Organization Science, 3*(2), 230–249.

Dubinskas, F. A. (1994). On the edge of chaos: A metaphor for transformative change. *Journal of Management Inquiry, 3*(4), 355–366.

Duncan, R., & Weiss, A. (1979). Organizational learning: Implications for organizational design. In L. Cummings & B. Staw (Eds.), *Research in organizational behavior* (Vol. 1, pp. 75–123). Greenwich, CT: JAI Press.

Dutton, J., & Dukerich, J. (1991). Keeping an eye on the mirror: Image and identity in organizational adaptation. *Academy of Management Journal, 34*(3), 517–554.

Dutton, J., & Duncan, R. (1987). The creation of momentum for change through the process of strategic issue diagnosis. *Strategic Management Journal, 8,* 279–295.

Dutton, J., & Jackson, S. (1987). Categorizing strategic issues: Links to organizational action. *Academy of Management Review, 12*(1), 76–91.

Edelman, M. (1966). *The symbolic uses of politics.* New York: Harper & Row.

Eisenberg, E., & Riley, P. (2001). Organizational culture. In F. Jablin & L. Putnam (Eds.), *The new handbook of organizational communication* (pp. 291–322). Thousand Oaks, CA: Sage.

Eisenhardt, K. M., Barr, P., Barry, B., Dacin, T., Dougherty, D., Glynn, M. A., et al. (Eds.). (2000). Special topic forum on change and development journeys in a pluralistic world. *Academy of Management Review, 25*(4).

Eisenhardt, K. M., & Bhatia, M. M. (2002). Organizational complexity and computation. In J. Baum (Ed.), *The Blackwell companion to organizations* (pp. 442–466). Oxford, UK: Blackwell.

Eisenhardt, K. M., & Sull, D. N. (2001). Strategy as simple rules. *Harvard Business Review, 79*(1), 106–116.

Eldredge, N., & Gould, S. (1972). Punctuated equilibria: An alternative to phyletic gradualism. In T. Schopf (Ed.), *Models in paleobiology* (pp. 82–115). San Francisco: Freeman, Cooper & Co.

Engeström, Y. (1987). *Learning by expanding: An activity-theoretical approach to developmental research.* Helsinki, Finland: Orienta-Konsultit.

Engeström, Y. (2000). Activity theory as a framework for analyzing and redesigning work. *Ergonomics, 43*(7), 960–974.

Epple, D., Argote, L., & Devadas, R. (1991). Organizational learning curves: A method for investigating intra-plant transfer of knowledge acquired through learning by doing. *Organization Science, 2*(1), 58–70.

Ezzamel, M., & Willmott, H. (2004). Rethinking strategy: Contemporary perspectives and debates. *European Management Review, 1*(1), 43–48.

Fahey, L., & Narayanan, V. K. (1989). Linking changes in revealed causal maps and environmental change. *Journal of Management Studies, 26*(4), 361–378.

Fairclough, N. (1992). *Discourse and social change.* Cambridge, UK: Polity.

Fairclough, N., & Thomas, P. (2004). The discourse of globalization and the globalization of discourse. In D. Grant, C. Hardy, C. Oswick, & L. Putnam (Eds.), *The Sage handbook of organizational discourse* (pp. 379–396). London: Sage.

Feldman, M. S. (1991). The meanings of ambiguity: Learning from stories and metaphors. In P. Frost, L. Moore, M. Louis, C. Lundberg, & J. Martin (Eds.), *Reframing organizational culture* (pp. 145–156). Newbury Park, CA: Sage.

Feldman, M. S. (2000). Organizational routines as a source of continuous change. *Organization Science, 11*(6), 611–629.

Feldman, M. S., & Pentland, B. T. (2003). Reconceptualizing organizational routines as a source of flexibility and change. *Administrative Science Quarterly, 48*(1), 94–118.

Feldman, S. P. (1990). Stories as cultural creativity: On the relation between symbolism and politics in organizational change. *Human Relations, 43*(9), 809–828.

Fincham, R. (2000). Management as magic: Reengineering and the search for business salvation. In D. Knights & H. Willmott (Eds.), *The reengineering revolution? Critical studies of corporate change.* London: Sage.

Fincham, R., & Evans, M. (1999). The consultants' offensive: Reengineering—from fad to technique. *New Technology, Work and Employment, 14*(1), 32–44.

Fiol, C. M., & Lyles, M. A. (1985). Organizational learning. *Academy of Management Review, 10*(4), 803–813.

Fiol, C. M., & O'Connor, E. (2002). When hot and cold collide in radical change processes: Lessons from community development. *Organization Science, 13*(5), 532–546.

Fisher, W. R. (1987). *Human communication as narration: Toward a philosophy of reason, value and action.* Columbia: University of South Carolina Press.

Fleetwood, S. (2005). Ontology in organization and management studies: A critical realist perspective. *Organization, 12*(2), 197–222.

Fletcher, K., & Huff, A. (1990). Strategic argument mapping: A study of strategy reformulation at AT&T. In A. Huff (Ed.), *Mapping strategic thought* (pp. 185–193). Chichester, Toronto, Canada: Wiley.

Flichy, P. (1995). *L'innovation technique.* Paris: Éditions La Découverte.

Flier, B., Van Den Bosch, F. A. J., & Volberda, H. W. (2003). Co-evolution in strategic renewal behaviour of British, Dutch and French financial incumbents: Interaction of environmental selection, institutional effects and managerial intentionality. *Journal of Management Studies, 40*(8), 2163–2187.

Ford, J. D. (1999). Organizational change as shifting conversations. *Journal of Organizational Change Management, 12*(6), 480–500.

Ford, J. D., & Baucus, D. A. (1987). Organizational adaptation to performance downturns: An interpretation-based perspective. *Academy of Management Review, 12*(2), 366–380.

Ford, J. D., & Ford, L. W. (1995). The role of conversations in producing intentional change in organizations. *Academy of Management Review, 20*(3), 541–570.

Forester, J. (1992). Critical ethnography: On fieldwork in a Habermasian way. In M. Alvesson & H. Willmott (Eds.), *Critical management studies* (pp. 46–65). London: Sage.

Forrester, J. (1961). *Industrial dynamics.* Cambridge: MIT Press.

Foucault, M. (1973). *Madness and civilization.* New York: Vintage Books.

Foucault, M. (1980). *Power/knowledge: Selected interviews and other writings, 1972–1977* (C. Gordon, Ed.). New York: Pantheon Books.

Fournier, V., & Grey, C. (2000). At the critical moment: Conditions and prospects for critical management studies. *Human Relations, 53*(1), 7–32.

Fox, S. (2000). Communities of practice, Foucault and actor-network theory. *Journal of Management Studies, 37*(6), 853–667.

Frances, J., & Garnsey, E. (2000). Reengineering the food chains. In D. Knights & H. Willmott (Eds.), *The reengineering revolution? Critical studies of corporate change* (pp. 88–113). London: Sage.

Francis, H., & Sinclair, J. (2003). A processual analysis of HRM-based change. *Organization, 10*(4), 685–706.

Freeman, J. H., Carroll, G. R., & Hannan, M. T. (1983). The liability of newness: Age dependence in organizational death rates. *American Sociological Review, 48,* 692–710.

Freeman, J. H., & Hannan, M. T. (1983). Niche width and the dynamics of organizational populations. *American Journal of Sociology, 88,* 1116–1145.

Frost, P., & Egri, C. (1991). The political process of innovation. In L. Cummings & B. Staw (Eds.), *Research in organizational behavior* (Vol. 13, pp. 229–295). Greenwich, CT: JAI Press.

Frost, P., Moore, L., Louis, M., Lundberg, C., & Martin, J. (Eds.). (1985). *Organizational culture.* Beverly Hills, CA: Sage.

Frost, P., Moore, L., Louis, M., Lundberg, C., & Martin, J. (Eds.). (1991). *Reframing organizational culture.* Newbury Park, CA: Sage.

Gagliardi, P. (1986). The creation and change of organizational cultures: A conceptual framework. *Organization Studies, 7*(2), 117–134.

Galunic, D. C., & Eisenhardt, K. M. (1996). The evolution of intracorporate domains: Divisional charter losses in high-technology, multidivisional corporations. *Organization Science, 7*(3), 255–282.

Galunic, D. C., & Eisenhardt, K. M. (2001). Architectural innovation and modular corporate forms. *Academy of Management Journal, 44*(6), 1229–1249.

Galunic, D. C., & Rodan, S. (1998). Resource recombinations in the firm: Knowledge structures and the potential for Schumpeterian recombination. *Strategic Management Journal, 19*(12), 1193–1201.

Galunic, D. C., & Weeks, J. R. (2002). Intraorganizational ecology. In J. Baum (Ed.), *The Blackwell companion to organizations* (pp. 75–97). Oxford, UK: Blackwell.

Garfinkel, H. (1967). *Studies on ethnomethodology.* Englewood Cliffs, NJ: Prentice Hall.

Garud, R., & Karnoe, P. (2001). *Path dependence and creation.* Mahwah, NJ: Lawrence Erlbaum.

Garud, R., & Van de Ven, A. H. (1992). An empirical evaluation of the internal corporate venturing process. *Strategic Management Journal, 13*(8), 93–109.

Gersick, C. (1988). Time and transition in work teams toward a new model of group development. *Academy of Management Journal, 31*(1), 9–41.

Gersick, C. (1991). Revolutionary change theories: A multilevel exploration of the punctuated equilibrium paradigm. *Academy of Management Review, 16*(1), 10–36.

Gersick, K., Lansberg, I., Desjardins, M., & Dunn, B. (1999). Staging and transitions: Managing change in the family business. *Family Business Review, 12*(4), 287–297.

Gherardi, S. (2000). Where learning is: Metaphors and situated learning in a planning group. *Human Relations, 53*(8), 1057–1080.

Gherardi, S., & Nicolini, D. (2000). To transfer is to transform: The circulation of safety knowledge. *Organization, 7*(2), 329–348.

Giddens, A. (1976). *New rules of sociological method: A positive critique of interpretative sociologies.* New York: Basic Books.

Giddens, A. (1979). *Central problems in social theory.* London: Macmillan.

Giddens, A. (1984). *The constitution of society: Outline of the theory of structuration.* Berkeley: University of California Press.

Ginsberg, A., Larsen, E., & Lomi, A. (1996). Generating strategy from individual behavior: A dynamic model of structural embeddedness. In J. Baum & J. Dutton (Eds.), *Advances in strategic management* (Vol. 13, pp. 121–147). Greenwich, CT: JAI Press.

Gioia, D. (1986). Symbols, scripts and sensemaking: Creating meaning in the organizational experience. In H. Sims, D. Gioia, & Associates (Eds.), *The thinking organization* (pp. 49–74). San Francisco: Jossey-Bass.

Gioia, D., & Chittipeddi, K. (1991). Sensemaking and sensegiving in strategic change initiation. *Strategic Management Journal, 12*, 433–448.

Gioia, D., & Thomas, J. B. (1996). Identity, image, and issue interpretation: Sensemaking during strategic change in academia. *Administrative Science Quarterly, 41*(3), 370–403.

Gioia, D., Thomas, J. B., Clark, S. M., & Chittipeddi, K. (1994). Symbolism and strategic change in academia: The dynamics of sensemaking and influence. *Organization Science, 5*(3), 363–383.

Giroux, H., & Taylor, J. R. (2002). The justification of knowledge: Tracking the translations of quality. *Management Learning, 33*(4), 497–517.

Giroux, N. (1998). La communication dans la mise en oeuvre du changement. *Management International, 3*(1), 1–14.

Giroux, N., & Marroquin, L. (2005). L'approche narrative des organisations. *Revue Française de Gestion, 31*, 15–42.

Glynn, M. A., Lant, T., & Milliken, F. J. (1994). Mapping learning processes in organizations: A multi-level framework linking learning and organizing. In C. Stubbard, J. R. Meindl, & J. F. Porac (Eds.), *Advances in managerial cognition and information processing* (pp. 43–83). Greenwich, CT: JAI Press.

Goodrick, E., & Salancik, G. R. (1996). Organizational discretion in responding to institutional practices: Hospitals and cesarean births. *Administrative Science Quarterly, 41*(1), 1–28.

Gouldner, A. (1950). *Patterns of industrial bureaucracy.* Glencoe, IL: Free Press.

Grant, D., Michelson, G., Oswick, C., & Wailes, N. (2005). Guest editorial: Discourse and organizational change. *Journal of Organizational Change Management, 18*(1), 6–15.

Greenwood, R., & Hinings, C. (1988). Organizational design types, tracks and the dynamics of strategic change. *Organization Studies, 9*(3), 293–316.

Greenwood, R., & Hinings, C. (1993). Understanding strategic change: The contribution of archetypes. *Academy of Management Journal, 36*(5), 1052–1081.

Greenwood, R., & Hinings, C. (1996). Understanding radical organizational change: Bringing together the old and the new institutionalism. *Academy of Management Review, 21*(4), 1022–1054.

Greenwood, R., Hinings, C., & Brown, J. (1990). "P2-form" strategic management: Corporate practices in professional partnerships. *Academy of Management Journal, 33*(4), 725–755.

Gregory, K. L. (1983). Native-view paradigms: Multiple cultures and culture conflicts in organizations. *Administrative Science Quarterly, 28*(3), 359–376.

Greiner, L. E. (1972). Evolution and revolution as organizations grow. *Harvard Business Review, 76*(3), 37–46.

Greiner, L. E., & Bhambri, A. (1989). New CEO intervention and dynamics of deliberate strategic change. *Strategic Management Journal, 10*(1), 67–86.

Greve, H. R. (2002). Interorganizational evolution. In J. Baum (Ed.), *The Blackwell companion to organizations* (pp. 557–578). Oxford, UK: Blackwell.

Grimm, C. M., Corsi, T. M., & Smith, R. D. (1993). Determinants of strategic change in the LTL motor carrier industry: A discrete choice analysis. *Transportation Journal, 32*(4), 56–64.

Grimm, C. M., & Smith, K. G. (1991). Management and organizational change: A note on the railroad industry. *Strategic Management Journal, 12*, 557–562.

Groleau, C. (2006). One phenomenon, two lenses: Understanding collective action from the perspectives of coorientation and activity theory. In F. Cooren, J. Taylor, & E. Van Every (Eds.), *Communication as organizing: Empirical and theoretical approaches to the dynamic of text and conversation* (pp. 157–177). Mahwah, NJ: Lawrence Erlbaum.

Gunge, S. P. (2000). Business process reengineering and "the new organization." In D. Knights & H. Willmott (Eds.), *The reengineering revolution? Critical studies of corporate change* (pp. 114–133). London: Sage.

Hafsi, T., & Demers, C. (1989). *Le changement radical dans les organisations complexes: Le cas d'Hydro-Québec*. Boucherville, Québec, Canada: Gaëtan Morin.

Hafsi, T., & Demers, C. (1997). *Mesurer la capacité de changer des organisations*. Montréal, Québec, Canada: Éditions Transcontinental.

Haire, M. (Ed.). (1959). *Modern organization theory*. New York: Wiley.

Hamel, G. (1991). Competition for competence and interpartner learning within international strategic alliances. *Strategic Management Journal, 12*, 83–103.

Hannan, M. T., & Freeman, J. H. (1977). The population ecology of organizations. *American Journal of Sociology, 83*, 929–984.

Hannan, M. T., & Freeman, J. H. (1984). Structural inertia and organizational change. *American Sociological Review, 49*, 149–164.

Hannan, M. T., & Freeman, J. H. (1989). *Organizational ecology*. Cambridge, MA: Harvard University Press.

Hardy, C. (1985). The nature of unobtrusive power. *Journal of Management Studies, 22*(4), 384–399.

Hardy, C. (1995). Managing strategic change: Power, paralysis and perspective. In J. Baum (Ed.), *Advances in strategic management* (pp. 3–30). Greenwich, CT: JAI Press.

Hardy, C. (1996). Understanding power: Bringing about strategic change. *British Journal of Management, 7*, S3.

Hardy, C., & Clegg, S. (1996). Some dare call it power. In S. Clegg, C. Hardy, & W. Nord (Eds.), *Handbook of organization studies* (pp. 622–641). London: Sage.

Hardy, C., Palmer, I., & Phillips, N. (2000). Discourse as a strategic resource. *Human Relations, 53*(9), 1227–1248.

Hardy, C., & Phillips, N. (2004). Discourse and power. In D. Grant, C. Hardy, C. Oswick, & L. Putnam (Eds.), *The Sage handbook of organizational discourse* (pp. 299–316). London: Sage.

Harrisson, D., Laplante, N., & St-Cyr, L. (2001). Cooperation and resistance in work innovation networks. *Human Relations, 54*(2), 215–255.

Hassard, J. (1999). Pop culture magicians seek honest-grappler-after-truth for marginal discussion. *Organization Studies, 20*(4), 561–578.

Hatch, M. J. (1993). The dynamics of organizational culture. *Academy of Management Review, 18*(4), 657–693.

Hatch, M. J., & Schultz, M. (2002). The dynamics of organizational identity. *Human Relations, 55*(8), 989–1018.

Hatch, M. J., & Yanow, D. (2003). Organization theory as an interpretive science. In H. Tsoukas & C. Knudsen (Eds.), *The Oxford handbook of organizational theory: Meta-theoretical perspectives* (pp. 63–87). Oxford, UK: Oxford University Press.

Heath, C., Luff, P., & Knoblauch, H. (2004). Tools, technologies and organizational interaction: The emergence of "workplace studies." In D. Grant, C. Hardy, C. Oswick, & L. Putnam (Eds.), *The Sage handbook of organizational discourse* (pp. 337–358). London: Sage.

Hedberg, B. (1974). *Reframing as a way to cope with organizational stagnation: A case study.* International Institute of Management, Berlin, Germany (Working Paper No. I/74–51).

Hedberg, B. (1981). How organizations learn and unlearn. In W. Starbuck & P. Nystrom (Eds.), *Handbook of organizational design: Vol. 1. Adapting organizations to their environments* (pp. 3–27). Oxford, UK: Oxford University Press.

Hedberg, B., & Jönsson, S. A. (1977). Strategy formulation as a discontinuous process. *International Studies of Management and Organizations, 7*(2), 88–109.

Hedberg, B., & Jönsson, S. A. (1978). Designing semi-confusing information systems for organizations in changing environments. *Accounting, Organizations and Society, 3*(1), 47–64.

Hedberg, B., Nystrom, P., & Starbuck, W. (1976). Camping on seesaws: Prescriptions for a self-designing organization. *Administrative Science Quarterly, 21*(1), 41–65.

Henderson, R. M., & Clark, K. B. (1990). Architectural innovation: The reconfiguration of existing product technologies and the failure of established firms. *Administrative Science Quarterly, 35*(1), 9–30.

Hendry, J. (2000). Strategic decision making, discourse, and strategy as social practice. *Journal of Management Studies, 37*(7), 955–977.

Heracleous, L., & Barrett, M. (2001). Organizational change as discourse: Communicative actions and deep structures in the context of information technology implementation. *Academy of Management Journal, 44*(4), 755–778.

Heracleous, L., & Hendry, J. (2000). Discourse and the study of organization: Toward a structurational perspective. *Human Relations, 53*(10), 1251–1286.

Heracleous, L., & Marshak, R. J. (2004). Conceptualizing organizational discourse as situated symbolic action. *Human Relations, 57*(10), 1285–1312.

Hickson, D., Hinings, C., Lee, C., & Schneck, R. (1971). A strategic contingencies theory of intraorganizational power. *Administrative Science Quarterly, 16*(2), 216–229.

Hinings, C., Brown, J., & Greenwood, R. (1991). Change in an autonomous professional organization. *Journal of Management Studies, 28*(4), 375–393.

Hinings, C., & Greenwood, R. (1988). The normative prescription of organizations. In L. Zucker (Ed.), *Institutional patterns and organizations: Culture and environment* (pp. 53–70). Cambridge, MA: Ballinger.

Hinings, C., Greenwood, R., Ranson, S., & Walsh, K. (1988). *The dynamics of strategic change.* Oxford, UK: Basil Blackwell.

Hinings, C., Hickson, D., Pennings, J., & Schneck, R. (1974). Structural conditions of intraorganizational power. *Administrative Science Quarterly, 19*(1), 22–44.

Hirsch, P. M., & Gillespie, J. J. (2001). Unpacking path dependence: Differential valuations accorded history across disciplines. In R. Garud & P. Karnoe (Eds.), *Path dependence and creation* (pp. 69–90). Mahwah, NJ: Lawrence Erlbaum.

Hirsch, P. M., & Lounsbury, M. (1997). Putting the organization back into organization theory. *Journal of Management Inquiry, 6*(1), 79–88.

Hislop, D., Newell, S., Scarborough, H., & Swan, J. (2000). Networks, knowledge and power: Decision making, politics and the process of innovation. *Technology Analysis & Strategic Management, 12,* 399–411.

Holmqvist, M. (2003). A dynamic model of intra- and interorganizational learning. *Organization Studies, 24*(1), 95–123.

Hrebeniak, L. G., & Joyce, W. F. (1985). Organizational adaptation: Strategic choice and environmental determinism. *Administrative Science Quarterly, 30*(3), 336–349.

Huber, G. P. (1991). Organizational learning: The contributing processes and the literatures. *Organization Science, 2*(1), 88–115.

Huff, A. (1983). A rhetorical examination of strategic change. In L. Pondy, P. Frost, G. Morgan, & T. Dandridge (Eds.), *Organizational symbolism* (pp. 167–183). Greenwich, CT: JAI Press.

Huff, A. (1988). Politics and argument as a means of coping with ambiguity and change. In L. R. Pondy, R. J. Boland, & H. Thomas (Eds.), *Managing ambiguity and change* (pp. 79–90). Chichester, Toronto, Canada: Wiley.

Huff, A. (1990a). Mapping strategic thought. In A. Huff (Ed.), *Mapping strategic thought* (pp. 11–59). Chichester, Toronto, Canada: Wiley.

Huff, A. (Ed.). (1990b). *Mapping strategic thought.* Chichester, Toronto, Canada: Wiley.

Huff, A., Huff, J. O., & Barr, P. (2000). *When firms change direction.* New York: Oxford University Press.

Hurst, D. K., & Zimmerman, B. J. (1994). From life cycle to ecocycle: A new perspective on the growth, maturity, destruction, and renewal of complex systems. *Journal of Management Inquiry, 3*(4), 339–354.

Hutchins, E. (1991). The social organization of distributed cognition. In L. B. Resnick, J. M. Levine, & S. D. Teasley (Eds.), *Perspectives on socially shared cognition.* Washington, DC: American Psychological Association.

Huy, Q. N. (1999). Emotional capability, emotional intelligence, and radical change. *Academy of Management Review, 24*(2), 325–346.

Huy, Q. N. (2001). Time, temporal capability, and planned change. *Academy of Management Review, 26*(4), 601–624.

Huygens, M., Baden-Fuller, C., Van Den Bosch, F. A. J., & Volberda, H. V. (2001). Coevolution of firm capabilities and industrial competition: Investigating the music industry, 1877–1997. *Organization Studies, 22*(6), 971–1011.

Iansiti, M. (2000). How the incumbent can win: Managing technological transitions in the semiconductor industry. *Management Science, 46*(2), 169–185.

Iansiti, M., & Clark, K. B. (1994). Integration and dynamic capability: Evidence from product development in automobiles and mainframe computers. *Industrial and Corporate Change, 3*, 557–605.

Ingram, P. (2002). Interorganizational learning. In J. Baum (Ed.), *The Blackwell companion to organizations* (pp. 642–663). Oxford, UK: Blackwell.

Inkpen, A. C., & Crossan, M. M. (1995). Believing is seeing: Joint ventures and organization learning. *Journal of Management Studies, 32*(5), 595–618.

Isabella, L. (1990). Evolving interpretations as a change unfolds: How managers construe key organizational events. *Academy of Management Journal, 33*(1), 7–41.

Isenberg, D. (1987). Drugs and drama: The effects of two dramatic events in a pharmaceutical company on managers' cognitions. *Columbia Journal of World Business, 22*(1), 43–50.

Jackson, S., & Dutton, J. (1988). Discerning threats and opportunities. *Administrative Science Quarterly, 33*(3), 370–388.

Jaques, E. (1952). *The changing culture of a factory*. New York: Dryden Press.

Jarzabkowski, P. (2003). Strategic practices: An activity theory perspective on continuity and change. *Journal of Management Studies, 40*(1), 23.

Joerges, B., & Czarniawska, B. (1998). The question of technology, or how organizations inscribe the world. *Organization Studies, 19*(3), 363–385.

Johnson, G. (1987). [Commentary on chapter 1]. In A. M. Pettigrew (Ed.), *The management of strategic change* (pp. 56–62). London: Basil Blackwell.

Johnson, G. (1988). Rethinking incrementalism. *Strategic Management Journal, 9*, 75–91.

Johnson, G., Melin, L., & Whittington, R. (2003). Micro strategy and strategizing: Towards an activity-based approach. *Journal of Management Studies, 40*(1), 3–22.

Johnson, J. L. (1994). Chaos and complexity: Theory for management. *Journal of Management Inquiry, 3*(4), 320–328.

Johnson, J. L., & Burton, B. K. (1994). Chaos and complexity theory for management: Caveat emptor. *Journal of Management Inquiry, 3*(4), 320–328.

Johnson, R. (1997). The board of directors over time: Composition and the organizational life cycle. *International Journal of Management, 11*(2), 339–343.

Jones, M. (1999). Structuration theory. In W. Currie & B. Galliers (Eds.), *Rethinking management information systems* (pp. 103–135). Oxford, UK: Oxford University Press.

Kanter, R. M. (1983). *The change masters*. New York: Simon & Schuster.

Karnoe, P., & Garud, R. (2001). Path creation and dependence in the Danish wind turbine field. In J. Porac & M. Ventresca (Eds.), *Constructing industries and markets*. New York: Pergamon Press.

Kauffman, S. A. (1995). *At home in the universe: The search for the laws of self-organization and complexity*. New York: Oxford University Press.

Keck, S., & Tushman, M. (1993). Environmental and organizational context and executive team structure. *Academy of Management Journal, 36*(6), 1314–1344.

Khandwalla, P. N. (1973). Viable and effective design of firms. *Academy of Management Journal, 16*(3), 481–495.

Kiesler, S., & Sproull, L. (1982). Managerial response to changing environments: Perspectives on problem sensing from social cognition. *Administrative Science Quarterly, 27*(4), 548–570.

Kilmann, R. H., Saxton, M. J., & Serpa, R. (1985). *Gaining control of the corporate culture*. San Francisco: Jossey-Bass.

Kim, D. H. (1993). The link between individual and organizational learning. *Sloan Management Review, Fall*, 37–50.

Kimberly, J. R. (1980). The life cycle analogy and the study of organizations: Introduction. In J. Kimberly, E. R. Miles, & Associates (Eds.), *The organizational life cycle: Issues in the creation, transformation, and decline of organizations* (pp. 1–14). San Francisco: Jossey-Bass.

Kimberly, J. R., Miles, R. E., & Associates. (1980). *The organizational life cycle: Issues in the creation, transformation, and decline of organizations.* San Francisco: Jossey-Bass.

Kirkpatrick, I., & Ackroyd, S. (2003). Archetype theory and the changing professional organization: A critique and alternative. *Organization, 10*(4), 731.

Kirsch, D. (2000). *The electric vehicle and the burden of history.* New Brunswick, NJ: Rutgers University Press.

Knights, D. (1997). Organization theory in the age of deconstruction: Dualism, gender and postmodernism revisited. *Organization Studies, 18*(1), 1–19.

Knights, D., & McCabe, D. (1998). When "life is but a dream": Obliterating politics through business process reengineering. *Human Relations, 51*(6), 761–798.

Knights, D., & McCabe, D. (1999). "Are there no limits to authority?" TQM and organizational power. *Organization Studies, 20*(2), 197–224.

Knights, D., & Willmott, H. (1989). Power and subjectivity at work: From degradation to subjugation in social relations. *Sociology, 23*(4), 535–558.

Knights, D., & Willmott, H. (Eds.). (2000). *The reengineering revolution: Critical studies of corporate change.* London: Sage.

Kogut, B., & Zander, U. (1992). Knowledge of the firm, combinative capabilities, and the replication of technology. *Organization Science, 3*(3), 383–397.

Koput, K. W. (1997). A chaotic model of innovative search: Some answers, many questions. *Organization Science, 8*(5), 528–542.

Kuhn, T. (1970). *The structure of scientific revolutions* (2nd ed.). Chicago: University of Chicago Press.

Lampel, J., & Shamsie, J. (2003). Capabilities in motion: New organizational forms and the reshaping of the Hollywood movie industry. *Journal of Management Studies, 40*(8), 2189–2210.

Langley, A., & Denis, J.-L. (2006). Neglected dimensions of organizational change: Towards a situated view. In R. Lines, I. G. Stensaker, & A. Langley (Eds.), *New perspectives on organizational change and learning.* Bergen: Fagbokforlaget.

Langton, J. (1979). Darwinism and a behavioral theory of sociocultural evolution: An analysis. *American Journal of Sociology, 85*(2), 288–309.

Lant, T., & Mezias, S. J. (1990). Managing discontinuous change: A simulation study of organizational learning and entrepreneurship. *Strategic Management Journal, 11*, 147–179.

Lant, T., & Mezias, S. J. (1992). An organizational learning model of convergence and reorientation. *Organization Science, 3*(1), 47–71.

Latour, B. (1991). *Nous n'avons jamais été modernes.* Paris: Éditions La Découverte.

Latour, B. (1995). *La science en action: Introduction à la sociologie des sciences* (M. Biezunski, Trans.). [Originally published (1987) as *Science in action: How to follow scientists and engineers through society*]. Paris: Gallimard.

Lave, J. (1988). *Cognition in practice.* New York: Cambridge University Press.

Lave, J., & Wenger, E. (1991). *Situated learning: Legitimate peripheral participation.* Cambridge, UK: Cambridge University Press.

Law, J. (1994). Organization, narrative and strategy. In J. Hassard & M. Parker (Eds.), *Towards a new theory of organizations* (pp. 248–268). London: Routledge.

Lawrence, P. R., & Lorsch, J. W. (1969). *Organization and environment: Managing differentiation and integration.* Homewood, IL: Richard D. Irwin.

Lawrence, T. B., & Phillips, N. (1998). Commentary: Separating play and critique: Postmodern and critical perspectives on TQM/BPR. *Journal of Management Inquiry, 7*(2), 154–160.

Lee, G. K., & Cole, R. E. (2003). From a firm-based to a community-based model of knowledge creation: The case of the Linux kernel development. *Organization Science, 14*(6), 633–649.

Leifer, R. (1989). Understanding organizational transformation using a dissipative structure model. *Human Relations, 42*(10), 899–916.

Leonard-Barton, D. (1988). Implementation as mutual adaptation of technology and organization. *Research Policy,* (17), 251–267.

Leonardi, P. M., & Jackson, M. H. (2004). Technological determinism and discursive closure in organizational mergers. *Journal of Organizational Change Management, 17*(6), 615.

Leroy, F., & Ramanantsoa, B. (1996). La fusion comme source d'évolution organisationnelle. *Proceedings of the 5th Annual Conference of the Association Internationale de Management Stratégique (AIMS).* Lille, France. Available from http://www.strategie-aims.com/lille/com4202.pdf

Leroy, F., & Ramanantsoa, B. (1997). The cognitive and behavioural dimensions of organizational learning in a merger: An empirical study. *Journal of Management Studies, 34*(6), 871–894.

Levie, J., & Hay, M. (1998). Progress or just proliferation? A historical review of stages models of early corporate growth. *London Business School* (Working Paper No. WP 98–5).

Levinthal, D. (1994). Surviving Schumpeterian environments: An evolutionary perspective. In J. Baum & J. Singh (Eds.), *Evolutionary dynamics of organizations* (pp. 167–178). New York: Oxford University Press.

Levinthal, D. (1997). Adaptation on rugged landscapes. *Management Science, 43,* 934–950.

Levinthal, D., & March, J. G. (1981). A model of adaptive organizational search. *Journal of Economic Behavior and Organization, 2,* 307–333.

Levinthal, D., & March, J. G. (1993). The myopia of learning. *Strategic Management Journal, 14,* 95–112.

Levinthal, D., & Myatt, J. (1994). Co-evolution of capabilities and industry: The evolution of mutual fund processing. *Strategic Management Journal, 15,* 45–62.

Levinthal, D., & Warglien, M. (1999). Landscape design: Designing for local action in complex worlds. *Organization Science, 10,* 342–357.

Levitt, B., & March, J. G. (1988). Organizational learning. *Annual Review of Sociology, 14,* 319–340.

Levy, D. (1994). Chaos theory and strategy: Theory, application, and managerial implications. *Strategic Management Journal, 15,* 167–178.

Lewin, A. Y., & Volberda, H. W. (1999). Prolegomena on coevolution: A framework for research on strategy and new organizational forms. *Organization Science, 10*(5), 519–534.

Lindblom, C. E. (1959). The science of "muddling through." *Public Administration Review, 19*(2), 79–88.

Lodahl, T., & Mitchell, S. (1980). Drift in the development of innovative organizations. In J. Kimberly, R. Miles, & Associates (Eds.), *The organizational life cycle* (pp. 184–207). San Francisco: Jossey-Bass.

Lok, J., & Willmott, H. (2006). Institutional theory, language, and discourse analysis: A comment on Phillips, Lawrence, and Hardy. *Academy of Management Review, 31*(2), 477–480.

Lomi, A., & Larsen, E. R. (1996). Interacting locally and evolving globally: A computational approach to the dynamics of organizational populations. *Academy of Management Journal, 39*(4), 1287–1321.

Lomi, A., Larsen, E. R., & van Ackere, A. (2003). Organization, evolution and performance in neighborhood-based systems. In J. Baum & O. Sorensen (Eds.), *Advances in strategic management* (Vol. 20, pp. 239–266). Amsterdam: Elsevier JAI.

Lovas, B., & Ghoshal, S. (2000). Strategy as guided evolution. *Strategic Management Journal, 21*(9), 875–896.

Luhmann, N. (1995). *Social systems.* Stanford: Stanford University Press.

Lundberg, C. (1985). On the feasibility of cultural intervention in organizations. In P. Frost, L. Moore, M. Louis, C. Lundberg, & J. Martin (Eds.), *Organizational culture* (pp. 169–185). Beverly Hills, CA: Sage.

Lyles, M. A., & Schwenk, C. R. (1992). Top management, strategy and organizational knowledge structures. *Journal of Management Studies, 29*(2), 155–175.

MacIntosh, R., & MacLean, D. (1999). Conditioned emergence: A dissipative structures approach to transformation. *Strategic Management Journal, 20,* 297–316.

Madsen, T. L., Mosakowski, E., & Zaheer, S. (2002). Knowledge retention and personnel mobility: The nondisruptive effects of inflows of experience. *Organization Science, 14*(2), 173–191.

Mahnke, V. (2001). The process of vertical dis-integration: An evolutionary perspective on outsourcing. *Journal of Management and Governance, 5,* 353–379.

March, J. G. (1965). *Handbook of organizations.* Chicago: Rand McNally.

March, J. G. (1981). Footnotes to organizational change. *Administrative Science Quarterly, 26*(4), 563–577.

March, J. G. (1991). Exploration and exploitation in organizational learning. *Organization Science, 2*(1), 71–87.

March, J. G. (1994). The evolution of evolution. In J. Baum & J. Singh (Eds.), *Evolutionary dynamics of organizations* (pp. 39–49). New York: Oxford University Press.

March, J. G., & Olsen, J. P. (1976). *Ambiguity and choice in organizations.* Bergen, Norway: Universitetsforlaget.

March, J. G., Schulz, M., & Zhou, X. (2000). *The dynamics of rules: Change in written organizational codes.* Stanford, CA: Stanford University Press.

Markoczy, L., & Goldberg, J. (1998). Management organization and human nature: An introduction. *Managerial and Decision Economics, 19,* 387–409.

Markus, M. L., & Pfeffer, J. (1983). Power and the design and implementation of accounting and control systems. *Accounting, Organizations, and Society, 8*(2/3), 205–218.

Martin, J. (1985). Can organizational culture be managed? In P. Frost, L. Moore, M. Louis, C. Lundberg, & J. Martin (Eds.), *Organizational culture* (pp. 95–98). Beverly Hills, CA: Sage.

Martin, J., & Frost, P. (1996). The organizational culture war games: A struggle for intellectual dominance. In S. Clegg, C. Hardy, & W. Nord (Eds.), *Handbook of organization studies* (pp. 599–641). London: Sage.

Martin, J., Sitkin, S., & Boehm, M. (1985). Founders and the elusiveness of a cultural legacy. In P. Frost, L. Moore, M. Louis, C. Lundberg, & J. Martin (Eds.), *Organizational culture* (pp. 99–124). Beverly Hills, CA: Sage.

Mathews, K. M., White, M. C., & Long, R. G. (1999). Why study the complexity sciences in the social sciences? *Human Relations, 52*(4), 439–462.

Maturana, H. (1991). Science in daily life: The ontology of scientific explanations. In F. Steier (Ed.), *Research and reflexivity: Self-reflexivity as social process* (pp. 30–52). Newbury Park, CA: Sage.

Maturana, H., & Varela, F. (1987). *The tree of knowledge: The biological roots of understanding.* Boston: Shambhala.

McCabe, D. (1996). The best laid schemes o' TQM: Strategy, politics and power. *New Technology, Work and Employment, 11*(1), 28–38.

McCabe, D., & Knights, D. (2000). "Such stuff as dreams are made on": BPR up against the wall of functionalism, hierarchy and specialization. In D. Knights & H. Willmott (Eds.), *The reengineering revolution: Critical studies of corporate change* (pp. 63–87). London: Sage.

McCabe, D., Knights, D., Kerfoot, D., Morgan, G., & Willmott, H. (1998). Making sense of quality: Towards a review and critique of quality initiatives in financial services. *Human Relations, 51*(3), 389–411.

McKelvey, B. (1982). *Organizational systematics: Taxonomy, evolution, classification.* Berkeley: University of California Press.

McKelvey, B. (1997). Quasi-natural organization science. *Organization Science, 8*(4), 352–380.

McKelvey, B. (1999). Avoiding complexity catastrophe in coevolutionary pockets: Strategies for rugged landscapes. *Organization Science, 10*(3), 294–321.

McKelvey, B. (2002). Model-centered organization science epistemology. In J. Baum (Ed.), *The Blackwell companion to organizations* (pp. 752–780). Oxford, UK: Blackwell.

McLoughlin, I., & Badham, R. (2005). Political process perspectives on organization and technological change. *Human Relations, 58*(7), 827–843.

Merton, R. (1948). Manifest and latent functions. In R. Merton (Ed.), *Social theory and social structure* (pp. 37–59). Glencoe, IL: Free Press.

Metzger, R. (1989). Organizational life cycles in banking. *Group & Organization Studies, 14*(4), 389–399.

Meyer, A. D. (1982). Adapting to environmental jolts. *Administrative Science Quarterly, 27*(4), 515–537.

Meyer, A. D., Frost, P., & Weick, K. (1998). The *Organization Science* jazz festival: Improvisation as a metaphor for organizing. *Organization Science, 9*(5), 540–542.

Meyer, A. D., Goes, J., & Brooks, G. (1990). Environmental jolts and industry revolutions: Organizational responses to discontinuous change. *Strategic Management Journal, 11,* 93–110.

Meyer, A. D., Goes, J., & Brooks, G. (1993). Organizations reacting to hyperturbulence. In G. P. Huber & W. H. Glick (Eds.), *Organizational change and redesign* (pp. 66–111). New York: Oxford University Press.

Meyer, A. D., Tsui, A., & Hinings, C. (1993). Configurational approaches to organizational analysis. *Academy of Management Journal, 36*(6), 1175–1195.

Meyer, J., & Rowan, B. (1977). Institutionalized organizations: Formal structure as myth and ceremony. *American Journal of Sociology, 83,* 340–363.

Meyer, M. (1979). Organizational structure as signaling. *Pacific Sociological Review, 22,* 481–500.

Meyer, M. (1994). Turning evolution inside the organization. In J. Baum & J. Singh (Eds.), *Evolutionary dynamics of organizations* (pp. 109–116). New York: Oxford University Press.

Meyerson, D. (1991). "Normal" ambiguity? A glimpse of an occupational culture. In P. Frost, L. Moore, M. Louis, C. Lundberg, & J. Martin (Eds.), *Reframing organizational culture* (pp. 131–144). Newbury Park, CA: Sage.

Meyerson, D., & Martin, J. (1987). Cultural change: An integration of three different views. *Journal of Management Studies, 24*(6), 623–647.

Mezias, S. J., & Glynn, M. A. (1993). The three faces of corporate renewal. *Strategic Management Journal, 14*(2), 77–101.

Miettinen, R., & Virkkunen, J. (2005). Epistemic objects, artefacts and organizational change. *Organization, 12*(3), 437–456.

Miles, R. E., & Snow, C. (1978). *Organizational strategy, structure, and process.* New York: McGraw-Hill.

Milgrom, P. R., & Roberts, J. (1990). The economics of modern manufacturing: Technology, strategy and organization. *American Economic Review, 80*, 511–528.

Miller, D. (1981). Toward a new contingency approach: The search for organizational gestalts. *Journal of Management Studies, 18*(1), 1–26.

Miller, D. (1982). Evolution and revolution: A quantum view of structural change in organizations. *Journal of Management Studies, 19*(2), 131–151.

Miller, D., & Friesen, P. (1978). Archetypes of strategy formulation. *Management Science, 24*, 921–933.

Miller, D., & Friesen, P. (1980). Archetypes of organizational transition. *Administrative Science Quarterly, 25*(2), 268–299.

Miller, D., & Friesen, P. (1982). Structural change and performance: Quantum versus piecemeal-incremental approaches. *Academy of Management Journal, 25*(4), 867–892.

Miller, D., & Friesen, P. (1984). *Organizations: A quantum view.* Englewood Cliffs, NJ: Prentice Hall.

Miller, D., Greenwood, R., & Hinings, C. (1997). Creative chaos versus munificent momentum: The schism between normative and academic views of organizational change. *Journal of Management Inquiry, 6*(1), 71–78.

Miller, D., & Shamsie, J. (2001). Learning across the life cycle: Experimentation and performance among the Hollywood studio heads. *Strategic Management Journal, 22*(8), 725–732.

Miner, A. S. (1990). Structural evolution through idiosyncratic jobs: The potential for unplanned learning. *Organization Science, 1*(2), 195–210.

Miner, A. S. (1991). Organizational evolution and the social ecology of jobs. *American Sociological Review, 56*(6), 772–785.

Miner, A. S. (1994). Seeking adaptive advantage: Evolutionary theory and managerial action. In J. Baum & J. Singh (Eds.), *Evolutionary dynamics of organizations* (pp. 76–89). New York: Oxford University Press.

Miner, A. S., & Mezias, S. J. (1996). Ugly duckling no more: Pasts and futures of organizational learning research. *Organization Science, 7*(1), 88–99.

Mintzberg, H. (1973). Strategy-making in three modes. *California Management Review, 16*(2), 44–53.

Mintzberg, H. (1979). *The structuring of organizations.* Englewood Cliffs, NJ: Prentice Hall.

Mintzberg, H. (1983). *Power in and around organizations* (Vol. 3). Englewood Cliffs, NJ: Prentice Hall.

Mintzberg, H. (1984). Power and organizational life cycles. *Academy of Management Review, 9*(2), 207–224.

Mintzberg, H., Ahlstrand, B., & Lampel, J. (1998). *Strategy safari.* New York: Free Press.

Mintzberg, H., & McHugh, A. (1985). Strategy formation in an adhocracy. *Administrative Science Quarterly, 30*(2), 160–197.

Mintzberg, H., & Waters, J. (1982). Tracking strategy in an entrepreneurial firm. *Academy of Management Journal, 25*(3), 465–499.

Mintzberg, H., & Waters, J. (1985). Of strategies, deliberate and emergent. *Strategic Management Journal, 6*(3), 257–272.

Mintzberg, H., & Westley, F. (1992). Cycles of organizational change. *Strategic Management Journal, 13*, 39–59.

Moldoveanu, M. C., & Bauer, R. (2004). On the relationship between organizational complexity and organizational dynamics. *Organization Science, 15*, 98–118.

Moldoveanu, M. C., & Baum, J. (2002). Contemporary debates in organizational epistemology. In J. Baum (Ed.), *The Blackwell companion to organizations* (pp. 733–751). Oxford, UK: Blackwell.

Moores, K., & Yuen, S. (2001). Management accounting systems and organizational configuration: A life-cycle perspective. *Accounting, organizations and society, 26*(4–5), 351–389.

Morel, B., & Ramanujam, R. (1999). Through the looking glass of complexity: The dynamics of organizations as adaptive and evolving systems. *Organization Science, 10*(3), 278–293.

Morgan, G. (1982). Cybernetics and organization theory: Epistemology or technique? *Human Relations, 35*, 521–537.

Morgan, G. (1986). *Images of organization.* Beverly Hills, CA: Sage.

Morgan, G., Frost, P., & Pondy, L. (1983). Organizational symbolism. In L. Pondy, P. Frost, G. Morgan, & T. Dandridge (Eds.), *Organizational symbolism* (pp. 3–35). Greenwich, CT: JAI Press.

Morris, D., Tasliyan, M., & Wood, G. (2003). The social and organizational consequences of the implementation of electronic data interchange systems: Reinforcing existing power relations or a contested domain? *Organization Studies, 24*(4), 557–574.

Mueller, F., & Carter, C. (2005). The "HRM project" and managerialism, or why some discourses are more equal than others. *Journal of Organizational Change Management, 18*(4), 369–382.

Mueller, F., Sillince, J., Harvey, C., & Howorth, C. (2004). "A rounded picture is what we need": Rhetorical strategies, arguments, and the negotiation of change in a UK hospital trust. *Organization Studies, 25*(1), 75–93.

Mumby, D. (2001). Power and politics. In F. Jablin & L. Putnam (Eds.), *The new handbook of organizational communication* (pp. 585–623). Thousand Oaks, CA: Sage.

Murmann, J. P., Aldrich, H., Levinthal, D., & Winter, S. G. (2003). Evolutionary thought in management and organization theory at the beginning of the new millennium. *Journal of Management Inquiry, 12*(1), 22–40.

Mutch, A. (2002). Actors and networks or agents and structures: Towards a realist view of information systems. *Organization, 9*(3), 477–496.

Mutch, A. (2003). Communities of practice and habitus: A critique. *Organization Studies, 24*(3), 383–401.

Mutch, A. (2005). Discussion of Willmott: Critical realism, agency and discourse: Moving the debate forward. *Organization, 12*(5), 781–786.

Neilsen, E. H., & Rao, H. (1987). The strategy-legitimacy nexus: A thick description. *Academy of Management Review, 12*(2), 523–533.

Nelson, R. R., & Winter, S. G. (1977). In search of a useful theory of innovation. *Research Policy, 6*, 36–76.

Nelson, R. R., & Winter, S. G. (1978). Forces generating and limiting concentration under Schumpeterian competition. *Bell Journal of Economics, 9,* 524–548.

Nelson, R. R., & Winter, S. G. (1982). *An evolutionary theory of economic change.* Cambridge, MA: Harvard University Press.

Noda, T., & Bower, J. L. (1996). Strategy making as iterated processes of resource allocation. *Strategic Management Journal, 17,* 159–192.

Nohria, N., & Eccles, R. G. (1992). *Networks and organizations.* Boston: Harvard Business School Press.

Nonaka, I. (1988). Creating order out of organizational chaos. *California Management Review, 30*(3), 57–71.

Nonaka, I. (1994). A dynamic theory of organizational knowledge creation. *Organization Science, 5*(1), 14–37.

Nord, W. (1985). Can organizational culture be managed? A synthesis. In P. Frost, L. Moore, M. Louis, C. Lundberg, & J. Martin (Eds.), *Organizational culture* (pp. 187–196). Beverly Hills, CA: Sage.

Normann, R. (1977). *Management for growth.* New York: Wiley.

Nystrom, P., & Starbuck, W. (Eds.). (1981). *Handbook of organizational design: Vol. 1. Adapting organizations to their environments.* New York: Oxford University Press.

O'Connor, E. S. (1995). Paradoxes of participation: Textual analysis and organizational change. *Organization Studies, 16*(5), 769–803.

O'Connor, E. S. (2000). Plotting the organization: The embedded narrative as a construct for studying change. *Journal of Applied Behavioral Science, 36*(2), 174–192.

Oliver, A. (2001). Strategic alliances and the learning life-cycle of biotechnology firms. *Organization Studies, 22*(3), 467–489.

Oliver, C. (1991). Strategic responses to institutional processes. *Academy of Management Review, 16*(1), 145–179.

Orlikowski, W. J. (1996). Improvising organizational transformation over time: A situated change perspective. *Information Systems Research, 7*(1), 63–92.

Orlikowski, W. J. (2000). Using technology and constituting structures: A practice lens for studying technology in organizations. *Organization Science, 11*(4), 404–428.

Orlikowski, W. J. (2002). Knowing in practice: Enacting a collective capability in distributed organizing. *Organization Science, 13*(3), 249–273.

Orlikowski, W. J., & Robey, D. (1991). Information technology and the structuring of organizations. *Information Systems Research, 2*(2), 143–169.

Orr, J. (1990). Sharing knowledge, celebrating identity: War stories and community memory in a service culture. In D. S. Middleton & D. Edwards (Eds.), *Collective remembering: Memory in society.* London: Sage.

Oswick, C., Grant, D., Michelson, G., & Wailes, N. (2005). Looking forwards: Discursive directions in organizational change. *Journal of Organizational Change Management, 18*(4), 383–390.

Park, O., Sims, H., & Motowidlo, S. (1986). Affect in organizations: How feelings and emotions influence managerial judgment. In H. Sims, D. Gioia, & Associates (Eds.), *The thinking organization* (pp. 215–237). San Francisco: Jossey-Bass.

Parsons, T. (1960). *Structure and process in modern societies.* Glencoe, IL: Free Press.

Penrose, E. (1952). Biological analogies in the theory of the firm. *American Economic Review, 42,* 804–819.

Perrow, C. (1984). *Normal accidents: Living with high-risk technologies.* New York: Basic Books.

Perrow, C. (1985). Comment on Langton's "ecological theory of bureaucracy." *Administrative Science Quarterly, 30*(2), 278–283.

Perrow, C. (1986). *Complex organizations: A critical essay* (3rd ed.). Glenview, IL: Scott, Foresman.

Peters, T., & Waterman, R. (1982). *In search of excellence : Lessons from America's best-run companies.* New York: Harper and Row.

Pettigrew, A. M. (1973). *The politics of organizational decision making.* London: Tavistock.

Pettigrew, A. M. (1977). Strategy formulation as a political process. *International Studies of Management and Organizations, 7*(2), 78–87.

Pettigrew, A. M. (1979). On studying organizational cultures. *Administrative Science Quarterly, 24*(4), 570–581.

Pettigrew, A. M. (1985a). *The awakening giant: Continuity and change in ICI.* Oxford, UK: Basil Blackwell.

Pettigrew, A. M. (1985b). Examining change in the long-term context of culture and politics. In J. Pennings & Associates (Eds.), *Organizational strategy and change* (pp. 269–318). San Francisco: Jossey-Bass.

Pettigrew, A. M. (1997). What is a processual analysis? *Scandinavian Management Journal, 13*(4), 337–348.

Pettigrew, A. M., Ferlie, E., & McKee, L. (1992). *Shaping strategic change: Making change in large organizations—the case of the National Health Service.* London: Sage.

Pettigrew, A. M., & Whipp, R. (1991). *Managing change for comprehensive success.* Oxford, UK: Basil Blackwell.

Pettigrew, A. M., Woodman, R., & Cameron, K. (2001). Studying organizational change and development: Challenges for future research. *Academy of Management Journal, 44*(4), 697–713.

Pfeffer, J. (1981). *Power in organizations.* Marshfield, MA: Pitman.

Pfeffer, J., & Salancik, G. R. (1974). Organizational decision making as a political process. *Administrative Science Quarterly, 19*(2), 135–151.

Pfeffer, J., & Salancik, G. R. (1978). *The external control of organizations: A resource dependence perspective.* New York: Harper and Row.

Phillips, N., Lawrence, T. B., & Hardy, C. (2004). Discourse and institutions. *Academy of Management Review, 29*(4), 635–652.

Pinnington, A., & Morris, T. (2002). Transforming the architect: Ownership form and archetype change. *Organization Studies, 23*(2), 189–210.

Polanyi, M. (1966). *The tacit dimension.* New York: Doubleday.

Polley, D. (1997). Turbulence in organizations: New metaphors for organizational research. *Organization Science, 8*(5), 445–457.

Pondy, L., Frost, P., Morgan, G., & Dandridge, T. (1983). *Organizational symbolism.* Greenwich, CT: JAI Press.

Pondy, L., & Huff, A. (1985). Achieving routine in organizational change. *Journal of Management, 11*, 103–116.

Pondy, L., & Mitroff, I. (1979). Beyond open systems models of organizations. In L. Cummings & B. Staw (Eds.), *Research in organizational behavior* (Vol. 1, pp. 3–39). Greenwich, CT: JAI Press.

Poole, M. S., & DeSanctis, G. (1990). Understanding the use of group decision support systems: The theory of adaptive structuration. In J. Fulk & C. W. Steinfield (Eds.), *Organizations and communication technology* (pp. 173–193). Newbury Park, CA: Sage.

Poole, M. S., Gioia, D., & Gray, B. (1989). Influence modes, schema change, and organizational transformation. *Journal of Applied Behavioral Science, 25,* 271–289.

Poole, M. S., Van de Ven, A., Dooley, K., & Holmes, M. E. (2000). *Organizational change and innovation processes.* New York: Oxford University Press.

Porac, J. F. (1994). On the concept of "organizational community." In J. Baum & J. Singh (Eds.), *Evolutionary dynamics of organizations* (pp. 451–456). New York: Oxford University Press.

Porac, J. F., Thomas, H., Wilson, F., Paton, D., & Kanfer, A. (1995). Rivalry and the industry model of Scottish knitwear producers. *Administrative Science Quarterly, 40*(2), 203–227.

Porter, M. (1980). *Competitive strategy: Techniques for analyzing industries and competitors.* New York: Free Press.

Powell, W. (1988). Institutional effects on organizational structure and performance. In L. Zucker (Ed.), *Institutional patterns and organizations: Culture and environment* (pp. 115–136). Cambridge, MA: Ballinger.

Powell, W., & DiMaggio, P. (Eds.). (1991). *The new institutionalism in organizational analysis.* Chicago: University of Chicago Press.

Prahalad, C. K., & Bettis, R. A. (1986). The dominant logic: A new linkage between diversity and performance. *Strategic Management Journal, 7,* 485–501.

Prahalad, C. K., & Hamel, G. (1990). The core competence of the corporation. *Harvard Business Review, 68*(3), 79–91.

Pugh, D., Hickson, D., Hinings, C., & Turner, C. (1971). The context of organizational structures. In W. Starbuck (Ed.), *Organizational growth and development* (pp. 327–368). Harmondsworth, UK: Penguin Books.

Quinn, J. B. (1978). Strategic change: "Logical incrementalism." *Sloan Management Review, 20*(1), 7–19.

Quinn, J. B. (1980). Managing strategic change. *Sloan Management Review, 22*(4), 3–20.

Rajagopalan, N., & Spreitzer, G. (1997). Toward a theory of strategic change: A multi-lens perspective and integrative framework. *Academy of Management Review, 22*(1), 48–79.

Ramaprasad, A. (1982). Revolutionary change and strategic management. *Behavioral Science, 27,* 387–392.

Ranson, S., Hinings, C., & Greenwood, R. (1980). The structuring of organizational structures. *Administrative Science Quarterly, 25*(1), 1–17.

Rao, H. (1998). Caveat emptor: The construction of nonprofit consumer watchdog organizations. *American Journal of Sociology, 103,* 912–961.

Reed, M. (1992). Introduction. In M. Reed & M. Hughes (Eds.), *Rethinking organization: New directions in organization theory and analysis* (pp. 1–16). London: Sage.

Reed, M. (1993). Organizations and modernity: Continuity and discontinuity in organization theory. In J. Hassard & M. Parker (Eds.), *Postmodernism and organization* (pp. 163–182). London: Sage.

Reed, M. (1996). Organizational theorizing: A historically contested terrain. In S. R. Clegg, C. Hardy, & W. R. Nord (Eds.), *Handbook of organization studies* (pp. 31–56). London: Sage.

Reed, M. (1997). In praise of duality and dualism: Rethinking agency and structure in organizational analysis. *Organization Studies, 18*(1), 21–42.

Reed, M. (2003). The agency/structure dilemma in organization theory. In H. Tsoukas & C. Knudsen (Eds.), *The Oxford handbook of organization theory* (pp. 289–309). Oxford, UK: Oxford University Press.

Reed, M. (2005). Reflections on the "realist turn" in organization and management studies. *Journal of Management Studies, 42*(8), 1621–1644.

Reed, M., & Hughes, M. (1992). *Rethinking organization*. London: Sage.

Reger, R. K., Gustafson, L. T., & Mullane, J. V. (1994). Reframing the organization: Why implementing total quality is easier said than done. *Academy of Management Review, 19*(3), 565–584.

Reitter, R., Chevalier, F., Laroche, H., Mendoza, C., & Pulicani, P. (1991). *Cultures d'entreprise*. Paris: Librairie Vuibert.

Rhenman, E. (1973). *Organizational theory for long-range planning*. London: John Wiley & Sons.

Rindova, V., & Kotha, S. (2001). Continuous "morphing": Competing through dynamic capabilities, form, and function. *Academy of Management Journal, 44*(6), 1263–1280.

Rivkin, J. W., & Siggelkow, N. (2003). Balancing search and stability: Interdependencies among elements of organizational design. *Management Science, 49*(3), 290–311.

Robey, D., & Boudreau, M.-C. (1999). Accounting for the contradictory organizational consequences of information technology: Theoretical directions and methodological implications. *Information Systems Research, 10*(2), 167–185.

Robichaud, D., Giroux, H., & Taylor, J. R. (2004). The metaconversation: The recursive property of language as a key to organizing. *Academy of Management Review, 29*(4), 617–634.

Rodrigues, S. B., & Child, J. (2003). Co-evolution in an institutionalized environment. *Journal of Management Studies, 40*(8), 2137–2162.

Romanelli, E., & Tushman, M. L. (1994). Organizational transformation as punctuated equilibrium: An empirical test. *Academy of Management Journal, 37*(5), 1141–1166.

Rosenkopf, L., & Tushman, M. L. (1994). The coevolution of technology and organization. In J. Baum & J. Singh (Eds.), *Evolutionary dynamics of organizations* (pp. 403–424). New York: Oxford University Press.

Rouleau, L. (2005). Micro-practices of strategic sensemaking and sensegiving: How middle managers interpret and sell change every day. *Journal of Management Studies, 42*(7), 1413–1441.

Ruelle, D. (1991). *Chance and chaos*. Princeton, NJ: Princeton University Press.

Salvato, C. (2003). The role of micro-strategies in the engineering of firm evolution. *Journal of Management Studies, 40*(1), 83–108.

Samra-Fredericks, D. (2003). Strategizing as lived experience and strategists' everyday efforts to shape strategic direction. *Journal of Management Studies, 40*(1), 141–174.

Sastry, A. (1997). Problems and paradoxes in a model of punctuated organizational change. *Administrative Science Quarterly, 42*(June), 237–275.

Schein, E. (1985). *Organizational culture and leadership*. San Francisco: Jossey-Bass.

Schein, E. (1990). Organizational culture: What it is and how to change it. In P. Evans, Y. Doz, & A. Laurent (Eds.), *Human resource management in international firms* (pp. 56–82). New York: St. Martin's Press.

Schein, E. (1991). What is culture? In P. Frost, L. Moore, M. Louis, C. Lundberg, & J. Martin (Eds.), *Reframing organizational culture* (pp. 243–253). Newbury Park, CA: Sage.

Schein, E. (1996). Culture: The missing concept in organization studies. *Administrative Science Quarterly, 41*(2), 229–240.

Schilling, M. (2000). Towards a general modular systems theory and its application to interfirm product modularity. *Academy of Management Review, 25*(2), 312–334.

Schön, D. (1979). Generative metaphor: A perspective on problem-setting in social policy. In A. Ortony (Ed.), *Metaphor and thought.* Cambridge, UK: Cambridge University Press.

Schulz, M. (1998). Limits to bureaucratic growth: The density dependence of organizational rule births. *Administrative Science Quarterly, 43*(4), 845–876.

Schulz, M. (2002). Organizational learning. In J. Baum (Ed.), *The Blackwell companion to organizations* (pp. 415–441). Oxford, UK: Blackwell.

Schumpeter, J. A. (1942). *Capitalism, socialism, and democracy.* New York: Harper.

Schwartz, H., & Davis, S. (1980). Matching corporate culture and business strategy. *Organizational Dynamics,* (Summer), 30–48.

Schwenk, C. R. (1988). The cognitive perspective on strategic decision making. *Journal of Management Studies, 25*(1), 41–55.

Scott, B. R. (1971). *Stages of corporate development, Part 1: Case No. 9-371-294.* Boston: Harvard Business School Press.

Scott, R. (1995). Institutional theory and organizations. In R. Scott & S. Christensen (Eds.), *The institutional construction of organizations* (pp. xi–xxiii). Thousand Oaks, CA: Sage.

Scott, R. (1998). *Organizations: Rational, natural and open systems* (4th ed.). Upper Saddle River, NJ: Prentice Hall.

Searle, J. R. (1969). *Speech acts: An essay in the philosophy of language.* Cambridge, UK: Cambridge University Press.

Selznick, P. (1949). *TVA and the grass roots.* Berkeley: University of California Press.

Selznick, P. (1957). *Leadership in administration: A sociological interpretation* (1984 reprint ed.). Berkeley: University of California Press.

Sewell, W. (1992). A theory of structure. Duality, agency and transformation. *American Journal of Sociology, 98, 1–29.*

Sewell, G., & Wilkinson, B. (1992). "Someone to watch over me": Surveillance, discipline and the just-in-time labour process. *Sociology, 26*(2), 271–289.

Sheldon, A. (1980). Organizational paradigms. *Organization Dynamics,* (8), 61–71.

Sherer, P., & Lee, K. (2002). Institutional change in large law firms: A resource dependency and institutional perspective. *Academy of Management Journal, 45*(1), 102–119.

Siehl, C. (1985). After the founder: An opportunity to manage culture. In P. Frost, L. Moore, M. Louis, C. Lundberg, & J. Martin (Eds.), *Organizational culture* (pp. 125–140). Beverly Hills, CA: Sage.

Siggelkow, N., & Levinthal, D. (2003). Temporarily divide to conquer: Centralized, decentralized, and reintegrated organizational approaches to exploration and adaptation. *Organization Science, 14*(6), 650–669.

Sillince, J. A. A. (1999). The role of political language forms and language coherence in the organizational change process. *Organization Studies, 20*(3), 485–518.

Sillince, J. A. A. (2000). Rhetorical power, accountability and conflict in committees: An argumentation approach. *Journal of Management Studies, 37*(8), 1125–1156.

Simon, H. A. (1996). *The sciences of the artificial* (3rd ed.). Cambridge: MIT Press.

Singh, J., House, R., & Tucker, D. (1986). Organizational change and organizational mortality. *Administrative Science Quarterly, 31*(4), 587–611.

Skoldberg, K. (1994). Tales of change: Public administration reform and narrative mode. *Organization Science, 5*(2), 219–238.

Smircich, L. (1983a). Concepts of culture and organizational analysis. *Administrative Science Quarterly, 28*(3), 339–358.

Smircich, L. (1983b). Organizations as shared meanings. In L. Pondy, P. Frost, G. Morgan, & T. Dandridge (Eds.), *Organizational symbolism* (pp. 55–65). Greenwich, CT: JAI Press.

Smith, K. G., & Grimm, C. M. (1987). Environmental change, strategic change and organizational performance: A study of railroad regulation. *Strategic Management Journal, 8,* 363–376.

Sorenson, O. (2002). Interorganizational complexity and computation. In J. Baum (Ed.), *The Blackwell companion to organizations* (pp. 664–685). Oxford, UK: Blackwell.

Spender, J.-C., & Grinyer, P. H. (1996). Organizational renewal. *International Studies of Management & Organization, 26*(1), 17–40.

Stacey, R. D. (1995). The science of complexity: An alternative perspective for strategic change processes. *Strategic Management Journal, 16,* 477–495.

Starbuck, W. (1965). Organizational growth and development. In J. G. March (Ed.), *Handbook of organizations* (pp. 451–533). Chicago: Rand McNally.

Starbuck, W. (1971a). *Organizational growth and development.* Harmondsworth, UK: Penguin Books.

Starbuck, W. (1971b). Organizational metamorphosis. In W. Starbuck (Ed.), *Organizational growth and development* (pp. 275–298). Harmondsworth, UK: Penguin Books.

Starbuck, W. (1983). Organizations as action generators. *American Sociological Review, 48,* 91–102.

Starkey, K. (1987). [Review of the book *The Awakening Giant* by A. M. Pettigrew]. *Journal of Management Studies, 24*(4), 413–420.

Stopford, J. M., & Wells, L. T. (1972). *Managing the multinational enterprise.* New York: Basic Books.

Sturdy, A., & Grey, C. (2003). Beneath and beyond organizational change management: Exploring alternatives. *Organization, 10*(4), 651–662.

Suchman, L. A. (1987). *Plans and situated actions: The problem of human-machine communication.* Cambridge, UK: Cambridge University Press.

Sutton, R. I. (1987). The process of organizational death: Disbanding and reconnecting. *Administrative Science Quarterly, 32*(4), 542–570.

Sztompka, P. (1993). *The sociology of social change.* Cambridge, UK: Basil Blackwell.

Taylor, J. R. (1993). La dynamique de changement organisationnel: Une théorie conversation/texte de la communication et ses implications. *Communication & Organisation, 1*(3), 51–93.

Taylor, J. R., Cooren, F., Giroux, H., & Robichaud, D. (1996). The communicational basis of organization: Between the conversation and the text. *Communication Theory, 6*(1), 1–39.

Taylor, J. R., & Giroux, H. (2004). The role of language in self-organizing. In G. A. Barnett & R. Houston (Eds.), *Advances in self-organizing systems* (pp. 131–168). Cresskill, NJ: Hampton Press.

Taylor, J. R., & Van Every, E. J. (2000). *The emergent organization: Communication as its site and interface.* Mahwah, NJ: Lawrence Erlbaum.

Teece, D. F., Pisano, G., & Shuen, A. (1997). Dynamic capabilities and strategic management. *Strategic Management Journal, 18*(7), 509–533.

Tenkasi, R. V., & Boland, R. J. (1993). Locating meaning making in organizational learning: The narrative basis of cognition. *Research in Organizational Change and Development, 7,* 77–103.

Thiétart, R.-A., & Forgues, B. (1995). Chaos theory and organization. *Organization Science, 6*(1), 19–31.

Thiétart, R.-A., & Forgues, B. (1997). Action, structure and chaos. *Organization Studies, 18*(1), 119–143.

Thomas, R., & Davies, A. (2005). Theorizing the micro-politics of resistance: New public management and managerial identities in the UK public services. *Organization Studies, 26*(5), 683–706.

Thompson, J. D. (1967). *Organizations in action.* New York: McGraw-Hill.

Thompson, P. (1993). Postmodernism: Fatal distraction. In J. Hassard & M. Parker (Eds.), *Postmodernism and organizations* (pp. 183–203). London: Sage.

Tichy, N. (1982). Managing change strategically: The technical, political and cultural keys. *Organizational Dynamics,* (Autumn), 59–80.

Tolbert, P. S. (1988). Institutional sources of culture in major law firms. In L. Zucker (Ed.), *Institutional patterns in organizations: Culture and environment* (pp. 101–113). Cambridge, MA: Ballinger.

Tolbert, P. S., & Zucker, L. (1983). Institutional sources of change in the formal structure of organizations: The diffusion of social service reform, 1880–1935. *Administrative Science Quarterly, 28*(3), 22–39.

Tolbert, P. S., & Zucker, L. (1996). The institutionalization of institutional theory. In S. Clegg, C. Hardy, & W. Nord (Eds.), *Handbook of organization studies* (pp. 175–190). London: Sage.

Townley, B. (1993). Foucault, power/knowledge, and its relevance for human resource management. *Academy of Management Review, 18*(3), 518–545.

Trice, H. M., & Beyer, J. M. (1984). Studying organizational cultures through rites and ceremonials. *Academy of Management Review, 9*, 653–669.

Trice, H. M., & Beyer, J. M. (1993). *The cultures of work organizations.* Englewood Cliffs, NJ: Prentice Hall.

Tsoukas, H., & Chia, R. (2002). On organizational becoming: Rethinking organizational change. *Organization Science, 13*(5), 567–582.

Tsoukas, H., & Hatch, M. J. (2001). Complex thinking, complex practice: The case for a narrative approach to organizational complexity. *Human Relations, 54*(8), 979–1013.

Tsoukas, H., & Knudsen, C. (2003). *The Oxford handbook of organization theory.* Oxford, UK: Oxford University Press.

Tunstall, W. B. (1985). Breakup of the Bell System: A case study of cultural transformation. In R. Kilmann, M. Saxton, R. Serpa, & Associates (Eds.), *Gaining control of the corporate culture* (pp. 44–65). San Francisco: Jossey-Bass.

Tushman, M. L., & Anderson, P. (1986). Technological discontinuities and organizational environments. *Administrative Science Quarterly, 31*(3), 439–465.

Tushman, M. L., & Romanelli, E. (1985). Organizational evolution: A metamorphosis model of convergence and reorientation. In L. Cummings & B. Staw (Eds.), *Research in organizational behavior* (Vol. 7, pp. 171–222). Greenwich, CT: JAI Press.

Vaara, E. (2002). On the discursive construction of success/failure in narratives of post-merger integration. *Organization Studies, 23*(2), 211–249.

Van de Ven, A. (1980). Early planning, implementation and performance of new organizations. In J. Kimberly, R. Miles, & Associates (Eds.), *The organizational life cycle* (pp. 83–134). San Francisco: Jossey-Bass.

Van de Ven, A. (1992). Suggestions for studying strategy process: A research note. *Strategic Management Journal, 13*, 169–191.

Van de Ven, A., & Poole, M. S. (1988). Paradoxical requirements for a theory of organizational change. In R. Quinn & K. Cameron (Eds.), *Paradox and transformation: Toward a theory of change in organization and management.* Cambridge, MA: Ballinger.

Van de Ven, A., & Poole, M. S. (1995). Explaining development and change in organizations. *Academy of Management Review, 20*(3), 510–540.

Van Maanen, J., & Barley, S. (1985). Cultural organizations: Fragments of a theory. In P. Frost, L. Moore, M. Louis, C. Lundberg, & J. Martin (Eds.), *Organizational culture* (pp. 31–53). Beverly Hills, CA: Sage.

Virany, B., Tushman, M., & Romanelli, E. (1992). Executive succession and organization outcomes in turbulent environments: An organization learning approach. *Organization Science, 3*(1), 72–91.

Volberda, H. W., & Lewin, A. Y. (2003). Co-evolutionary dynamics within and between firms: From evolution to co-evolution. *Journal of Management Studies, 40*(8), 2111–2136.

Walsh, J. (1995). Managerial and organizational cognition: Notes from a trip down memory lane. *Organization Science, 6*(3), 280–321.

Walsham, G., & Sahay, S. (1999). GIS for district-level administration in India: Problems and opportunities. *MIS Quarterly, 23*(1), 39–65.

Warglien, M. (1995). Hierarchical selection and organizational adaptation. *Industrial and Corporate Change, 4*, 161–185.

Warglien, M. (2002). Intraorganizational evolution. In J. Baum (Ed.), *The Blackwell companion to organizations* (pp. 98–118). Oxford, UK: Blackwell.

Watson, T. J. (1982). Group ideologies and organizational change. *Journal of Management Studies, 19*(3), 259–275.

Watzlawick, P., Weakland, J. H., & Fisch, R. (1974). *Change: Principles of problem formation and problem resolution.* New York: Horton.

Weaver, G. R., & Gioia, D. (1994). Paradigms lost: Incommensurability vs structurationist inquiry. *Organization Studies, 15*(4), 565–590.

Weber, M. (1947). *Theory of social and economic organization.* New York: Free Press.

Weeks, J., & Galunic, C. (2003). A theory of the cultural evolution of the firm: The intraorganizational ecology of memes. *Organization Studies, 24*(8), 1309–1352.

Weick, K. E. (1969). *The social psychology of organizing.* Reading, MA: Addison-Wesley.

Weick, K. E. (1979a). Cognitive processes in organizations. In L. Cummings & B. Staw (Eds.), *Research in organizational behavior* (Vol. 1, pp. 41–74). Greenwich, CT: JAI Press.

Weick, K. E. (1979b). *The social psychology of organizing* (2nd ed.). Reading, MA: Addison-Wesley.

Weick, K. E. (1989). Organized improvisation: 20 years of organizing. *Communication Studies, 40*, 241–248.

Weick, K. E. (1993). Organizational redesign as improvisation. In G. Huber & W. Glick (Eds.), *Organizational change and redesign* (pp. 346–379). New York: Oxford University Press.

Weick, K. E. (1995). *Sensemaking in organizations.* Thousands Oaks, CA: Sage.

Weick, K. E. (1998). Improvisation as a mindset for organizational analysis. *Organization Science, 9*(5), 543–555.

Weick, K. E., & Quinn, R. (1999). Organizational change and development. *Annual Review of Psychology, 50*, 361–386.

Weick, K. E., & Westley, F. (1996). Organizational learning: Affirming an oxymoron. In S. Clegg, C. Hardy, & W. Nord (Eds.), *Handbook of organization studies* (pp. 440–458). London: Sage.

Weitzel, W., & Jönsson, E. (1989). Decline in organizations: A literature integration and extension. *Administrative Science Quarterly, 34*(1), 91–110.

Wenger, E. (1998). *Communities of practice: Learning, meaning and identity.* Cambridge, UK: Cambridge University Press.

Wenger, E. (2000). Communities of practice and social learning systems. *Organization, 7*(2), 225–246.

Whipp, R., Rosenfeld, R., & Pettigrew, A. (1987). Understanding strategic change processes: Some preliminary British findings. In A. Pettigrew (Ed.), *The management of strategic change* (pp. 14–55). London: Basil Blackwell.

White, H. (1981). The narrativization of real events. In W. J. T. Mitchell (Ed.), *On narrative* (pp. 249–254). Chicago: University of Chicago Press.

Whittington, R. (1988). Environmental structure and theories of strategic choice. *Journal of Management Studies, 25*(6), 521–537.

Whittington, R. (1992). Putting Giddens into action: Social systems and managerial agency. *Journal of Management Studies, 29*(6), 693–712.

Whittington, R. (1994). Sociological pluralism, institutions and managerial agency. In J. Hassard & M. Parker (Eds.), *Towards a new theory of organizations* (pp. 53–54). New York: Routledge.

Whittington, R. (1996). Strategy as practice. *Long Range Planning, 29*(5), 731–736.

Whittington, R. (2030). The work of strategizing and organizing. For a practice perspective. *Strategic Organization, 1*(1), 119–127.

Whittington, R. (2004). Strategy after modernism: Recovering practice. *European Management Review, 1*(1), 62–68.

Whittington, R., & Melin, L. (2003). Organizing/strategizing. In A. Pettigrew, R. Whittington, L. Melin, W. Ruigrok, C. Sanchez-Runde, & F. Van den Bosch (Eds.), *Innovative forms of organizing.* London: Sage.

Whittington, R., & Pettigrew, A. (2003). Complementarities thinking. In A. Pettigrew, R. Whittington, L. Meilin, C. Sanchez-Runde, F. van den Bosch, W. Ruigrok, & T. Numagami (Eds.), *Innovative forms of organizing* (pp. 125–132). London: Sage.

Wiersema, M. F., & Bantel, K. A. (1992). Top management team demography and corporate strategic change. *Academy of Management Journal, 35*(1), 91–121.

Wildavsky, H. (1968). Budgeting as a political process. In D. Sills (Ed.), *International encyclopedia of the social sciences* (Vol. 2). New York: Crowell Collier Macmillan.

Wilkins, A. L., & Dyer, W. G. (1988). Toward culturally sensitive theories of cultural change. *Academy of Management Review, 13*(4), 522–533.

Willmott, H. (1981). The structuring of organizational structure: A note. *Administrative Science Quarterly, 26*(3), 470–474.

Willmott, H. (1987). Studying managerial work: A critique and a proposal. *Journal of Management Studies, 24*(3), 249–270.

Willmott, H. (1993). Strength is ignorance, slavery is freedom: Managing culture in modern organizations. *Journal of Management Studies, 30*(4), 515–552.

Willmott, H. (1995). The odd couple? Re-engineering business processes; managing human relations. *New Technology, Work and Employment, 10*(2), 89–98.

Willmott, H. (2003). Organization theory as a critical science? Forms of analysis and new organizational forms. In H. Tsoukas & C. Knudsen (Eds.), *The Oxford handbook of organization theory: Meta-theoretical perspectives* (pp. 88–112). Oxford, UK: Oxford University Press.

Willmott, H. (2005). Theorizing contemporary control: Some post-structuralist responses to some critical realist questions. *Organization, 12*(5), 747–780.

Wilson, E. O. (1975). *Sociobiology: The new synthesis.* Cambridge, MA: Harvard University Press.

Winter, S. G. (1990). Survival, selection, and inheritance in evolutionary theories of organization. In J. Singh (Ed.), *Organizational evolution: New directions* (pp. 269–297). Thousand Oaks, CA: Sage.

Winter, S. G. (2003). Understanding dynamic capabilities. *Strategic Management Journal, 24*(10), 991–995.

Woodward, J. (1965). *Industrial organization: Theory and practice.* London: Oxford University Press.

Wren, D. (1994). *The evolution of management thought* (4th ed.). New York: Wiley.

Yanow, D. (2000). Seeing organizational learning: A cultural view. *Organization, 7*(2), 247–268.

Zajac, E. J., & Shortell, S. M. (1989). Changing generic strategies: Likelihood, direction, and performance implications. *Strategic Management Journal, 10,* 413–430.

Zald, M., & Berger, M. A. (1978). Social movements in organizations: Coup d'etat, insurgency, and mass movements. *American Journal of Sociology, 83*(4), 823–861.

Zhou, X. (1993). The dynamics of organizational rules. *American Journal of Sociology, 98*(5), 1134–1166.

Zollo, M., & Winter, S. G. (2002). Deliberate learning and the evolution of dynamic capabilities. *Organization Science, 13*(3), 339–351.

Zucker, L. (1977). The role of institutionalization in cultural persistence. *American Sociological Review, 42,* 726–743.

Zucker, L. (Ed.). (1988a). *Institutional patterns and organizations.* Cambridge, MA: Ballinger.

Zucker, L. (1988b). Institutional theories of organization: Conceptual developments and research agenda. In L. Zucker (Ed.), *Institutional patterns and organizations* (pp. xiii–xix). Cambridge, MA: Ballinger.

Index

Academy of Management Journal, 37, 57
Ackroyd, S., 189
Action, purposeful (approaches), 11–13
Activity theory, 213–214, 220
    (n18), 221 (n22)
Actor-network theory (ANT), 199,
    202–205, 216, 220 (n19), 226–227
Actors and Systems (Crozier and
    Friedberg), 102
Adaptation perspective, of
    organizational change, 1–3
    life-cycle, 17–23
    organic, 6, 13–17, 14 (table)
    rational, 5, 6–13, 7 (table)
    selection versus, 1–3, 3 (figure),
        41 (table)
    theory, 188
Adaptive learning theory, 124
Agency, in organizational change, 223
Ahlstrand, B., 48, 97
Aldrich, H., 21, 77, 132, 136,
    142–143, 148, 152
Allison, G. T., 16
Alvesson, M., 79, 90, 180, 182–183, 189,
    216, 219 (n3), 219 (n4)
Amblard, H., 107
Amburgey, T., 31
Anderson, D. L., 158–161, 163, 206
ANT. *See* Actor-network theory
Archer, M., 189
Archer's morphogenetic theory, 189
Argote, L., 127
Argyris, C., 74 (n5)
Astley, G., 30
Autogenic perspective, 158
Azevedo, J., 216

Bacdayan, P., 127
Bacharach, S. B., 107
Badham, R, 107
Bamberger, P., 107
Bantel, K. A., 10
Barker, J. R., 187
Barley, S., 81
Barr, P. S., 67, 71
Barrett, M., 201
Bartunek, J., 56, 70, 88
Bassanini, A. P., 172 (n16)
Baum, J., 30–31, 120 (n1), 135,
    138, 145–148, 150, 152, 171
    (n2), 173 (n21), 173 (n25),
    173 (n26), 174 (n32)
Baumard, P., 131
Behavioral learning approach,
    121–134, 125 (table),
    153, 170–171, 224 (table)
Berg, P. O., 82–83
Berger, M. A., 99
Beyer, J. M., 90
Bhaskar, R., 120 (n3)
Bhatia, M. M., 168
Biggart, N. W., 56
Blackler, F., 221 (n23)
Blau, P., 23 (n)
Boehm, M., 86
Boland, R. J., 197
Bourdieu, P., 54, 58 (n4), 213
Bower, J., 145
BPR. *See* Business Process
    Reengineering
Braybrooke, D., 13–16, 48, 96–97
Bretton Woods Agreement, 4 (n2)
Brocklehurst, M., 187

Brown, A. D., 105, 155, 159–160, 166, 197, 201
Brown, J. S., 208–210, 217
Brown, S. L., 160
Bruner, J., 195
Brunsson, N., 37, 69–70
Buchanan, D., 107
Burgelman, R. A., 57, 143–145, 149, 152–153, 166, 171 (n4), 173 (n25)
Burns, T., 6, 8
Burrell, G., 188
Burton, B. K., 169
Business Process Reengineering (BPR), 116, 185–186, 219 (n7)

Calás, M. B., 89, 184
Caldwell, R., 216, 234
Cameron, K., 18, 21–22
Campbell, D. T., 120 (n3), 135, 173 (n26)
Carley, K. M., 127, 163, 166, 168, 172 (n8), 174 (n39), 174 (n40)
Carter, C., 202
CAS theory. See Complex adaptive system theory
Catastrophe theory, 174 (n30)
Causal maps, 67
Cellular automata, 164, 169, 175 (n41)
Chandler, A. D., 19, 21, 24 (n4)
Change, organizational
    adaptation perspective of, 1–3, 5–23, 41 (table), 188
    agency in, 223
    as an emergent phenomenon, 162–168
    as practical and social performance, 208–215
    as reframing, 62–71
    cognitive approach to, 61–73, 63 (table), 73 (n1), 86, 91, 92 (n9), 111 (table), 113 (table), 121, 128–131, 132
    configurational approach to, 47–58, 51 (table), 86, 109 (n10), 111 (table), 113 (table)
    cultural approach to, 75–91, 77 (table), 92 (n5), 92 (n9), 111 (table), 113 (table)

discourse and, 193–207
emancipation, 180–185
evolutionary approach to, 135–154
evolutionary perspective of, 43–114
first-order, 64
formal structural perspective of, 55
functionalist framework of, 79–81
future of, 233–234
history of, xi–xii, 231 (figure)
incremental, 96–101
intraorganizational ecology and, 143–147
natural evolution perspective of, 115–171, 222–227
political approach to, 93–108, 94 (table), 111 (table), 113 (table)
power law patterns of, and complex adaptive system, 158–162
process perspective on, 116
quantum structural, 50
routine-based, 124–126
second-order, 64. See also Reframing
selection perspective of, 25–38, 61
situated, 207–215
social dynamics perspective of, 118, 119 (figure), 177–227
transformative perspective of, 43–114
viewed from above, 110–114
viewed from the inside, 222–227
viewed from the outside, 40–42
Change Masters, The (Kanter), 99
Changing Culture of a Factory, The (Jaques), 76
Chaos
    edge of, 155, 159–161, 163, 168, 170
    punctuated change and, 155–158
    theory, 155, 162–163, 174 (n30)
Chaotic equilibrium, 155–157
Cheng, Y. T., 162, 174 (n38)
Chevalier, F., 97
Child, J., xii, 1–2, 5–6, 9, 11–13, 19–21, 30, 42, 55, 61
Chittipeddi, K., 69
Choice, strategic, 11–13
Clark, P., 189, 190
Clegg, S., 93, 105–106, 120 (n1), 219 (n3)
Coactivational view, 103

Coevolution, 105, 147–150
Cognitive approach, to organizational
    change, 61–73, 63 (table), 73 (n1),
    86, 91, 92 (n9), 111 (table), 113
    (table), 121, 128–131, 132
Cohen, M. D., 127, 174 (n40)
Cole, R. E., 134
Collective learning, 129
Complementarities theory, 57
Complex adaptive system (CAS)
    theory, 155, 158–167
Complexity
    approach, 121–122, 154–171,
        224 (table)
    theory, 156 (table), 161, 165–166, 223
Configuration theorists, 48, 86
Configurational approach, to
    organizational change, 47–58,
    51 (table), 86, 109 (n10),
    111 (table), 113 (table)
Contextualism, 104–105, 149
Contingency theory, 6–11, 7 (table)
Contu, A., 217, 220 (n18)
Convergent change, 68
Corsi, T. M., 10
Coser, L., 35
Covaleski, M., 36
Critical approach, 93
Critical discourse analysis, 190, 199
Critical realist epistemology, 120 (n3)
Critical theorists, 90
Cross-level learning, 126–128
Crossan, M. M., 131, 133
Crozier, M., 9, 13, 101–103, 106–108,
    108 (n1), 109 (n6)
Cultural approach, to organizational
    change, 75–91, 77 (table), 92 (n5),
    92 (n9), 111 (table), 113 (table)
Currie, G., 201
Cybernetics, 154
Cyert, R., 11, 13–14, 28, 97, 122–124
Czarniawska, B., 37, 202, 204

Darwinian theory, 148
David, P., 174 (n39)
Deetz, S., 180, 182–184, 219 (n3),
    219 (n4), 219 (n5)
Dent, J. F., 88

Design archetypes, 54–55
Deterministic chaos.
    See Chaotic equilibrium
Devadas, R., 127
Discursive approach, 177–179, 190–218,
    194 (table), 225 (table)
Differentiation studies, 87–89, 92 (n3)
DiMaggio, P., 25, 33–36, 150
Discontinuous change, 68
Discourse, and change, 193–207
Donaldson, L., 9, 12, 56, 187
Dooley, K., 155, 157–161, 174 (n32)
Doolin, B., 202–203
Dosi, G., 172 (n16)
Dow, G., 103
Doz, Y., 108
Drazin, R., 158
Dubinskas, F. A., 161, 169
Duguid, P., 208–210, 217
Dutton, J., 66
Dyer, W. G., 89

Ecology
    intraorganizational, 143–147
    population, 25–32, 27 (table)
Edelman, M., 196
Edge of chaos, 155, 159–161, 163, 168, 170
Egri, C., 95
Eisenhardt, K. M., 149, 155, 159–160,
    166–168, 173 (n25)
Electronic data interchange (EDI), 186
Emergent processes, in organizations, 54
Emotion, cognitive perspective and, 72
Enactment, concept of, 61, 63, 68
Engeström, Y., 213–214, 221
    (n22), 221 (n23)
Environmental determinism, 2
Epple, D., 127
Equilibrium, punctuated, 50–53
Ethnographic methods, 81
Evolutionary approach, to natural
    evolution, 121–122, 135–154,
    170–171, 224 (table)
Evolutionary perspective, of
    organizational change, 43–114.
    See also Natural evolution
Explicit knowledge, 130–131
Ezzamel, M., 217

Fairclough, N, 190, 199–200, 220 (n16)
Feldman, M. S., 89, 208, 211–212, 214
Fisch, R., 64
Fisher, W. R., 195
Fleetwood, S., 188
For Positivist Organization Theory
    (Donaldson), 9
Ford, J. D., 195
Ford, L. W., 195
Forgues, B., 156, 159, 174 (n32)
Formal structural perspective, of
    organizational change, 55
Foucault, M., 180, 183–184, 187, 191,
    200, 219 (n7), 220 (n11)
Fournier, V., 188, 219 (n1), 219 (n3)
Fragmentation studies, 87, 88–90
Frances, J., 186
Francis, H., 191, 200, 202
Freeman, J. H., 2, 6, 25–26, 28–32
Friedberg, E., 9, 13, 102–103,
    106–108, 109 (n6)
Friesen, P., 48–53, 56, 58
Frost, P., 81, 90, 95
Functionalist perspective, 64, 76–84,
    87, 89–90, 91 (n2), 96

Gagliardi, P., 85
Galunic, D. C., 142, 149, 173 (n25)
Garbage can model, 175 (n40)
Garnsey, E., 186
Garud, R., 128, 174 (n39)
Genealogy, organizational,
    137–143
General systems theory, 154
Gersick, C., 67, 174 (n30)
Ghoshal, S., 145, 147, 149, 173 (n25)
Giddens, A., 54, 58 (n4), 103, 162,
    182–183, 189, 191, 201, 207–208,
    211, 213, 220 (n17)
Gillespie, J. J., 172 (n16)
Gioia, G., 69, 82, 92 (n9)
Giroux, H., 143
Glynn, M. A., 124–125, 128–129, 171
    (n4)
Goodrick, E., 36
Gouldner, A., 23 (n1)
Greenwood, R., 32, 37, 50, 53–55, 57–58,
    58 (n3), 109 (n10)
Greiner, L. E., 20, 44

Grey, C., 188, 219 (n1), 219 (n3)
Grimm, C. M., 10
Grinyer, P. H., 212
Groupthink, 66
Growth perspective, of organizational
    change. *See* Adaptation perspective,
    of organizational change

Haire, M., 17
Handbook of Organizations
    (March), 5
Hannan, M. T., 2, 6, 25–26, 28–32,
    173 (n21)
Hardy, C., 93, 96, 104–106, 120 (n1),
    188, 200, 219 (n3)
Hatch, M. J., 79, 82, 89, 91, 169
Hay, M., 21
Hedberg, B., 48–49, 82, 87
Hendry, J., 191
Heracleous, L., 191, 201, 206
Hinings, C., 32, 37, 47, 50, 53–55, 57–58,
    58 (n3), 109 (n10)
Hirsch, P. M., 5, 13, 15, 172 (n16)
Hislop, D., 105
Holmqvist, M., 131
Huber, G. P., 127
Huff, A., 65–66, 71, 98–99, 101
Huff, J. O., 71
Human cognition, 62
Humphreys, M., 197
Hypertext organization, 161

Imitation perspective, of organizational
    change. *See* Selection perspective,
    of organizational change
Incremental change, 93, 94 (table),
    105, 108, 109 (n2)
    bottom-up, 98–101
    top-down, 96–98
Innovation, 100–101
Institutional school, 76
Institutionalism, New, 25, 32–38,
    33 (table), 41 (table), 61
Institutionalization, process
    of, 34–35
Integrative thinking, 100
Intel Corporation, 143
Interpretation process, social
    nature of, 73

Interpretive perspective, 71, 77–78, 81–82, 84, 89–90, 91 (n2), 92 (n6)
Interpretivist-subjectivist perspective, 112
Intraorganizational ecology, 143–147
Isabella, L., 68
Isomorphism, 61
   mimetic, 34–35
   normative, 35

Jackson, M. H., 197
Jaques, E., 76
Jarzabkowski, P., 214, 221 (n23)
Joerges, B., 202
Johnson, G., 57, 104–105
Johnson, J. L., 169
Jones, M., 182, 211
Jönsson, S. A., 82, 87
Just-in-time manufacturing (JIT), 185

Kadushin, C., 35
Kanter, R. M., 99–101, 106, 109 (n4), 171 (n4)
Karnoe, P., 174 (n39)
Kärreman, D., 189, 216
Kauffman, S. A., 160, 164–165
Kieser, A., xii, 1, 5–6, 9, 11, 19–21, 30
Kimberly, J. R., 21–22
Kirkpatrick, I., 189
Kirsch, D., 174 (n39)
Knights, D., 182, 186
Knowledge
   development, 122
   explicit, 130–131
   management, 116
   structure, 65–68
   tacit, 130–131
Koput, K. W., 163
Kuhn, T., 46 (n2), 67–68

Lampel, J., 48, 97
Language games, 180-185
Lant, T., 125
Laroche, H., 97
Larsen, E. R., 164
Latour, B., 202–204
Lave, J., 208, 213, 217
Lawrence, P. R., 6

Learning
   adaptive, 124
   approach, 72, 73 (n1)
   behavioral, 128–132
   cognitive, 128–132
   collective, 129
   cross-level, 126–128
   school, 109 (n2)
   social constructionist perspective on, 133
   See also Behavioral learning approach
Lee, G. K., 134
Lee, J. L., 166
Leifer, R., 174 (n30)
Leonardi, P. M., 197
Leroy, F., 129–131
Levie, J., 21
Levinthal, D., 124–125, 152–153, 155, 164–165, 173 (n25), 175 (n43)
Lewin, A. Y., 85
Lewin, K., 92 (n8)
Life-cycle approach, 6, 17, 18 (table), 21–23, 41 (table), 53, 84
   patterns of change, 20–21
   stages of development, 18–20
Lindblom, C. E., 13–16, 48, 96–97
Lodahl, T., 79, 86
Logical incrementalism, 96–97, 99, 105
Lok, J., 217
Lomi, A., 164
Long, R. G., 162
Lounsbury, M., 5, 15, 37
Lovas, B., 145, 147, 149, 173 (n25)
Luhmann, N., 213
Lyles, M. A., 67

MacIntosh, R., 174 (n30)
MacLean, D., 174 (n30)
Mapping Strategic Thought (Huff), 65
March, J. G., 5, 11, 13–14, 28, 37, 97, 121–124, 125, 128, 132, 146–147, 150, 172 (n9), 174 (n40)
Marshak, R. J., 206
Martin, J., 83–84, 86–90, 92 (n3)
Marx, K., 93
Mathews, K. M., 162
McCabe, D., 186
McHugh, A., 57, 145

McKelvey, B., 136, 148, 152, 155,
   164–165, 168, 170, 172 (n12),
   174 (n40), 175 (n44), 188
Melin, L., 213
Memes, 138, 142–143, 147, 153
Mendoza, C., 97
Mental maps, 65, 67.
Merton, R., 23 (n)
Meyer, A. D., 47
Meyer, J., 9, 32–34, 36–37,
   58 (n3), 150–151
Meyerson, D., 83, 84, 86–89
Mezias, S. J., 125, 132, 171 (n4)
Miettinen, R., 214, 217
Miles, R. E., 48
Milgrom, P. R., 57
Miller, D., 32, 47–53, 56–58
Mimetic isomorphism, 34–35
Miner, A. S., 132, 145–146, 152
Mintzberg, H., 47–48, 56–57, 97, 99, 145
Mitchell, S., 79, 86
Moch, M., 88
Modular organization, 161
Momentum, 49, 50–53, 54, 56
Morel, B., 155–156, 158–159,
   168, 174 (n35)
Morgan, G., 82
Morphogenesis, 189–190
Mueller, F., 196, 202
Mumby, D., 219 (n3)
Mutch, A., 189, 216
Myatt, J., 173 (n25)

Narrative analysis, 195
Natural evolution perspective, of
   organizational change, 115–122,
   222–227, 224 (table)
   behavioral learning approach,
      121–134, 125 (table), 153,
      170–171, 224 (table)
   complexity approach, 121–122,
      154–171, 224 (table)
   evolutionary approach, 121–122,
      135–154, 170–171, 224 (table)
Neilsen, E. H., 70–71
Nelson, R. R., 121–122, 124, 136,
   138–139, 141–142, 172 (n13),
   172 (n17)

Neo-institutional theory, 25, 32–38,
   33 (table), 41 (table), 61
Neo-Marxism, 219 (n2)
Newell, S., 105
NK models, 164–165, 169
Nonaka, I., 130–131, 134,
   142, 172 (n10)
Nonlinear systems, 155
Nord, W., 83, 87, 120 (n1)
Normann, R., 16
Normative isomorphism, 35
Nystrom, P., 48–49

Objective-functionalist perspective, 61
Objectivist research, 73 (n2)
OD. See Organizational development
Olsen, J. P., 128, 174 (n40)
Organic adaptation approach, 6, 13–17,
   14 (table), 41 (table)
Organization Science, 207
Organizational change. See Change,
   organizational
Organizational Culture (Frost et al.), 81
Organizational development (OD), xii, 2
Organizational forms, new,
   161, 185–187
Organizational genealogy, 137–143
Organizational Growth and Development
   (Starbuck), 1
Organizational learning,
   108, 122–123, 126
Organizational Life Cycle,
   The (Kimberly), 21
Organizations: A Quantum View (Miller
   and Friesen), 49
Organizations, self-renewal, 115–120
Orientation, strategic, 51
Orlikowski, W. J., 210–212, 214
Orr, J., 208

Park, O., 74 (n7)
Parsons, T., 29
Penrose, E., 5, 21
Pentland, B. T., 212
Perrow, C., 17, 174 (n39)
Pettigrew, A. M., xii, 55, 57, 79–80, 101,
   103–108, 115, 149
Pfeffer, J., 5, 11–12

Phillips, N., 200, 217
Pink noise, 161, 163. *See also*
    Edge of chaos
Polanyi, M., 130, 172 (n10)
Political approach, to organizational
    change, 93–96, 94 (table), 106–108,
    111 (table), 113 (table)
    as a force against change, 96–98
    as a force for change, 98–101
    as a reproduction and
        transformational
        process, 101–106
Pondy, L., 98
Poole, M. S., xiii, 22, 27, 69, 133,
    157, 174 (n34)
Population ecology, 25–32,
    27 (table), 41 (table)
Porac, J. F., 150, 152
Porter, M., 48
Postmodern approach, 177–190, 181
    (table), 218–219, 225 (table)
Postmodernism, 183, 188, 207, 226
Poststructuralism, 191
Powell, W., 25, 33–35
Power, change and, 95–106
Practice-centered approach, 177–179,
    190–218, 209 (table), 225 (table)
Prahalad, C. K., 108
Pulicani, P., 97
Punctuated change, chaos
    and, 155–158
Punctuated equilibrium model, 49–53,
    57–58, 73, 85–86, 104–105, 125,
    144, 149, 153, 160, 173 (n22), 230
Purposeful action approaches,
    7 (table), 11–13

Quantum structural change, 50
Quinn, R., xiii, 48, 57, 96–99, 101,
    105–106, 109 (n11), 145

Radical approach, 177–190, 181 (table),
    218–219, 225 (table)
Rajagopalan, N., 10
Ramanantsoa, B., 129–131
Ramanujam, R., 155–156, 158–159,
    168, 174 (n35)
Rao, H., 70, 71, 72

Rational adaptation approaches,
    5, 7 (table), 41 (table)
    contingency theory, 6–11
    purposeful action approaches, 11–13
Rational lens perspective, 10
Reed, M., 189, 215
Reframing
    as a change of knowledge
        structure, 65–68
    as a social interaction process, 68–71
    organizational change as, 62–71
Reitter, R., 97
Reorientations, 52–53
Represented voice, 206
Resource dependency theory,
    7 (table), 11–13, 95
Return map, 174 (n33)
Revolution, 49, 50–53, 54, 56
Rhenman, E., 16
Rhetorical analysis, 195
Roberts, J., 57
Robichaud, D., 205–206
Romanelli, E., 49–54, 56, 58, 85,
    125, 160
Rouleau, L., 213
Routine-based change, 124–126
Rowan, B., 9, 32–34, 36
Ruelle, D., 169

Salancik, G. R., 5, 11–12, 36
Salvato, C., 141, 145
Sandelands, L. E., 158
Scarborough, H., 105
Schein, E., 79, 80–82, 84–86, 89–90,
    92 (n4), 92 (n8)
Schön, D., 74 (n5)
Schultz, M., 91
Schulz, M., 123
Schumpeter, J. A., 139
Schwenk, C. R., 65, 67
SCOT (social construction of
    technology), 210
Scott, R., 33, 38 (n)
Searle, J. R., 220 (n14)
Second-order change, 64.
    See also Reframing
Sectoral archetypes, 54
Segmentalism, 100

Selection perspective, of organizational change, 25–38
  population ecology, 25–32, 27 (table)
Self-organized criticality (SOC), 159
Selznick, P., 13–16, 28, 32, 39 (n2), 42, 76, 80
Sense-making, 70
Sevon, G., 37, 204
Sewell, W., 208
Siggelkow, N., 155
Sillince, J. A. A., 196
Silverman, B. S., 174 (n32)
Simon, H. A., 154
Sinclair, J., 191, 200, 202
Singh, J., 135, 138, 145–148, 150, 173 (n21), 173 (n25), 173 (n26)
Sitkin, S., 86
Situated action theory, 208
Situated learning theory, 213
Situated practice, 120 (n2)
Smircich, L., 78, 89, 184
Smith, C., 55
Smith, K. G., 10
Smith, R. D., 10
Snow, C., 48
SOC (self-organized criticality), 159
Social construction, 55
Social construction of technology (SCOT), 210
Social interaction process, 68–71
Social dynamics perspective, of organizational change, 118, 119 (figure), 177–179, 218–227, 225 (table)
  discursive and practice-centered approaches, 190–218, 225 (table)
  radical and postmodern approaches, 179–190, 225 (table)
Sociobiology, 150
"Some Dare Call It Power" (Hardy and Clegg), 93
Sonnenstuhl, W. J., 107
Sorenson, O., 168–169, 174 (n39)
Speech act theory, 195
Spender, J. C., 212
Spreitzer, G., 10
Stacey, R. D., 160, 162
Stalker, G. M., 6, 8

Stanford University, 146
Starbuck, W., xii, 1, 5, 21, 48, 130
Strategic choice model, 7 (table), 11–12, 61
Strategic contingency theory, 95
Strategic continuity, 143
Strategic orientation, 51
Structural contingency, 56
"Structural Inertia and Organizational Change" (Hannan and Freeman), 28–29
Structuration theory, 103, 149, 162, 180, 182, 189, 191, 199, 207–208, 214, 220 (n17)
Subjective-interpretive perspective, 61, 73 (n2)
Suchman, L. A., 208, 220 (n18)
Sull, D. N., 167
Swan, J., 105

Tacit knowledge, 130–131
Taylor, J. R., 143, 200, 204–205
Tenkasi, R. V., 197
Theories, of organizational change. See Change, organizational
Thiétart, R. A., 156, 159, 174 (n32)
Thomas, P., 199
Thompson, J. D., 5–6, 188–189
Time-pacing, 167
Tolbert, P. S., 35–36
Total Quality Management (TQM), 34, 37, 185, 186
Townley, B., 184
Transformative perspective, of organizational change, 43–114
Translation, 203
Trice, H. M., 90
Tsoukas, H., 169
Tsui, A., 47, 58 (n3)
Tunstall, W. B., 86
Tushman, M. L., 49–54, 56, 58, 85, 125, 160

United Way, 26

Vaara, E., 197
Van de Ven, A., xiii, 22, 27, 30, 128, 133, 155, 157–162, 174 (n32), 174 (n38)

Van Every, E. J., 200
Van Maanen, J., 81, 92 (n6)
Vikkunen, J., 214, 217
Voluntarism, 2

Walsh, J., 61, 65–66, 72
Warglien, M., 138, 143, 144,
    148, 172 (n11)
Watzlawick, P., 64
Weakland, J. H., 64
Weber, M., 48, 93, 187
Weeks, J., 142
Weick, K. E., xiii, 15–16, 61, 63, 68, 124,
    130, 135, 142, 158, 191, 200,
    204–205, 207, 211, 217
Wenger, E., 208, 213, 217, 220 (n18)
Whetten, D., 18, 21–22
White, H., 195

White, M. C., 162
Whittington, R., 16, 57, 183,
    189, 213, 217
Wiersema, M. F., 10
Wildavsky, H., 48
Wilkins, A. L., 89
Willmott, H., 182–183, 186, 189,
    216–217, 220 (n16), 220 (n18)
Winter, S. G., 121–122, 124,
    136, 138–139, 141–142,
    172 (n13), 172 (n17)
Woodward, J., 6

Yanow, D., 209

Zald, M., 99
Zollo, M., 142
Zucker, L., 35–36

About the Author

Christiane Demers is a professor in the Department of Management at HEC Montréal, where she has been teaching courses on organizational change theories, strategic change management, and strategy for more than 15 years. She holds a Ph.D. in administration from HEC Montréal and received her M.Sc. in communication sciences from the University of Montréal. Her research focuses on organizational transformation, with particular emphasis on its links with strategic dynamics and communication processes. Another topic that interests her is the evolution of the field of organizational change. She has published, both individually and collaboratively, a number of books and journal articles on these subjects and has presented her work at international conferences.